SRA Reading Mastery

CLASSIC EDITION

Presentation Book B

Level I

Siegfried Engelmann
Elaine C. Bruner

SRA

A Division of The McGraw-Hill Companies

Columbus, Ohio

www.sra4kids.com

SRA/McGraw-Hill

A Division of The McGraw-Hill Companies

Send all inquiries to:
SRA/McGraw-Hill
8787 Orion Place
Columbus, OH 43240-4027

Printed in the United States of America.

ISBN 0-07-569288-0

11 12 13 14 WCE 13 12 11 10

Table of Contents

*Individual Checkout Lessons

Lesson 57

SOUNDS

TASK 1 Teacher and children play the sounds game

a. Use acetate and crayon. Write the sounds in the symbol box. Keep score in the score box.
b. **I'm smart. I bet I can beat you in a game.**
c. **Here's the rule. When I touch a sound, you say it.**
d. Play the game.
Make one symbol at a time in the symbol box. Use the symbols **t, o, a,** and **i.**
Make each symbol quickly.
(Pause.) Touch the symbol.
Play the game for about two minutes.
Then ask: **Who won?** Draw a mouth on the face in the score box.

TASK 2 Sounds firm-up

a. Point to **a. When I touch the sound, you say it.**
b. (Pause.) **Get ready.** Touch **a.** *aaa.*
c. **Again.** Repeat *b* until firm.
d. **Get ready to say all the sounds when I touch them.**
e. Alternate touching **r, ē, d, i, th, o, c,** and **a** three or four times.
   Point to the sound. (Pause one second.) Say: **Get ready.**
   Touch the sound. *The children respond.*

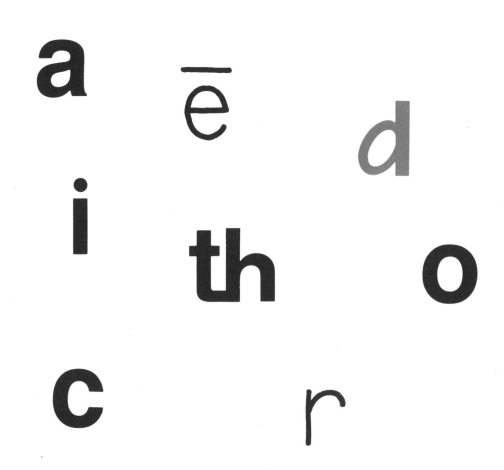

TASK 3 Individual test

Call on different children to identify one or more sounds in task 2.

READING VOCABULARY
Get ready to read all the words on this page without making a mistake.

Do not touch any small letters.

TASK 4   Children sound out word and tell what word

a. Touch the ball for **ēat.** Sound it out.
b. Get ready. Touch **ē, t** as the children say *ēēēt.*
c. Again. Repeat *b* until firm.
d. Yes, what word? (Signal.) *Eat.*

TASK 5   Children sound out the word and tell what word

a. Touch the ball for **sock.** Sound it out.
b. Get ready. Touch **s, o, c** as the children say *sssoooc.*
c. Again. Repeat *b* until firm.
d. Yes, what word? (Signal.) *Sock.*

TASK 6   Children sound out the word and tell what word

a. Touch the ball for **on.** Sound it out.
b. Get ready. Touch **o, n** as the children say *ooonnn.*
c. Again. Repeat *b* until firm.
d. Yes, what word? (Signal.) *On.*

TASK 7   Children sound out the word and tell what word

a. Touch the ball for **fēēt.** Sound it out.
b. Get ready. Touch **f, ē, t** as the children say *fffēēēt.*
c. Again. Repeat *b* until firm.
d. Yes, what word? (Signal.) *Feet.*

TASK 8 Individual test

Call on different children to sound out one word and tell what word.

ēat

sock

on

fēēt

Get ready to read all the words on this page without making a mistake.

Do not touch any small letters.

TASK 9   Children sound out the word and tell what word

a. Touch the ball for **in.**   Sound it out.
b. Get ready.   Touch **i, n** as the children say *iiinnn.*
c. Again.   Repeat *b* until firm.
d. Yes, what word?   (Signal.) *In.*

TASK 10   Children sound out the word and tell what word

a. Touch the ball for **if.**   Sound it out.
b. Get ready.   Touch **i, f** as the children say *iiifff.*
c. Again.   Repeat *b* until firm.
d. Yes, what word?   (Signal.) *If.*

TASK 11   Children sound out the word and tell what word

a. Touch the ball for **sēat.**   Sound it out.
b. Get ready.   Touch **s, ē, t** as the children say *sssēēēt.*
c. Again.   Repeat *b* until firm.
d. Yes, what word?   (Signal.) *Seat.*

TASK 12   Children rhyme with an

a. Point to **an** and **man.**   These words rhyme, but the part that rhymes is not written in red.
b. Touch the ball for **an.**   Sound it out.
c. Get ready.   Touch **a, n** as the children say *aaannn.*
d. Return to the ball for **an.**   Again.   Repeat *c* until firm.
e. Yes, what word?   (Signal.) *An.*
f. Quickly touch the ball for **man.**   This word rhymes with   (pause) **aann.** Get ready.   Touch **m.** *mmm.* Move your finger quickly along the arrow. *Mmman.*
g. Yes, what word?   (Signal.) *Man.*

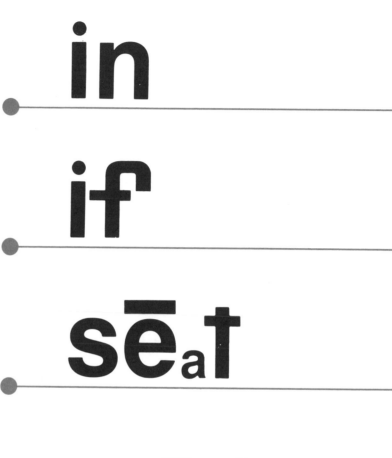

Take-Home 57

STORY

TASK 13   First reading—children sound out each word and say it fast

a. Pass out Take-Home 57. Do not let the children look at the picture until task 17.   **There are no balls under the sounds on this take-home. But I'll clap for each sound. You touch under each sound.**

b. **Finger on the ball of the top arrow.** Check children's responses.

c. **Touch the first word.** Check children's responses.   **Sound it out. Get ready.** Clap for each sound. *Iiit.*

d. **Again. (Pause.)   Get ready.** Clap for each sound. *Iiit.*   **Say it fast.** (Signal.) *It.*   **Yes, what word?** (Signal.) *It.*

e. **Touch the next word.** Check children's responses.   **Sound it out. Get ready.** Clap for each sound. *Iiisss.*

f. **Again. (Pause.)   Get ready.** Clap for each sound. *Iiisss.*   **Say it fast.** (Signal.) *Is.*   **Yes, what word?** (Signal.) *Is.*

g. Repeat *e* and *f* for the word **on.**

h. Repeat *b* through *g* until firm.

TASK 14   Second reading—children sound out each word and say it fast

a. **Get ready to read the words again. Everybody, finger on the ball.**   Check children's responses.

b. Repeat *c* through *g* in task 13 until firm.

TASK 15   Individual test

Call on different children to read each word. The child sounds out the word as you clap, then says it fast. The other children are to point under the sounds that are said.

TASK 16   Teacher and children read the fast way

a. Point to the words on the first arrow. Touch under **on.**   **Everybody, this word is** (pause) **on. What word?** (Signal.)   *On.*   **Yes, on. Remember that.**

b. **We're going to read this story the fast way.**

c. Point to **it is.**   **I'll read these words the fast way.**

d. Point to **on.**   **When I touch this word, you're going to say . . . .**   (Signal.) *On.*   **Yes, on.**

e. Repeat *d* until firm.

f. Touch the ball of the arrow.   **Reading the fast way. (Pause three seconds.) Touch under it is and say: It is . . . .**

g. Then touch under **on.**   *On.*

h. Repeat *f* and *g* until firm.

i. **Yes, it is on.**

TASK 17   Picture comprehension

a. **You're going to see a picture of something. And . . . .** (Signal.)   *It is on.*

b. Repeat *a* until firm.

c. **Yes, you will see something and** (pause) **it is on.**   **I wonder what you'll see.**

d. **Turn your take-home over and look at the picture.**

e. **Ask these questions:**
   1. **Is something on in the picture?** *The children respond.*   *Yes, something is on.*
   2. **What is on?** *The children respond.*   *Yes, the light is on.*
   3. **That light is pretty big, isn't it?** *Yes.*
   4. **What would you do with a great big light bulb like that?**   *The children respond.*

TASK 18 Word finding

a. **Turn your take-home back to side 1. Point to the words on the first arrow. I'm going to read all these words the fast way.**

b. **Touch the ball of the arrow. Touch under each word and read:**
It (pause) is (pause) on.

c. **I'll do it again. Touch under each word and read:**
It (pause) is (pause) on.

d. **Everybody, look at the words in your story.**

e. **Look for the word (pause) it. Iiit.**

f. **Everybody, point to iiit. Get your finger right over the word**
iiit. Check children's responses.

g. **Get ready to touch (pause) it when I clap. Get ready. Clap.**
(The children touch it.)

h. **Fingers up. Repeat** *f* **and** *g* **until firm.**

i. **Everybody, look at the words in your story.**

j. **Look for the word (pause) on. Ooonnn.**

k. **Everybody, point to ooonnn. Get your finger right over the word**
ooonnn. Check children's responses.

l. **Get ready to touch (pause) on when I clap. Get ready. Clap.**
(The children touch on.)

m. **Repeat** *j* **through** *l* **until firm.**

n. Direct the children to find the words in this order:
it   (Repeat *e*, *f*, and *g*.)
on   (Repeat *j*, *k*, and *l*.)
on   (Repeat *j*, *k*, and *l*.)
it   (Repeat *e*, *f*, and *g*.)

SUMMARY OF INDEPENDENT ACTIVITY

TASK 19 Introduction to independent activity

a. Hold up Take-Home 57.

b. **Everybody, you're going to finish this take-home on your own.**
Tell the children when they will work the remaining items.
Let's go over the things you're going to do.

TASK 20 Story copying

Point to the dotted words below the story on side 1. **You're going to write the dotted words on this arrow. Then you're going to write those words on the other arrows.**

TASK 21 Pair relations

a. Point to the first box in the top row of the pair-relations exercise.

b. **Everybody, what does this first box say?** (Signal.) $\bar{e}\bar{e}\bar{e}$—*nnn*.
Yes, $\bar{e}\bar{e}\bar{e}$—nnn. You're going to fix up every box with $\bar{e}\bar{e}\bar{e}$ to say . . . . (Signal.) $\bar{e}\bar{e}\bar{e}$—*nnn*.

c. Point to the second box in the top row. **What does this box say?** (Signal.) *c*—*ooo*. **Yes, c—ooo. You're going to fix up every box with c to say . . . .** (Signal.) *c*—*ooo*.

TASK 22 Cross-out game

Point to the boxed sounds in the Cross-out Game on side 2.
Everybody, what sound are you going to circle today? (Signal.) *ththth*. **What sound are you going to cross out?** (Signal.) *ooo*.

TASK 23 Matching

Point to the first column of sounds in the Matching Game.
You're going to draw lines for every sound over here.

TASK 24 Sound writing

a. Point to the sound-writing exercise. **Here are the sounds you're going to write today. I'll touch the sounds. You say them.**

b. Touch each sound. *The children respond.*

c. Repeat the series until firm.

TASK 25 Story picture

Point to the story picture. **After you finish your take-home, you can color the story picture.**

END OF LESSON 57

Lesson 58

SOUNDS

TASK 1   Teacher firms up a

a. Point to **a**. Everybody, get ready to tell me this sound. Get ready. Touch **a**. *aaa.*

b. Point to **ā**. Everybody, look at the line over this sound. This is not **aaa**. Is it **aaa**? (Signal.) *No.*

c. Point to each sound and ask: Is this **aaa**? *The children respond.*

d. Repeat c until firm.

TASK 2   Teaching ā as in āte; children discriminate a—ā

a. Point to the first **ā**. Everybody, this is **āāā**.

b. When I touch it, you say it. (Pause.) Get ready. Touch **ā**. *āāā.*

c. Again. Touch **ā**. *āāā.*

d. Repeat c until firm.

e. Get ready to do all these sounds. When I touch the sound, you say it. Alternate touching the sounds. Before touching each **ā,** trace the line and say: Remember—this is not **aaa**.

f. Repeat e until all the sounds are firm.

TASK 3   Sounds firm-up

a. Point to **ā**. When I touch the sound, you say it.

b. (Pause.) Get ready.   Touch **ā**. *āāā.*

c. Again.   Repeat b until firm.

d. Get ready to say all the sounds when I touch them.

e. Alternate touching **o, ā, c,** and **n** three or four times. Point to the sound. (Pause one second.) Say: Get ready.   Touch the sound. *The children respond.*

TASK 4   Individual test

Call on different children to identify one or more sounds in task 3.

6

READING VOCABULARY
Get ready to read all the words on this page without making a mistake.

Do not touch any small letters.

TASK 5   Children sound out the word and tell what word

a. Touch the ball for **if.** Sound it out.
b. Get ready. Touch **i, f** as the children say *iiifff.*
c. Again. Repeat *b* until firm.
d. Yes, what word? (Signal.) *If.*

if

TASK 6   Children sound out the word and tell what word

a. Touch the ball for **on.** Sound it out.
b. Get ready. Touch **o, n** as the children say *ooonnn.*
c. Again. Repeat *b* until firm.
d. Yes, what word? (Signal.) *On.*

on

TASK 7   Children sound out the word and tell what word

a. Touch the ball for **sam.** Sound it out.
b. Get ready. Touch **s, a, m** as the children say *Sssaaammm.*
c. Again. Repeat *b* until firm.
d. Yes, what word? (Signal.) *Sam.*

sam

TASK 8   Children sound out the word and tell what word

a. Touch the ball for **sick.** Sound it out.
b. Get ready. Touch **s, i, c** as the children say *sssiiic.*
c. Again. Repeat *b* until firm.
d. Yes, what word? (Signal.) *Sick.*

sick

TASK 9   Children sound out and tell what word

a. Touch the ball for **can.** Sound it out.
b. Get ready. Touch **c, a, n** as the children say *caaannn.*
c. Again. Repeat *b* until firm.
d. Yes, what word? (Signal.) *Can.*

Individual test

Call on different children to sound out one word and tell what word.

can

58

Get ready to read all the words on this page without making a mistake.

TASK 10   Children sound out the word and tell what word

a. Touch the ball for **in.** Sound it out.
b. Get ready. Touch **i, n** as the children say *iiinnn*.
c. Again. Repeat *b* until firm.
d. Yes, what word? (Signal.) *In.*

in

TASK 11   Children sound out the word and tell what word

a. Touch the ball for **fēēt.** Sound it out.
b. Get ready. Touch **f, ē, t** as the children say *fffēēēt*.
c. Again. Repeat *b* until firm.
d. Yes, what word? (Signal.) *Feet.*

fēēt

TASK 12   Children rhyme with it

a. Point to **it** and **sit.** These words rhyme.
b. Touch the ball for **it.** Sound it out.
c. Get ready. Touch **i, t** as the children say *iiit*.
d. Return to the ball for **it.** Again. Repeat *c* until firm.
e. Yes, what word? (Signal.) *It.*
f. Quickly touch the ball for **sit.** This word rhymes with (pause) **iit.**
   Get ready. Touch **s.** *sss*. Move your finger quickly along the arrow. *Sssit.*

g. Yes, what word? (Signal.) *Sit.*

it

TASK 13   Children sound out the word and tell what word

a. Touch the ball for **sit.** Sound it out.
b. Get ready. Touch **s, i, t** as the children say *sssiiit*.
c. Again. Repeat *b* until firm.
d. Yes, what word? (Signal.) *Sit.*

sit

8

Take-Home 58

STORY

TASK 14 First reading—children sound out each word and say it fast

a. Pass out Take-Home 58. Do not let the children look at the picture until task 18.

b. Finger on the ball of the top arrow. Check children's responses.

c. Touch the first word. Check children's responses. Sound it out. Get ready. Clap for each sound. *Sssiiit.*

d. Again. (Pause.) Get ready. Clap for each sound. *Sssiiit.* Say it fast. (Signal.) *Sit.* Yes, what word? (Signal.) *Sit.*

e. Touch the next word Check children's responses. Sound it out. Get ready. Clap for each sound. *Ooonnn.*

f. Again. (Pause.) Get ready. Clap for each sound. *Ooonnn.* Say it fast. (Signal.) *On.* Yes, what word? (Signal.) *On.*

g. Repeat *e* and *f* for the word **it.**

h. Repeat *b* through *g* until firm.

TASK 15 Second reading—children sound out each word and say it fast

a. Get ready to read the words again. Everybody, finger on the ball. Check children's responses.

b. Repeat *c* through *g* in task 14 until firm.

TASK 16 Individual test

Call on different children to read each word. The child sounds out the word as you clap, then says it fast. The other children are to point under the sounds that are said.

TASK 17 Teacher and children read the fast way

a. Point to the words on the first arrow. Touch under **it.** Everybody, this word is (pause) **it.** What word? (Signal.) *It.* Yes, **it.** Remember that.

b. We're going to read this story the fast way.

c. Point to **sit on.** I'll read these words the fast way.

d. Point to **it.** When I touch this word, you're going to say . . . . (Signal.) *It.* Yes, **it.**

e. Repeat *d* until firm.

f. Touch the ball of the arrow. Reading the fast way. (Pause three seconds.) Touch under **sit on** and say: Sit on . . . .

g. Then touch under **it.** *It.*

h. Repeat *f* and *g* until firm.

i. Yes, **sit on it.**

TASK 18 Picture comprehension

a. In the picture, you'll see what happened to a boy. His grandmother said, "Don't . . . ." (Signal.) *Sit on it.*

b. Repeat *a* until firm.

c. Yes, his grandmother said, "Don't (pause) **sit on it.**" I wonder if the boy listened to his grandmother.

d. Turn your take-home over and look at the picture.

e. Ask these questions:

  1. Did the boy listen to his grandmother? *The children respond.* No, he didn't.

  2. Is he sitting on it? (Signal.) *Yes.*

  3. What is he sitting on? *The children respond.*

  4. What do you think his grandmother will say? *The children respond.*

TASK 19   Word finding

a. **Turn your take-home back to side 1.** Point to the words on the first arrow. **I'm going to read all these words the fast way.**

b. Touch the ball of the arrow. Touch under each word and read:
Sit (pause) on (pause) it.

c. I'll do it again. Touch under each word and read:
Sit (pause) on (pause) it.

d. **Everybody, look at the words in your story.**

e. **Look for the word** (pause) **it. Iiit.**

f. **Everybody, point to iiit. Get your finger right over the word iiit.**
Check children's responses.

g. **Get ready to touch** (pause) **it when I clap. Get ready. Clap.**
(The children touch it.)

h. **Fingers up.** Repeat *f* and *g* until firm.

i. **Everybody, look at the words in your story.**

j. **Look for the word** (pause) **on. Ooonnn.**

k. **Everybody, point to ooonnn. Get your finger right over the word ooonnn.** Check children's responses.

l. **Get ready to touch** (pause) **on when I clap. Get ready. Clap.**
(The children touch on.)

m. Repeat *j* through *l* until firm.

n. Direct the children to find the words in this order:
on   (Repeat *j*, *k*, and *l*.)
it   (Repeat *e*, *f*, and *g*.)
on   (Repeat *j*, *k*, and *l*.)
it   (Repeat *e*, *f*, and *g*.)

SUMMARY OF INDEPENDENT ACTIVITY

TASK 20   Introduction to independent activity

a. Hold up Take-Home 58.

b. **Everybody, you're going to finish this take-home on your own.**
Tell the children when they will work the remaining items.
Let's go over the things you're going to do.

TASK 21   Story copying

Point to the dotted words below the story on side 1. **You're going to write the dotted words on this arrow. Then you're going to write those words on the other arrows.**

TASK 22   Pair relations

a. Point to the first box in the top row of the pair-relations exercise.

b. **Everybody, what does this first box say?** (Signal.) *t—fff.*
Yes, t—fff. You're going to fix up every box with t to say . . . .
(Signal.) *t—fff.*

c. Point to the second box in the top row. **What does this box say?** (Signal.) *rrr—ththth.* **Yes, rrr—ththth. You're going to fix up every box with rrr to say . . . .** (Signal.) *rrr—ththth.*

TASK 23   Cross-out game

Point to the boxed sounds in the Cross-out Game on side 2.
Everybody, what sound are you going to circle today? (Signal.)
c. **What sound are you going to cross out?** (Signal.) *t.*

TASK 24   Matching

Point to the first column of sounds in the Matching Game.
You're going to draw lines for every sound over here.

TASK 25   Sound writing

a. Point to the sound-writing exercise. **Here are the sounds you're going to write today. I'll touch the sounds. You say them.**

b. Touch each sound. *The children respond.*

c. Repeat the series until firm.

TASK 26   Story picture

Point to the story picture. **After you finish your take-home, you can color the story picture.**

END OF LESSON 58

Lesson 59

ā

a

i

o

SOUNDS

TASK 1 Teaching ā as in āte

a. Point to ā. **My turn.** (Pause.) Touch ā and say: āāā.
b. Point to ā. **Your turn. When I touch it, you say it.** (Pause.) **Get ready.** Touch ā. *āāā.* Lift your finger.
c. **Again.** Touch ā. *āāāā.* Lift your finger.
d. Repeat *c* until firm.

TASK 2 Sounds firm-up

a. **Get ready to say the sounds when I touch them.**
b. Alternate touching ā and **a.** Point to the sound. (Pause one second.) Say: **Get ready.** Touch the sound. *The children respond.*
c. When ā and **a** are firm, alternate touching **a, i, ā,** and **o** until all four sounds are firm.

TASK 3 Individual test

Call on different children to identify **a, i, ā,** or **o.**

TASK 4 Sounds firm-up

a. Point to ā. **When I touch the sound, you say it.**
b. (Pause.) **Get ready.** Touch ā. *āāā.*
c. **Again.** Repeat *b* until firm.
d. **Get ready to say all the sounds when I touch them.**
e. Alternate touching **o, c, ē, t, ā, th, n,** and **f** three or four times. Point to the sound. (Pause one second.) Say: **Get ready.** Touch the sound. *The children respond.*

TASK 5 Individual test

Call on different children to identify one or more sounds in task 4.

Take-Home 107

SUMMARY OF INDEPENDENT ACTIVITY

TASK 24   Introduction to independent activity

a. Pass out Take-Home 107 to each child.
b. Everybody, you're going to do this take-home on your own.
Tell the children when they will work the items.
Let's go over the things you're going to do.

TASK 25   Sentence copying

a. Hold up side 1 of your take-home and point to the first line in the sentence-copying exercise.
b. Everybody, here's the sentence you're going to write on the lines below.
c. Get ready to read the words in this sentence the fast way.
First word. Check children's responses. Get ready. Clap. Thē.
d. Next word. Check children's responses. Get ready. Clap. Man.
e. Repeat d for the remaining words.
f. After you finish your take-home, you get to draw a picture about the sentence, thē man was cōld.

TASK 26   Sound writing

a. Point to the sound-writing exercise. Here are the sounds you're going to write today. I'll touch the sounds. You say them.
b. Touch each sound. The children respond.
c. Repeat the series until firm.

TASK 27   Matching

a. Point to the column of words in the Matching Game.
b. Everybody, you're going to follow the lines and write these words.
c. Reading the fast way.
d. Point to the first word. (Pause.) Get ready. (Signal.)
The children respond.
e. Repeat d for the remaining words.
f. Repeat d and e until firm.

TASK 28   Cross-out game

Point to the boxed word in the Cross-out Game. Everybody, here's the word you're going to cross out today. What word? (Signal.)
Need. Yes, need.

TASK 29   Pair relations

a. Point to the pair-relations exercise on side 2. You're going to circle the picture in each box that shows what the words say.
b. Point to the space at the top of the page. After you finish, remember to draw a picture that shows thē man was cōld.

END OF LESSON 107

END OF PRESENTATION BOOK B

59

READING VOCABULARY

Get ready to read all the words on this page without making a mistake.

Do not touch any small letters.

āte

TASK 6   Children sound out the word and tell what word

a. Touch the ball for **āte.** Sound it out.
b. **Get ready.** Touch **ā, t** as the children say *āāāt.*
c. **Again.** Repeat *b* until firm.
d. **Yes, what word?** (Signal.) *Ate.*

this

TASK 7   Children sound out the word and tell what word

a. Touch the ball for **this.** Sound it out.
b. **Get ready.** Touch **th, i, s** as the children say *thththiiisss.*
c. **Again.** Repeat *b* until firm.
d. **Yes, what word?** (Signal.) *This.*

not

TASK 8   Children sound out the word and tell what word

a. Touch the ball for **not.** Sound it out.
b. **Get ready.** Touch **n, o, t** as the children say *nnnooot.*
c. **Again.** Repeat *b* until firm.
d. **Yes, what word?** (Signal.) *Not.*

nāme

TASK 9   Children sound out the word and tell what word

a. Touch the ball for **nāme.** Sound it out.
b. **Get ready.** Touch **n, ā, m** as the children say *nnnāāāmmm.*
c. **Again.** Repeat *b* until firm.
d. **Yes, what word?** (Signal.) *Name.*

TASK 10   Individual test

Call on different children to sound out one word and tell what word.

12

Story 107

TASK 20   First reading—children read the story the fast way

Have the children reread any sentences containing words that give them trouble. Keep a list of these words.

a. Pass out Storybook 1.
b. Open your book to page 35 and get ready to read.
c. We're going to read this story the fast way.
d. Touch the first word. Check children's responses.
e. Reading the fast way. First word. (Pause three seconds.)
Get ready. Clap. *Thē.*
f. Next word. Check children's responses. (Pause three seconds.)
Get ready. Clap. *Old.*
g. Repeat *f* for the remaining words in the first sentence. Pause at least three seconds between claps. The children are to identify each word without sounding it out.
h. Repeat *d* through *g* for the next two sentences. Have the children reread the first three sentences until firm.
i. The children are to read the remainder of the story the fast way, stopping at the end of each sentence.
j. After the first reading of the story, print on the board the words that the children missed more than one time. Have the children sound out each word one time and tell what word.
k. After the group's responses are firm, call on individual children to read the words.

TASK 21   Individual test

a. I'm going to call on different children to read a whole sentence the fast way.
b. Call on different children to read a sentence. Do not clap for each word.

TASK 22   Second reading—children read the story the fast way and answer questions

a. You're going to read the story again the fast way and I'll ask questions.
b. First word. Check children's responses. Get ready. Clap. *Thē.*
c. Clap for each remaining word. Pause at least three seconds between claps. Pause longer before words that gave the children trouble during the first reading.
d. Ask the comprehension questions below as the children read.

After the children read:	You say:
The old man was cold.	How did he feel? (Signal.) *Cold.*
He did not have a hat or a coat or socks.	Tell me what he didn't have. (Signal.) *Hat, coat, socks.*
So he got a goat with lots of hats and coats and socks.	What did he get? (Signal.) *A goat.* What did the goat have? (Signal.) *Lots of hats and coats and socks.*
Now the old man is not cold	Is the old man cold now? (Signal.) *No.*
and the goat is not cold.	Is the goat cold? (Signal.) *No.*

TASK 23   Picture comprehension

a. What do you think you'll see in the picture? *The children respond.*
b. Turn the page and look at the picture.
c. Show me the goat's hats. *(The children respond.)*
d. Show me the goat's coats. *(The children respond.)*
e. Show me the goat's socks. *(The children respond.)*
f. Ask these questions:
  1. Why is that goat giving the old man a coat? *The children respond.* Yes, the man is cold.
  2. What would you do if you were that goat? *The children respond.*

Get ready to read all the words on this page without making a mistake.

Do not touch any small letters.

TASK 11 Children sound out the word and tell what word

a. Touch the ball for **mad.** Sound it out.
b. Get ready. Touch **m, a, d** as the children say *mmmaaad.*
c. Again. Repeat *b* until firm.
d. Yes, what word? (Signal.) *Mad.*

TASK 12 Children sound out the word and tell what word

a. Touch the ball for **that.** Sound it out.
b. Get ready. Touch **th, a, t** as the children say *thththaaat.*
c. Again. Repeat *b* until firm.
d. Yes, what word? (Signal.) *That.*

TASK 13 Children sound out the word and tell what word

a. Touch the ball for **ēat.** Sound it out.
b. Get ready. Touch **ē, t** as the children say *ēēēt.*
c. Again. Repeat *b* until firm.
d. Yes, what word? (Signal.) *Eat.*

TASK 14 Children sound out the word and tell what word

a. Touch the ball for **sam.** Sound it out.
b. Get ready. Touch **s, a, m** as the children say *Sssaaammm.*
c. Again. Repeat *b* until firm.
d. Yes, what word? (Signal.) *Sam.*

mad

that

ēat

sam

TASK 17   Children identify, then sound out an irregular word (said)

a. Touch the ball for **said.** Everybody, you're going to read this
word the fast way. (Pause three seconds.) Get ready.
Move your finger quickly along the arrow. *Said.* Yes, **said.**
b. Now you're going to sound out the word. Get ready.
Quickly touch **s, a, i, d** as the children say *sssaaaiiid.*
c. Again. Repeat *b.*
d. How do we say the word? (Signal.) *Said.* Yes, **said.**
e. Repeat *b* and *d* until firm.

said

TASK 18   Individual test

Call on different children to do *b* and *d* in task 17.

cōld

TASK 19   Children sound out the word and tell what word

a. Touch the ball for **cōld.** Sound it out.
b. Get ready. Touch **c, ō, l, d** as the children say *cōōōllld.*
If sounding out is not firm, repeat *b.*
c. What word? (Signal.) *Cold.* Yes, **cold.**

Take-Home 59

STORY

TASK 15 First reading—children sound out each word and say it fast

a. Pass out Take-Home 59. Do not let the children look at the picture until task 19.

b. Finger on the ball of the top arrow. Check children's responses.

c. Touch the first word. Check children's responses. Sound it out. Get ready. Clap for each sound. *Sssaaammm.*

d. Again. (Pause.) Get ready. Clap for each sound. *Sssaaammm.* Say it fast. (Signal.) *Sam.* Yes, what word? (Signal.) *Sam.*

e. Touch the next word. Check children's responses. Sound it out. Get ready. Clap for each sound. *Iiisss.*

f. Again. (Pause.) Get ready. Clap for each sound. *Iiisss.* Say it fast. (Signal.) *Is.* Yes, what word? (Signal.) *Is.*

g. Repeat e and f for the word **mad.**

h. Repeat b through g until firm.

TASK 16 Second reading—children sound out each word and say it fast

a. Get ready to read the words again. Everybody, finger on the ball. Check children's responses.

b. Repeat c through g in task 15 until firm.

TASK 17 Individual test

Call on different children to read each word. The child sounds out the word as you clap, then says it fast. The other children are to point under the sounds that are said.

TASK 18 Teacher and children read the fast way

a. Point to the words on the first arrow. Touch under **mad.** Everybody, this word is (pause) **mad.** What word? (Signal.) *Mad.* Yes, **mad.** Remember that.

b. We're going to read this story the fast way.

c. Point to **sam is.** I'll read these words the fast way.

d. Point to **mad.** When I touch this word, you're going to say . . . . (Signal.) *Mad.* Yes, **mad.**

e. Repeat d until firm.

f. Touch the ball of the arrow. Reading the fast way. (Pause three seconds.) Touch under **sam is** and say: Sam is . . . .

g. Then touch under **mad.** *Mad.*

h. Repeat f and g until firm.

i. Yes, **Sam is mad.**

TASK 19 Picture comprehension

a. What do you think the picture will show? (Signal.) *Sam is mad.*

b. Repeat a until firm.

c. Yes, the picture will show (pause) **Sam is mad.**

d. Turn your take-home over and look at the picture.

e. Ask these questions:

1. Which boy is Sam? *The children respond.*

2. How do you know that the boy in the striped shirt is Sam? *The children respond.* Yes, he's mad.

3. Why do you think Sam is mad? *The children respond.*

4. If you were the other boy, would you share your fruit with Sam? *The children respond.*

TASK 11   Children identify, then sound out an irregular word (was)

a. Touch the ball for **was.** Everybody, you're going to read this
word the fast way.   (Pause three seconds.) Get ready.
Move your finger quickly along the arrow. *Was.* Yes, **was.**
b. Now you're going to sound out the word. Get ready.
Quickly touch **w, a, s** as the children say *wwwaaasss.*
c. Again.   Repeat *b.*
d. How do we say the word?   (Signal.) *Was.* Yes, **was.**
e. Repeat *b* and *d* until firm.

was

TASK 12   Individual test

Call on different children to do *b* and *d* in task 11.

TASK 13   Children read the fast way

Touch the ball for **ōld.** Get ready to read this word the fast way.
(Pause three seconds.) Get ready.   (Signal.) *Old.*

ōld

TASK 14   Children read the fast way.

Touch the ball for **now.** Get ready to read this word the fast way.
(Pause three seconds.) Get ready.   (Signal.) *Now.*

now

TASK 15   Children read the words the fast way

a. Now you get to read the words on this page the fast way.
b. Touch the ball for **was.** (Pause three seconds.) Get ready.
Move your finger quickly along the arrow. *Was.*
c. Repeat *b* for each word on the page.

TASK 16   Individual test

Call on different children to read one word the fast way.

59

TASK 20 Word finding

a. **Turn your take-home back to side 1.** Point to the words on the first arrow. **I'm going to read all these words the fast way.**

b. Touch the ball of the arrow. Touch under each word and read:
Sam (pause) is (pause) mad.

c. **I'll do it again.** Touch under each word and read:
Sam (pause) is (pause) mad.

d. **Everybody, look at the words in your story.**

e. **Look for the word** (pause) **is. Iiisss.**

f. **Everybody, point to iiisss. Get your finger right over the word iiisss.** Check children's responses.

g. **Get ready to touch** (pause) **is when I clap. Get ready.** Clap.
(The children touch is.)

h. **Fingers up.** Repeat *f* and *g* until firm.

i. **Everybody, look at the words in your story.**

j. **Look for the word** (pause) **mad. Mmmaaad.**

k. **Everybody, point to mmmaaad. Get your finger right over the word mmmaaad.** Check children's responses.

l. **Get ready to touch** (pause) **mad when I clap. Get ready.** Clap.
(The children touch mad.)

m. Repeat *j* through *l* until firm.

n. Direct the children to find the words in this order:
is   (Repeat *e*, *f*, and *g*.)
mad (Repeat *j*, *k*, and *l*.)
is   (Repeat *e*, *f*, and *g*.)
mad (Repeat *j*, *k*, and *l*.)

SUMMARY OF INDEPENDENT ACTIVITY

TASK 21 Introduction to independent activity

a. Hold up Take-Home 59.

b. **Everybody, you're going to finish this take-home on your own.**
Tell the children when they will work the remaining items.
Let's go over the things you're going to do.

TASK 22 Story copying

Point to the dotted words below the story on side 1. **You're going to write the dotted words on this arrow. Then you're going to write those words on the other arrows.**

TASK 23 Pair relations

a. Point to the first box in the top row of the pair-relations exercise.

b. **Everybody, what does this first box say?** (Signal.) *sss—iii.*
Yes, sss—iii. You're going to fix up every box with sss to say . . . . (Signal.) *sss—iii.*

c. Point to the second box in the top row. **What does this box say?** (Signal.) *aaa—ooo.* **Yes, aaa—ooo. You're going to fix up every box with aaa to say . . . .** (Signal.) *aaa—ooo.*

TASK 24 Cross-out game

Point to the boxed sounds in the Cross-out Game on side 2.
Everybody, what sound are you going to circle today?
(Signal.) *nnn.* **What sound are you going to cross out?**
(Signal.) *rrr.*

TASK 25 Matching

Point to the first column of sounds in the Matching Game.
You're going to draw lines for every sound over here.

TASK 26 Sound writing

a. Point to the sound-writing exercise. **Here are the sounds you're going to write today. I'll touch the sounds. You say them.**

b. Touch each sound. *The children respond.*

c. Repeat the series until firm.

TASK 27 Story picture

Point to the story picture. **After you finish your take-home, you can color the story picture.**

END OF LESSON 59

READING VOCABULARY

Do not touch any small letters.

TASK 6   Children rhyme with ōats

a. Touch the ball for **ōats.** You're going to read this word the fast way. (Pause three seconds.) Get ready. Move your finger quickly along the arrow. *Oats.*

b. Touch the ball for **gōats.** This word rhymes with (pause) **oats.** Move to **g,** then quickly along the arrow. *Goats.* Yes, what word? (Signal.) *Goats.*

c. Touch the ball for **cōats.** This word rhymes with (pause) **oats.** Move to **c,** then quickly along the arrow. *Coats.* Yes, what word? (Signal.) *Coats.*

TASK 7   Children sound out an irregular word (to)

a. Touch the ball for **to.** Sound it out.
b. Get ready. Quickly touch each sound as the children say *tooo.*
c. Again. Repeat *b* until firm.
d. That's how we <u>sound out</u> the word. Here's how we <u>say</u> the word. **To.** How do we <u>say</u> the word? (Signal.) *To.*
e. Now you're going to <u>sound out</u> the word. Get ready. Touch each sound as the children say *tooo.*
f. Now you're going to say the word. Get ready. (Signal.) *To.*
g. Repeat *e* and *f* until firm.
h. Yes, this word is **to.** I want **to** eat lunch.

TASK 8   Individual test

Call on different children to do *e* and *f* in task 7.

TASK 9   Children read the words the fast way

a. Now you get to read the words on this page the fast way.
b. Touch the ball for **ōats.** (Pause three seconds.) Get ready. Move your finger quickly along the arrow. *Ōats.*
c. Repeat *b* for each word on the page.

TASK 10   Individual test

Call on different children to read one word the fast way.

Lesson 60

$\bar{a}$

$\bar{e}$

o

d

SOUNDS

TASK 1 Teaching ā as in āte

a. Point to **ā**. **My turn.** (Pause.) Touch **ā** and say: *āāā*.

b. Point to **ā**. **Your turn. When I touch it, you say it.** (Pause.) **Get ready.** Touch **ā**. *āāā*. Lift your finger.

c. **Again.** Touch **ā**. *āāāā*. Lift your finger.

d. Repeat *c* until firm.

TASK 2 Sounds firm-up

a. **Get ready to say the sounds when I touch them.**

b. Alternate touching **ā** and **ē**. Point to the sound. (Pause one second.) Say: **Get ready.** Touch the sound. *The children respond.*

c. When **ā** and **ē** are firm, alternate touching **d, ē, ā,** and **o** until all four sounds are firm.

TASK 3 Individual test

Call on different children to identify **d, ē, ā,** or **o**.

TASK 4 Teacher introduces cross-out game

a. Use acetate and crayon.

b. **I'll cross out the sounds on this page when you can tell me every sound.**

c. **Remember—when I touch it, you say it.**

d. Go over the sounds until the children can identify all the sounds in order.

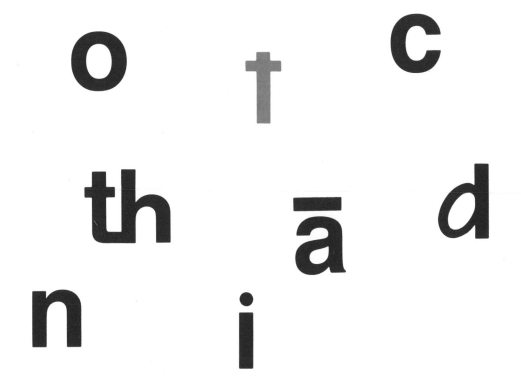

TASK 5 Individual test

Call on different children to identify two or more sounds in task 4.

TASK 6 Teacher crosses out sounds

a. **You told me every sound. Get ready to do it again. This time I'll cross out each sound when you tell me what it is.**

b. Point to each sound. (Pause.) Say: **Get ready.** Touch the sound. *The children respond.* As you cross out the sound, say: **Goodbye, _____.**

16

Lesson 107

SOUNDS

TASK 1   Teacher introduces cross-out game

a. Use acetate and crayon.
b. I'll cross out the sounds on this page when you can tell me every
sound.

c. Remember—when I touch it, you say it.
d. Go over the sounds until the children can identify all the sounds
in order.

ē   i

l   sh   I

n   t   d

TASK 2   Individual test

Call on different children to identify two or more sounds in task 1.

TASK 3   Teacher crosses out sounds

a. You told me every sound. Get ready to do it again. This time I'll
cross out each sound when you tell me what it is.
b. Point to each sound. (Pause.) Say: Get ready.   Touch the sound.
The children respond. As you cross out the sound, say:
Goodbye, _____ .

TASK 4   Child plays teacher

a. Use acetate and crayon.
b. [Child's name] is going to be the
teacher.
c. [He or She] is going to touch
the sounds. When [he or she]
touches a sound, you say it.
d. The child points to and touches
the sounds. You circle any sound
that is not firm.
e. After the child has completed the
page, present all the circled
sounds to the children.

TASK 5   Individual test

Call on different children.
If you can say the sound when I call
your name, you may cross it out.

ā

k

v

u

g

w

ō   o

323

READING VOCABULARY

Get ready to read the words on this page without making a mistake.

TASK 7   Children sound out the word and tell what word

---

a. Touch the ball for **fat**. Sound it out.
b. Get ready. Touch **f, a, t** as the children say *fffaaat*. If sounding out
is not firm, repeat *b*.
c. What word? (Signal.) *Fat*. Yes, **fat**.

TASK 8   Children sound out the word, then read it the fast way

---

a. Touch the ball for **thē**. Sound it out.
b. Get ready. Touch **th, ē** as the children say *thththēēē*. If sounding out
is not firm, repeat *b*.
c. What word? (Signal.) *Thē*. Yes, **thē**.
d. Return to the ball. Get ready to read the word the fast way.
Don't sound it out. Just tell me the word.
e. (Pause at least three seconds.) Get ready. Move your finger quickly
along the arrow. *Thē*. Yes, **thē**. Good reading.

To correct	If the children sound out the word instead of reading it the fast way
	1. Say: **I'll read the word the <u>fast</u> way. Thē.**
	2. Repeat *d* and *e* until firm.
	3. Repeat *a* through *e*.

f. Repeat *d* and *e* until firm.

TASK 9   Individual test

Call on different children to do *d* and *e* in task 8.

Take-Home 106

SUMMARY OF INDEPENDENT ACTIVITY

TASK 19   Introduction to independent activity

a. Pass out Take-Home 106 to each child.
b. Everybody, you're going to do this take-home on your own. Tell the children when they will work the items. Let's go over the things you're going to do.

TASK 20   Sentence copying

a. Hold up side 1 of your take-home and point to the first line in the sentence-copying exercise.
b. Everybody, here's the sentence you're going to write on the lines below.
c. Get ready to read the words in this sentence the fast way. First word. Check children's responses. Get ready. Clap. *Give.*
d. Next word. Check children's responses. Get ready. Clap. *Me.*
e. Repeat *d* for the remaining words.
f. After you finish your take-home, you get to draw a picture about the sentence, **give mē a sock.**

TASK 21   Sound writing

a. Point to the sound-writing exercise. Here are the sounds you're going to write today. I'll touch the sounds. You say them.
b. Touch each sound. *The children respond.*
c. Repeat the series until firm.

TASK 22   Matching

a. Point to the column of words in the Matching Game.
b. Everybody, you're going to follow the lines and write these words.
c. Reading the fast way.
d. Point to the first word. (Pause.) Get ready. (Signal.)
The children respond.
e. Repeat *d* for the remaining words.
f. Repeat *d* and *e* until firm.

TASK 23   Cross-out game

Point to the boxed word in the Cross-out Game. Everybody, here's the word you're going to cross out today. What word? (Signal.)
Hats. Yes, **hats.**

TASK 24   Pair relations

a. Point to the pair-relations exercise on side 2. You're going to circle the picture in each box that shows what the words say.
b. Point to the space at the top of the page. After you finish, remember to draw a picture that shows **give mē a sock.**

END OF LESSON 106

Do not touch any small letters.

60

TASK 10   Children sound out the word and tell what word

a. Touch the ball for **sick**. Sound it out.
b. Get ready. Touch **s, i, c** as the children say *sssiiic*.
                              If sounding out is not firm, repeat *b*.
c. What word? (Signal.) *Sick*. **Yes, sick.**

TASK 11   Children sound out the word, then read it the fast way

a. Touch the ball for **rat**. Sound it out.
b. Get ready. Touch **r, a, t** as the children say *rrraaat*. If sounding out
                              is not firm, repeat *b*.
c. What word? (Signal.) *Rat*. **Yes, rat.**
d. Return to the ball. **Get ready to read the word the fast way.**
                              Don't sound it out. Just tell me the word.
e. (Pause at least three seconds.) **Get ready.** Move your finger
                    quickly along the arrow. *Rat*. **Yes, rat. Good reading.**

To correct	If the children sound out the word instead of reading it the fast way
	1. Say: **I'll read the word the <u>fast</u> way. Rat.**
	2. Repeat *d* and *e* until firm.
	3. Repeat *a* through *e*.

f. Repeat *d* and *e* until firm.

TASK 12   Individual test

Call on different children to do *d* and *e* in task 11.

TASK 15 Second reading—children read the story the fast way and answer questions

a. Now you're going to read the story the fast way and I'll ask some more questions.

b. Finger on the ball of the top line. Check children's responses.
Remember to stop when you get to a period.

c. Get ready. Clap for each word in the first sentence. Pause at least three seconds between claps. Pause longer before words that gave the children trouble during the first reading.

d. Clap for the word following **sock.** Praise children who do not read the word.

e. Again. Repeat *b* through *d* until firm.

f. Then ask: What did he say? (Signal.) *Give me a hat or a sock.*
Who said that? (Signal.) *He did.*

g. Reading the words in the next sentence the fast way.

h. Get ready. Clap for each word in the second sentence. Pause at least three seconds between claps. Pause longer before words that gave the children trouble during the first reading.

i. Clap for the word following **nōse.** Praise children who do not read the word.

j. Let's read that sentence again the fast way. Repeat *h* and *i* until firm.

k. Then ask: What kind of sock did she give him? (Signal.)
A sock for his nose.
Is that the kind of sock he wanted? (Signal.) *No.*
What kind of a sock did he want? *The children respond.*

l. Use the procedure in *g* through *j* for the remaining sentences.
Ask the comprehension questions below as the children read.

After the children read:	You say:
He said, "I need socks on the feet, not on the nose."	What did he say? (Signal.) *I need socks on the feet, not on the nose.*
So she gave him socks for his feet.	What did she do? (Signal.) *She gave him socks for his feet.*

TASK 16 Picture comprehension

a. I wonder what kind of socks she gave him. *The children respond.*

b. Turn the page and look at the picture.

c. Ask these questions:
  1. Did she give him socks for his feet? *Yes.*
  2. What kind of socks did she give him? *The children respond.*
Big, striped socks.

TASK 17 Individual test

a. Turn back to page 33. I'm going to call on different children to read a whole sentence the fast way.

b. Call on different children to read one of the first three sentences.
Do not clap for each word.

TASK 18 Sentence saying

Good reading. Now, everybody, say all the words in that sentence without looking. (Signal.) *The children repeat the sentence at a normal speaking rate.*

60

Get ready to read all the words on this page without making a mistake. Do not touch any small letters.

TASK 13   Children sound out the word and tell what word

a. Touch the ball for **that.**   Sound it out.
b. Get ready.   Touch **th, a, t** as the children say *thththaaat.*
If sounding out is not firm, repeat *b.*
c. What word?   (Signal.) *That.*   Yes, **that.**

that

TASK 14   Children sound out the word and tell what word

a. Touch the ball for **this.**   Sound it out.
b. Get ready.   Touch **th, i, s** as the children say *thththiiisss.*
If sounding out is not firm, repeat *b.*
c. What word?   (Signal.) *This.*   Yes, **this.**

this

TASK 15   Children rhyme with āte

a. Point to **āte** and **rāte.**   These words rhyme.
b. Touch the ball for **āte.**   Sound it out.
c. Get ready.   Touch **ā, t** as the children say *āāāt.* If sounding out is not firm repeat *c.*
d. What word?   (Signal.) *Ate.*   Yes, **ate.**
e. Quickly touch the ball for **rāte.**   This word rhymes with (pause) **āat.** Get ready.   Touch **r.** *rrr.* Move your finger quickly along the arrow. *Rrrāte.*
f. What word?   (Signal.) *Rate.*   Yes, **rate.**

āte

TASK 16   Individual test

Call on different children to sound out one word and tell what word.

rāte

Story 106

Do not clap for any small letters.

TASK 13   Quotation finding

a. Pass out Storybook 1.
b. Open your book to page 33.
c. Hold up your storybook. Underline the first sentence with your finger. Somebody is saying something in this sentence. Touch the marks that show the words that he is saying. *(The children touch the quotation marks around* **give mē a hat ōr a sock.***)*
d. Underline the third sentence with your finger. Somebody is saying something in this sentence. Touch the marks that show the words that he is saying. *(The children touch the quotation marks around* **I nēēd socks on thē fēēt, not on thē nōse.***)*
e. Repeat *c* and *d* until firm.

TASK 14   First reading—children read the story and answer questions

Have the children reread any sentences containing words that give them trouble. Keep a list of these words.

a. You're going to read the story and I'll ask questions.
b. Clap for the sounds in each word as the children sound out each word one time and tell what word.
c. Present the items below as the children read.

After the children read:	You say:
He said,	**Now we're going to read what he said.**
"Give me a hat or a sock."	**What did he say?** (Signal.) *Give me a hat or a sock.*
He said,	**Now we're going to read what he said.**
"I need socks on the feet, not on the nose."	**What did he say?** (Signal.) *I need socks on the feet, not on the nose.*

d. After the first reading of the story, print on the board the words that the children missed more than one time. Have the children sound out each word one time and tell what word.
e. After the group's responses are firm, call on individual children to read the words.

Take-Home 60

STORY
Do not clap for any small letters.

TASK 17   First reading—children sound out each word and say it fast

a. Pass out Take-Home 60. Do not let the children look at the picture
                                                                 until task 21.
b. **Finger on the ball of the top arrow.** Check children's responses.
c. **Touch the first word.** Check children's responses. **Sound it out.**
                    Get ready. Clap for each sound. *Thththēēē.*
d. **Again.** (Pause.) **Get ready.** Clap for each sound. *Thththēēē.*
                Say it fast. (Signal.) *Thē.* **Yes, what word?** (Signal.) *Thē.*
e. **Touch the next word.** Check children's responses. **Sound it out.**
                    Get ready. Clap for each sound. *Rrraaat.*
f. **Again.** (Pause.) **Get ready.** Clap for each sound. *Rrraaat.*
                Say it fast. (Signal.) *Rat.* **Yes, what word?** (Signal.) *Rat.*
g. Repeat *e* and *f* for the word **āte.**
h. Repeat *b* through *g* until firm.

TASK 18   Second reading—children sound out each word and say it fast

a. **Get ready to read the words again. Everybody, finger on the ball.**
                                              Check children's responses.
b. Repeat *c* through *g* in task 17 until firm.

TASK 19   Individual test

Call on different children to read each word. The child sounds out the
            word as you clap, then says it fast. The other children are to point
                    under the sounds that are said.

TASK 20   Teacher and children read the fast way

a. Point to the words on the first arrow. Touch under **āte.**
                Everybody, this word is (pause) **ate. What word?** (Signal.)
                                        Ate. **Yes, ate. Remember that.**
b. **We're going to read this story the fast way.**
c. Point to **thē rat. I'll read these words the fast way.**
d. Point to **āte. When I touch this word, you're going to say . . . .**
                                        (Signal.) *Ate.* **Yes, ate.**
e. Repeat *d* until firm.
f. Touch the ball of the arrow. **Reading the fast way.** (Pause three
                seconds.) Touch under **thē rat** and say: **Thē rat . . . .**
g. Then touch under **āte.** *Ate.*
h. Repeat *f* and *g* until firm.
i. **Yes, thē rat ate.**

TASK 21   Picture comprehension

a. **What do you think the picture will show?** (Signal.) *Thē rat ate.*
b. Repeat *a* until firm.
c. **Yes, the picture will show** (pause) **thē rat ate.**
d. **Turn your take-home over and look at the picture.**
e. **Ask these questions:**
  1. **There's the rat. What did the rat eat?** *The children respond.*
  2. **What did the rat drink?** (Signal.) *Milk.*
  3. **Does the rat look sad to you?** *The children respond.* **No.**
  4. **Does the rat look pretty full?** *The children respond.*

TASK 7 Children sound out the word and tell what word

a. Touch the ball for **gōat. Sound it out.**
b. Get ready. Touch **g, ō, t** as the children say *gōōōt.*

If sounding out is not firm, repeat *b.*

c. What word? (Signal.) *Goat.* Yes, **goat.**

Do not touch any small letters.

TASK 8 Children sound out an irregular word (to)

a. Touch the ball for **to. Sound it out.**
b. Get ready. Quickly touch each sound as the children say *tooo.*

To correct	If the children do not say the sounds you touch
	1. Say: **You've got to say the sounds I touch.**
	2. Repeat *a* and *b* until firm.

c. Again. Repeat *b* until firm.
d. That's how we <u>sound out</u> the word. Here's how we <u>say</u> the word.

To. How do we <u>say</u> the word? (Signal.) *To.*

e. Now you're going to <u>sound out</u> the word. Get ready.

Touch each sound as the children say *tooo.*

f. Now you're going to say the word. Get ready. (Signal.) *To.*
g. Repeat *e* and *f* until firm.
h. Yes, this word is to. Go to school.

TASK 9 Individual test

Call on different children to do *e* and *f* in task 8.

TASK 10 Children rhyme with socks

a. Touch the ball for **socks. You're going to read this word the fast way.** (Pause three seconds.) **Get ready.** Move your finger quickly along the arrow. *Socks.*
b. Touch the ball for **rocks. This word rhymes with** (pause) **socks.**
Move to **r,** then quickly along the arrow. *Rrrocks.*
Yes, **what word?** (Signal.) *Rocks.*

TASK 11 Children read the words the fast way

Have the children read the words on this page the fast way.

TASK 12 Individual test

Call on different children to read one word the fast way.

TASK 22　Word finding

a. Turn your take-home back to side 1.　Point to the words on the first arrow.　I'm going to read all these words the fast way.

b. Touch the ball of the arrow. Touch under each word and read:

The (pause) rat (pause) ate.

c. I'll do it again.　Touch under each word and read:

The (pause) rat (pause) ate.

d. Everybody, look at the words in your story.

e. Look for the word　(pause)　**thē. Thththēēē.**

f. Everybody, point to **thththēēē.** Get your finger right over the word **thththēēē.** Check children's responses.

g. Get ready to touch　(pause)　**thē** when I clap. Get ready.　Clap.

*(The children touch **thē**.)*

h. Fingers up.　Repeat *f* and *g* until firm.

i. Everybody, look at the words in your story.

j. Look for the word　(pause)　**ate. Aāāte.**

k. Everybody, point to **āāāte.** Get your finger right over the word **āāāte.** ·Check children's responses.

l. Get ready to touch　(pause)　**ate** when I clap. Get ready.　Clap.

*(The children touch **āte**.)*

m. Repeat *j* through *l* until firm.

n. Direct the children to find the words in this order:

thē (Repeat *e*, *f*, and *g*.)
āte (Repeat *j*, *k*, and *l*.)
āte (Repeat *j*, *k*, and *l*.)
thē (Repeat *e*, *f*, and *g*.)

SUMMARY OF INDEPENDENT ACTIVITY

TASK 23　Introduction to independent activity

a. Hold up Take-Home 60.

b. Everybody, you're going to finish this take-home on your own.
Tell the children when they will work the remaining items.
Let's go over the things you're going to do.

TASK 24　Story copying

Point to the dotted words below the story on side 1.　You're going to write the dotted words on this arrow. Then you're going to write those words on the other arrows.

TASK 25　Pair relations

a. Point to the first box in the top row of the pair-relations exercise.

b. Everybody, what does this first box say? (Signal.) ēēē—āāā.
Yes, ēēē—āāā. You're going to fix up every box with ēēē to say . . . . (Signal.) ēēē—āāā.

c. Point to the second box in the top row.　What does this box say? (Signal.) t—thththt. Yes, **t—thththt.** You're going to fix up every box with **t** to say . . . . (Signal.) t—thththt.

TASK 26　Cross-out game

Point to the boxed sounds in the Cross-out Game on side 2.
Everybody, what sound are you going to circle today?　(Signal.)
aaa.　What sound are you going to cross out?　(Signal.) *nnn.*

TASK 27　Matching

Point to the first column of sounds in the Matching Game.
You're going to draw lines for every sound over here.

TASK 28　Sound writing

a. Point to the sound-writing exercise.　Here are the sounds you're going to write today. I'll touch the sounds. You say them.

b. Touch each sound. *The children respond.*

c. Repeat the series until firm.

TASK 29　Story picture

Point to the story picture. After you finish your take-home,
you can color the story picture.

END OF LESSON 60

Before presenting lesson 61, give Mastery Test 11 to each child.
Do not present lesson 61 to any groups that are not firm on this test.

READING VOCABULARY

Do not touch any small letters.

TASK 4 Children read the fast way

a. Get ready to read these words the fast way.

b. Touch the ball for **nōse.** (Pause three seconds.) Get ready.

(Signal.) *Nose.*

c. Repeat *b* for the remaining words on the page.

TASK 5 Children read the fast way again

a. Get ready to do these words again. Watch where I point.

b. Point to a word. (Pause one second.) Say: Get ready. (Signal.)

The children respond. Point to the words in this order:

nēēd, nōse, ōr, fēēt, not.

c. Repeat *b* until firm.

TASK 6 Individual test

Call on different children to read one word the fast way.

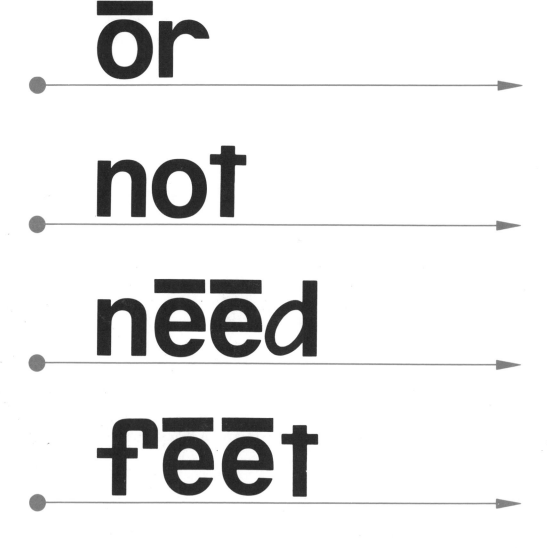

Mastery Test 11 after lesson 60, before lesson 61

a. When I touch the sound, you say it.
b. **(test item)** Point to **o**. Get ready. Touch **o**. *ooo.*
c. **(test item)** Point to **n**. Get ready. Touch **n**. *nnn.*
d. **(test item)** Point to **c**. Get ready. Touch **c**. *c.*

 o   n   c

e. Point to **ēat, mēat, nēat.** These words rhyme.
f. **(test item)** Touch the ball for **ēat**. Sound it out. Get ready.
Touch **ē, t**. *Eēēt.*
g. **(test item)** What word? *Eat.*
h. **(test item)** Quickly touch the ball for **mēat.**
This word rhymes with (pause) **ēēt**. Get ready. Touch **m**. Move
your finger quickly along the arrow. *Mmmēat.*
i. **(test item)** What word? *Meat.*
j. **(test item)** Quickly touch the ball for **nēat**. This word rhymes with
(pause) **ēēt**. Get ready.   Touch **n**. Move your finger quickly along the
arrow. *Nnnēat.*
k. **(test item)** What word? *Neat.*

Total number of test items: **9**

A group is weak if more than one-third of the children missed any of
the items on the test.

WHAT TO DO

If the group is firm on Mastery Test 11 and was firm on Mastery Test 10:

Skip lesson 61, present lesson 62 to the group during the next reading
period, and then skip lesson 63. If more than one child missed any of
the items on the test, present the firming procedures specified in the
next column to those children.

If the group is firm on Mastery Test 11 but was weak on Mastery Test 10:

Present lesson 61 to the group during the next reading period. If more
than one child missed any of the items on the test, present the firming
procedures specified below to those children.

If the group is weak on Mastery Test 11:

A. Present these firming procedures to the group during the next
reading period.
  1. Lesson 57, Reading Vocabulary, page 3, task 12.
  2. Lesson 58, Sounds, page 6, tasks 3, 4.
  3. Lesson 58, Reading Vocabulary, page 8, tasks 12, 13.
  4. Lesson 59, Sounds, page 11, tasks 4, 5.
  5. Lesson 60, Reading Vocabulary, page 19, tasks 15, 16.
B. After presenting the above tasks, again give Mastery Test 11
individually to members of the group who failed the test.
C. If the group is firm (less than one-third of the total group missed
any of the items on the retest), present lesson 61 to the group
during the next reading period.
D. If the group is still weak (more than one-third of the total group
missed any items on the retest), repeat *A* and *B* during the next
reading period.

Lesson 106

SOUNDS

TASK 1   Child plays teacher

a. Use acetate and crayon.
b. [Child's name] is going to be the teacher.
c. [He or She] is going to touch the sounds. When [he or she] touches a sound, you say it.
d. The child points to and touches the sounds. You circle any sound that is not firm.
e. After the child has completed the page, present all the circled sounds to the children.

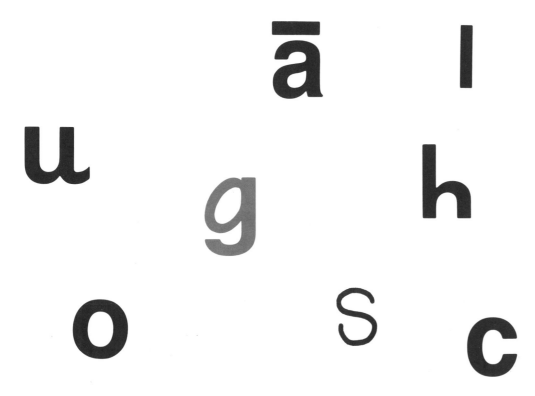

TASK 2   Individual test

Call on different children. If you can say the sound when I call your name, you may cross it out.

TASK 3   Teacher and children play the sounds game

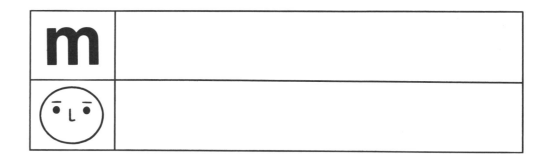

a. Use acetate and crayon. Write the sounds in the symbol box. Keep score in the score box.
b. I'm smart. I bet I can beat you in a game.
c. Here's the rule. When I touch a sound, you say it.
d. Play the game.
Make one symbol at a time in the symbol box. Use the symbols **v, k, th,** and **ō.**
Make each symbol quickly. (Pause.) Touch the symbol.
Play the game for about two minutes.
Then ask: Who won? Draw a mouth on the face in the score box.

Planning Pages: *For Lessons 61–80*

Making Progress

	Since Lesson 1	Since Lesson 41
Word Reading	14 sounds 59 regular words Reading words the fast way	5 sounds 44 regular words Reading words the fast way
Comprehension	**Picture Comprehension** Predicting what the picture will show	

What to Use

Teacher	Students
Presentation Book B (pages 23–155) **Teacher's Guide** (pages 32–33, 42–43) **Teacher's Take-Home Book and Answer Key** **Spelling Book**	**Take-Home Book B** lined paper (Spelling)

Keep in Mind:

The correction for all word misidentification errors is to have the children "Sound it out." Be sure to repeat any task on which the children have made an error.

What's Ahead in Lessons 61–80

New Skills
- Story length will increase from 4 to 15 words.
- Children begin to answer *who, what, when, where* and *why* questions about the story (Lesson 75).
- Children will answer questions about the picture.
- Words are read "the fast way" without first sounding out (Lesson 65).
- Children begin reading sentences in a story the fast way (Lesson 78).
- Comprehension activities are introduced on Take-Homes, with children crossing out a picture that does not match the word (Lesson 70).

New Sounds
- Lesson 61 – **h** as in *hat* (quick sound)
- Lesson 64 – **u** as in *under*
- Lesson 68 – **g** as in *gate* (quick sound)
- Lesson 72 – **l** as in *lock*
- Lesson 76 – **w** as in *wish* (This is a tricky one! Check the tape for proper pronunciation.)
- Lesson 80 – **sh** as in *shut*

New Vocabulary
- *Regular words:*

(62) mack	(71) and
(63) he, his, hit, hot	(73) came, fig
(64) mitt	(74) late
(65) had, ham	(75) hate, lick, rain, sand
(66) fun, run, sun	(76) hand, land, lock
(67) cut, nut	(77) game, mail, same
(68) dot, has, hat, sin	(78) nail, sail, we
(69) ant, mud, us	(79) ill, lid, mill, rut, sag, will
(70) fade, made, rag, rug	

Mastery Test 20 after lesson 105, before lesson 106

a. **Get ready to read the story.**
b. **First word.** (Pause.) **Get ready.** Clap for each sound as the child sounds out **she** one time.
c. **(test item)** **What word?** (Signal.) *She.*
d. **Next word.** (Pause.) **Get ready.** Clap for each sound as the child sounds out **can** one time.
e. **(test item)** **What word?** (Signal.) *Can.*
f. **(11 test items)** Repeat *d* and *e* for the remaining 11 words in the story.

Total number of test items: **13**

A group is weak if more than one-third of the children missed two or more words on the test.

If the group is firm on Mastery Test 20:

Present lesson 106 to the group during the next reading period. If more than one child missed two or more words on the test, present the firming procedures specified below to those children.

If the group is weak on Mastery Test 20:

A. Present these firming procedures to the group during the next reading period. Have the children read the story. Clap for the sounds in each word as the children sound out a word one time and tell what word. Then call on individual children to sound out a word and tell what word. Present each story until the children make no more than two mistakes. Then proceed to the next story.
   1. Story 103.
   2. Story 104.
   3. Story 105.
B. After presenting the above stories, again give Mastery Test 20 individually to members of the group who failed the test.
C. If the group is firm (less than one-third of the total group missed two or more words in the story on the retest), present lesson 106 to the group during the next reading period.
D. If the group is still weak (more than one-third of the total group missed two or more words in the story on the retest), repeat *A* and *B* during the next reading period.

shē can kick.

shē can lick.

shē said, "I am

not a cat."

Look Ahead

Mastery Tests

Skill Tested	Implications
Test 12 (Lesson 65) Reading a story, sounding out	Children will be reading sentences "the fast way" in upcoming lessons; children should be firm in sounding.
Test 13 (Lesson 70) Sounds $\bar{a}$, a, h, u, i	Be sure the children are firm on the difference between the sounds $\bar{a}$ and **a**.
Test 14 (Lesson 75) Reading a story, sounding out	Some children may need additional practice in reading the fast way.
Test 15 (Lesson 80) Word reading, sounding out, and reading the fast way	

Skills

	Lessons 61–80
Word Reading	6 sounds
	47 regular words
	Reading words the fast way
Comprehension	Answering questions about the picture
	Answering *who, what, when, where* and *why* questions orally

Reading Activities

Help children develop decoding and comprehension skills by using the following reading activities.

Fun with New Words (Lesson 79)

After the children complete Lesson 79, have them reinforce both current vocabulary and vocabulary that was previously introduced. On the chalkboard, randomly list the words from two or three lists below. Have children sort the words, using the chosen categories of outdoor things, indoor things, animals, feelings, people, and foods.

✷	⊞	🐱	😊😦	🧍🧍	🌭
roc𝗄s	fan	ram	mad	m$\bar{e}$	s$\bar{e}\bar{e}$d
sun	soc𝗄	cat	sad	t$\bar{e}$am	m$\bar{e}$at
mud	lid	rat	miss	sam	ham
r$\bar{a}$in	rag	ant	f$\bar{e}$ar	dan	nut
sand	sac𝗄		m$\bar{e}$an	man	fig
s$\bar{a}$il	rug		h$\bar{a}$te	mac𝗄	

Rhyming Books (Lesson 78)

Make a book by folding a sheet of white drawing paper into uneven pages. With the book closed, write a line and the rhyming word part on the exposed side (right). Draw a line for the beginning sound on the front page. Children fill in the beginning sound on the front page. They also make a beginning sound on the inside page. Children illustrate both pictures. Some example rhyming combinations are listed below.

hit	dot	sic𝗄
sit	hot	lic𝗄

fun	s$\bar{a}$il	loc𝗄
run	n$\bar{a}$il	soc𝗄
sun	m$\bar{a}$il	roc𝗄

More Than One Meaning (Lessons 63, 67, 73, 78)

In Lessons 63, 67, 73 and 78, the children learn words that have multiple meanings. Have children fold a piece of drawing paper in half and choose a word with multiple meanings from the vocabulary word list. Example words are as follows: cut, f$\bar{e}\bar{e}$t, fan, can, roc𝗄. Have children write the word on the bottom of each half. Then have children draw or cut out pictures to show the different meanings. Make a display of the drawings or bind the children's work into a class book.

Lessons 61–80

Take-Home 105

SUMMARY OF INDEPENDENT ACTIVITY

TASK 24   Introduction to independent activity

a. Pass out sides 1 and 2 of Take-Home 105 to each child.

b. Everybody, do a good job on your take-home today and I'll give you a bonus take-home. That is an extra take-home for doing a good job.

c. Hold up side 1 of your take-home.   You're going to do this take-home on your own. Tell the children when they will work the items.   Let's go over the things you're going to do.

TASK 25   Sentence copying

a. Point to the first line in the sentence-copying exercise.

b. Everybody, here's the sentence you're going to write on the lines below.

c. Get ready to read the words in this sentence the fast way.
   First word. Check children's responses.   Get ready. Clap. *The.*

d. Next word. Check children's responses.   Get ready. Clap. *Old.*

e. Repeat *d* for the remaining words.

f. After you finish your take-home, you get to draw a picture about the sentence, **thē ōld man shāves.**

TASK 26   Sound writing

a. Point to the sound-writing exercise.   Here are the sounds you're going to write today. I'll touch the sounds. You say them.

b. Touch each sound. *The children respond.*

c. Repeat the series until firm.

TASK 27   Matching

a. Point to the column of words in the Matching Game.

b. Everybody, you're going to follow the lines and write these words.

c. Reading the fast way.

d. Point to the first word. (Pause.)   Get ready. (Signal.)
The children respond.

e. Repeat *d* for the remaining words.

f. Repeat *d* and *e* until firm.

TASK 28   Cross-out game

Point to the boxed word in the Cross-out Game.   Everybody, here's the word you're going to cross out today. What word? (Signal.)
Now. Yes, **now.**

TASK 29   Pair relations

a. Point to the pair-relations exercise on side 2.   You're going to circle the picture in each box that shows what the words say.

b. Point to the space at the top of the page.   After you finish, remember to draw a picture that shows **thē ōld man shāves.**

TASK 30   Bonus take-home

After the children have completed their take-home exercises, give them sides 3 and 4 of Take-Home 105. Tell them they may keep the stories and read them.

END OF LESSON 105

Before presenting lesson 106, give Mastery Test 20 to each child.
Do not present lesson 106 to any groups that are not firm on this test.

Lesson 61

Groups that are firm on Mastery Tests 10 and 11 should skip this lesson and do lesson 62 today.

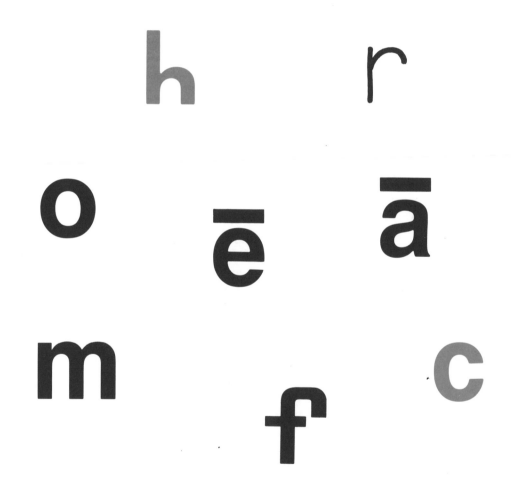

SOUNDS

TASK 1 Teaching **h** as in **hat**

a. Point to **h**. Here's a new sound. It's a quick sound.
b. My turn. (Pause.) Touch **h** for an instant, saying: *h*.
Do not say **huh** or **hih**.
c. Again. Touch **h** and say: *h*.
d. Point to **h**. Your turn. When I touch it, you say it. (Pause.) Get ready. Touch **h**. *h*.
e. Again. Touch **h**. *h*.
f. Repeat *e* until firm.

TASK 2 Individual test

Call on different children to identify **h**.

TASK 3 Sounds firm-up

a. Get ready to say the sounds when I touch them.
b. Alternate touching **h** and **ā**. Point to the sound. (Pause one second.) Say: Get ready. Touch the sound. *The children respond.*
c. When **h** and **ā** are firm, alternate touching **h, ā, th,** and **n** until all four sounds are firm.

TASK 4 Individual test

Call on different children to identify **h, ā, th,** or **n**.

TASK 5 Sounds firm-up

a. Point to **h**. When I touch the sound, you say it.
b. (Pause.) Get ready. Touch **h**. *h*.
c. Again. Repeat *b* until firm.
d. Get ready to say all the sounds when I touch them.
e. Alternate touching **m, r, o, ē, ā, h, f,** and **c** three or four times.
Point to the sound. (Pause one second.) Say: Get ready.
Touch the sound. *The children respond.*

TASK 6 Individual test

Call on different children to identify one or more sounds in task 5.

TASK 20 Second reading—children read the story the fast way and answer questions

a. Now you're going to read the story the fast way and I'll ask some more questions.

b. Finger on the ball of the top line. Check children's responses. Remember to stop when you get to a period.

c. Get ready. Clap for each word in the first sentence. Pause at least three seconds between claps. Pause longer before words that gave the children trouble during the first reading.

d. Clap for the word following **cat**. Praise children who do not read the word.

e. Again. Repeat *b* through *d* until firm.

f. Then ask: What did he say? (Signal.) *I can shave a cat.* Who said that? (Signal.) *The old man.*

g. Reading the words in the next sentence the fast way.

h. Get ready. Clap for each word in the second sentence. Pause at least three seconds between claps. Pause longer before words that gave the children trouble during the first reading.

i. Clap for the word following **did**. Praise children who do not read the word.

j. Let's read that sentence again the fast way. Repeat *h* and *i* until firm.

k. Then ask: What did he do? (Signal.) *He shaved a cat.*

l. Use the procedures in *g* through *j* for the remaining sentences. Ask the comprehension questions below as the children read.

m. Use the procedures in *h* through *l* for the remaining sentences in the story. Ask the comprehension questions below as the children read.

After the children read:	You say:
The old man said, "I can shave a cow."	What did he say? (Signal.) *I can shave a cow.*
So he did.	What did he do? (Signal.) *He shaved a cow.*
The old man said, "I can shave a rock."	What did he say? (Signal.) *I can shave a rock.* That's silly.
Did he shave a rock?	What do you think? *The children respond.* Let's read and find out.
No.	Did he shave a rock? (Signal.) *No.*

TASK 21 Picture comprehension

a. What do you think you'll see in the picture? *The children respond.*

b. Turn the page and look at the picture.

c. Ask these questions:
1. What is the old man holding? *The children respond.* A rock and a razor.
2. What is he doing? *The children respond.* Trying to shave a rock.
3. Did he shave that cat? *The children respond.* Yes.
4. Do you think he shaves his beard? *The children respond.* No.
5. Who can show me how a man shaves his face? *The children respond.*

TASK 22 Individual test

a. Turn back to page 30. I'm going to call on different children to read a whole sentence the fast way.

b. Call on different children to read one of the first three sentences. Do not clap for each word.

TASK 23 Sentence saying

Good reading. Now, everybody, say all the words in that sentence without looking. (Signal.) *The children repeat the sentence at a normal speaking rate.*

READING VOCABULARY

Get ready to read all the words on this page without making a mistake.

TASK 7 Children sound out the word and tell what word

a. Touch the ball for **sick.** Sound it out.
b. Get ready. Touch **s, i, c** as the children say *sssiiic.*

If sounding out is not firm, repeat *b.*

c. What word? (Signal.) *Sick.* Yes, **sick.**

TASK 8 Children sound out the word and tell what word

a. Touch the ball for **sit.** Sound it out.
b. Get ready. Touch **s, i, t** as the children say *sssiiit.*

If sounding out is not firm, repeat *b.*

c. What word? (Signal.) *Sit.* Yes, **sit.**

TASK 9 Children sound out the word, then read it the fast way

a. Touch the ball for **not.** Sound it out.
b. Get ready. Touch **n, o, t** as the children say *nnnooot.*

If sounding out is not firm, repeat *b.*

c. What word? (Signal.) *Not.* Yes, **not.**
d. Return to the ball. Get ready to read the word the fast way.

Don't sound it out. Just tell me the word.

e. (Pause at least three seconds.) Get ready. Move your finger quickly
along the arrow. *Not.* Yes, **not.** Good reading.

To correct	If the children sound out the word instead of reading it the fast way **1.** Say: **I'll read the word the <u>fast</u> way. Not.** **2.** Repeat *d* and *e* until firm. **3.** Repeat *a* through *e.*

f. Repeat *d* and *e* until firm.

TASK 10 Individual test

Call on different children to do *d* and *e* in task 9.

TASK 11 Individual test

Call on different children to sound out one word and tell what word.

Do not touch any small letters.

siCk

sit

not

Story 105

Do not clap for any small letters.

TASK 18   Quotation finding

a. Pass out Storybook 1.

b. **Open your book to page 30.**

c. Hold up your storybook. Underline the first sentence with your finger. **Somebody is saying something in this sentence. Touch the marks that show the words that he is saying.** *(The children touch the quotation marks around* **I can shāve a cat.***)*

d. Underline the third sentence with your finger. **Somebody is saying something in this sentence. Touch the marks that show the words that he is saying.** *(The children touch the quotation marks around* **I can shāve a cow.***)*

e. Underline the fifth sentence with your finger. **Somebody is saying something in this sentence. Touch the marks that show the words that he is saying.** *(The children touch the quotation marks around* **I can shāve a rock.***)*

f. Repeat *c* through *e* until firm.

TASK 19   First reading—children read the story and answer questions

Have the children reread any sentences containing words that give them trouble. Keep a list of these words.

a. **This is a pretend story. It's funny. You're going to read the story and I'll ask questions.**

b. Clap for the sounds in each word as the children sound out each word one time and tell what word.

c. Present the items below as the children read.

After the children read:	You say:
The old man said,	**Now we're going to read what the old man said.**
"I can shave a cat."	**What did he say?** (Signal.) *I can shave a cat.* **That's silly.**
The old man said,	**Now we're going to read what the old man said.**
"I can shave a cow."	**What did he say?** (Signal.) *I can shave a cow.* **That's silly too.**
The old man said,	**Now we're going to read what the old man said.**
"I can shave a rock."	**What did he say?** (Signal.) *I can shave a rock.* **Now that's really silly.**

d. After the first reading of the story, print on the board the words that the children missed more than one time. Have the children sound out each word one time and tell what word.

e. After the group's responses are firm, call on individual children to read the words.

Get ready to read all the words on this page without making a mistake.

Do not touch any small letters.

TASK 12   Children sound out the word and tell what word

a. Touch the ball for **this.** Sound it out.
b. Get ready.   Touch **th, i, s** as the children say *thththiiiisss.*
                              If sounding out is not firm, repeat *b.*
c. What word?   (Signal.) *This.* Yes, **this.**

TASK 13   Children sound out the word and tell what word

a. Touch the ball for **sack.** Sound it out.
b. Get ready.   Touch **s, a, c** as the children say *sssaaac.*
                              If sounding out is not firm, repeat *b.*
c. What word?   (Signal.) *Sack.* Yes, **sack.**

TASK 14   Children sound out the word, then read it the fast way

a. Touch the ball for **it.** Sound it out.
b. Get ready.   Touch **i, t** as the children say *iiit.*
                              If sounding out is not firm, repeat *b.*
c. What word?   (Signal.) *It.* Yes, **it.**
d. Return to the ball. Get ready to read the word the fast way.
                    Don't sound it out. Just tell me the word.
e. (Pause at least three seconds.) Get ready.   Move your finger quickly
                    along the arrow. *It.* Yes, **it.** Good reading.

To correct	If the children sound out the word instead of reading it the fast way
	1. Say: **I'll read the word the <u>fast</u> way. It.**
	2. Repeat *d* and *e* until firm.
	3. Repeat *a* through *e.*

f. Repeat *d* and *e* until firm.

TASK 15   Individual test

Call on different children to do *d* and *e* in task 14.

TASK 15   Children read the fast way

a. Get ready to read these words the fast way.
b. Touch the ball for **fōr.** (Pause three seconds.)   Get ready.
(Signal.) *For.*

c. Repeat *b* for the remaining words on the page.

TASK 16   Children read the fast way again

a. Get ready to do these words again. Watch where I point.
b. Point to a word. (Pause one second.) Say: Get ready. (Signal.)
The children respond. Point to the words in this order:
fōr, ōld, not, shāve, rugs.

c . Repeat *b* until firm.

TASK 17   Individual test

Call on different children to read one word in task 16 the fast way.

Do not touch any small letters.

fōr

shāve

ōld

not

rugs

Do not touch any small letters.

TASK 16   Children rhyme with ock

a. Point to the first sound of **rock.**   What sound? (Signal.) *rrr.*
Point to the first sound of **sock.**   What sound? (Signal.) *sss.*

b. These words rhyme with (pause)   **ock.**
What do they rhyme with? (Signal.) *Ock.*
Yes, rhymes with (pause)   **ock.**

c. Touch the ball for **rock.**   Get ready. Touch **r.** *rrr.*
Move your finger quickly along the arrow. *Rrrock.*

d. What word? (Signal.) *Rock.*   Yes, **rock.**

e. Touch the ball for **sock.**   This word rhymes with (pause)   **ock.**
What does it rhyme with? (Signal.) *Ock.*

f. Get ready. Touch **s.** *sss.*
Move your finger quickly along the arrow. *Sssock.*

g. What word? (Signal.) *Sock.*   Yes, **sock.**

TASK 17   Children sound out the word and tell what word

a. Touch the ball for **cat.**   Sound it out.

b. Get ready. Touch **c, a, t** as the children say *caaat.*

c. Again. Repeat *b* until firm.

d. Yes, what word? (Signal.) *Cat.*

TASK 10   Children identify, then sound out an irregular word (said)

a. Touch the ball for **said.** Everybody, you're going to read this word the fast way. (Pause three seconds.) Get ready. Move your finger quickly along the arrow. *Said.* Yes, **said.**

b. Now you're going to sound out the word. Get ready. Quickly touch **s, a, i, d** as the children say *sssaaaiiid.*

c. Again. Repeat *b.*

d. How do we say the word? (Signal.) *Said.* Yes, **said.**

e. Repeat *b* and *d* until firm.

TASK 11   Individual test

Call on different children to do *b* and *d* in task 10.

TASK 12   Children read the fast way

a. Get ready to read these words the fast way.

b. Touch the ball for **this.** (Pause three seconds.) Get ready. (Signal.) *This.*

c. Repeat *b* for **shē.**

TASK 13   Children read the fast way again

a. Get ready to do these words again. Watch where I point.

b. Point to a word. (Pause one second.) Say: Get ready. (Signal.) *The children respond.* Point to the words in this order: **this, said, shē.**

c. Repeat *b* until firm.

TASK 14   Individual test

Call on different children to read one word in task 13 the fast way.

Take-Home 61

STORY

TASK 18   Children follow the arrow to the bottom line

a. Pass out Take-Home 61. Do not let the children look at the picture
until task 22.

b. Point to the story.   **These words are on two lines. Watch me touch
all the words.**

c. Touch **this** and **is.**   **Now I follow the arrow to the ball on the next
line.** Follow the arrow.

d. **Now I touch the rest of the words. Touch not and me.**

e. Repeat *b* through *d* two times.

f. **Your turn. Finger on the ball of the <u>top</u> line.**
Check children's responses.

g. **Touch the words when I clap. Get ready. Clap for this and is.**
(The children respond.)

h. **Now follow the arrow to the next ball.** Check children's responses.

i. Repeat *f* through *h* until firm.

j. **Touch the words on the bottom line when I clap. Get ready.**
Clap for **not** and **me.** *(The children respond.)*

k. **This time you're going to touch all the words in the story.**
Finger on the ball of the <u>top</u> line. Check children's responses.
Get ready. Clap for this and is.

l. Do not clap for **not** until the children have followed the arrow to the
ball on the bottom line. Then clap for **not** and **me.**

m. Repeat *k* and *l* until firm.

TASK 19   First reading—children sound out each word and tell what word

a. **Finger on the ball of the top line.** Check children's responses.

b. **Touch the first word.** Check children's responses.   **Sound it out.**
Get ready. Clap for each sound. *Thththiiisss.*

c. **Again.** (Pause.)   **Get ready.** Clap for each sound. *Thththiiisss.*
What word? (Signal.) *This.*   **Yes, this.**

d. **Next word.** Check children's responses.   **Get ready.**
Clap for each sound. *Iiisss.*

e. **Again.** (Pause.)   **Get ready.** Clap for each sound. *Iiisss.*
What word? (Signal.) *Is.*   **Yes, is.**

f. **Follow the arrow all the way to the next word.**
Check children's responses.

g. **Get ready.** Clap for each sound. *Nnnooot.*

h. **Again.** (Pause.)   **Get ready.** Clap for each sound. *Nnnooot.*
What word? (Signal.) *Not.*   **Yes, not.**

i. **Next word.** Check children's responses.   **Get ready.**
Clap for each sound. *Mmmēēē.*

j. **Again.** (Pause.)   **Get ready.** Clap for each sound. *Mmmēēē.*
What word? (Signal.) *Me.*   **Yes, me.**

TASK 20   Second reading—children sound out each word and tell what word

a. **Let's read the story again. Everybody, touch the first word.**
Check children's responses.

b. **Get ready.** Clap for each sound. *Thththiiisss.*   **What word?** (Signal.)
This.   **Yes, this.**

c. **Next word.** Check children's responses.   **Get ready.** Clap for each
sound. *Iiisss.*   **What word?** (Signal.) *Is.*   **Yes, is.**

d. Repeat *c* for the words **not, me.**

Individual test

Call on different children to read one word. The child sounds out the
word only one time, then tells what word. The other children are to
point under the sounds that are said.

READING VOCABULARY

Do not touch any small letters.

TASK 4   Children sound out an irregular word (to)

a. Touch the ball for **to.** Sound it out.
b. Get ready.   Quickly touch each sound as the children say *tooo*.

To correct	If the children sound out the word as **too**oo (as in **two**) **1.** Say: **You've got to say the sounds I touch.** **2.** Repeat *a* and *b* until firm.

c. Again.   Repeat *b* until firm.
d. That's how we <u>sound out</u> the word. Here's how we <u>say</u> the word.
          To. How do we <u>say</u> the word?   (Signal.) *To*.
e. Now you're going to <u>sound out</u> the word. Get ready.
          Touch each sound as the children say *tooo*.
f. Now you're going to say the word. Get ready.   (Signal.) *To*.
g. Repeat *e* and *f* until firm.
h. Yes, this word is **to.** I went **to** the store.

TASK 5   Individual test

Call on different children to do *e* and *f* in task 4.

TASK 6   Children read the fast way

Touch the ball for **sāve.** Get ready to read this word the fast way.
          (Pause three seconds.) **Get ready.**   (Signal.) *Save*.

TASK 7   Children sound out the word and tell what word

a. Touch the ball for **hugs.** Sound it out.
b. Get ready.   Touch **h, u, g, s** as the children say *huuugsss*.
                    If sounding out is not firm, repeat *b*.
c. What word?   (Signal.) *Hugs*. Yes, **hugs.**

TASK 8   Children read the words the fast way

a. Now you get to read the words on this page the fast way.
b. Touch the ball for **to.** (Pause three seconds.) **Get ready.**
                    Move your finger quickly along the arrow. *To.*
c. Repeat *b* for each word on the page.

TASK 9   Individual test

Call on different children to read one word the fast way.

to

sāve

hugs

TASK 21 Teacher and children read the fast way

a. Point to the words on the first two arrows. Touch under **mē.**
Everybody, this word is (pause)**me. What word?** (Signal.) *Me.*
Yes, **me. Remember that.**

b. We're going to read this story the fast way.

c. Point to **this is not.** I'll read these words the fast way.

d. Point to **mē.** When I touch this word, you're going to say . . . .
(Signal.) *Me.* Yes, **me.**

e. Repeat *d* until firm.

f. Touch the ball of the first arrow. **Reading the fast way.**
(Pause three seconds.) Touch under **this is not** and say:
This is not . . . .

g. Then touch under **mē.** *Me.*

h. Repeat *f* and *g* until firm.

i. Yes, **this is not me.**

TASK 22 Picture comprehension

a. When you look at the picture, you'll say . . . . (Signal.)
This is not me.

b. Yes, when you look at the picture, you'll say . . . . (Signal.)
This is not me.

c. Turn your take-home over and look at the picture.

d. Ask these questions:
1. What do you say when you look at the picture? *This is not me.*
2. What's that thing in the picture? *The children respond.*
Yes, that's an alligator.
3. How would you like to have him for a pet? *The children respond.*

TASK 23 Word finding

a. Turn your take-home back to side 1.   Point to the words on the first
two arrows. I'm going to read all these words the fast way.

b. Touch the ball of the first arrow. Touch under each word and read:
This   (pause) is   (pause) not   (pause) me.

c. I'll do it again.   Touch under each word and read:
This   (pause) is   (pause) not   (pause) me.

d. Everybody, look at the words in your story.

e. Look for the word   (pause) **not. Nnnooot.**

f. Everybody, point to **nnnooot.** Get your finger right over the word
nnnooot.   Check children's responses.

g. Get ready to touch   (pause) **not** when I clap. Get ready.   Clap.
*(The children touch **not.**)*

h. Fingers up.   Repeat *f* and *g* until firm.

i. Everybody, look at the words in your story.

j. Look for the word   (pause) **me. Mmmēēē.**

k. Everybody, point to **mmmēēē.** Get your finger right over the word
mmmēēē.   Check children's responses.

l. Get ready to touch   (pause) **me** when I clap. Get ready.   Clap.
*(The children touch **mē.**)*

m. Repeat *j* through *l* until firm.

n. Direct the children to find the words in this order:
not (Repeat *e, f,* and *g*.)
mē (Repeat *j, k,* and *l*.)
mē (Repeat *j, k,* and *l*.)
not (Repeat *e, f,* and *g*.)

Lesson 105

SOUNDS

TASK 1 Child plays teacher

a. Use acetate and crayon.
b. [Child's name] is going to be the teacher.
c. [He or She] is going to touch the sounds. When [he or she] touches a sound, you say it.
d. The child points to and touches the sounds. You circle any sound that is not firm.
e. After the child has completed the page, present all the circled sounds to the children.

TASK 2 Individual test

Call on different children. If you can say the sound when I call your name, you may cross it out.

TASK 3 Teacher and children play the sounds game

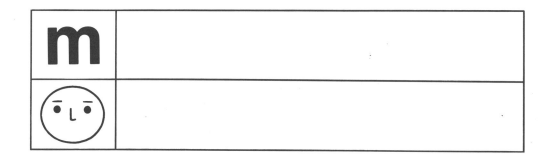

a. Use acetate and crayon. Write the sounds in the symbol box. Keep score in the score box.
b. I'm smart. I bet I can beat you in a game.
c. Here's the rule. When I touch a sound, you say it.
d. Play the game.
Make one symbol at a time in the symbol box. Use the symbols **n, ē, sh**, and **g**.
Make each symbol quickly. (Pause.) Touch the symbol.
Play the game for about two minutes.
Then ask: Who won? Draw a mouth on the face in the score box.

SUMMARY OF INDEPENDENT ACTIVITY

TASK 24   Introduction to independent activity

a. Hold up Take-Home 61.
b. Everybody, you're going to finish this take-home on your own.
Tell the children when they will work the remaining items.
Let's go over the things you're going to do.

TASK 25   Story copying

Point to the dotted words below the story on side 1. You're going to
write the dotted words on this arrow. Then you're going to write
those words on the other arrow.

TASK 26   Pair relations

a. Point to the first box in the top row of the pair-relations exercise.
b. Everybody, what does this box say?   (Signal.) $\bar{a}\bar{a}\bar{a}$—$\bar{e}\bar{e}\bar{e}$.
Yes, $\bar{a}\bar{a}\bar{a}$—$\bar{e}\bar{e}\bar{e}$. You're going to fix up every box with $\bar{a}\bar{a}\bar{a}$ to
say . . . .   (Signal.) $\bar{a}\bar{a}\bar{a}$—$\bar{e}\bar{e}\bar{e}$.
c. Point to the second box in the top row. What does this box say?
(Signal.) nnn—ooo. Yes, nnn—ooo. You're going to fix up every
box with nnn to say . . . .   (Signal.) nnn—ooo.

TASK 27   Cross-out game

Point to the boxed sounds in the Cross-out Game on side 2.
Everybody, what sound are you going to circle today?   (Signal.) c.
What sound are you going to cross out?   (Signal.) aaa.

TASK 28   Matching

Point to the first column of sounds in the Matching Game.
You're going to draw lines for every sound over here.

TASK 29   Sound writing

a. Point to the sound-writing exercise. Here are the sounds you're
going to write today. I'll touch the sounds. You say them.
b. Touch each sound. *The children respond.*
c. Repeat the series until firm.

TASK 30   Story picture

Point to the story picture. After you finish your take-home,
you can color the story picture.

END OF LES

TASK 17 **Picture comprehension**

a. Everybody, look at the picture.
b. Show me the sacks. *(The children respond.)*
c. Ask these questions:
 1. What are the children doing with the rocks? *The children respond.*
 2. What would you do with a sack of rocks? *The children respond.*

TASK 18 **Individual test**

a. Turn back to page 28. I'm going to call on different children to read a whole sentence the fast way.
b. Call on different children to read one of the first three sentences. Do not clap for each word.

TASK 19 **Sentence saying**

Good reading. Now, everybody, say all the words in that sentence without looking. (Signal.) *The children repeat the sentence at a normal speaking rate.*

Take-Home 104

SUMMARY OF INDEPENDENT ACTIVITY

TASK 20 **Introduction to independent activity**

a. Pass out Take-Home 104 to each child.
b. Everybody, you're going to do this take-home on your own. Tell the children when they will work the items. Let's go over the things you're going to do.

TASK 21 **Sentence copying**

a. Hold up side 1 of your take-home and point to the first line in the sentence-copying exercise.
b. Everybody, here's the sentence you're going to write on the lines below.
c. Get ready to read the words in this sentence the fast way. First word. Check children's responses. Get ready. Clap. *We.*
d. Next word. Check children's responses. Get ready. Clap. *Have.*
e. Repeat *d* for the remaining word.
f. After you finish your take-home, you get to draw a picture about the sentence, **wē have sacks.**

TASK 22 **Sound writing**

a. Point to the sound-writing exercise. Here are the sounds you're going to write today. I'll touch the sounds. You say them.
b. Touch each sound. *The children respond.*
c. Repeat the series until firm.

TASK 23 **Matching**

a. Point to the column of words in the Matching Game.
b. Everybody, you're going to follow the lines and write these words.
c. Reading the fast way.
d. Point to the first word. (Pause.) Get ready. (Signal.) *The children respond.*
e. Repeat *d* for the remaining words.
f. Repeat *d* and *e* until firm.

TASK 24 **Cross-out game**

Point to the boxed word in the Cross-out Game. Everybody, here's the word you're going to cross out today. What word? (Signal.) *Can.* Yes, **can**.

TASK 25 **Pair relations**

a. Point to the pair-relations exercise on side 2. You're going to circle the picture in each box that shows what the words say.
b. Point to the space at the top of the page. After you finish, remember to draw a picture that shows **wē have sacks.**

END OF LESSON 104

Lesson 62

h

th

r

n

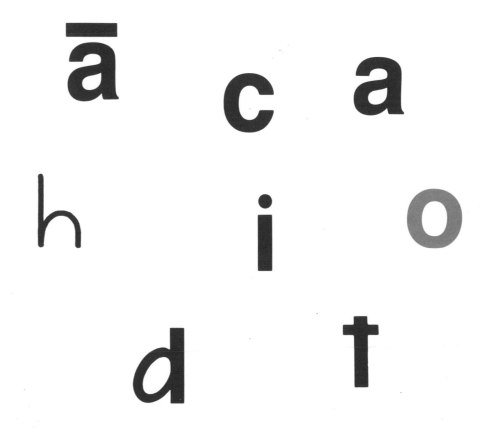

SOUNDS

TASK 1   Teaching **h** as in **hat**

a. Point to **h.** My turn. When I touch it, I'll say it. (Pause.) Touch **h** for an instant, saying: h. Do not say **huh** or **hih.**

b. Point to **h.** Your turn. When I touch it, you say it. (Pause.) Get ready. Touch **h.** *h.*

c. Again. Touch **h.** *h.*

d. Repeat *c* until firm.

TASK 2   Sounds firm-up

a. Get ready to say the sounds when I touch them.

b. Alternate touching **th** and **h.** Point to the sound. (Pause one second.) Say: Get ready. Touch the sound. *The children respond.*

c. When **th** and **h** are firm, alternate touching **n, th, r,** and **h** until all four sounds are firm.

TASK 4   Teacher introduces cross-out game

a. Use acetate and crayon.

b. I'll cross out the sounds on this page when you can tell me every sound.

c. Remember—when I touch it, you say it.

d. Go over the sounds until the children can identify all the sounds in order.

TASK 3   Individual test

Call on different children to identify **n, th, r,** or **h.**

TASK 5   Individual test

Call on different children to identify two or more sounds in task 4.

TASK 6   Teacher crosses out sounds

a. You told me every sound. Get ready to do it again. This time I'll cross out each sound when you tell me what it is.

b. Point to each sound. (Pause.) Say: Get ready. Touch the sound. *The children respond.* As you cross out the sound, say: Goodbye, _____ .

Story 104

Do not clap for any small letters.

TASK 15 First reading—children sound out each word and tell what word

Have the children reread any sentences containing words that give them trouble. Keep a list of these words.

a. Pass out Storybook 1.
b. Open your book to page 28 and get ready to read.
c. Clap for the sounds in each word of the story as the children sound out each word one time and tell what word.
d. After the first reading of the story, print on the board the words that the children missed more than one time. Have the children sound out each word one time and tell what word.
e. After the group's responses are firm, call on individual children to read the words.

TASK 16 Second reading—children read the story the fast way and answer questions

a. Now you're going to read the story the fast way and I'll ask questions.
b. Finger on the ball of the top line. Check children's responses. Remember to stop when you get to a period.
c. Get ready. Clap for each word in the first sentence. Pause at least three seconds between claps. Pause longer before words that gave the children trouble during the first reading.
d. Clap for the word following **rocks.** Praise children who do not read the word.
e. Again. Repeat *b* through *d* until firm.
f. Then ask: What do we do? (Signal.) *Save rocks.*
g. Reading the words in the next sentence the fast way.
h. Get ready. Clap for each word in the second sentence. Pause at least three seconds between claps. Pause longer before words that gave the children trouble during the first reading.
i. Clap for the word following **rocks.** Praise children who do not read the word.
j. Let's read that sentence again the fast way. Repeat *h* and *i* until firm.
k. Then ask: What do we do? (Signal.) *Save sacks and sacks of rocks.*
l. Use the procedures in *g* through *j* for the remaining sentences. Ask the comprehension questions below as the children read.

After the children read:	You say:
We save lots and lots of rocks.	What do we do? (Signal.) *Save lots and lots of rocks.*
We have lots of little rocks.	What do we have? (Signal.) *Lots of little rocks.*
And we give an old man lots of rocks.	Name two things we do with rocks. (Signal.) *Sit on rocks and give an old man lots of rocks.*

READING VOCABULARY

Get ready to read all the words on this page without making a mistake.

Do not touch any small letters.

TASK 7   Children sound out the word and tell what word

a. Touch the ball for **sack.** Sound it out.
b. Get ready.   Touch **s, a, c** as the children say *sssaaac.*
      If sounding out is not firm, repeat *b.*
c. What word?   (Signal.) *Sack.* **Yes, sack.**

sac_k

TASK 8   Children sound out the word and tell what word

a. Touch the ball for **sick.** Sound it out.
b. Get ready.   Touch **s, i, c** as the children say *sssiiic.*
      If sounding out is not firm, repeat *b.*
c. What word?   (Signal.) *Sick.* **Yes, sick.**

sic_k

TASK 9   Children sound out the word, then read it the fast way

a. Touch the ball for **is.** Sound it out.
b. Get ready.   Touch **i, s** as the children say *iiisss.*
      If sounding out is not firm, repeat *b.*
c. What word?   (Signal.) *Is.* **Yes, is.**
d. Return to the ball. Get ready to read the word the fast way.
      Don't sound it out. Just tell me the word.
e. (Pause at least three seconds.) Get ready.   Move your finger quickly
      along the arrow. *Is.* **Yes, is. Good reading.**

is

To correct	If the children sound out the word instead of reading it the fast way
	1. Say: **I'll read the word the <u>fast</u> way. Is.**
	2. Repeat *d* and *e* until firm.
	3. Repeat *a* through *e.*

f. Repeat *d* and *e* until firm.

TASK 10   Individual test

Call on different children to do *d* and *e* in task 9.

TASK 13   Children sound out the word and tell what word

a. Touch the ball for **give**.   Sound it out.
b. Get ready.   Touch **g, i, v** as the children say *giiivvv*.
If sounding out is not firm, repeat b.
c. What word? (Signal.) *Give.*   Yes, **give**.

TASK 14   Children rhyme with sāve

a. Touch the ball for **sāve**.   You're going to read this word the fast
way. (Pause three seconds.)   Get ready.
Move your finger quickly along the arrow. Save.
b. Touch the ball for **gāve**.   This word rhymes with (pause)   **save**.
Move to g, then quickly along the arrow. Gave.
Yes, what word? (Signal.) Gave.

Do not touch any small letters.

giv_e

sāv_e

gāv_e

Get ready to read all the words on this page without making a mistake.

Do not touch any small letters.

TASK 11   Children rhyme with ack

a. Point to the first sound of **rack.** What sound?   (Signal.) *rrr.*
Point to the first sound of **mack.** What sound?   (Signal.) *mmm.*
b. These words rhyme with   (pause) **ack.**
What do they rhyme with?   (Signal.) *Ack.*
Yes, rhymes with   (pause) **ack.**
c. Touch the ball for **rack.** Get ready.   Touch **r.** *rrr.*
Move your finger quickly along the arrow. *Rrrack.*
d. What word?   (Signal.) *Rack.* Yes, **rack.**
e. Touch the ball for **mack.** This word rhymes with   (pause) **ack.**
What does it rhyme with?   (Signal.) *Ack.*
f. Get ready.   Touch **m.** *mmm.*
Move your finger quickly along the arrow. *Mmmack.*
g. What word?   (Signal.) *Mack.* Yes, **mack.**

TASK 12   Children sound out the word and tell what word

a. Touch the ball for **tack.** Sound it out.
b. Get ready.   Touch **t, a, c** as the children say *taaac.*
If sounding out is not firm, repeat *b.*
c. What word?   (Signal.) *Tack.* Yes, **tack.**
d. Repeat *a, b,* and *c* for **if.**

To correct	For all mistakes, have the children sound out the word and say it fast. Then say: **Remember this word.**

Do not touch any small letters.

TASK 10   Children read the fast way

a. Get ready to read these words the fast way.
b. Touch the ball for **lots.** (Pause three seconds.) **Get ready.**
(Signal.) *Lots.*
c. Touch the ball for **sacks.** (Pause three seconds.) **Get ready.**
(Signal.) *Sacks.*
d. Repeat *c* for the remaining words on the page.

TASK 11   Children read the fast way again

a. Get ready to do these words again. Watch where I point.
b. Point to a word. (Pause one second.) Say: **Get ready.** (Signal.)
The children respond. Point to the words in this order:
sacks, have, rocks, wē, lots.
c. Repeat *b* until firm.

TASK 12   Individual test

Call on different children to read one word the fast way.

lots

sacₖs

rocₖs

wē

haveₑ

Get ready to read all the words on this page without making a mistake.

Do not touch any small letters.

TASK 13   Children sound out the word and tell what word

a. Touch the ball for **in**.   Sound it out.
b. Get ready. Touch **i, n** as the children say *iiinnn*.
　　　　　　　　　　If sounding out is not firm, repeat *b*.
c. What word? (Signal.) *In*.   Yes, **in**.

TASK 14   Children sound out the word and tell what word

a. Touch the ball for **rock**.   Sound it out.
b. Get ready. Touch **r, o, c** as the children say *rrroooc*.
　　　　　　　　　　If sounding out is not firm, repeat *b*.
c. What word? (Signal.) *Rock*.   Yes, **rock**.

TASK 15   Children sound out the word, then read it the fast way

a. Touch the ball for **it**.   Sound it out.
b. Get ready. Touch **i, t** as the children say *iiit*.
　　　　　　　　　　If sounding out is not firm, repeat *b*.
c. What word? (Signal.) *It*.   Yes, **it**.
d. Return to the ball.   Get ready to read the word the fast way.
　　　　　　　　Don't sound it out. Just tell me the word.
e. (Pause at least three seconds.)   Get ready. Move your finger quickly
　　　　　　　　along the arrow. *It*.   Yes, **it**. Good reading.

To correct	If the children sound out the word instead of reading it the fast way
	1. Say: **I'll read the word the <u>fast</u> way. It.**
	2. Repeat *d* and *e* until firm.
	3. Repeat *a* through *e*.

f. Repeat *d* and *e* until firm.

TASK 16   Individual test

Call on different children to do *d* and *e* in task 15.

TASK 17   Individual test

Call on different children to sound out one word and tell what word.

READING VOCABULARY

Do not touch any small letters.

To correct	For all mistakes, have the children sound out the word and say it fast. Then say: **Remember this word.**

TASK 7   Children read the fast way

a. Get ready to read these words the fast way.

b. Touch the ball for **shē**. (Pause three seconds.) Get ready.
                                                            (Signal.) *She.*

c. Touch the ball for **thē**. (Pause three seconds.) Get ready.
                                                            (Signal.) *Thē.*

d. Repeat *c* for **thōse**.

TASK 8   Children read the fast way again

a. Get ready to do these words again. Watch where I point.

b. Point to a word. (Pause one second.) Say: Get ready. (Signal.)
    The children respond. Point to the words in this order:
                                    thōse, thē, shē.

c. Repeat *b* until firm.

TASK 9   Individual test

Call on different children to read one word the fast way.

Take-Home 62

STORY

Do not clap for any small letters.

TASK 18 Children follow the arrow to the bottom line

a. Pass out Take-Home 62. Do not let the children look at the picture until task 23.

b. Point to the story. These words are on two lines. Watch me touch all the words.

c. Touch **this** and **is**. Now I follow the arrow to the ball on the next line. Follow the arrow.

d. Now I touch the rest of the words. Touch **a** and **rock**.

e. Repeat *b* through *d* two times.

f. Your turn. Finger on the ball of the top line.
Check children's responses.

g. Touch the words when I clap. Get ready. Clap for **this** and **is**.
(The children respond.)

h. Now follow the arrow to the next ball. Check children's responses.

i. Repeat *f* through *h* until firm.

j. Touch the words on the bottom line when I clap. Get ready. Clap for **a** and **rock**. (The children respond.)

k. This time you're going to touch all the words in the story. Finger on the ball of the top line. Check children's responses. Get ready. Clap for **this** and **is**.

l. Do not clap for **a** until the children have followed the arrow to the ball on the bottom line. Then clap for **a** and **rock**.

m. Repeat *k* and *l* until firm.

TASK 19 First reading—children sound out each word and tell what word

a. Finger on the ball of the top line. Check children's responses.

b. Touch the first word. Check children's responses. Sound it out.
Get ready. Clap for each sound. *Thththiiisss.*

c. Again. (Pause.) Get ready. Clap for each sound. *Thththiiisss.*
What word? (Signal.) *This.* Yes, **this**.

d. Next word. Check children's responses. Get ready.
Clap for each sound. *Iiisss.*

e. Again. (Pause.) Get ready. Clap for each sound. *Iiisss.*
What word? (Signal.) *Is.* Yes, **is**.

f. Follow the arrow all the way to the next word.
Check children's responses.

g. Get ready. Clap for the sound. *Aaa.*

h. Again. (Pause.) Get ready. Clap for the sound. *Aaa.*
What word? (Signal.) *A.* Yes, **a**.

i. Next word. Check children's responses. Get ready.
Clap for each sound. *Rrroooc.*

j. Again. (Pause.) Get ready. Clap for each sound. *Rrroooc.*
What word? (Signal.) *Rock.* Yes, **rock**.

TASK 20 Second reading—children sound out each word and tell what word

a. Let's read the story again. Everybody, touch the first word.
Check children's responses.

b. Get ready. Clap for each sound. *Thththiiisss.* What word? (Signal.)
This. Yes, **this**.

c. Next word. Check children's responses. Get ready. Clap for each sound. *Iiisss.* What word? (Signal.) *Is.* Yes, **is**.

d. Repeat *c* for the words **a, rock**.

TASK 21 Individual test

Call on different children to read one word. The child sounds out the word only one time, then tells what word. The other children are to point under the sounds that are said.

Lesson 104

SOUNDS

TASK 1 Teaching **v** as in **very**

a. Point to **v**. My turn. (Pause.) Touch **v** and say: *vvv*.
b. Point to **v**. Your turn. When I touch it, you say it. (Pause.)
Get ready. Touch **v**. *vvv*. Lift your finger.
c. Again. Touch **v**. *vvv*. Lift your finger.
d. Repeat *c* until firm.

TASK 2 Sounds firm-up

a. Get ready to say the sounds when I touch them.
b. Alternate touching **v** and **l**. Point to the sound. (Pause one second.)
Say: Get ready. Touch the sound. *The children respond.*
c. When **v** and **l** are firm, alternate touching **l, v, w,** and **f** until all
four sounds are firm.

TASK 3 Individual test

Call on different children to identify **l, v, w,** or **f.**

TASK 4 Teacher introduces cross-out game

a. Use acetate and crayon.
b. I'll cross out the sounds on this
page when you can tell me every
sound.
c. Remember—when I touch it,
you say it.
d. Go over the sounds until the
children can identify all the
sounds in order.

TASK 5 Individual test

Call on different children to identify
two or more sounds in task 4.

TASK 6 Teacher crosses out sounds

a. You told me every sound. Get
ready to do it again. This time
I'll cross out each sound when
you tell me what it is.
b. Point to each sound. (Pause.) Say:
Get ready. Touch the sound.
The children respond. As you
cross out the sound, say:
Goodbye, _____.

TASK 22 Teacher and children read the fast way

a. Point to the words on the first two arrows. Touch under **rock**.

Everybody, this word is (pause) **rock**. What word? (Signal.) *Rock.*

Yes, **rock**. Remember that.

b. We're going to read this story the fast way.

c. Point to **this is a.** I'll read these words the fast way.

d. Point to **rock.** When I touch this word, you're going to say . . . .

(Signal.) *Rock. Yes,* **rock**.

e. Repeat *d* until firm.

f. Touch the ball of the first arrow. Reading the fast way.

. (Pause three seconds.) Touch under **this is a** and say:

This is a . . .

g. Then touch under **rock**. *Rock.*

h. Repeat *f* and *g* until firm.

i. Yes, **this is a rock**.

TASK 23 Picture comprehension

a. When you look at the picture, you'll say . . . . (Signal.)

This is a rock.

b. Yes, when you look at the picture, you'll say . . . . (Signal.)

This is a rock.

c. Turn your take-home over and look at the picture.

d. Ask these questions:

  1. What do you say when you look at the picture? *This is a rock.*

  2. What is that rock doing? *The children respond.*

  3. How would you like to be that woman? *The children respond.*

TASK 24 Word finding

a. Turn your take-home back to side 1. Point to the words on the

first two arrows. I'm going to read all these words the fast way.

b. Touch the ball of the first arrow. Touch under each word and read:

This (pause) is (pause) a (pause) rock.

c. I'll do it again. Touch under each word and read:

This (pause) is (pause) a (pause) rock.

d. Everybody, look at the words in your story.

e. Look for the word (pause) **is. liisss.**

f. Everybody, point to **iiisss**. Get your finger right over the word

iiisss. Check children's responses.

g. Get ready to touch (pause) **is** when I clap. Get ready. Clap.

(The children touch **is.***)*

h. Fingers up. Repeat *f* and *g* until firm.

i. Everybody, look at the words in your story.

j. Look for the word (pause) **rock. Rrroooc.**

k. Everybody, point to **rrroooc**. Get your finger right over the word

rrroooc. Check children's responses.

l. Get ready to touch (pause) **rock** when I clap. Get ready. Clap.

(The children touch **rock.***)*

m. Repeat *j* through *l* until firm.

n. Direct the children to find the words in this order:

rock (Repeat *j, k,* and *l*.)

is (Repeat *e, f,* and *g*.)

is (Repeat *e, f,* and *g*.)

rock (Repeat *j, k,* and *l*.)

TASK 22 Picture comprehension

a. Everybody, look at the picture.
b. Ask these questions:
  1. Is that rat holding the hats? *Yes.*
  2. What's he doing? *The children respond.*   He's holding the hats.
  3. If you could have one of those hats, which one would you take?
                                    The children respond.

TASK 23 Individual test

a. Everybody, look at the story. I'm going to call on different children
                          to read a whole sentence the fast way.
b. Call on different children to read one of the first three sentences.
                          Do not clap for each word.

TASK 24 Sentence saying

Good reading. Now, everybody, say all the words in that sentence
          without looking. (Signal.) *The children repeat the sentence at a
                          normal speaking rate.*

Take-Home 103

SUMMARY OF INDEPENDENT ACTIVITY

TASK 25 Introduction to independent activity

a. Pass out Take-Home 103 to each child.
b. Everybody, you're going to do this take-home on your own.
          Tell the children when they will work the items.
          Let's go over the things you're going to do.

TASK 26 Sentence copying

a. Hold up side 1 of your take-home and point to the first line in the
                          sentence-copying exercise.
b. Everybody, here's the sentence you're going to write on the lines
                          below.
c. Get ready to read the words in this sentence the fast way.
          First word. Check children's responses. Get ready. Clap. *I.*
d. Next word. Check children's responses. Get ready. Clap. *Can.*
e. Repeat *d* for the remaining words.
f. After you finish your take-home, you get to draw a picture about
                          the sentence, **I can hōld thē hats.**

TASK 27 Sound writing

a. Point to the sound-writing exercise. Here are the sounds you're
                          going to write today. I'll touch the sounds. You say them.
b. Touch each sound. *The children respond.*
c. Repeat the series until firm.

TASK 28 Matching

a. Point to the column of words in the Matching Game.
b. Everybody, you're going to follow the lines and write these words.
c. Reading the fast way.
d. Point to the first word. (Pause.) Get ready. (Signal.)
                          The children respond.
e. Repeat *d* for the remaining words.
f. Repeat *d* and *e* until firm.

TASK 29 Cross-out game

Point to the boxed word in the Cross-out Game. Everybody, here's
                  the word you're going to cross out today. What word? (Signal.)
                          Cow. Yes, **cow.**

TASK 30 Pair relations

a. Point to the pair-relations exercise on side 2. You're going to
                  circle the picture in each box that shows what the words say.
b. Point to the space at the top of the page. After you finish,
                  remember to draw a picture that shows **I can hōld thē hats.**

END OF LESSON 103

SUMMARY OF INDEPENDENT ACTIVITY

TASK 25   Introduction to independent activity

a. Hold up Take-Home 62.
b. **Everybody, you're going to finish this take-home on your own.** Tell the children when they will work the remaining items. **Let's go over the things you're going to do.**

TASK 26   Story copying

Point to the dotted words below the story on side 1. **You're going to write the dotted words on this arrow. Then you're going to write those words on the other arrow.**

TASK 27   Pair relations

a. Point to the first box in the top row of the pair-relations exercise.
b. **Everybody, what does this box say?** (Signal.) *ooo—c.* **Yes, ooo—c. You're going to fix up every box with ooo to say . . . .** (Signal.) *ooo—c.*
c. Point to the second box in the top row. **What does this box say?** (Signal.) *fff—nnn.* **Yes, fff—nnn. You're going to fix up every box with fff to say . . . .** (Signal.) *fff—nnn.*

TASK 28   Cross-out game

Point to the boxed sounds in the Cross-out Game on side 2. **Everybody, what sound are you going to cross out today?** (Signal.) *t.* **What sound are you going to circle?** (Signal.) *fff.*

TASK 29   Matching

Point to the first column of sounds in the Matching Game. **You're going to draw lines for every sound over here.**

TASK 30   Sound writing

a. Point to the sound-writing exercise. **Here are the sounds you're going to write today. I'll touch the sounds. You say them.**
b. Touch each sound. *The children respond.*
c. Repeat the series until firm.

TASK 31   Story picture

Point to the story picture. **After you finish your take-home, you can color the story picture.**

END OF LESSON 62

Story 103

Do not clap for any small letters.

TASK 20   First reading—question mark finding

Have the children reread any sentences containing words that give them trouble. Keep a list of these words.

a. Pass out Storybook 1.
b. Open your book to page 26 and get ready to read.
c. Clap for the sounds in each word of the first paragraph as the children sound out each word one time and tell what word.
d. After the children read **an ōld man can hōld thē hats,** say:
Everybody, move along the lines until you come to the next period. Oh, oh. There's no period in this sentence. There's a funny mark called a question mark.
e. Everybody, touch the question mark.   Check children's responses.
f. There's a question mark in this sentence because this sentence asks a question. Everybody, get ready to read the question.
g. Finger on the first word.   Check children's responses.
Clap for the sounds in each word of the sentence as the children sound out each word one time and tell what word.
h. After the children read **can a fat rat hōld thē hats?** say:
Everybody, say that question.   *The children repeat the question at a normal speaking rate.*
i. Can a fat rat hold the hats? We'll find out later.
j. After the first reading of the story, print on the board the words that the children missed more than one time. Have the children sound out each word one time and tell what word.
k. After the group's responses are firm, call on individual children to read the words.

TASK 21   Second reading—children read the story the fast way and answer questions

a. Now you're going to read the story the fast way and I'll ask some more questions.
b. Finger on the ball of the top line.   Check children's responses. Remember to stop when you get to a period.
c. Get ready.   Clap for each word in the first sentence. Pause at least three seconds between claps. Pause longer before words that gave the children trouble during the first reading.
d. Clap for the word following **hats.** Praise children who do not read the word.
e. Again.   Repeat *b* through *d* until firm.
f. What do we have?   (Signal.) *Hats.*
g. Reading the words in the next sentence the fast way.
h. Get ready.   Clap for each word in the next sentence. Pause at least three seconds between claps. Pause longer before words that gave the children trouble during the first reading.
i. Clap for the word following **hats.** Praise children who do not read the word.
j. Let's read that sentence again the fast way.   Repeat *h* and *i* until firm.
k. What can I do?   (Signal.) *Hold the hats.*
l. Use the procedures in *g* through *j* for the remaining sentences. Ask the comprehension questions below as the children read.

After the children read:	You say:
The cow can hold the hats.	Who else can hold the hats? (Signal.) *The cow.*
An old man can hold the hats.	Name everybody who can hold the hats. *The children respond. The cow can, an old man can, and I can hold the hats.*
Can a fat rat hold the hats?	What do you think? *The children respond.*

Lesson 63

Groups that are firm on Mastery Tests 10 and 11 should skip this lesson and do lesson 64 today.

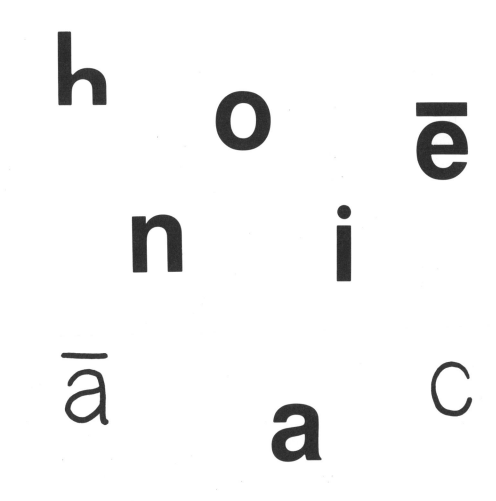

SOUNDS

TASK 1   Teaching **h** as in **hat**

a. Point to **h.**   **My turn. When I touch it, I'll say it.** (Pause.) Touch **h** for an instant, saying: **h.** Do not say **huh** or **hih.**

b. Point to **h.**   **Your turn. When I touch it, you say it.** (Pause.) **Get ready.** Touch **h.** *h.*

c.   **Again.** Touch **h.** *h.*

d. Repeat *c* until firm.

TASK 2   Sounds firm-up

a.   **Get ready to say the sounds when I touch them.**

b. Alternate touching **f** and **h.** Point to the sound. (Pause one second.) Say: **Get ready.** Touch the sound. *The children respond.*

c. When **f** and **h** are firm, alternate touching **th, f, h,** and **ā** until all four sounds are firm.

TASK 3   Individual test

Call on different children to identify **th, f, h,** or **ā.**

TASK 4   Sounds firm-up

a. Point to **h.**   **When I touch the sound, you say it.**

b. (Pause.)   **Get ready.** Touch **h.** *h.*

c.   **Again.** Repeat *b* until firm.

d.   **Get ready to say all the sounds when I touch them.**

e. Alternate touching **a, o, ē, n, i, ā, h,** and **c** three or four times. Point to the sound. (Pause one second.) Say: **Get ready.** Touch the sound. *The children respond.*

TASK 5   Individual test

Call on different children to identify one or more sounds in task 4.

TASK 15 Children identify, then sound out an irregular word (was)

a. Touch the ball for **was.** Everybody, you're going to read this word the fast way. (Pause three seconds.) Get ready. Move your finger quickly along the arrow. *Was.* Yes, **was.**

b. Now you're going to sound out the word. Get ready. Quickly touch **w, a, s** as the children say *wwwaaasss.*

c. Again. Repeat *b.*

d. How do we say the word? (Signal.) *Was.* Yes, **was.**

e. Repeat *b* and *d* until firm.

TASK 16 Individual test

Call on different children to do *b* and *d* in task 15.

To correct	For all mistakes, have the children sound out the word and say it fast. Then say: Remember this word.

TASK 17 Children read the fast way

a. Get ready to read these words the fast way.

b. Touch the ball for **hē.** (Pause three seconds.) Get ready. (Signal.) *He.*

c. Touch the ball for **shē.** (Pause three seconds.) Get ready. (Signal.) *She.*

d. Repeat *c* for the remaining words on the page.

TASK 18 Children read the fast way again

a. Get ready to do these words again. Watch where I point.

b. Point to a word. (Pause one second.) Say: Get ready. (Signal.) *The children respond.* Point to the words in this order: **thē, shē, was, thōse, hē.**

c. Repeat *b* until firm.

TASK 19 Individual test

Call on different children to read one word the fast way.

Do not touch any small letters.

was

hē

shē

thē

thōse

READING VOCABULARY

Get ready to read all the words on this page without making a mistake.

TASK 6 **Children sound out the word and tell what word**

a. Touch the ball for **sēē.** Sound it out.
b. Get ready. Touch **s, ē** as the children say *sssēēē.*
                        If sounding out is not firm, repeat *b.*
c. What word? (Signal.) *See.* Yes, **see.**

TASK 7 **Children sound out the word and tell what word**

Repeat the procedures in task 6 for **it.**

TASK 8 **Children sound out the word, then read it the fast way**

a. Touch the ball for **mē.** Sound it out.
b. Get ready. Touch **m, ē** as the children say *mmmēēē.*
                        If sounding out is not firm, repeat *b.*
c. What word? (Signal.) *Me.* Yes, **me.**
d. Return to the ball. Get ready to read the word the fast way.
                  Don't sound it out. Just tell me the word.
e. (Pause at least three seconds.) Get ready. Move your finger
                  quickly along the arrow. *Me.* Yes, **me.** Good reading.

To correct	If the children sound out the word instead of reading it the fast way
	1. Say: I'll read the word the <u>fast</u> way. **Me.**
	2. Repeat *d* and *e* until firm.
	3. Repeat *a* through *e.*

f. Repeat *d* and *e* until firm.

TASK 9 **Individual test**—Have children do *d* and *e* in task 8.

TASK 10 **Children sound out the word, then read it the fast way**

Repeat the procedures in task 8 for **is.**

TASK 11 **Individual test**—Have children do *d* and *e* in task 8 for **is.**

TASK 12 **Individual test**

Call on different children to sound out one word and tell what word.

sēē

it

mē

is

TASK 9   Children sound out an irregular word (of)

a. Touch the ball for **of.** **Sound it out.**

b. **Get ready.** Quickly touch each sound as the children say *ooofff*.

To correct	If the children sound out the word as **ooovvv** **1.** Say: **You've got to say the sounds I touch.** **2.** Repeat *a* and *b* until firm.

c. **Again.** Repeat *b* until firm.

d. **That's how we** sound out **the word. Here's how we** say **the word.**
            Of. How do we say **the word?** (Signal.) *Of.*

e. **Now you're going to** sound out **the word. Get ready.**
                  Touch each sound as the children say *ooofff*.

f. **Now you're going to say the word. Get ready.** (Signal.) *Of.*

g. Repeat *e* and *f* until firm.

h. **Yes, this word is of. A handle is part of a cup.**

TASK 10   Individual test

Call on different children to do *e* and *f* in task 9.

TASK 11   Children sound out the word and tell what word

a. Touch the ball for **hōld.** **Sound it out.**

b. **Get ready.** Touch **h, ō, l, d** as the children say *hōōōllld*.
                  If sounding out is not firm, repeat *b*.

c. **What word?** (Signal.) *Hold.* **Yes, hold.**

TASK 12   Children read the fast way

Touch the ball for **ōr.** **Get ready to read this word the fast way.**
            (Pause three seconds.) **Get ready.** (Signal.) *Or.*

TASK 13   Children read the words the fast way

a. **Now you get to read the words on this page the fast way.**

b. Touch the ball for **of.** (Pause three seconds.) **Get ready.**
                  Move your finger quickly along the arrow. *Of.*

c. Repeat *b* for each word on the page.

TASK 14   Individual test—Have children read one word the fast way.

Get ready to read all the words on this page without making a mistake.

TASK 13   Children rhyme with ot

---

a. Point to the first sound of **not**. What sound?   (Signal.) *nnn.*
Point to the first sound of **hot**. What sound?   (Signal.) *h.*

b. These words rhyme with   (pause) **ot**.
What do they rhyme with?   (Signal.) *Ot.*
Yes, rhyme with   (pause) **ot**.

c. Touch the ball for **not**. Get ready.   Touch **n**. *nnn.*
Move your finger quickly along the arrow. *Not.*

d. What word?   (Signal.) *Not.* Yes, **not**.

e. Touch the ball for **hot**. This word rhymes with   (pause) **ot**.
What does it rhyme with?   (Signal.) *Ot.*

f. Get ready.   Move your finger quickly along the arrow. *Hot.*

g. What word?   (Signal.) *Hot.* Yes, **hot**.

TASK 14   Children sound out the word and tell what word

---

a. Touch the ball for **hot**. Sound it out.

b. Get ready.   Touch **h, ˙o, t** as the children say *hooot.*

c. Again.   Repeat *b* until firm.

d. Yes, what word?   (Signal.) *Hot.* Yes, **hot**. The sun is **hot**.

TASK 15   Children read a word beginning with a stop sound (hē)

---

a. Point under **ē**. What's this sound?   (Signal.) *ēēē.*

b. Touch the ball for **hē**. This word rhymes with   (pause) **ēē**.
Get ready.   Move quickly along the arrow. *Hēēē.*

c. What word?   (Signal.) *He.* Yes, **he**.

d. Again.   Repeat *b* and *c* until firm.

e. Return to the ball. Sound it out. Remember—say the sounds when
I touch them. Get ready.   Quickly touch **h, ē** as the children
say *hēēē.*

f. What word?   (Signal.) *He.* Yes, **he**. Good reading. **He** is a boy.

g. Repeat *e* and *f* until firm.

TASK 16   Individual test

Call on different children to sound out the word in task 15 and
tell what word.

READING VOCABULARY

Do not touch any small letters.

To correct	For all mistakes, have the children sound out the word and say it fast. Then say: **Remember this word.**

TASK 6   Children read the fast way

a. Get ready to read these words the fast way.

b. Touch the ball for **have.** (Pause three seconds.) **Get ready.**
(Signal.) *Have.*

c. Touch the ball for **ōld.** (Pause three seconds.) **Get ready.**
(Signal.) *Old.*

d. Repeat *c* for the remaining words on the page.

TASK 7   Children read the fast way again

a. Get ready to do these words again. Watch where I point.

b. Point to a word. (Pause one second.) Say: **Get ready.** (Signal.)
The children respond. Point to the words in this order:
hats, sōld, wē, have, ōld.

c. Repeat *b* until firm.

TASK 8   Individual test

Call on different children to read one word the fast way.

haVe

ōld

wē

hats

sōld

Get ready to read the words on this page without making a mistake.

TASK 17   Children read a word beginning with a stop sound (hit)

a. Run your finger under **it.** You're going to sound out this part.
Get ready. Touch **i, t** as the children say *iiit.*

b. Say it fast. (Signal.) *It.* Yes, this part says (pause) **it.**

c. Repeat *a* and *b* until firm.

d. Touch the ball for **hit.** This word rhymes with (pause) **it.**
Get ready. Move quickly along the arrow. *Hit.*

e. What word? (Signal.) *Hit.* Yes, **hit.**

f. Repeat *d* and *e* until firm.

g. Return to the ball. Now you're going to sound out (pause) **hit.**
Get ready. Quickly touch **h, i, t** as the children say *hiiit.*

h. What word? (Signal.) *Hit.* Yes, **hit.** Good reading. She **hit** me.

i. Repeat *g* and *h* until firm.

TASK 18   Individual test

Call on different children to do *g* and *h* in task 17.

TASK 19   Children read a word beginning with a stop sound (his)

a. Run your finger under **is.** You're going to sound out this part.
Get ready. Touch **i, s** as the children say *iiisss.*

b. Say it fast. (Signal.) *Is.* Yes, this part says (pause) **is.**

c. Repeat *a* and *b* until firm.

d. Touch the ball for **his.** This word rhymes with (pause) **is.**
Get ready. Move quickly along the arrow. *His.*

e. What word? (Signal.) *His.* Yes, **his.**

f. Repeat *d* and *e* until firm.

g. Return to the ball. Now you're going to sound out (pause) **his.**
Get ready. Quickly touch **h, i, s** as the children say *hiiisss.*

h. What word? (Signal.) *His.* Yes, **his.** Good reading.
His brother is big.

i. Repeat *g* and *h* until firm.

TASK 20   Individual test

Call on different children to do *g* and *h* in task 19.

Lesson 103

SOUNDS

TASK 1   Teaching v as in very

a. Point to **v**. My turn.   (Pause.) Touch **v** and say: *vvv.*
b. Point to **v**. Your turn. When I touch it, you say it.   (Pause.)
Get ready.   Touch **v**. *vvv.* Lift your finger.
c. Again.   Touch **v**. *vvvv.* Lift your finger.
d. Repeat *c* until firm.

V

v

th

sh

f

TASK 2   Sounds firm-up

a. Get ready to say the sounds when I touch them.
b. Alternate touching **v** and **th**. Point to the sound. (Pause one second.)
Say: Get ready.   Touch the sound. *The children respond.*
c. When **v** and **th** are firm, alternate touching **th, sh, v,** and **f**
until all four sounds are firm.

TASK 3   Individual test

Call on different children to identify **th, sh, v,** or **f.**

TASK 4   Sounds firm-up

a. Point to **v**. When I touch the
sound, you say it.
b. (Pause.) Get ready.   Touch **v**.
vvv.
c. Again.   Repeat *b* until firm.
d. Get ready to say all the sounds
when I touch them.
e. Alternate touching **k, ō, ā, o, c, i,
v,** and **g** three or four times. Point
to the sound. (Pause one second.)
Say: Get ready.   Touch the
sound. *The children respond.*

TASK 5   Individual test

Call on different children to identify
one or more sounds in task 4.

v

k

ō

ā

c

i

o

g

Take-Home 63

STORY
Do not clap for any small letters.

TASK 21   Children follow the arrow to the bottom line

a. Pass out Take-Home 63. Do not let the children look at the picture.
until task 26.

b. Point to the story.   These words are on two lines. Watch me touch
all the words.

c. Touch **this** and **sack**.   Now I follow the arrow to the ball on the
next line.   Follow the arrow.

d. Now I touch the rest of the words.   Touch **is** and **fat**.

e. Repeat *b* through *d* two times.

f. Your turn. Finger on the ball of the <u>top</u> line.
Check children's responses.

g. Touch the words when I clap. Get ready.   Clap for **this** and **sack**.
(The children respond.)

h. Now follow the arrow to the next ball.   Check children's responses.

i. Repeat *f* through *h* until firm.

j. Touch the words on the bottom line when I clap. Get ready.
Clap for **is** and **fat**. *(The children respond.)*

k. This time you're going to touch all the words in the story.
Finger on the ball of the <u>top</u> line. Check children's responses.
Get ready.   Clap for **this** and **sack**.

l. Do not clap for **is** until the children have followed the arrow to the
ball on the bottom line. Then clap for **is** and **fat**.

m. Repeat *k* and *l* until firm.

TASK 22   First reading—children sound out each word and tell what word

a. Finger on the ball of the top line.   Check children's responses.

b. Touch the first word.   Check children's responses.   Sound it out.
Get ready.   Clap for each sound. *Thththiiisss.*

c. Again. (Pause.)   Get ready.   Clap for each sound. *Thththiiisss.*
What word? (Signal.) *This.*   Yes, **this.**

d. Next word.   Check children's responses.   Get ready.
Clap for each sound. *Sssaaac.*

e. Again. (Pause.)   Get ready.   Clap for each sound. *Sssaaac.*
What word? (Signal.) *Sack.*   Yes, **sack.**

f. Follow the arrow all the way to the next word.
Check children's responses.

g. Get ready.   Clap for each sound. *Iiisss.*

h. Again. (Pause.)   Get ready.   Clap for each sound. *Iiisss.*
What word? (Signal.) *Is.*   Yes, **is.**

i. Next word.   Check children's responses.   Get ready.   Clap for each
sound. *Fffaaat.*

j. Again. (Pause.)   Get ready.   Clap for each sound. *Fffaaat.*
What word? (Signal.) *Fat.*   Yes, **fat.**

TASK 23   Second reading—children sound out each word and tell what word

a. Let's read the story again. Everybody, touch the first word.
Check children's responses.

b. Get ready.   Clap for each sound. *Thththiiisss.*   What word? (Signal.)
This.   Yes, **this.**

c. Next word.   Check children's responses.   Get ready.   Clap for each
sound. *Sssaaac.*   What word? (Signal.) *Sack.*   Yes, **sack.**

d. Repeat *c* for the words **is, fat.**

TASK 24   Individual test

Call on different children to read one word. The child sounds out the
word only one time, then tells what word. The other children are to
point under the sounds that are said.

TASK 18   Picture comprehension

a. Everybody, look at the picture.
b. Ask these questions:
   1. Who is sitting on who?   *The children respond.*
                  The cat is sitting on the cow.
   2. What's one way to take the cow and the cat with you?
        The children respond. Put the cat on top of the cow.
   3. How could you do it another way?   *The children respond.*

TASK 19   Individual test

a. Everybody, look at the story. I'm going to call on different children
            to read a whole sentence the fast way.
b. Call on different children to read one of the first three
            sentences. Do not clap for each word.

TASK 20   Sentence saying

Good reading. Now, everybody, say all the words in that sentence
      without looking.   (Signal.) *The children repeat the sentence at a
            normal speaking rate.*

Take-Home 102

SUMMARY OF INDEPENDENT ACTIVITY

TASK 21   Introduction to independent activity

a. Pass out Take-Home 102 to each child.
b. Everybody, you're going to do this take-home on your own.
         Tell the children when they will work the items.
         Let's go over the things you're going to do.

TASK 22   Sentence copying

a. Hold up side 1 of your take-home and point to the first line in the
            sentence-copying exercise.
b. Everybody, here's the sentence you're going to write on the lines
            below.
c. Get ready to read the words in this sentence the fast way.
      First word.   Check children's responses. Get ready.   Clap. *A.*
d. Next word.   Check children's responses. Get ready.   Clap. *Cat.*
e. Repeat *d* for the remaining words.
f. After you finish your take-home, you get to draw a picture about
          the sentence, **a cat is on thē cow**.

TASK 23   Sound writing

a. Point to the sound-writing exercise. Here are the sounds you're
        going to write today. I'll touch the sounds. You say them.
b. Touch each sound. *The children respond.*
c. Repeat the series until firm.

TASK 24   Matching

a. Point to the column of words in the Matching Game.
b. Everybody, you're going to follow the lines and write these words.
c. Reading the fast way.
d. Point to the first word. (Pause.) Get ready.   (Signal.)
           The children respond.
e. Repeat *d* for the remaining words.
f. Repeat *d* and *e* until firm.

TASK 25   Cross-out game

Point to the boxed word in the Cross-out Game. Everybody, here's
      the word you're going to cross out today. What word?   (Signal.)
          And. Yes, **and**.

TASK 26   Pair relations

a. Point to the pair-relations exercise on side 2. You're going to
      circle the picture in each box that shows what the words say.
b. Point to the space at the top of the page. After you finish,
      remember to draw a picture that shows **a cat is on thē cow**.

END OF LESSON 102

TASK 25 Teacher and children read the fast way

a. Point to the words on the first two arrows. Touch under **fat.**
Everybody, this word is (pause) **fat.** What word? (Signal.) *Fat.*
Yes, **fat.** Remember that.

b. We're going to read this story the fast way.

c. Point to **this sack is.** I'll read these words the fast way.

d. Point to **fat.** When I touch this word, you're going to say . . . .
(Signal.) *Fat.* Yes, **fat.**

e. Repeat *d* until firm.

f. Touch the ball of the first arrow. Reading the fast way.
(Pause three seconds.) Touch under **this sack is** and say:
This sack is . . . .

g. Then touch under **fat.** *Fat.*

h. Repeat *f* and *g* until firm.

i. Yes, **this sack is fat.**

TASK 26 Picture comprehension

a. When you look at the picture, you'll say . . . . (Signal.)
This sack is fat.

b. Yes, when you look at the picture, you'll say . . . . (Signal.)
This sack is fat.

c. Turn your take-home over and look at the picture.

d. Ask these questions:

1. What do you say when you look at the picture? (Signal.) *This sack is fat.*

2. What is in that sack? *The children respond.* Yes, **food.**

3. Are the man and the girl sad? (Signal.) *No.*

4. What are they going to do with all the food in the sack?
The children respond.

5. What would you do with that sack of food?
The children respond.

TASK 27 Word finding

a. Turn your take-home back to side 1. Point to the words on the
first two arrows. I'm going to read all these words the fast way.

b. Touch the ball of the first arrow. Touch under each word and read:
This (pause) **sack** (pause) **is** (pause) **fat.**

c. I'll do it again. Touch under each word and read:
This (pause) **sack** (pause) **is** (pause) **fat.**

d. Everybody, look at the words in your story.

e. Look for the word (pause) **this. Thththiiisss.**

f. Everybody, point to **thththiiisss.** Get your finger right over the
word **thththiiisss.** Check children's responses.

g. Get ready to touch (pause) **this** when I clap. Get ready. Clap.
*(The children touch **this.**)*

h. Fingers up. Repeat *f* and *g* until firm.

i. Everybody, look at the words in your story.

j. Look for the word (pause) **fat. Fffaaat.**

k. Everybody, point to **fffaaat.** Get your finger right over the word
fffaaat. Check children's responses.

l. Get ready to touch (pause) **fat** when I clap. Get ready. Clap.
*(The children touch **fat.**)*

m. Repeat *j* through *l* until firm.

n. Direct the children to find the words in this order:
this (Repeat *e, f,* and *g.*)
fat (Repeat *j, k,* and *l.*)
this (Repeat *e, f,* and *g.*)
fat (Repeat *j, k,* and *l.*)

Story 102

Do not clap for any small letters.

TASK 16 First reading—question mark finding

Have the children reread any sentences containing words that give them trouble. Keep a list of these words.

a. Pass out Storybook 1.
b. Open your book to page 24 and get ready to read.
c. Clap for the sounds in each word of the first paragraph as the children sound out each word one time and tell what word.
d. After the children read **thē cat is fat,** say: Everybody, move along the lines until you come to the next period. Oh, oh. There's no period in this sentence. There's a funny mark called a question mark.
e. Everybody, touch the question mark. Check children's responses.
f. There's a question mark in this sentence because this sentence asks a question. Everybody, get ready to read the question.
g. Finger on the first word. Check children's responses. Clap for the sounds in each word of the sentence as the children sound out each word one time and tell what word.
h. After the children read **how can I tāke thē cow and thē cat with mē?** say: Everybody, say that question. *The children repeat the question at a normal speaking rate.*
i. Everybody, get ready to read the next sentence. Repeat *g* and *h* for the sentence: **can thē cow sit on thē cat?**
j. Yes, **can the cow sit on the cat**? Let's read the next sentence and find out.
k. Finger on the first word. Check children's responses. Clap for the sounds as the children sound out the word one time and tell what word.
l. Can the cow sit on the cat? (Signal.) *No.*
m. After the first reading of the story, print on the board the words that the children missed more than one time. Have the children sound out each word one time and tell what word.
n. After the group's responses are firm, call on individual children to read the words.

TASK 17 Second reading—children read the story the fast way and answer questions

a. Now you're going to read the story the fast way and I'll ask some more questions.
b. Finger on the ball of the top line. Check children's responses. Remember to stop when you get to a period.
c. Get ready. Clap for each word in the first sentence. Pause at least three seconds between claps. Pause longer before words that gave the children trouble during the first reading.
d. Clap for the word following **cow.** Praise children who do not read the word.
e. Again. Repeat *b* through *d* until firm.
f. What do I have? (Signal.) *A cow.*
g. Reading the words in the next sentence the fast way.
h. Get ready. Clap for each word in the next sentence. Pause at least three seconds between claps. Pause longer before words that gave the children trouble during the first reading.
i. Clap for the word following **fat.** Praise children who do not read the word.
j. Let's read that sentence again the fast way. Repeat *h* and *i* until firm.
k. Tell me about the cow. (Signal.) *The cow is fat.*
l. Use the procedures in *g* through *j* for the remaining sentences. Ask the comprehension questions below as the children read.

After the children read:	You say:
I have a cat.	What do I have? (Signal.) *A cat.*
The cat is fat.	Tell me about the cat. (Signal.) *The cat is fat.*
How can I take the cow and the cat with me?	Maybe the cow can sit on the cat.
Can the cow sit on the cat?	Let's read and find out.
No.	Can the cow sit on the cat? (Signal.) *No.*

PAIR RELATIONS

The children will need pencils.

TASK 28 Children cross out the incorrect boxes

a. Hold up Take-Home 63. Point to the pair-relations exercise on side 1. **Here's a new Cross-out Game.**

b. Touch the first box in the top row. **Everybody, all the boxes in the top row should say what this box says. What does this box say?** (Signal.) *aaa—aaa.* **Yes, aaa—aaa. That means you have to cross out every box that does not say aaa—aaa.**

c. Point to each box in the top row and ask: **Does this box say aaa—aaa?** (Signal.) *The children respond.* If the answer is no, say: **So you have to cross out this box.** The children are not to cross out the boxes now.

d. **Everybody, touch the first box in the top row.** Check children's responses.

e. **Pick up your pencil. Cross out the boxes in the top row that do not say aaa—aaa.** Check children's responses.

f. **Everybody, touch the first box in the next row.** Check children's responses. **What does that box say?** (Signal.) *rrr—c.* **Yes, rrr—c. That means you have to cross out every box in that row that does not say rrr—c. Do it.** Check children's responses.

g. **You will do the other rows of boxes later.**

SUMMARY OF INDEPENDENT ACTIVITY

TASK 29 Introduction to independent activity

Everybody, you're going to finish this take-home on your own. Tell the children when they will work the remaining items. **Let's go over the things you're going to do.**

TASK 30 Story copying

Point to the dotted words below the story on side 1. **You're going to write the dotted words on this arrow. Then you're going to write those words on the other arrow.**

TASK 31 Pair relations

a. Point to the first box in the third row in the pair-relations exercise.

b. **You're going to cross out the boxes in this row that don't say what this box says. What does this box say?** (Signal.) *sss—mmm.* **Yes, sss—mmm.**

c. Point to the third row. **So what are you going to do with every box in this row that doesn't say sss—mmm?** (Signal.) *Cross it out.* **Yes, cross it out.**

d. Repeat *a* through *c* for the fourth row.

TASK 32 Cross-out game

Point to the boxed sounds in the Cross-out Game on side 2. **Everybody, what sound are you going to circle today?** (Signal.) *nnn.* **What sound are you going to cross out?** (Signal.) *rrr.*

TASK 33 Matching

Point to the first column of sounds in the Matching Game. **You're going to draw lines for every sound over here.**

TASK 34 Sound writing

a. Point to the sound-writing exercise. **Here are the sounds you're going to write today. I'll touch the sounds. You say them.**

b. Touch each sound. *The children respond.*

c. Repeat the series until firm.

TASK 35 Story picture

Point to the story picture. **After you finish your take-home, you can color the story picture.**

END OF LESSON 63

TASK 13   Children sound out the word and tell what word

a. Touch the ball for **have.** Sound it out.
b. Get ready. Touch **h, a, v** as the children say *haaavvv.*
If sounding out is not firm, repeat *b.*
c. What word? (Signal.) *Have.* Yes, **have.**

TASK 14   Children sound out an irregular word (of)

a. Touch the ball for **of.** Sound it out.
b. Get ready. Quickly touch each sound as the children say *ooofff.*

To correct	If the children sound out the word as **ooovvv**
	1. Say: **You've got to say the sounds I touch.**
	2. Repeat *a* and *b* until firm.

c. Again. Repeat *b* until firm.
d. That's how we <u>sound out</u> the word. Here's how we <u>say</u> the word.
Of. How do we <u>say</u> the word? (Signal.) *Of.*
e. Now you're going to <u>sound out</u> the word. Get ready.
Touch each sound as the children say *ooofff.*
f. Now you're going to say the word. Get ready. (Signal.) *Of.*
g. Repeat *e* and *f* until firm.
h. Yes, this word is **of.** He ate a dish **of** ice cream.

TASK 15   Individual test

Call on different children to do *e* and *f* in task 14.

Do not touch any small letters.

Lesson 64

SOUNDS

TASK 1 Teaching **u** as in **under**

a. Point to **u.** Here's a new sound.

b. My turn. (Pause.) Touch **u** and say: *uuu.*

c. Again. Touch **u** for a longer time. *uuuuu.* Lift your finger.

d. Point to **u.** Your turn. When I touch it, you say it. (Pause.) Get ready. Touch **u.** *uuu.* Lift your finger.

e. Again. Touch **u.** *uuuuuu.* Lift your finger.

f. Repeat *e* until firm.

TASK 2 Individual test

Call on different children to identify **u.**

TASK 3 Sounds firm-up

a. Get ready to say the sounds when I touch them.

b. Alternate touching **a** and **u.** Point to the sound. (Pause one second.) Say: Get ready. Touch the sound. *The children respond.*

c. When **a** and **u** are firm, alternate touching **u, a, o,** and **i** until all four sounds are firm.

TASK 4 Individual test

Call on different children to identify **u, a, o,** or **i.**

TASK 5 Teacher introduces cross-out game

a. Use acetate and crayon.

b. I'll cross out the sounds on this page when you can tell me every sound.

c. Remember—when I touch it, you say it.

d. Go over the sounds until the children can identify all the sounds in order.

TASK 6 Individual test

Call on different children to identify two or more sounds in task 5.

TASK 7 Teacher crosses out sounds

a. You told me every sound. Get ready to do it again. This time I'll cross out each sound when you tell me what it is.

b. Point to each sound. (Pause.) Say: Get ready. Touch the sound. *The children respond.* As you cross out the sound, say: Goodbye, _____.

To correct	For all mistakes, have the children sound out the word and say it fast. Then say: **Remember this word.**

Do not touch any small letters.

TASK 10 Children read the fast way

a. **Get ready to read these words the fast way.**
b. Touch the ball for **gō.** (Pause three seconds.) **Get ready.**
(Signal.) *Go.*
c. Touch the ball for **thōse.** (Pause three seconds.) **Get ready.**
(Signal.) *Those.*

d. Repeat *c* for the remaining words on the page.

TASK 11 Children read the fast way again

a. **Get ready to do these words again. Watch where I point.**
b. Point to a word. (Pause one second.) Say: **Get ready.** (Signal.)
The children respond. Point to the words in this order:
ōld, gō, thōse, thē, this.

c. Repeat *b* until firm.

TASK 12 Individual test

Call on different children to read one word the fast way.

gō

thōse

thē

this

ōld

READING VOCABULARY

Get ready to read all the words on this page without making a mistake.

TASK 8   Children sound out the word and tell what word

a. Touch the ball for **it.** Sound it out.
b. Get ready. Touch **i, t** as the children say *iiit.*
　　　　　　　　　If sounding out is not firm, repeat *b.*
c. What word? (Signal.) *It.* Yes, **it.**

TASK 9   Children sound out the word, then read it the fast way

a. Touch the ball for **thē.** Sound it out.
b. Get ready. Touch **th, ē** as the children say *thththēēē.*
　　　　　　　　　If sounding out is not firm, repeat *b.*
c. What word? (Signal.) *Thē.* Yes, **thē.**
d. Return to the ball. **Get ready to read the word the fast way.**
　　　　　　　　　Don't sound it out. Just tell me the word.
e. (Pause at least three seconds.) **Get ready.** Move your finger
　　　quickly along the arrow. *Thē.* Yes, **thē.** Good reading.

To correct	If the children sound out the word instead of reading it the fast way
	1. Say: **I'll read the word the <u>fast</u> way. Thē.**
	2. Repeat *d* and *e* until firm.
	3. Repeat *a* through *e.*

f. Repeat *d* and *e* until firm.

TASK 10   Individual test

Call on different children to do *d* and *e* in task 9.

TASK 11   Children sound out the word, then read it the fast way

Repeat the procedures in task 9 for **sit.**

TASK 12   Individual test

Call on different children to do *d* and *e* in task 9 for **sit.**

READING VOCABULARY

To correct	For all mistakes, have the children sound out the word and say it fast. Then say: **Remember this word.**

TASK 7   Children read the fast way

a. Get ready to read these words the fast way.
b. Touch the ball for **had.** (Pause three seconds.) **Get ready.**
(Signal.) *Had.*
c. Touch the ball for **sāve.** (Pause three seconds.) **Get ready.**
(Signal.) *Save.*
d. Repeat *c* for the remaining words on the page.

TASK 8   Children read the fast way again

a. Get ready to do these words again. Watch where I point.
b. Point to a word. (Pause one second.) Say: **Get ready.** (Signal.)
The children respond. Point to the words in this order:
with, now, nuts, sāve, had.
c. Repeat *b* until firm.

TASK 9   Individual test

Call on different children to read one word the fast way.

Do not touch any small letters.

had

sāve

nuts

now

with

Get ready to read all the words on this page without making a mistake.

TASK 13 Children read a word beginning with a stop sound (hē)

a. Point under **ē**. What's this sound? (Signal.) *ēēē*.
b. Touch the ball for **hē**. This word rhymes with (pause) **ēē**.
   Get ready. Move quickly along the arrow. *Hēēē*.
c. What word? (Signal.) *He.* Yes, **he**.
d. Again. Repeat *b* and *c* until firm.
e. Return to the ball. Sound it out. Remember—say the sounds when
         I touch them. Get ready. Quickly touch **h**, **ē** as the children
                        say *hēēē*.
f. What word? (Signal.) *He.* Yes, **he**. Good reading. **He** can run fast.
g. Repeat *e* and *f* until firm.

TASK 14 Individual test

Call on different children to sound out the word in task 13 and tell
                                    what word.

TASK 15 Children read a word beginning with a stop sound (hot)

a. Run your finger under **ot**. You're going to sound out this part.
                    Get ready. Touch **o**, **t** as the children say *ooot*.
b. Say it fast. (Signal.) *Ot.* Yes, this part says (pause) **ot**.
c. Repeat *a* and *b* until firm.
d. Touch the ball for **hot**. This word rhymes with (pause) **ot**.
   Get ready. Move quickly along the arrow. *Hot*.
e. What word? (Signal.) *Hot.* Yes, **hot**.
f. Repeat *d* and *e* until firm.
g. Return to the ball. Now you're going to sound out (pause) **hot**.
            Get ready. Quickly touch **h**, **o**, **t** as the children say *hooot*.
h. What word? (Signal.) *Hot.* Yes, **hot**. Good reading. The sun is **hot**.
i. Repeat *g* and *h* until firm.

TASK 16 Individual test

Call on different children to do *g* and *h* in task 15.

TASK 17 Individual test

Call on different children to sound out one word and tell what word.

Lesson 102

v

f

w

th

SOUNDS

TASK 1 Teaching v as in very

a. Point to **v.** Here's a new sound.

b. My turn. (Pause.) Touch **v** and say: vvv.

c. Again. Touch **v** for a longer time. vvvvv. Lift your finger.

d. Point to **v.** Your turn. When I touch it, you say it. (Pause.) Get ready. Touch **v.** vvv. Lift your finger.

e. Again. Touch **v.** vvvvvv. Lift your finger.

f. Repeat e until firm.

TASK 2 Individual test

Call on different children to identify **v.**

TASK 3 Sounds firm-up

a. Get ready to say the sounds when I touch them.

b. Alternate touching **f** and **v.** Point to the sound. (Pause one second.) Say: Get ready. Touch the sound. *The children respond.*

c. When **f** and **v** are firm, alternate touching **f, v, w,** and **th** until all four sounds are firm.

TASK 4 Individual test

Call on different children to identify **f, v, w,** or **th.**

TASK 5 Sounds firm-up

a. Point to **v.** When I touch the sound, you say it.

b. (Pause.) Get ready. Touch **v.** vvv.

c. Again. Repeat b until firm.

d. Get ready to say all the sounds when I touch them.

e. Alternate touching **ō, k, l, sh, v, ā, n,** and **u** three or four times.
Point to the sound. (Pause one second.) Say: Get ready.
Touch the sound. *The children respond.*

v   **ō**   **k**

I   **sh**

ā   **n**   **u**

TASK 6 Individual test

Call on different children to identify one or more sounds in task 5.

TASK 18   Children rhyme with it

a. Point to the first sound of **mitt.** What sound? (Signal.) *mmm.*
Point to the first sound of **hit.** What sound? (Signal.) *h.*

b. These words rhyme with (pause) **it.**
What do they rhyme with? (Signal.) *It.*
Yes, rhymes with (pause) **it.**

c. Touch the ball for **mitt.** Get ready. Touch **m.** *mmm.*
Move your finger along the arrow. *Mmmit.*

d. What word? (Signal.) *Mitt.* Yes, **mitt.**

e. Touch the ball for **hit.** This word rhymes with (pause) **it.**
What does it rhyme with? (Signal.) *It.*

f. Get ready. Move your finger quickly along the arrow. *Hit.*

g. What word? (Signal.) *Hit.* Yes, **hit.**

TASK 19   Children sound out the word and tell what word

a. Touch the ball for **hit.** Sound it out.

b. Get ready. Touch **h, i, t** as the children say *hiiit.*

c. Again. Repeat *b* until firm.

d. Yes, what word? (Signal.) *Hit.*

TASK 18   Picture comprehension

a. Everybody, look at the picture.
b. Ask these questions:
   1. Can a cat lick a kitten? *Yes.*
   2. Why is that mother cat licking the kitten? *The children respond.*
   3. How do you get clean when you're dirty? *The children respond.*

TASK 19   Individual test

a. Everybody, look at the story. I'm going to call on different children to read a whole sentence the fast way.
b. Call on different children to read one of the first three sentences. Do not clap for each word.

TASK 20   Sentence saying

Good reading. Now, everybody, say all the words in that sentence without looking. (Signal.) *The children repeat the sentence at a normal speaking rate.*

Take-Home 101

SUMMARY OF INDEPENDENT ACTIVITY

TASK 21   Introduction to independent activity

a. Pass out Take-Home 101 to each child.
b. Everybody, you're going to do this take-home on your own.
   Tell the children when they will work the items.
   Let's go over the things you're going to do.

TASK 22   Sentence copying

a. Hold up side 1 of your take-home and point to the first line in the sentence-copying exercise.
b. Everybody, here's the sentence you're going to write on the lines below.
c. Get ready to read the words in this sentence the fast way.
   First word. Check children's responses. Get ready. Clap. *I.*
d. Next word. Check children's responses. Get ready. Clap. *Can.*
e. Repeat *d* for the remaining words.
f. After you finish your take-home, you get to draw a picture about the sentence, **I can kiss a cat**.

TASK 23   Sound writing

a. Point to the sound-writing exercise. Here are the sounds you're going to write today. I'll touch the sounds. You say them.
b. Touch each sound. *The children respond.*
c. Repeat the series until firm.

TASK 24   Matching

a. Point to the column of words in the Matching Game.
b. Everybody, you're going to follow the lines and write these words.
c. Reading the fast way.
d. Point to the first word. (Pause.) Get ready. (Signal.)
   The children respond.
e. Repeat *d* for the remaining words.
f. Repeat *d* and *e* until firm.

TASK 25   Cross-out game

Point to the boxed word in the Cross-out Game. Everybody, here's the word you're going to cross out today. What word? (Signal.)
Him. Yes, **him**.

TASK 26   Pair relations

a. Point to the pair-relations exercise on side 2. You're going to circle the picture in each box that shows what the words say.
b. Point to the space at the top of the page. After you finish, remember to draw a picture that shows **I can kiss a cat**.

END OF LESSON 101

Take-Home 64

STORY

TASK 20 First reading—children sound out each word and tell what word

a. Pass out Take-Home 64. Do not let the children look at the picture until task 24.

b. Get ready to read the story. Everybody, touch the first word. Check children's responses.

c. Get ready. Clap for each sound. *Iiisss.*

d. Again. (Pause.) Get ready. Clap for each sound. *Iiisss.* What word? (Signal.) *Is.* Yes, is.

e. Next word. Check children's responses. Get ready. Clap for each sound. *Thththiiisss.*

f. Again. (Pause.) Get ready. Clap for each sound. *Thththiiisss.* What word? (Signal.) *This.* Yes, this.

g. Repeat e and f for the words **a, mitt.**

TASK 21 Second reading—children sound out each word and tell what word

a. Let's read the story again. Everybody, touch the first word. Check children's responses.

b. Get ready. Clap for each sound. *Iiisss.* What word? (Signal.) *Is.* Yes, is.

c. Next word. Check children's responses. Get ready. Clap for each sound. *Thththiiisss.* What word? (Signal.) *This.* Yes, this.

d. Repeat c for the words **a, mitt.**

TASK 22 Individual test

Call on different children to read one word. The child sounds out the word only one time, then tells what word. The other children are to point under the sounds that are said.

TASK 23 Teacher and children read the fast way

a. Let's read the fast way. Touch under **a.** This word is **a.** Touch under **mitt.** This word is **mitt.**

b. Point to **a.** What are you going to say when I touch this word? (Signal.) *A.*

c. Point to **mitt.** What are you going to say when I touch this word? (Signal.) *Mitt.*

d. Repeat b and c until firm.

e. My turn. Touch under the words as you say: Is this . . . .

f. Your turn. Touch under the words as the children say *a mitt.*

g. Repeat e and f until firm.

TASK 24 Picture comprehension

a. The girl in the picture wants to know . . . . (Signal.) *Is this a mitt?*

b. Yes, she wants to know . . . . (Signal.) *Is this a mitt?*

c. Turn your take-home over and look at the picture.

d. Ask these questions:
1. Is this a mitt? (Signal.) *Yes.*
2. Is the girl good at catching a ball? *The children respond.*
3. What kind of mitt is she wearing? (Signal.) *A baseball mitt.*
4. Did you ever play baseball? *The children respond.*

TASK 25 Word finding

a. Turn your take-home back to side 1. Everybody, let's play Find-the-Words. Look at the words in your story and get ready.

b. One of the words is (pause) **is.** Get ready to touch **is** when I clap. (Pause three seconds.) Get ready. Clap. *(The children touch **is**.)*

c. Repeat b for these words: **mitt, is, mitt, is.**

d. Repeat b and c until firm.

Story 101

Do not clap for any small letters.

TASK 16   First reading—question mark finding

Have the children reread any sentences containing words that give them trouble. Keep a list of these words.

a. Pass out Storybook 1.

b. Open your book to page 22 and get ready to read.

c. Clap for the sounds in each word of the first paragraph as the children sound out each word one time and tell what word.

d. After the children read **I can kiss a kitten**, say: **Everybody, move along the lines until you come to the next period. Oh, oh. There's no period in this sentence. There's a funny mark called a question mark.**

e. Everybody, touch the question mark. Check children's responses.

f. There's a question mark in this sentence because this sentence asks a question. Everybody, get ready to read the question.

g. Finger on the first word. Check children's responses. Clap for the sounds in each word of the sentence as the children sound out each word one time and tell what word.

h. After the children read **can a cow kiss mē?** say: **Everybody, say that question.** *The children repeat the question at a normal speaking rate.*

i. Yes, can a cow kiss me? Let's read the next sentence and find out.

j. Finger on the first word. Check children's responses. Clap for the sounds as the children sound out the word one time and tell what word.

k. Can a cow kiss me? (Signal.) *No.*

l. Everybody, get ready to read the next sentence. Repeat *g* for the sentence: **a cow can not kiss mē.**

m. Everybody, get ready to read the next sentence. Repeat *g* for the sentence: **a cow can lick me.**

n. What can a cow do? (Signal.) *A cow can lick me.*

o. Everybody, get ready to read the next sentence. Repeat *g* and *h* for the sentence: **can a cat lick a kitten?**

p. Can a cat lick a kitten? We'll find out later.

q. After the first reading of the story, print on the board the words that the children missed more than one time. Have the children sound out each word one time and tell what word.

r. After the group's responses are firm, call on individual children to read the words.

TASK 17   Second reading—children read the story the fast way and answer questions

a. Now you're going to read the story the fast way and I'll ask some more questions.

b. Finger on the ball of the top line. Check children's responses. **Remember to stop when you get to a period.**

c. Get ready. Clap for each word in the first sentence. Pause at least three seconds between claps. Pause longer before words that gave the children trouble during the first reading.

d. Clap for the word following **cat.** Praise children who do not read the word.

e. Again. Repeat *b* through *d* until firm.

f. What can I do? (Signal.) *Kiss a cat.*

g. Reading the words in the next sentence the fast way.

h. Get ready. Clap for each word in the next sentence. Pause at least three seconds between claps. Pause longer before words that gave the children trouble during the first reading.

i. Clap for the word following **kitten.** Praise children who do not read the word.

j. Let's read that sentence again the fast way. Repeat *h* and *j* until firm.

k. What else can I do? (Signal.) *Kiss a kitten.*

l. Use the procedures in *g* through *j* for the remaining sentences. Ask the comprehension questions below as the children read.

After the children read:	You say:
Can a cow kiss me?	I don't know. Let's read and find out.
A cow can not kiss me.	Can a cow kiss me? (Signal.) *No.*
A cow can lick me.	What can a cow do? (Signal.) *Lick me.*
Can a cat lick a kitten?	What do you think? *The children respond.*

PAIR RELATIONS

The children will need pencils.

TASK 26 Children cross out the incorrect boxes

a. Hold up Take-Home 64. Point to the pair-relations exercise on side 1.
Here's the new Cross-out Game.

b. Touch the first box in the top row. Everybody, all the boxes in the
top row should say what this box says. What does this box say?
(Signal.) *c—nnn.* Yes, **c—nnn**. That means you have to cross out
every box that does not say **c—nnn**.

c. Point to each box in the top row and ask: Does this box say
c—nnn? (Signal.) *The children respond.* If the answer is no, say:
So you have to cross out this box. The children are not to cross
out the boxes now.

d. Everybody, touch the first box in the top row.
Check children's responses.

e. Pick up your pencil. Cross out the boxes in the top row that do
not say **c—nnn**. Check children's responses.

f. Everybody, touch the first box in the next row.
Check children's responses.
What does that box say? (Signal.) *d—ooo.* Yes, **d—ooo**.
That means you have to cross out every box in that row that does
not say **d—ooo**. Do it. Check children's responses.

g. You will do the other rows of boxes later.

SUMMARY OF INDEPENDENT ACTIVITY

TASK 27 Introduction to independent activity

Everybody, you're going to finish this take-home on your own.
Tell the children when they will work the remaining items.
Let's go over the things you're going to do.

TASK 28 Story copying

Point to the dotted words below the story on side 1. You're going
to write the dotted words on this arrow. Then you're going to write
those words on the other arrow.

TASK 29 Pair relations

a. Point to the first box in the third row in the pair-relations exercise.

b. You're going to cross out the boxes in this row that don't say what
this box says. What does this box say? (Signal.) *fff—ēēē.*
Yes, **fff—ēēē**.

c. Point to the third row. So what are you going to do with every box
in this row that doesn't say **fff—ēēē**? (Signal.) *Cross it out.*
Yes, cross it out.

d. Repeat a through c for the fourth row.

TASK 30 Cross-out game

Point to the boxed sounds in the Cross-out Game on side 2.
Everybody, what sound are you going to cross out today?
(Signal.) *nnn.* What sound are you going to circle? (Signal.) *mmm.*

TASK 31 Matching

Point to the first column of sounds in the Matching Game. You're
going to draw lines for every sound over here.

TASK 32 Sound writing

a. Point to the sound-writing exercise. Here are the sounds you're
going to write today. I'll touch the sounds. You say them.

b. Touch each sound. *The children respond.*

c. Repeat the series until firm.

TASK 33 Story picture

Point to the story picture. After you finish your take-home,
you can color the story picture.

END OF LESSON 64

TASK 11 **Children sound out the word and tell what word**

a. Touch the ball for **kitten.** Sound it out.
b. Get ready. Touch **k, i,** between the **t**'s, **n** as the children say *kiiitnnn.*
If sounding out is not firm, repeat *b.*
c. What word? (Signal.) *Kitten.* Yes, **kitten.** A **kitten** is a baby cat.

TASK 12 **Children sound out the word and tell what word**

a. Touch the ball for **kiss.** Sound it out.
b. Get ready. Touch **k, i,** between the **s**'s as the children say *kiiisss.*
If sounding out is not firm, repeat *b.*
c. What word? (Signal.) *Kiss.* Yes, **kiss.**

To correct	For all mistakes, have the children sound out the word and say it fast. Then say: **Remember this word.**

TASK 13 **Children read the fast way**

a. Get ready to read these words the fast way.
b. Touch the ball for **this.** (Pause three seconds.) Get ready.
(Signal.) *This.*
c. Touch the ball for **thōse.** (Pause three seconds.) Get ready.
(Signal.) *Those.*

d. Repeat *c* for **that.**

TASK 14 **Children read the fast way again**

a. Get ready to do these words again. Watch where I point.
b. Point to a word. (Pause one second.) Say: Get ready. (Signal.)
The children respond. Point to the words in this order:
thōse, this, that.

c. Repeat *b* until firm.

TASK 15 **Individual test**

Call on different children to read one word on the page the fast way.

Do not touch any small letters.

kitten

kiss

this

thōse

that

Lesson 65

u

ē

d

SOUNDS

u

TASK 1   Teaching u as in under

a. Point to **u**. My turn. (Pause.)
   Touch **u** and say: uuu.
b. Point to **u**. Your turn. When I
   touch it, you say it. (Pause.)
   Get ready. Touch **u**. *uuu.*
   Lift your finger.
c. Again. Touch **u**. *uuuu.*
   Lift your finger.
d. Repeat *c* until firm.

h

o

f

TASK 2   Sounds firm-up

a. Get ready to say the sounds
   when I touch them.
b. Alternate touching **u** and **o**. Point
   to the sound. (Pause one second.)
   Say: Get ready. Touch the
   sound. *The children respond.*
c. When **u** and **o** are firm, alternate
   touching **o, i, u,** and **a** until all
   four sounds are firm.

ā

c

i

a

TASK 4   Sounds firm-up

a. Point to **u**. When I touch the sound, you say it.
b. (Pause.) Get ready. Touch **u**. *uuu.*
c. Again. Repeat *b* until firm.
d. Get ready to say all the sounds when I touch them.
e. Alternate touching **o, ē, d, h, u, f, ā,** and **c** three or four times.
   Point to the sound. (Pause one second.) Say: Get ready.
   Touch the sound. *The children respond.*

TASK 3   Individual test

Call on different children to identify **o, i, u,** or **a**.

TASK 5   Individual test

Call on different children to identify one or more sounds in task 4.

50

TASK 7 Children sound out an irregular word (of)

a. Touch the ball for **of**. **Sound it out.**

b. **Get ready.** Quickly touch each sound as the children say *ooofff*.

To correct	If the children sound out the word as **ooovvv**
	1. Say: **You've got to say the sounds I touch.**
	2. Repeat *a* and *b* until firm.

c. **Again.** Repeat *b* until firm.

d. **That's how we** <u>sound out</u> **the word. Here's how we** <u>say</u> **the word. Of. How do we say the word?** (Signal.) *Of.*

e. **Now you're going to** <u>sound out</u> **the word. Get ready.** Touch each sound as the children say *ooofff*.

f. **Now you're going to say the word. Get ready.** (Signal.) *Of.*

g. Repeat *e* and *f* until firm.

h. **Yes, this word is of. This part of the table is the top.**

TASK 8 Individual test

Call on different children to do *e* and *f* in task 7.

To correct	For all mistakes, have the children sound out the word and say it fast. Then say: **Remember this word.**

TASK 9 Children read the fast way

a. **Get ready to read these words the fast way.**

b. Touch the ball for **hit**. (Pause three seconds.) **Get ready.** (Signal.) *Hit.*

c. Touch the ball for **nō**. (Pause three seconds.) **Get ready.** (Signal.) *No.*

TASK 10 Children read the fast way again

a. **Get ready to do these words again. Watch where I point.**

b. Point to a word. (Pause one second.) Say: **Get ready.** (Signal.) *The children respond.* Point to the words in this order: **of, hit, nō.**

c. Repeat *b* until firm.

of

hit

nō

READING VOCABULARY

TASK 6   Children sound out the word, then read it the fast way

a. Touch the ball for **thē.** Sound it out.
b. Get ready. Touch **th, ē** as the children say *thththēēē.*
                         If sounding out is not firm, repeat *b.*
c. What word? (Signal.) *Thē.* Yes, **thē.**
d. Return to the ball. Get ready to read the word the fast way.
     I'm going to count to five. See if you can remember the word.
e. 1, 2, 3, 4, 5. Get ready. Move your finger quickly along the arrow.
                   Thē. Yes, **thē.** Good reading.

f. Again. Repeat *e* until firm.

TASK 7   Individual test

Call on different children to do *e* in task 6.

TASK 8   Children sound out the word, then read it the fast way

a. Touch the ball for **man.** Sound it out.
b. Get ready. Touch **m, a, n** as the children say *mmmaaannn.*
                        If sounding out is not firm, repeat *b.*
c. What word? (Signal.) *Man.* Yes, **man.**
d. Return to the ball. Get ready to read the word the fast way.
     I'm going to count to five. See if you can remember the word.
e. 1, 2, 3, 4, 5. Get ready. Move your finger quickly along the arrow.
                 Man. Yes, **man.** Good reading.

f. Again. Repeat *e* until firm.

TASK 9   Individual test

Call on different children to do *e* in task 8.

READING VOCABULARY

To correct	For all mistakes, have the children sound out the word and say it fast. Then say: **Remember this word.**

TASK 4   Children read the fast way

a. Get ready to read these words the fast way.
b. Touch the ball for **fōr.** (Pause three seconds.)   **Get ready.**
(Signal.) *For.*
c. Touch the ball for **ōr.** (Pause three seconds.)   **Get ready.**
(Signal.) *Or.*
d. Repeat *c* for the remaining words on the page.

TASK 5   Children read the fast way again

a. Get ready to do these words again. Watch where I point.
b. Point to a word. (Pause one second.) Say: **Get ready.** (Signal.)
The children respond. Point to the words in this order:
fōr, hits, not, ōr, will.
c. Repeat *b* until firm.

TASK 6   Individual test

Call on different children to read one word the fast way.

fōr

ōr

not

hits

will

TASK 10   Children sound out the word, then read it the fast way

a. Touch the ball for **not.** **Sound it out.**
b. **Get ready.**   Touch **n, o, t** as the children say *nnnooot.*
                              If sounding out is not firm, repeat *b.*
c. **What word?** (Signal.) *Not.* **Yes, not.**
d. Return to the ball. **Get ready to read the word the fast way.**
            I'm going to count to five. See if you can remember the word.
e. 1, 2, 3, 4, 5. **Get ready.** Move your finger quickly along the arrow.
                              Not. **Yes, not. Good reading.**
f. **Again.** Repeat *e* until firm.

not

TASK 11   Individual test

Call on different children to do *e* in task 10.

ad

TASK 12   Children rhyme with ad

a. Point to **ad** and **had.** **These words rhyme.**
b. Touch the ball for **ad.** **Sound it out.**
c. **Get ready.** Touch **a, d** as the children say *aaad.*
                              If sounding out is not firm, repeat *c.*
d. **What word?** (Signal.) *Ad.* **Yes, ad.**
e. Quickly touch the ball for **had.** **This word rhymes with** (pause) **ad.**
       Get ready. Move your finger quickly along the arrow. *Had.*
f. **What word?** (Signal.) *Had.* **Yes, had. I had** five dollars.

had

Lesson 101

Groups that are firm on Mastery Tests 18 and 19 should skip this lesson and do lesson 102 today.

SOUNDS

TASK 1   Child plays teacher

a. Use acetate and crayon.
b. [Child's name] is going to be the teacher.
c. [He or She] is going to touch the sounds. When [he or she] touches a sound, you say it.
d. The child points to and touches the sounds. You circle any sound that is not firm.
e. After the child has completed the page, present all the circled sounds to the children.

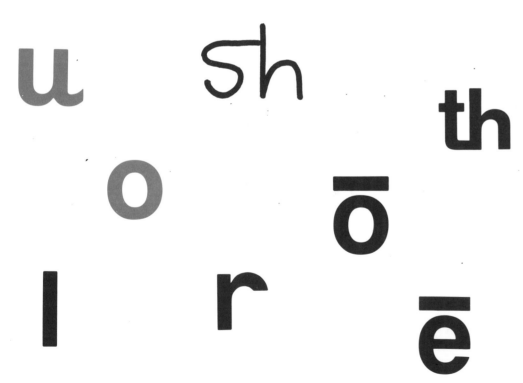

TASK 2   Individual test

Call on different children. If you can say the sound when I call your name, you may cross it out.

TASK 3   Teacher and children play the sounds game

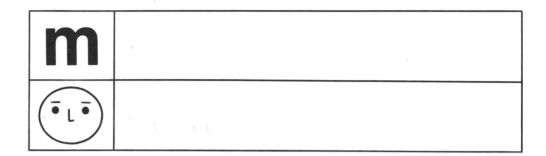

a. Use acetate and crayon. Write the sounds in the symbol box. Keep score in the score box.
b. I'm smart. I bet I can beat you in a game.
c. Here's the rule. When I touch a sound, you say it.
d. Play the game.
Make one symbol at a time in the symbol box. Use the symbols **c, g, k,** and **d.**
Make each symbol quickly. (Pause.) Touch the symbol.
Play the game for about two minutes.
Then ask: Who won? Draw a mouth on the face in the score box.

TASK 13 **Children read a word beginning with a stop sound (ham)**

a. Run your finger under **am.** You're going to sound out this part.
Get ready. Touch **a, m** as the children say *aaammm.*

b. Say it fast. (Signal.) *Am.* Yes, this part says (pause) **am.**

c. Repeat *a* and *b* until firm.

d. Touch the ball for **ham.** This word rhymes with (pause) **am.**
Get ready. Move quickly along the arrow. *Ham.*

e. What word? (Signal.) *Ham.* Yes, **ham.**

f. Repeat *d* and *e* until firm.

g. Return to the ball. Now you're going to sound out (pause) **ham.**
Get ready. Quickly touch **h, a, m** as the children say *haaammm.*

h. What word? (Signal.) *Ham.* Yes, **ham.** Good reading. She ate a
ham sandwich.

i. Repeat *g* and *h* until firm.

ham

TASK 14 **Individual test**

Call on different children to do *g* and *h* in task 13.

TASK 15 **Children sound out the word, then read it the fast way**

a. Touch the ball for **sat.** Sound it out.

b. Get ready. Touch **s, a, t** as the children say *sssaaat.*
If sounding out is not firm, repeat *b.*

c. What word? (Signal.) *Sat.* Yes, **sat.**

d. Return to the ball. Get ready to read the word the fast way.
I'm going to count to five. See if you can remember the word.

e. 1, 2, 3, 4, 5. Get ready. Move your finger quickly along the arrow.
Sat. Yes, **sat.** Good reading.

f. Again. Repeat *e* until firm.

sat

TASK 16 **Individual test**

Call on different children to do *e* in task 15.

Look Ahead

Mastery Tests

Skill Tested	Implications
Test 20 (Lesson 105) Reading a story, sounding out the words	Beginning in Lesson 107, stories will be read the fast way.
Test 21 (Lesson 110) Reading words the fast way	More words will be introduced in each lesson.
Test 22 (Lesson 115) Reading the story the fast way	Story length will increase.
Test 23 (Lesson 120) Sounds	Be sure children are firm.

Reading Checkouts

Lessons 108–110, 115, 120

• Beginning at Lesson 108, students will begin doing checkouts on the story or part of the story, reading the passage within a specified time and error limit.

Prior to lesson 108

• Develop a plan for managing and recording checkouts. Initially, you will need at least 4–5 minutes per child to explain and conduct checkouts.
• Plan to conduct checkouts while children are completing Take-Homes or other independent work.
• Paraprofessionals or classroom volunteers can assist with checkouts.
• For children who need additional practice in reading the stories, partner readings may be an option. Seat children side by side with their chairs facing in opposite directions. One child reads while the other follows along, and they then switch.
• Checkouts, along with mastery tests, will provide important information about the children's progress.

Skills

	Lessons 101–120
Word Reading	4 sounds 53 regular words 13 irregular words Reading stories the fast way

Reading Activities

Help children develop comprehension skills by using the following activities.

Fun with New Words (Lessons 101–120)

On the chalkboard, list these words from Lessons 101–110. Direct children to write all the words that tell about more than one thing. Direct children to write another list with all the words that rhyme with *old*.

-ōld	**-s**
tōld	lots
sōld	cōats
cōld	rocks
mōld	socks
hōld	hats
	sacks

On the chalkboard, list these words from Lessons 111–120. Direct children to write all the words that rhyme with *make* and all the words that rhyme with *late*. Then direct children to make lists for other words that rhyme.

-ā	**-ar**
gāve	are
cāke	car
tāke	tar
lāke	farm
hāte	arm
gāte	part

A So-So Story (Lessons 106–108)

After children have read stories 106–108, play a game of so-so. Have children use the story lines from these stories to discuss the events and fill in the sequence chart. Have children retell the story in their own words using the so-so clues.

thē ōld man said, "give mē socks."
   sō

shē gāve him socks for his fēet.

thē ōld man was cōld.
   sō

hē got a gōat with hats and cōats and socks.

thē ōld gōat āte his ōld cōat.
   sō

now thē ōld gōat is cōld and sad.

TASK 17 Children read the word in the box the fast way

a. Touch the ball for **not.**

b. You're going to read this word the fast way. I'll move down the arrow and stop under the sounds. But don't say the sounds out loud. Just figure out what you're going to say. Touch under each sound. *Children do not respond.*

c. Return to the ball. (Pause at least three seconds.) Read it the fast way. Get ready. Slash. *Not.* Yes, **not.**

TASK 18 Individual test

Call on different children to read the word in task 17 the fast way.

TASK 19 Children read the word in the box the fast way

a. Touch the ball for **man.**

b. You're going to read this word the fast way. I'll move down the arrow and stop under the sounds. But don't say the sounds out loud. Just figure out what you're going to say. Touch under each sound. *Children do not respond.*

c. Return to the ball. (Pause at least three seconds.) Read it the fast way. Get ready. Slash. *Man.* Yes, **man.**

TASK 20 Individual test

Call on different children to read the word in task 19 the fast way.

TASK 21 Children reread the words in the box the fast way

Repeat tasks 17 and 19.

TASK 22 Children sound out the word and tell what word

a. Touch the ball for **sit.** Sound it out.

b. Get ready. Touch **s, i, t** as the children say *sssiiit.*

If sounding out is not firm, repeat *b.*

c. What word? (Signal.) *Sit.* Yes, **sit.**

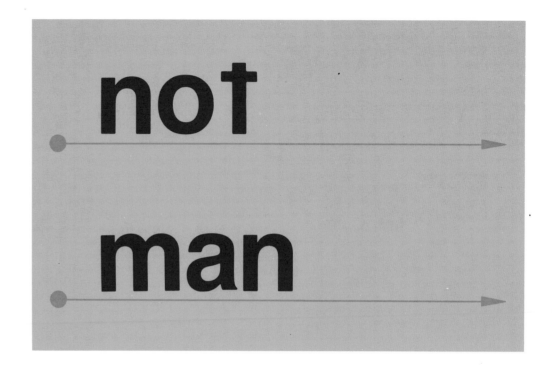

Planning Pages: For Lessons 101–120

Making Progress

	Since Lesson 1	Since Lesson 81
Word Reading	23 sounds 161 irregular words 2 irregular words Reading words the fast way	3 sounds 55 regular words 2 irregular words Reading words the fast way
Comprehension	**Picture Comprehension** Predicting what the picture will show Answering questions about the picture **Story Comprehension** Answering questions orally Making predictions Finding periods, question marks, and quotation marks	**Story Comprehension** Finding periods, question marks, and quotation marks

What to Use

Teacher	Students

Presentation Book B (pages 285–382)
  Lessons 101–107
Presentation Book C (pages 1–77)
  Lessons 108–120
Teacher's Guide (page 46)
Teacher's Take-Home Book and Answer Key
Spelling Book
	Storybook 1 (pages 22–64)
	  Lessons 101–117
	Storybook 2 (pages 1–9)
	  Lessons 118–120
	Take-Home Book B
	Take-Home Book C
	plain paper (Lesson 120)
	lined paper (Spelling)

Keep in Mind:

When children sound out irregular words, make sure they say the sounds for the letters. Also, when students encounter a new word, make sure they sound it out.

What's Ahead in Lessons 101–120

New Skills
- Story length will increase from 33 to 82 words.
- Titles for stories will be introduced (Lesson 115).
- Beginning at Lesson 107, all stories will be read "the fast way."

New Sounds
- Lesson 102 – **v** as in *love*
- Lesson 108 – **p** as in *sap* (quick sound)
- Lesson 113 – **ch** as in *chin* (quick sound)
- Lesson 118 – **e** as in *end*

New Vocabulary
- *Regular words:*
  - (101) kitten
  - (102) have
  - (103) hold
  - (104) give, save, gave
  - (105) hugs, shave, rugs
  - (106) goat
  - (107) oats, goats, coats, cold
  - (108) mop, cop, top
  - (109) ship, dip, down
  - (110) fog, lot, log, dog
  - (112) pot
  - (113) chops, shops
  - (114) chips, road
  - (115) each, teach
  - (116) caves, waves, saves
  - (117) cows, cats, cave, pots,
  - (118) tops, home
  - (119) corn, takes, pigs, here, all, more, lake
  - (120) met, there, wet, let, get, went

- *Irregular words:*
  - (101) of
  - (105) to
  - (112) are, car, tar
  - (113) art, part
  - (114) far, farm
  - (115) arm, cars
  - (116) girl
  - (117) do

Take-Home 65

STORY

TASK 23 **First reading—children sound out each word and tell what word**

a. Pass out Take-Home 65. Do not let the children look at the picture
until task 27.

b. Get ready to read the story. Everybody, touch the first word.
Check children's responses.

c. Get ready. Clap for each sound. *Thththēēē.*

d. Again. (Pause.) Get ready. Clap for each sound. *Thththēēē.*
What word? (Signal.) *Thē.* Yes, **thē.**

e. Next word. Check children's responses. Get ready.
Clap for each sound. *Mmmaaannn.*

f. Again. (Pause.) Get ready. Clap for each sound. *Mmmaaannn.*
What word? (Signal.) *Man.* Yes, **man.**

g. Repeat *e* and *f* for the words **is, not, sad.**

TASK 24 **Second reading—children sound out each word and tell what word**

a. Let's read the story again. Everybody, touch the first word.
Check children's responses.

b. Get ready. Clap for each sound. *Thththēēē.* What word? (Signal.)
Thē. Yes, **thē.**

c. Next word. Check children's responses. Get ready. Clap for each
sound. *Mmmaaannn.* What word? (Signal.) *Man.* Yes, **man.**

d. Repeat *c* for the words **is, not, sad.**

TASK 25 **Individual test**

Call on different children to read one word. The child sounds out the
word only one time, then tells what word. The other children are
to point under the sounds that are said.

TASK 26 **Teacher and children read the fast way**

a. Let's read the fast way. Touch under **not.** This word is **not.**
Touch under **sad.** This word is **sad.**

b. Point to **not.** What are you going to say when I touch this word?
(Signal.) *Not.*

c. Point to **sad.** What are you going to say when I touch this word?
(Signal.) *Sad.*

d. Repeat *b* and *c* until firm.

e. My turn. Touch under the words as you say: Thē man is . . . .

f. Your turn. Touch under the words as the children say *not sad.*

g. Repeat *e* and *f* until firm.

TASK 27 **Picture comprehension**

a. What do you know about the person you'll see in the picture?
(Signal.) *The man is not sad.*

b. Yes, what do you know about him? (Signal.) *The man is not sad.*

c. Turn your take-home over and look at the picture.

d. Ask these questions:
   1. Does the man look sad to you? *No.*
   2. I wonder why he's so happy? *The children respond.*
   3. He looks as if he can't stop laughing. Did you ever start
      laughing so hard that you couldn't stop? *The children respond.*

TASK 28 **Word finding**

a. Turn your take-home back to side 1. Everybody, let's play
Find-the-Words. Look at the words in your story and get ready.

b. One of the words is (pause) **thē.** Get ready to touch **thē** when I
clap. (Pause three seconds.) Get ready. Clap.
*(The children touch **thē.**)*

c. Repeat *b* for these words: **sad, thē, sad, thē.**

d. Repeat *b* and *c* until firm.

Mastery Test 19 after lesson 100, before lesson 101

WHAT TO DO

a. When I touch the sound, you say it.
b. **(test item)** Point to **I**. Get ready. Touch **I**. *III.*
c. **(test item)** Point to **k**. Get ready. Touch **k**. *k.*
d. **(test item)** Point to **sh**. Get ready. Touch **sh**. *shshsh.*
e. **(test item)** Point to **u**. Get ready. Touch **u**. *uuu.*

Total number of test items: **4**

A group is weak if more than one-third of the children missed any of the items on the test.

I

k

sh

u

If the group is firm on Mastery Test 19 and was firm on Mastery Test 18:

Skip lesson 101 and present lesson 102 to the group during the next reading period. If more than one child missed any of the items on the test, present the firming procedures specified below to those children.

If the group is firm on Mastery Test 19 but was weak on Mastery Test 18:

Present lesson 101 to the group during the next reading period. If more than one child missed any of the items on the test, present the firming procedures specified below to those children.

If the group is weak on Mastery Test 19:

A. Present these firming procedures to the group during the next reading period.
  1. Lesson 99, Sounds, page 272, tasks 2 through 5.
  2. Lesson 99, Reading Vocabulary, page 273, tasks 6 through 11.
  3. Lesson 100, Reading Vocabulary, page 280, tasks 10, 11, 12.
  4. Lesson 100, Sounds, page 278, tasks 4, 5, 6.
B. After presenting the above tasks, again give Mastery Test 19 individually to members of the group who failed the test.
C. If the group is firm (less than one-third of the total group missed any items on the retest), present lesson 101 to the group during the next reading period.
D. If the group is still weak (more than one-third of the total group missed any items on the retest), repeat *A* and *B* during the next reading period.

MATCHING

The children will need pencils.

TASK 29   Children match words

a. Hold up Take-Home 65. Point to the matching exercise on side 2.
b. Here's a new Matching Game. You're going to match words. I'll point to the words in the first column. You read them.
c. Point to the word **fat** in the first column. Sound it out. Get ready. Touch the sounds as the children sound out the word. *Fffaaat.* What word? (Signal.) *Fat.*
d. Repeat *c* for the remaining words in the first column.
e. Touch **fat** in the first column. This word is (pause) **fat.** Everybody, get ready to touch another word **fat.** (Pause four seconds.) Get ready. (Signal.) Check children's responses.
f. Draw a line from one **fat** to the other **fat.** Check children's responses.
g. Repeat *e* and *f* for **is.**
h. Now match the rest of the words by yourselves. Check children's responses.

SUMMARY OF INDEPENDENT ACTIVITY

TASK 30   Introduction to independent activity

Everybody, you're going to finish this take-home on your own. Tell the children when they will work the remaining items. Let's go over the things you're going to do.

TASK 31   Story copying

Point to the dotted words below the story on side 1. You're going to write the dotted words on this arrow. Then you're going to write those words on the other arrow.

TASK 32   Pair relations

a. Point to the left column of boxes in the pair-relations exercise.
b. You're going to cross out the boxes in each row that don't say what these boxes say.
c. Point to the first box. What does this box say? (Signal.) *ēēē—mmm.*
d. Point to the first row. So what are you going to do with every box in this row that doesn't say *ēēē—mmm?* (Signal.) *Cross it out.* Yes, cross it out.
e. If the children's responses are not firm, repeat *a* through *d* for other rows.

TASK 33   Cross-out game

Point to the boxed sounds in the Cross-out Game on side 2. Everybody, what sound are you going to circle today? (Signal.) *aaa.* What sound are you going to cross out? (Signal.) *āāā.*

TASK 34   Sound writing

a. Point to the sound-writing exercise. Here are the sounds you're going to write today. I'll touch the sounds. You say them.
b. Touch each sound. *The children respond.*
c. Repeat the series until firm.

TASK 35   Story picture

Point to the story picture. After you finish your take-home, you can color the story picture.

END OF LESSON 65

Before presenting lesson 66, give Mastery Test 12 to each child.
Do not present lesson 66 to any groups that are not firm on this test.

TASK 16 Picture comprehension

a. Everybody, look at the picture.

b. Ask these questions:
1. What is he? *The children respond.* A worm.
2. Does he have feet? *No.*
3. Does he have teeth? *No.*
4. Does he have a nose? *No.*
5. Is he a cow? *No.*
6. Is he a cat? *No.*
7. What is he? *The children respond.* Yes, a worm.
8. Did you ever eat an apple with a worm in it? *Children respond.*

TASK 17 Individual test

a. Everybody, look at the story. I'm going to call on different children to read a whole sentence the fast way.

b. Call on different children to read one of the first three sentences. Do not clap for each word.

TASK 18 Sentence saying

Good reading. Now, everybody, say all the words in that sentence without looking. (Signal.) *The children repeat the sentence at a normal speaking rate.*

Take-Home 100

SUMMARY OF INDEPENDENT ACTIVITY

TASK 19 Introduction to independent activity

a. Pass out sides 1 and 2 of Take-Home 100 to each child.

b. Everybody, do a good job on your take-home today and I'll give you a bonus take-home. It's an extra take-home for doing a good job.

c. Hold up side 1 of your take-home. You're going to do this take-home on your own. Tell the children when they will work the items. Let's go over the things you're going to do.

TASK 20 Sentence copying

a. Point to the first line in the sentence-copying exercise.

b. Everybody, here's the sentence you're going to write on the lines below.

c. Get ready to read the words in this sentence the fast way. First word. Check children's responses. Get ready. Clap. *He.*

d. Next word. Check children's responses. Get ready. Clap. *Has.*

e. Repeat *d* for the remaining words.

f. After you finish your take-home, you get to draw a picture about the sentence, **hē has nō tēēth.**

TASK 21 Sound writing

a. Point to the sound-writing exercise. Here are the sounds you're going to write today. I'll touch the sounds. You say them.

b. Touch each sound. *The children respond.* Repeat until firm.

TASK 22 Matching

a. Point to the column of words in the Matching Game.

b. Everybody, you're going to follow the lines and write these words.

c. Reading the fast way.

d. Point to the first word. (Pause.) Get ready. (Signal.) *The children respond.*

e. Repeat *d* for the remaining words.

f. Repeat *d* and *e* until firm.

TASK 23 Cross-out game

Point to the boxed word in the Cross-out Game. Everybody, here's the word you're going to cross out today. What word? (Signal.) *If.* Yes, if.

TASK 24 Pair relations

a. Point to the pair-relations exercise on side 2. You're going to circle the picture in each box that shows what the words say.

b. Point to the space at the top of the page. After you finish, remember to draw a picture that shows **hē has nō tēēth.**

TASK 25 Bonus take-home

After the children have completed their take-home exercises, give them sides 3 and 4 of Take-Home 100. Tell them they may keep the stories and read them.

END OF LESSON 100

Before presenting lesson 101, give Mastery Test 19 to each child.
Do not present lesson 101 to any groups that are not firm on this test.

Mastery Test 12 after lesson 65, before lesson 66

a. (test item) Finger on the ball of the top line. *(The child responds.)*
b. (test item) Touch the first word. *(The child is to touch under **this.**)*
c. Sound it out. Get ready. Clap for each sound. *Thththiiisss.*
d. Again. (Pause.) Get ready. Clap for each sound. *Thththiiisss.*
e. (test item) What word? (Signal.) *This.*
f. Next word. *(The child responds.)* Get ready. Clap for each sound. *Iiisss.*
g. Again. (Pause.) Get ready. Clap for each sound. *Iiisss.*
h. (test item) What word? (Signal.) *Is.*
i. Next word. *(The child responds.)* Get ready. Clap for each sound. *Nnnooot.*
j. Again. (Pause.) Get ready. Clap for each sound. *Nnnooot.*
k. (test item) What word? (Signal.) *Not.*
l. Next word. *(The child responds.)* Get ready. Clap for each sound. *Mmmēēē.*
m. Again. (Pause.) Get ready. Clap for each sound. *Mmmēēē.*
n. (test item) What word? (Signal.) *Me.*

Total number of test items: **6**

A group is weak if more than one-third of the children missed any of the items on the test.

WHAT TO DO

If the group is firm on Mastery Test 12:

Present lesson 66 to the group during the next reading period. If more than one child missed any of the items on the test, present the firming procedures specified below to those children.

If the group is weak on Mastery Test 12:

A. Present these firming procedures to the group during the next reading period. Present each story until the children can read it without making a mistake. Then proceed to the next story.
  1. Lesson 63, Story, page 41, tasks 22, 23, 24.
  2. Lesson 64, Story, page 48, tasks 20, 21, 22.
  3. Lesson 65, Story, page 55, tasks 23, 24, 25.
  Duplicate stories for lessons 63, 64, and 65 are provided in the Teacher's Guide. You may reproduce these stories for use in presenting the firming procedures.
B. After presenting the above tasks, again give Mastery Test 12 individually to members of the group who failed the test.
C. If the group is firm (less than one-third of the total group missed any items on the retest), present lesson 66 to the group during the next reading period.
D. If the group is still weak (more than one-third of the total group missed any items on the retest), repeat *A* and *B* during the next reading period.

this∎is
not∎mē.

Story 100

Do not clap for any small letters.

TASK 14 First reading—question mark finding

Have the children reread any sentences containing words that give them trouble. Keep a list of these words.

a. Pass out Storybook 1.

b. Open your book to page 20 and get ready to read.

c. Clap for the sounds in each word of the first paragraph as the children sound out each word one time and tell what word.

d. After the children read **and hē is not a cat,** say: **Everybody, move along the lines until you come to the next period. Oh, oh. There's no period in this sentence. There's a funny mark called a question mark.**

e. **Everybody, touch the question mark.** Check children's responses.

f. **There's a question mark in this sentence because this sentence asks a question. Everybody, get ready to read the question.**

g. **Finger on the first word.** Check children's responses. Clap for the sounds in each word of the sentence as the children sound out each word one time and tell what word.

h. After the children read **is hē a rat?** say: **Everybody, say that question.** *The children repeat the question at a normal speaking rate.*

i. **Yes, is he a rat? Let's read the next sentence and find out.**

j. **Finger on the first word.** Check children's responses. Clap for the sounds as the children sound out the word one time and tell what word.

k. **Is he a rat?** (Signal.) *No.*

l. **Everybody, get ready to read the next sentence. Repeat g.**

m. After the first reading of the story, print on the board the words that the children missed more than one time. Have the children sound out each word one time and tell what word.

n. After the group's responses are firm, call on individual children to read the words.

TASK 15 Second reading—children read the story the fast way and answer questions

a. **Now you're going to read the story the fast way and I'll ask some more questions.**

b. **Finger on the ball of the top line.** Check children's responses. **Remember to stop when you get to a period.**

c. **Get ready.** Clap for each word in the first sentence. Pause at least three seconds between claps. Pause longer before words that gave the children trouble during the first reading.

d. Clap for the word following **fēēt.** Praise children who do not read the word.

e. **Again.** Repeat *b* through *d* until firm.

f. **Tell me what he doesn't have.** (Signal.) *Feet.*

g. **Reading the words in the next sentence the fast way.**

h. **Get ready.** Clap for each word in the next sentence. Pause at least three seconds between claps. Pause longer before words that gave the children trouble during the first reading.

i. Clap for the word following **nōse.** Praise children who do not read the word.

j. **Let's read that sentence again the fast way.** Repeat *h* and *i* until firm.

k. **Name two things he doesn't have.** (Signal.) *Feet and a nose.*

l. Use the procedures in *g* through *j* for the remaining sentences. Ask the comprehension questions below as the children read.

After the children read:	You say:
He has no teeth.	**Name three things he doesn't have.** (Signal.) *Feet, a nose, and teeth.*
And he is not a cat.	**Is he a cow or a cat?** (Signal.) *No.*
Is he a rat?	**What do you think?** *The children respond.* **Let's read and find out.**
He is not a rat.	**Is he a rat?** (Signal.) *No.*

Lesson 66

u

i

o

a

SOUNDS

TASK 1   Teaching **u** as in **under**

a. Point to **u**. My turn. (Pause.)
Touch **u** and say: uuu.
b. Point to **u**. Your turn. When I touch it, you say it. (Pause.)
Get ready. Touch **u**. uuu.
Lift your finger.
c. Again. Touch **u**. uuuu.
Lift your finger.
d. Repeat c until firm.

TASK 2   Sounds firm-up

a. Get ready to say the sounds when I touch them.
b. Alternate touching **i** and **u**. Point to the sound. (Pause one second.) Say: Get ready. Touch the sound. *The children respond.*
c. When **i** and **u** are firm, alternate touching **u, o, a,** and **i** until all four sounds are firm.

TASK 3   Individual test

Call on different children to identify **u, o, a,** or **i**.

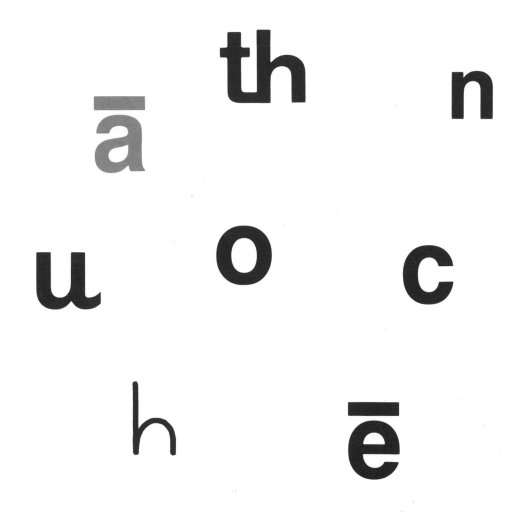

TASK 4   Child plays teacher

a. Use acetate and crayon.
b. [Child's name] is going to be the teacher.
c. [He or She] is going to touch the sounds. When [he or she] touches a sound, you say it.
d. The child points to and touches the sounds. You circle any sound that is not firm.
e. After the child has completed the page, present all the circled sounds to the children.

TASK 5   Individual test

Call on different children. If you can say the sound when I call your name, you may cross it out.

TASK 13 **Children sound out the word and tell what word**

a. Touch the ball for **tēēth.** Sound it out.

b. Get ready. Touch **t,** between the **ē**'s, **th** as the children say
tēēēththth. If sounding out is not firm, repeat *b*.

c. What word? (Signal.) *Teeth*. Yes, we say **teeth**. Here are my **teeth**.

d. Get ready to read this word the fast way.

e. Touch the ball for **tēēth.** (Pause three seconds.) Get ready.
Move your finger quickly along the arrow. *Teeth*.

READING VOCABULARY

TASK 6   Children sound out the word and tell what word

a. Touch the ball for **fit.** Sound it out.
b. Get ready. Touch **f, i, t** as the children say *fffiiit.*
> If sounding out is not firm, repeat *b.*
c. What word? (Signal.) *Fit.* Yes, **fit.**

TASK 7   Children sound out the word, then read it the fast way

a. Touch the ball for **is.** Sound it out.
b. Get ready. Touch **i, s** as the children say *iiisss.*
> If sounding out is not firm, repeat *b.*
c. What word? (Signal.) *Is.* Yes, **is.**
d. Return to the ball. Get ready to read the word the fast way.
> I'm going to count to five. See if you can remember the word.
e. 1, 2, 3, 4, 5. Get ready. Move your finger quickly along the arrow.
> *Is.* Yes, **is.** Good reading.

f. Again. Repeat *e* until firm.

TASK 8   Individual test

Call on different children to do *e* in task 7.

TASK 9   Children sound out the word, then read it the fast way

a. Touch the ball for **in.** Sound it out.
b. Get ready. Touch **i, n** as the children say *iiinnn.*
> If sounding out is not firm, repeat *b.*
c. What word? (Signal.) *In.* Yes, **in.**
d. Return to the ball. Get ready to read the word the fast way.
> I'm going to count to five. See if you can remember the word.
e. 1, 2, 3, 4, 5. Get ready. Move your finger quickly along the arrow.
> *In.* Yes, **in.** Good reading.

f. Again. Repeat *e* until firm.

TASK 10   Individual test

Call on different children to do *e* in task 9.

| To correct | For all mistakes, have the children sound out the word and say it fast. Then say: **Remember this word.** |

Do not touch any small letters.

TASK 10   Children read the fast way

a. Get ready to read these words the fast way.
b. Touch the ball for **fōr.** (Pause three seconds.) Get ready.
(Signal.) *For.*
c. Touch the ball for **ōld.** (Pause three seconds.) Get ready.
(Signal.) *Old.*

d. Repeat *c* for the remaining words on the page.

TASK 11   Children read the fast way again

a. Get ready to do these words again. Watch where I point.
b. Point to a word. (Pause one second.) Say: Get ready. (Signal.)
The children respond. Point to the words in this order:
fōr, ōld, has, thōse, hat.

c. Repeat *b* until firm.

TASK 12   Individual test

Call on different children to read one word the fast way.

fōr

ōld

thōse

hat

has

TASK 11   Children rhyme with un

a. Point to the first sound of **run**. What sound? (Signal.) *rrr*.
Point to the first sound of **fun**. What sound? (Signal.) *fff*.

b. These words rhyme with (pause) **un**.
What do they rhyme with? (Signal.) *Un*.
Yes, rhymes with (pause) **un**.

c. Touch the ball for **run**. Get ready. Touch **r**. *rrr*.
Move your finger quickly along the arrow. *Rrrun*.

d. What word? (Signal.) *Run*. Yes, **run**.

e. Touch the ball for **fun**. This word rhymes with (pause) **un**.
What does it rhyme with? (Signal.) *Un*.

f. Get ready. Touch **f**. *fff*.
Move your finger quickly along the arrow. *Fffun*.

g. What word? (Signal.) *Fun*. Yes, **fun**.

run

fun

TASK 12   Children sound out the word, then read it the fast way

a. Touch the ball for **sat**. Sound it out.

b. Get ready. Touch **s, a, t** as the children say *sssaaat*.
If sounding out is not firm, repeat *b*.

c. What word? (Signal.) *Sat*. Yes, **sat**.

d. Return to the ball. Get ready to read the word the fast way.
I'm going to count to five. See if you can remember the word.

e. 1, 2, 3, 4, 5. Get ready. Move your finger quickly along the arrow.
Sat. Yes, **sat**. Good reading.

f. Again. Repeat *e* until firm.

sat

TASK 13   Individual test

Call on different children to do *e* in task 12.

READING VOCABULARY

To correct	For all mistakes, have the children sound out the word and say it fast. Then say: **Remember this word.**

TASK 7   Children read the fast way

a. Get ready to read these words the fast way.

b. Touch the ball for **nō.** (Pause three seconds.) Get ready.

(Signal.) *No.*

c. Touch the ball for **rocks.** (Pause three seconds.) Get ready.

(Signal.) *Rocks.*

d. Repeat *c* for the remaining words on the page.

TASK 8   Children read the fast way again

a. Get ready to do these words again. Watch where I point.

b. Point to a word. (Pause one second.) Say: Get ready.   (Signal.)

The children respond. Point to the words in this order:

nō, nōse, ōr, rocks, socks.

c. Repeat *b* until firm.

TASK 9   Individual test

Call on different children to read one word the fast way.

Do not touch any small letters.

nō

rocₖs

ōr

nōsₑ

socₖs

TASK 14   Children sound out the word, then read it the fast way

a. Touch the ball for **sun.** **Sound it out.**

b. **Get ready.** Touch **s, u, n** as the children say *sssuuunnn.*

If sounding out is not firm, repeat *b.*

c. **What word?** (Signal.) *Sun.* **Yes, sun.**

d. Return to the ball. **Get ready to read the word the fast way.**

I'm going to count to five. See if you can remember the word.

e. **1, 2, 3, 4, 5. Get ready.** **Move your finger quickly along the arrow.**

Sun. **Yes, sun. Good reading.**

f. **Again.** Repeat *e* until firm.

sun

TASK 15   Individual test

Call on different children to do *e* in task 14.

TASK 16   Children read a word beginning with a stop sound (hē)

a. Point under **ē.** **What's this sound?** (Signal.) *ēēē.*

b. Touch the ball for **hē.** **This word rhymes with** (pause) **ēē.**
Get ready. Move quickly along the arrow. *Hēēē.*

c. **What word?** (Signal.) *He.* **Yes, he.**

d. **Again.** Repeat *b* and *c* until firm.

e. Return to the ball. **Sound it out. Remember—say the sounds when
I touch them. Get ready.** Quickly touch **h, ē** as the children
say *hēēē.*

f. **What word?** (Signal.) *He.* **Yes, he. Good reading. He is my friend.**

g. Repeat *e* and *f* until firm.

hē

TASK 17   Individual test

Call on different children to sound out the word in task 16 and
tell what word.

Lesson 100

SOUNDS

TASK 1   Teaching ō as in ōver

a. Point to ō. **My turn.** (Pause.) Touch ō and say: ōōō.
b. Point to ō. **Your turn. When I touch it, you say it.** (Pause.) **Get ready.** Touch ō. ōōō. Lift your finger.
c. **Again.** Touch. ō. ōōōō. Lift your finger.
d. Repeat c until firm.

ō

i

o

ā

TASK 2   Sounds firm-up

a. **Get ready to say the sounds when I touch them.**
b. Alternate touching **i** and **ō.** Point to the sound. (Pause one second.) Say: **Get ready.** Touch the sound. *The children respond.*
c. When **i** and **ō** are firm, alternate touching **i, ō, o,** and **ā** until all four sounds are firm.

TASK 3   Individual test

Call on different children to identify **i, ō, o,** or **ā.**

TASK 4   Teacher introduces cross-out game

a. Use acetate and crayon.
b. **I'll cross out the sounds on this page when you can tell me every sound.**
c. **Remember—when I touch it, you say it.**
d. Go over the sounds until the children can identify all the sounds in order.

TASK 5   Individual test

Call on different children to identify two or more sounds in task 4.

TASK 6   Teacher crosses out sounds

a. **You told me every sound. Get ready to do it again. This time I'll cross out each sound when you tell me what it is.**
b. Point to each sound. (Pause.) Say: **Get ready.** Touch the sound. *The children respond.* As you cross out the sound, say: **Goodbye, _____ .**

g

ō

w

ā

s

t

u

k

TASK 18   Children read the word in the box the fast way

a. Touch the ball for **in**.
b. You're going to read this word the fast way. I'll move down the arrow and stop under the sounds. But don't say the sounds out loud. Just figure out what you're going to say. Touch under each sound. *Children do not respond.*
c. Return to the ball. (Pause at least three seconds.) Read it the fast way. Get ready. Slash. *In.* Yes, **in.**

TASK 19   Individual test

Call on different children to read the word in task 18 the fast way.

TASK 20   Children read the word in the box the fast way

a. Touch the ball for **sat**.
b. You're going to read this word the fast way. I'll move down the arrow and stop under the sounds. But don't say the sounds out loud. Just figure out what you're going to say. Touch under each sound. *Children do not respond.*
c. Return to the ball. (Pause at least three seconds.) Read it the fast way. Get ready. Slash. *Sat.* Yes, **sat.**

TASK 21   Individual test

Call on different children to read the word in task 20 the fast way.

TASK 22   Children reread the words in the box the fast way

Repeat tasks 18 and 20.

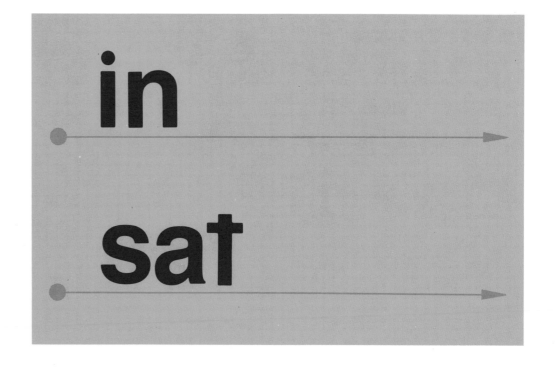

Take-Home 99

SUMMARY OF INDEPENDENT ACTIVITY

TASK 21 Introduction to independent activity

a. Pass out Take-Home 99 to each child.
b. Everybody, you're going to do this take-home on your own.
                    Tell the children when they will work the items.
                    Let's go over the things you're going to do.

TASK 22 Sentence copying

a. Hold up side 1 of your take-home and point to the first line in the
                                        sentence-copying exercise.
b. Everybody, here's the sentence you're going to write on the lines
                                                                below.

c. Get ready to read the words in this sentence the fast way.
            First word.   Check children's responses. Get ready.   Clap. *He.*
d. Next word. Check children's responses. Get ready.   Clap. *Sat.*
e. Repeat *d* for the remaining words.
f. After you finish your take-home, you get to draw a picture about
                            the sentence, **hē sat with a cat.**

TASK 23 Sound writing

a. Point to the sound-writing exercise. Here are the sounds you're
                going to write today. I'll touch the sounds. You say them.
b. Touch each sound. *The children respond.*
c. Repeat the series until firm.

TASK 24 Matching

a. Point to the column of words in the Matching Game.
b. Everybody, you're going to follow the lines and write these words.
c. Reading the fast way.
d. Point to the first word. (Pause.) Get ready. (Signal.)
                                        The children respond.
e. Repeat *d* for the remaining words.
f. Repeat *d* and *e* until firm.

TASK 25 Cross-out game

Point to the boxed word in the Cross-out Game. Everybody, here's
            the word you're going to cross out today. What word? (Signal.)
                                        Thē. Yes, **thē.**

TASK 26 Pair relations

a. Point to the pair-relations exercise on side 2. You're going to
                circle the picture in each box that shows what the words say.
b. Point to the space at the top of the page. After you finish,
                remember to draw a picture that shows **he sat with a cat.**

END OF LESSON 99

Take-Home 66

STORY

TASK 23 First reading—children sound out each word and tell what word

a. Pass out Take-Home 66. Do not let the children look at the picture
until task 27.

b. Get ready to read the story. Everybody, touch the first word.
Check children's responses.

c. Get ready. Clap for each sound. *Thththēēē.*

d. Again. (Pause.) Get ready. Clap for each sound. *Thththēēē.*
What word? (Signal.) *Thē.* Yes, **thē.**

e. Next word. Check children's responses. Get ready.
Clap for each sound. *Mmmaaannn.*

f. Again. (Pause.) Get ready. Clap for each sound. *Mmmaaannn.*
What word? (Signal.) *Man.* Yes, **man.**

g. Repeat *e* and *f* for the words **sat, on, me.**

TASK 24 Second reading—children sound out each word and tell what word

a. Let's read the story again. Everybody, touch the first word.
Check children's responses.

b. Get ready. Clap for each sound. *Thththēēē.* What word? (Signal.)
Thē. Yes, **thē.**

c. Next word. Check children's responses. Get ready. Clap for each
sound. *Mmmaaannn.* What word? (Signal.) *Man.* Yes, **man.**

d. Repeat *c* for the words **sat, on, me.**

TASK 25 Individual test

Call on different children to read one word. The child sounds out the
word only one time, then tells what word. The other children are to
point under the sounds that are said.

TASK 26 Teacher and children read the fast way

a. Let's read the fast way. Touch under **on.** This word is **on.**
Touch under **mē.** This word is **me.**

b. Point to **on.** What are you going to say when I touch this word?
(Signal.) *On.*

c. Point to **mē.** What are you going to say when I touch this word?
(Signal.) *Me.*

d. Repeat *b* and *c* until firm.

e. My turn. Touch under the words as you say: Thē man sat . . . .

f. Your turn. Touch under the words as the children say *on me.*

g. Repeat *e* and *f* until firm.

TASK 27 Picture comprehension

a. What will the picture show? (Signal.) *Thē man sat on me.*

b. Yes, what will the picture show? (Signal.) *Thē man sat on me.*

c. Turn your take-home over and look at the picture.

d. Ask these questions:
1. Oh, oh. What is that man doing? *The children respond.*
Yes, sitting on the boy.
2. How does that boy feel? *The children respond.*
3. What would you do if you were that boy? *The children respond.*

TASK 28 Word finding

a. Turn your take-home back to side 1. Everybody, let's play
Find-the-Words. Look at the words in your story and get ready.

b. One of the words is (pause) **man.** Get ready to touch **man** when
I clap. (Pause three seconds.) Get ready. Clap.
*(The children touch **man.**)*

c. Repeat *b* for these words: **on, man, man, on.**

d. Repeat *b* and *c* until firm.

TASK 17   Second reading—children read the story the fast way and answer questions

a. Now you're going to read the story the fast way and I'll ask some more questions.

b. Remember to stop when you get to a question mark.

c. First word. Check children's responses. Get ready. Clap. *He*.

d. Next word. Check children's responses. Get ready. Clap. *Said*.

e. Clap for the remaining words in the first sentence. Pause at least three seconds between claps. Pause longer before words that gave the children trouble during the first reading.

f. Again. Repeat c through e until firm.

g. Then ask: What did he say? (Signal.) *Can I eat a nut?*

h. Reading the words in the next sentence the fast way.

i. First word. Check children's responses. Get ready. Clap. *She*.

j. Clap for each remaining word in the second sentence. Pause at least three seconds between claps. Pause longer before words that gave the children trouble during the first reading.

k. Read that sentence again the fast way. Repeat i and j until firm.

l. Then ask: What did she say? (Signal.) *Go sit with the cow.*

m. Use the procedures in h through l for the remaining sentences in the story. Ask the comprehension questions below as the children read.

After the children read:	You say:
He said, "No. I will not go."	What did he say? (Signal.) *No. I will not go.*
She said, "Go sit with the cat."	What did she say? (Signal.) *Go sit with the cat.*
He said, "The cat can eat a nut."	What did he say? (Signal.) *The cat can eat a nut.*
She said, "Go sit with the cat and eat."	What did she say? (Signal.) *Go sit with the cat and eat.*

TASK 18   Picture comprehension

a. Everybody, look at the picture.

b. Ask these questions:
1. Did he do what she said? *The children respond.* Yes.
2. What's he doing? *The children respond.*
   Sitting with the cat and eating.

TASK 19   Individual test

a. Everybody, look at the story. I'm going to call on different children to read a whole sentence the fast way.

b. Call on different children to read one of the first three sentences.
   Do not clap for each word.

TASK 20   Sentence saying

Good reading. Now, everybody, say all the words in that sentence without looking. (Signal.) *The children repeat the sentence at a normal speaking rate.*

66

MATCHING
The children will need pencils.

TASK 29   Children match words

a. Hold up Take-Home 66. Point to the matching exercise on side 2.
b. Here's the new Matching Game. You're going to match words. I'll point to the words in the first column. You read them.
c. Point to the word **not** in the first column. Sound it out. Get ready. Touch the sounds as the children sound out the word. *Nnnooot.* What word? (Signal.) *Not.*
d. Repeat *c* for the remaining words in the first column.
e. Touch **not** in the first column. This word is (pause) **not.** Everybody, get ready to touch another word **not.** (Pause four seconds.) Get ready. (Signal.) Check children's responses.
f. Draw a line from one **not** to the other **not.**
Check children's responses.
g. Repeat *e* and *f* for **is.**
h. Now match the rest of the words by yourselves.
Check children's responses.

SUMMARY OF INDEPENDENT ACTIVITY

TASK 30   Introduction to independent activity

Everybody, you're going to finish this take-home on your own. Tell the children when they will work the remaining items. Let's go over the things you're going to do.

TASK 31   Story copying

Point to the dotted words below the story on side 1. You're going to write the dotted words on this arrow. Then you're going to write those words on the other arrow.

TASK 32   Pair relations

a. Point to the left column of boxes in the pair-relations exercise.
b. You're going to cross out the boxes in each row that don't say what these boxes say.
c. Point to the first box. What does this box say? (Signal.) *rrr—iii.*
d. Point to the first row. So what are you going to do with every box in this row that doesn't say **rrr—iii**? (Signal.) *Cross it out.* Yes, cross it out.
e. If the children's responses are not firm, repeat *a* through *d* for other rows.

TASK 33   Cross-out game

Point to the boxed sounds in the Cross-out Game on side 2. Everybody, what sound are you going to cross out today? (Signal.) *c.* What sound are you going to circle? (Signal.) *ooo.*

TASK 34   Sound writing

a. Point to the sound-writing exercise. Here are the sounds you're going to write today. I'll touch the sounds. You say them.
b. Touch each sound. *The children respond.*
c. Repeat the series until firm.

TASK 35   Story picture

Point to the story picture. After you finish your take-home, you can color the story picture.

END OF LESSON 66

Story 99

Do not clap for any small letters.

TASK 15   Quotation finding

a. Pass out Storybook 1.
b. Open your book to page 17.
c. Hold up your storybook. Underline the first sentence with your finger. Somebody is saying something in this sentence. Touch the marks that show the words that he is saying. *(The children touch the quotation marks around* **can I ēat a nut?***)*
d. Underline the second sentence with your finger. Somebody is saying something in this sentence. Touch the marks that show the words that she is saying. *(The children touch the quotation marks around* **gō sit with thē cow.***)*
e. Repeat *d* for the following quotations:
  1. **nō, I will not gō.**
  2. **gō sit with thē cat.**
  3. **thē cat can ēat a nut.**
  4. **gō sit with thē cat and ēat.**
  5. **this is fun.**
f. Repeat *c* through *e* until firm.

TASK 16   First reading—children read the story and answer questions

Have the children reread any sentences containing words that give them trouble. Keep a list of these words.

a. You're going to read the story and I'll ask questions.
b. Clap for the sounds in each word as the children sound out each word one time and tell what word.
c. Present the items below as the children read.

After the children read:	You say:
He said,	Now we're going to read what he said.
"Can I eat a nut?"	What did he say? (Signal.) *Can I eat a nut?*
She said,	Now we're going to read what she said.
"Go sit with the cow."	What did she say? (Signal.) *Go sit with the cow.*
He said,	Now we're going to read what he said.
"No. I will not go."	What did he say? (Signal.) *No. I will not go.*

d. After the first reading of the story, print on the board the words that the children missed more than one time. Have the children sound out each word one time and tell what word.
e. After the group's responses arè firm, call on individual children to read the words.

Lesson 67

SOUNDS

TASK 1 Teacher and children play the sounds game

m	

a. Use acetate and crayon. Write the sounds in the symbol box. Keep score in the score box.
b. I'm smart. I bet I can beat you in a game.
c. Here's the rule. When I touch a sound, you say it.
d. Play the game.
   Make one symbol at a time in the symbol box. Use the symbols **ā, ē, th,** and **h.**
   Make each symbol quickly. (Pause.) Touch the symbol. Play the game for about two minutes.
   Then ask: Who won? Draw a mouth on the face in the score box.

TASK 2 Teacher introduces cross-out game

a. Use acetate and crayon.
b. I'll cross out the sounds on this page when you can tell me every sound.
c. Remember—when I touch it, you say it.
d. Go over the sounds until the children can identify all the sounds in order.

TASK 3 Individual test

Call on different children to identify two or more sounds in task 2.

TASK 4 Teacher crosses out sounds

a. You told me every sound. Get ready to do it again. This time I'll cross out each sound when you tell me what it is.
b. Point to each sound. (Pause.) Say: Get ready. Touch the sound. *The children respond.* As you cross out the sound, say: Goodbye, _____.

m

o

c

a

t

d   u   r

To correct	For all mistakes, have the children sound out the word and say it fast. Then say: **Remember this word.**

TASK 12   Children read the fast way

a. Get ready to read these words the fast way.

b. Touch the ball for **nō.** (Pause three seconds.) Get ready.

(Signal.) *No.*

c. Touch the ball for **with.** (Pause three seconds.) Get ready.

(Signal.) *With.*

d. Repeat *c* for the remaining words on the page.

TASK 13   Children read the fast way again

a. Get ready to do these words again. Watch where I point.

b. Point to a word. (Pause one second.) Say: Get ready.   (Signal.)
The children respond. Point to the words in this order:
nō, not, with, sit, sō.

c. Repeat *b* until firm.

TASK 14   Individual test

Call on different children to read one word the fast way.

nō

with

sit

sō

not

READING VOCABULARY

Do not touch any small letters.

TASK 5 **Children sound out the word and tell what word**

a. Touch the ball for **nut.** Sound it out.
b. Get ready. Touch **n, u, t** as the children say *nnnuuut.*
c. Again. Repeat *b* until firm.
d. Yes, what word? (Signal.) *Nut.*

nut

TASK 6 **Children sound out the word and tell what word**

a. Touch the ball for **cut.** Sound it out.
b. Get ready. Touch **c, u, t** as the children say *cuuut.*
c. Again. Repeat *b* until firm.
d. Yes, what word? (Signal.) *Cut.*

cut

TASK 7 **Children sound out the word, then read it the fast way**

a. Touch the ball for **sock.** Sound it out.
b. Get ready. Touch **s, o, c** as the children say *sssoooc.*
   If sounding out is not firm, repeat *b.*
c. What word? (Signal.) *Sock.* Yes, **sock.**
d. Return to the ball. Get ready to read the word the fast way.
   I'm going to count to five. See if you can remember the word.
e. 1, 2, 3, 4, 5. Get ready. Move your finger quickly along the arrow.
   Sock. Yes, **sock.** Good reading.
f. Again. Repeat *e* until firm.

sock

TASK 8 **Individual test**

Call on different children to do *e* in task 7.

TASK 9 **Children sound out the word and tell what word**

Repeat the procedures in task 7 for **rock.**

rock

READING VOCABULARY

Do not touch any small letters.

TASK 6   Children sound out the word and tell what word

a. Touch the ball for **cākes. Sound it out.**
b. Get ready.   Touch **c, ā, k, s** as the children say *cāāāksss*.
                     If sounding out is not firm, repeat *b*.
c. What word?   (Signal.) *Cakes*. **Yes, cakes.**

cākₑs

TASK 7   Children sound out the word and tell what word

a. Touch the ball for **gō. Sound it out.**
b. Get ready.   Touch **g, ō** as the children say *gōōō*.
                     If sounding out is not firm, repeat *b*.
c. What word?   (Signal.) *Go*. **Yes, go.**

gō

TASK 8   Children rhyme with ōr

a. Touch the ball for **ōr. You're going to read this word the**
               fast way.   (Pause three seconds.) **Get ready.**
                Move your finger quickly along the arrow. *Or*.
b. Touch the ball for **fōr. This word rhymes with**   (pause) **or.**
                   Move to **f,** then quickly along the arrow. *For*.
                         Yes, what word?   (Signal.) *For*.

ōr

TASK 9   Children sound out the word and tell what word

a. Touch the ball for **thōse. Sound it out.**
b. Get ready.   Touch **th, ō, s** as the children say *thththōōōsss*.
                  If sounding out is not firm, repeat *b*.
c. What word?   (Signal.) *Those*. **Yes, those.** I like **those** shoes.

fōr

TASK 10   Children read the words the fast way

a. Now you get to read the words on this page the fast way.
b. Touch the ball for **cākes.** (Pause three seconds.) **Get ready.**
                Move your finger quickly along the arrow. *Cakes*.
c. Repeat *b* for each word on the page.

thōsₑ

TASK 11   Individual test

Call on different children to read one word the fast way.

TASK 10 Children rhyme with **un**

a. Point to the first sound of **fun**. What sound? (Signal.) *fff.*
Point to the first sound of **sun**. What sound? (Signal.) *sss.*

b. These words rhyme with (pause) **un**.
What do they rhyme with? (Signal.) *Un.*
Yes, rhymes with (pause) **un**.

c. Touch the ball for **fun**. Get ready. Touch **f**. *fff.*
Move your finger quickly along the arrow. *Fffun.*

d. What word? (Signal.) *Fun.* Yes, **fun**.

e. Touch the ball for **sun**. This word rhymes with (pause) **un**.
What does it rhyme with? (Signal.) *Un.*

f. Get ready. Touch **s**. *sss.*
Move your finger quickly along the arrow. *Sssun.*

g. What word? (Signal.) *Sun.* Yes, **sun**.

TASK 11 Children sound out the word, then read it the fast way

a. Touch the ball for **sick**. Sound it out.

b. Get ready. Touch **s, i, c** as the children say *sssiiic.*
If sounding out is not firm, repeat *b.*

c. What word? (Signal.) *Sick.* Yes, **sick**.

d. Return to the ball. Get ready to read the word the fast way.
I'm going to count to five. See if you can remember the word.

e. 1, 2, 3, 4, 5. Get ready. Move your finger quickly along the arrow.
Sick. Yes, **sick**. Good reading.

f. Again. Repeat *e* until firm.

TASK 12 Individual test

Call on different children to do *e* in task 11.

TASK 13 Children sound out the word and tell what word

a. Touch the ball for **sack**. Sound it out.

b. Get ready. Touch **s, a, c** as the children say *sssaaac.*
If sounding out is not firm, repeat *b.*

c. What word? (Signal.) *Sack.* Yes, **sack**.

Do not touch any small letters.

fun

sun

sick

sack

Lesson 99

SOUNDS

TASK 1 Teaching ō as in ōver

a. Point to ō. **My turn.** (Pause.) Touch ō and say: *ōōō.*
b. Point to ō. **Your turn. When I touch it, you say it.** (Pause.) **Get ready.** Touch ō. *ōoō.* Lift your finger.
c. **Again.** Touch ō. *ōōōō.* Lift your finger.
d. Repeat c until firm.

ō

ā

I

o

TASK 2 Sounds firm-up

a. **Get ready to say the sounds when I touch them.**
b. Alternate touching ō and ā. Point to the sound. (Pause one second.) Say: **Get ready.** Touch the sound. *The children respond.*
c. When ō and ā are firm, alternate touching o, I, ō, and ā until all four sounds are firm.

TASK 3 Individual test

Call on different children to identify o, I, ō, or ā.

TASK 4 Sounds firm-up

a. Point to ō. **When I touch the sound, you say it.**
b. (Pause.) **Get ready.** Touch ō. *ōōō.*
c. **Again.** Repeat b until firm.
d. **Get ready to say all the sounds when I touch them.**
e. Alternate touching i, k, ō, ē, u, a, w, and sh three or four times. Point to the sound. (Pause one second.) Say: **Get ready.** Touch the sound. *The children respond.*

TASK 5 Individual test

Call on different children to identify one or more sounds in task 4.

ō

i

k

ē

u

a

w

TASK 14 Children read the word in the box the fast way

a. Touch the ball for **nut.**
b. You're going to read this word the fast way. I'll move down the arrow and stop under the sounds. But don't say the sounds out loud. Just figure out what you're going to say. Touch under each sound. *Children do not respond.*
c. Return to the ball. (Pause at least three seconds.) Read it the fast way. Get ready. Slash. *Nut.* Yes, **nut.**

TASK 15 Individual test

Call on different children to read the word in task 14 the fast way.

TASK 16 Children read the word in the box the fast way

a. Touch the ball for **sick.**
b. You're going to read this word the fast way. I'll move down the arrow and stop under the sounds. But don't say the sounds out loud. Just figure out what you're going to say. Touch under each sound. *Children do not respond.*
c. Return to the ball. (Pause at least three seconds.) Read it the fast way. Get ready. Slash. *Sick.* Yes, **sick.**

TASK 17 Individual test

Call on different children to read the word in task 16 the fast way.

TASK 18 Children reread the words in the box the fast way

Repeat tasks 14 and 16.

TASK 19 Children sound out the word, then read it the fast way

a. Touch the ball for **run.** Sound it out.
b. Get ready. Touch **r, u, n** as the children say *rrruuunnn.*
　　　　　　　　　If sounding out is not firm, repeat *b.*
c. What word? (Signal.) *Run.* Yes, **run.**
d. Return to the ball. Get ready to read the word the fast way.
　　I'm going to count to five. See if you can remember the word.
e. 1, 2, 3, 4, 5. Get ready. Move your finger quickly along the arrow.
　　　　　　　　　　　Run. Yes, **run.** Good reading.
f. Again. Repeat *e* until firm.

TASK 20 Individual test

Call on different children to do *e* in task 19.

Do not touch any small letters.

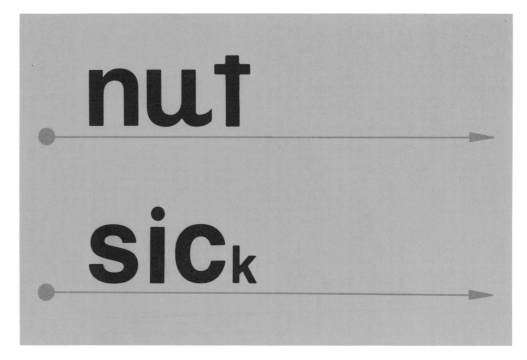

TASK 20 Picture comprehension

a. **What do you think you'll see in the picture?** *The children respond.*
b. **Will she be hugging him?** *The children respond.*
c. **Will she be kissing him?** *The children respond.*
d. **Turn the page and look at the picture.**
e. Ask these questions:
   1. Is she hitting him? *No.*
   2. Is she hugging him? *No.*
   3. What's she doing? *The children respond.* **Yes, she's kissing him.**
   4. Did you ever kiss somebody? *The children respond.*

TASK 21 Individual test

a. **Turn back to page 15. I'm going to call on different children to read a whole sentence the fast way.**
b. Call on different children to read one of the first three sentences. Do not clap for each word.

TASK 22 Sentence saying

Good reading. Now, everybody, say all the words in that sentence without looking. (Signal.) *The children repeat the sentence at a normal speaking rate.*

Take-Home 98

SUMMARY OF INDEPENDENT ACTIVITY

TASK 23 Introduction to independent activity

a. Pass out Take-Home 98 to each child.
b. **Everybody, you're going to do this take-home on your own.** Tell the children when they will work the items. **Let's go over the things you're going to do.**

TASK 24 Sentence copying

a. Hold up side 1 of your take-home and point to the first line in the sentence-copying exercise.
b. **Everybody, here's the sentence you're going to write on the lines below.**
c. **Get ready to read the words in this sentence the fast way. First word.** Check children's responses. **Get ready.** Clap. *She.*
d. **Next word.** Check children's responses. **Get ready.** Clap. *Was.*
e. Repeat *d* for the remaining words.
f. **After you finish your take-home, you get to draw a picture about the sentence, shē was not mad.**

TASK 25 Sound writing

a. Point to the sound-writing exercise. **Here are the sounds you're going to write today. I'll touch the sounds. You say them.**
b. **Touch each sound.** *The children respond.*
c. **Repeat the series until firm.**

TASK 26 Matching

a. Point to the column of words in the Matching Game.
b. **Everybody, you're going to follow the lines and write these words.**
c. **Reading the fast way.**
d. **Point to the first word.** (Pause.) **Get ready.** (Signal.) *The children respond.*
e. **Repeat *d* for the remaining words.**
f. **Repeat *d* and *e* until firm.**

TASK 27 Cross-out game

Point to the boxed word in the Cross-out Game. **Everybody, here's the word you're going to cross out today. What word?** (Signal.) *No.* **Yes, no.**

TASK 28 Pair relations

a. Point to the pair-relations exercise on side 2. **You're going to circle the picture in each box that shows what the words say.**
b. Point to the space at the top of the page. **After you finish, remember to draw a picture that shows shē was not mad.**

END OF LESSON ~

Take-Home 67

TASK 21 First reading—children sound out each word and tell what word

a. Pass out Take-Home 67. Do not let the children look at the picture
until task 25.

b. Get ready to read the story. Everybody, touch the first word.
Check children's responses.

c. Get ready. Clap for each sound. *Hēēē.*

d. Again. (Pause.) Get ready. Clap for each sound. *Hēēē.*

e. Next word. Check children's responses. Get ready.
Clap for each sound. *Iiisss.*

f. Again. (Pause.) Get ready. Clap for each sound. *Iiisss.*
What word? (Signal.) *Is.* Yes, is.

g. Repeat *e* and *f* for the words **sick, and, sad.**

TASK 22 Second reading—children sound out each word and tell what word

a. Let's read the story again. Everybody, touch the first word.
Check children's responses.

b. Get ready. Clap for each sound. *Hēēē.* What word? (Signal.) *He.*
Yes, **he.**

c. Next word. Check children's responses. Get ready. Clap for each
sound. *Iiisss.* What word? (Signal.) *Is.* Yes, is.

d. Repeat *c* for the words **sick, and, sad.**

TASK 23 Individual test

Call on different children to read one word. The child sounds out
the word only one time, then tells what word. The other children
are to point under the sounds that are said.

TASK 24 Teacher and children read the fast way

a. Let's read the fast way. Touch under **and.** This word is **and.**
Touch under **sad.** This word is **sad.**

b. Point to **and.** What are you going to say when I touch this word?
(Signal.) *And.*

c. Point to **sad.** What are you going to say when I touch this word?
(Signal.) *Sad.*

d. Repeat *b* and *c* until firm.

e. My turn. Touch under the words as you say: He is sick . . . .

f. Your turn. Touch under the words as the children say *and sad.*

g. Repeat *e* and *f* until firm.

TASK 25 Picture comprehension

a. What do you know about the person you'll see in the picture?
(Signal.) *He is sick and sad.*

b. Yes, what do you know about him? (Signal.) *He is sick and sad.*

c. Turn your take-home over and look at the picture.

d. Ask these questions:

   1. Does he look sick and sad? *Yes.* I wonder why.
   The children respond.

   2. Look around him and see if you can tell what he ate.
   The children respond.

   3. Did you ever eat so much that you got sick?
   The children respond.

TASK 26 Word finding

a. Turn your take-home back to side 1. Everybody, let's play
Find-the-Words. Look at the words in your story and get ready.

b. One of the words is (pause) **and.** Get ready to touch **and** when I
clap. (Pause three seconds.) Get ready. Clap.
*(The children touch **and.**)*

c. Repeat *b* for these words: **hē, and, hē, sick, and, sick, hē, sick, and,
sick, hē, and.**

d. Repeat *b* and *c* until firm.

Story 98

TASK 18 First reading—question mark finding

Have the children reread any sentences containing words that give them trouble. Keep a list of these words.

a. Pass out Storybook 1.
b. Open your book to page 15 and get ready to read.
c. Clap for the sounds in each word of the first sentence as the children sound out each word one time and tell what word.
d. After the children read **shē was not mad at him,** say: Everybody, move along the lines until you come to the next period. Oh, oh. There's no period in this sentence. There's a funny mark called a question mark.
e. Everybody, touch the question mark. Check children's responses.
f. There's a question mark in this sentence because this sentence asks a question. Everybody, get ready to read the question.
g. Finger on the first word. Check children's responses. Clap for the sounds in each word of the sentence as the children sound out each word one time and tell what word.
h. After the children read **did shē hit him?** say: Everybody, say that question. *The children repeat the question at a normal speaking rate.*
i. Yes, **did she hit him**? Let's read the next sentence and find out.
j. Finger on the first word. Check children's responses. Clap for the sounds in each word of the sentence as the children sound out each word one time and tell what word.
k. Did she hit him? (Signal.) *No.*
l. Everybody, get ready to read the next sentence. Repeat g through k for the sentences: **did shē hug him? nō, nō, nō.**
m. Everybody, get ready to read the next sentence. Repeat g and h for the last sentence: **did shē kiss him?**
n. Did she kiss him? We'll find out later.
o. After the first reading of the story, print on the board the words that the children missed more than one time. Have the children sound out each word one time and tell what word.
p. After the group's responses are firm, call on individual children to read the words.

TASK 19 Second reading—children read the story the fast way and answer questions

a. Now you're going to read the story the fast way and I'll ask some more questions.
b. Remember to stop when you get to a period.
c. First word. Check children's responses. Get ready. Clap. *She.*
d. Next word. Check children's responses. Get ready. Clap. *Was.*
e. Clap for the remaining words in the first sentence. Pause at least three seconds between claps. Pause longer before words that gave the children trouble during the first reading.
f. Again. Repeat c through e until firm.
g. Then ask: Was she mad at him? (Signal.) *No.*
h. Reading the words in the next sentence the fast way.
i. First word. Check children's responses. Get ready. Clap. *Did.*
j. Clap for each remaining word in the sentence. Pause at least three seconds between claps. Pause longer before words that gave the children trouble during the first reading.
k. Read that sentence again the fast way. Repeat i and j until firm.
l. Then ask: Did she hit him? Let's read and find out.
m. Repeat h through k for the next sentence. Then ask: Did she hit him? (Signal.) *No.*
n. Use the procedures in h through k for the remaining sentences in the story. Ask the comprehension questions below as the children read.

After the children read:	You say:
Did she hug him?	What do you think? *The children respond.* Let's read and find out.
No, no, no.	Did she hug him? (Signal.) *No.*
Did she kiss him?	What do you think? *The children respond.*

67

SUMMARY OF INDEPENDENT ACTIVITY

TASK 27   Introduction to independent activity

a. Hold up Take-Home 67.
b. Everybody, you're going to finish this take-home on your own.
Tell the children when they will work on the remaining items.
Let's go over the things you're going to do.

TASK 28   Story copying

Point to the dotted words below the story on side 1. You're going to
write the dotted words on this arrow. Then you're going to write
those words on the other arrow.

TASK 29   Pair relations

a. Point to the left column of boxes in the pair-relations exercise.
b. You're going to cross out the boxes in each row that don't say
what these boxes say.
c. Point to the first box. What does this box say? (Signal.) *aaa—rrr.*
d. Point to the first row. So what are you going to do with every box
in this row that doesn't say **aaa—rrr**? (Signal.) *Cross it out.*
Yes, cross it out.
e. If the children's responses are not firm, repeat *a* through *d* for
other rows.

TASK 30   Cross-out game

Point to the boxed sounds in the Cross-out Game on side 2.
Everybody, what sound are you going to circle today?
(Signal.) *nnn.* What sound are you going to cross out?
(Signal.) *h.*

TASK 31   Matching

a. Point to the first column of words in the Matching Game.
b. Everybody, get ready to read each of the words over here.
Touch the sounds as the children sound out the word.
Then ask: What word? (Signal.) *The children respond.*
c. Point to the first column. You're going to make lines for every
word over here.

TASK 32   Sound writing

a. Point to the sound-writing exercise. Here are the sounds you're
going to write today. I'll touch the sounds. You say them.
b. Touch each sound. *The children respond.*
c. Repeat the series until firm.

TASK 33   Story picture

Point to the story picture. After you finish your take-home,
you can color the story picture.

END OF LESSON 67

TASK 14   Children sound out the word and tell what word

a. Touch the ball for **thōse.** Sound it out.
b. Get ready. Touch **th, ō, s** as the children say *thththōōōsss*.
If sounding out is not firm, repeat *b*.
c. What word? (Signal.) *Those.* Yes, **those. Those** books are big.
d. Get ready to read this word the fast way.
e. Touch the ball for **thōse.** (Pause three seconds.) Get ready.
Move your finger quickly along the arrow. *Those.*

To correct	For all mistakes, have the children sound out the word and say it fast. Then say: Remember this word.

TASK 15   Children read the fast way

a. Get ready to read these words the fast way.
b. Touch the ball for **hit.** (Pause three seconds.) Get ready.
(Signal.) *Hit.*
c. Touch the ball for **him.** (Pause three seconds.) Get ready.
(Signal.) *Him.*

TASK 16   Children read the fast way again

a. Get ready to do these words again. Watch where I point.
b. Point to a word. (Pause one second.) Say: Get ready. (Signal.)
The children respond. Point to the words in this order:
thōse, him, hit.

c. Repeat *b* until firm.

TASK 17   Individual test

Call on different children to read one word on the page the fast way.

Do not touch any small letters.

Lesson 68

g

c

d

t

SOUNDS

TASK 1   Teaching g as in go

a. Point to **g.** Here's a new sound. It's a quick sound.
b. **My turn.** (Pause.) Touch **g** for an instant, saying: g. Do not say **guuh.**
c. **Again.** Touch **g** and say: g.
d. Point to **g.** Your turn. When I touch it, you say it. (Pause.) **Get ready.** Touch **g.** *g.*
e. **Again.** Touch **g.** *g.*
f. Repeat *e* until firm.

TASK 2   Individual test

Call on different children to identify **g.**

TASK 3   Sounds firm-up

a. **Get ready to say the sounds when I touch them.**
b. Alternate touching **g** and **c.** Point to the sound. (Pause one second.) Say: **Get ready.** Touch the sound. *The children respond.*
c. When **g** and **c** are firm, alternate touching **g, d, t,** and **c** until all four sounds are firm.

TASK 4   Individual test

Call on different children to identify **g, d, t,** or **c.**

TASK 5   Sounds firm-up

a. Point to **g.** When I touch the sound, you say it.
b. (Pause.) **Get ready.** Touch **g.** *g.*
c. **Again.** Repeat *b* until firm.
d. **Get ready to say all the sounds when I touch them.**
e. Alternate touching **n, u, h, ē, g, ā, o,** and **i** three or four times. Point to the sound. (Pause one second.) Say: `Get ready. Touch the sound. *The children respond.*

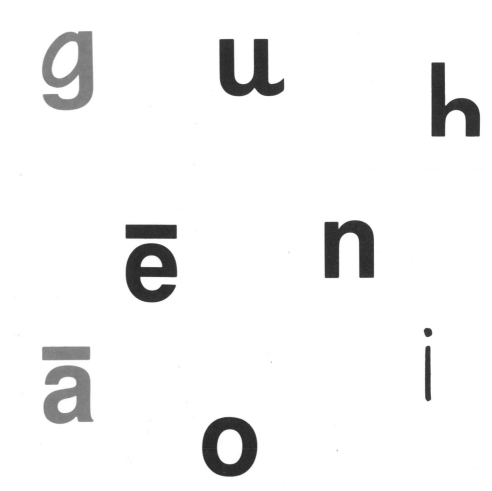

TASK 6   Individual test

Call on different children to identify one or more sounds in task 5.

TASK 8   Children sound out the word and tell what word

a. Touch the ball for **kiss.** Sound it out.

b. Get ready.   Touch **k, i,** between the **s**'s as the children say *kiiisss*.
If sounding out is not firm, repeat *b*.

c. What word?   (Signal.) *Kiss*.   Yes, **kiss.**

TASK 9 Children identify, then sound out an irregular word (was)

a. Touch the ball for **was.** Everybody, you're going to read this
word the fast way.   (Pause three seconds.)   Get ready.
Move your finger quickly along the arrow. *Was*.   Yes, **was.**

b. Now you're going to sound out the word. Get ready.   Quickly touch
w, a, s as the children say *wwwaaasss*.

c. Again.   Repeat *b*.

d. How do we say the word?   (Signal.) *Was*.   Yes, **was.**

e. Repeat *b* and *d* until firm.

TASK 10   Individual test

Call on different children to do *b* and *d* in task 9.

TASK 11   Children rhyme with rug

a. Touch the ball for **rug.**   You're going to read this word the
fast way.   (Pause three seconds.)   Get ready.
Move your finger quickly along the arrow. *Rug*.

b. Touch the ball for **hug.**   This word rhymes with   (pause)   **rug.**
Move quickly along the arrow. *Hug*.
Yes, what word?   (Signal.) *Hug*.

TASK 12   Children read the words the fast way

a. Now you get to read the words on this page the fast way.

b. Touch the ball for **kiss.** (Pause three seconds.)   Get ready.
Move your finger quickly along the arrow. *Kiss*.

c. Repeat *b* for each word on the page.

TASK 13   Individual test

Call on different children to read one word the fast way.

kiss

was

rug

hug

68

READING VOCABULARY

TASK 7 Children sound out the word, then read it the fast way

a. Touch the ball for **fun.** Sound it out.

b. Get ready. Touch **f, u, n** as the children say *fffuuunnn.*

If sounding out is not firm, repeat *b.*

c. What word? (Signal.) *Fun.* Yes, **fun.**

d. Return to the ball. Get ready to read the word the fast way.

I'm going to count to five. See if you can remember the word.

e. 1, 2, 3, 4, 5. Get ready. Move your finger quickly along the arrow.

Fun. Yes, **fun.** Good reading.

f. Again. Repeat *e* until firm.

TASK 8 Individual test

Call on different children to do *e* in task 7.

TASK 9 Children sound out the word, then read it the fast way

a. Touch the ball for **in.** Sound it out.

b. Get ready. Touch **i, n** as the children say *iiinnn.*

If sounding out is not firm, repeat *b.*

c. What word? (Signal.) *In.* Yes, **in.**

d. Return to the ball. Get ready to read the word the fast way.

I'm going to count to five. See if you can remember the word.

e. 1, 2, 3, 4, 5. Get ready. Move your finger quickly along the arrow.

In. Yes, **in.** Good reading.

f. Again. Repeat *e* until firm.

TASK 10 Individual test

Call on different children to do *e* in task 9.

TASK 11 Children sound out the word and tell what word

a. Touch the ball for **fin.** Sound it out.

b. Get ready. Touch **f, i, n** as the children say *fffiiinnn.*

If sounding out is not firm, repeat *b.*

c. What word? (Signal.) *Fin.* Yes, **fin.**

READING VOCABULARY

To correct	For all mistakes, have the children sound out the word and say it fast. Then say: **Remember this word.**

TASK 5 Children read the fast way

a. Get ready to read these words the fast way.

b. Touch the ball for **rats.** (Pause three seconds.) **Get ready.**
(Signal.) *Rats*.

c. Touch the ball for **nō.** (Pause three seconds.) **Get ready.**
(Signal.) *No*.

d. Repeat *c* for the remaining words on the page.

TASK 6 Children read the fast way again

a. Get ready to do these words again. Watch where I point.

b. Point to a word. (Pause one second.) Say: **Get ready.** (Signal.)
The children respond. Point to the words in this order:
nō, rats, thē, this, that.

c. Repeat *b* until firm.

TASK 7 Individual test

Call on different children to read one word the fast way.

rats

nō

that

this

thē

68

TASK 12   Children rhyme with ot

a. Point to the first sound of **not**. What sound? (Signal.) *nnn*.
Point to the first sound of **dot**. What sound? (Signal.) *d*.

b. These words rhyme with (pause) **ot**.
What do they rhyme with? (Signal.) *Ot*.
Yes, rhymes with (pause) **ot**.

c. Touch the ball for **not**. Get ready. Touch **n**. *nnn*.
Move your finger quickly along the arrow. *Nnnot*.

d. What word? (Signal.) *Not*. Yes, **not**.

e. Touch the ball for **dot**. This word rhymes with (pause) **ot**.
What does it rhyme with? (Signal.) *Ot*.

f. Get ready. Move your finger quickly along the arrow.

g. What word? (Signal.) *Dot*. Yes, **dot**.

not

TASK 13   Children sound out the word and tell what word

a. Touch the ball for **dot**. Sound it out.

b. Get ready. Touch **d, o, t** as the children say *dooot*.

c. Again. Repeat *b* until firm.

d. Yes, what word? (Signal.) *Dot*.

dot

TASK 14   Children sound out the word, then read it the fast way

a. Touch the ball for **sin**. Sound it out.

b. Get ready. Touch **s, i, n** as the children say *sssiiinnn*.
If sounding out is not firm, repeat *b*.

c. What word? (Signal.) *Sin*. Yes, **sin**.

d. Return to the ball. Get ready to read the word the fast way.
I'm going to count to five. See if you can remember the word.

e. 1, 2, 3, 4, 5. Get ready. Move your finger quickly along the arrow.
Sin. Yes, **sin**. Good reading.

f. Again. Repeat *e* until firm.

sin

TASK 15   Individual test

Call on different children to do *e* in task 14.

Lesson 98

SOUNDS

TASK 1   Teacher firms up o

a. Point to **o**. **Everybody, get ready to tell me this sound. Get ready. Touch o.** *ooo.*

b. Point to **ō**. **Everybody, look at the line over this sound. This is not ooo. Is it ooo?** (Signal.) *No.*

c. Point to each sound and ask: **Is this ooo?** *The children respond.*

d. Repeat *c* until firm.

TASK 2   Teaching ō as in ōver; children discriminate o—ō

a. Point to the first **ō**. **Everybody, this is ōōō.**

b. **When I touch it, you say it.** (Pause.) **Get ready. Touch ō.** *ōōō.*

c. **Again. Touch ō.** *ōōō.*

d. Repeat *c* until firm.

e. **Get ready to do all these sounds. When I touch the sound, you say it.** Alternate touching the sounds. Before touching each **ō,** trace the line and say: **Remember—this is not ooo.**

f. Repeat *e* until all the sounds are firm.

TASK 3   Sounds firm-up

a. Point to **ō**. **When I touch the sound, you say it.**

b. (Pause.) **Get ready.** Touch **ō**. *ōōō.*

c. **Again.** Repeat *b* until firm.

d. **Get ready to say all the sounds when I touch them.**

e. Alternate touching **ē, ā, ō,** and **k** three or four times. Point to the sound. (Pause one second.) Say: **Get ready.** Touch the sound. *The children respond.*

TASK 4   Individual test

Call on different children to identify one or more sounds in task 3.

266

TASK 16   Children sound out the word, then read it the fast way

a. Touch the ball for **run.** Sound it out.

b. Get ready.   Touch **r, u, n** as the children say *rrruuunnn.*

If sounding out is not firm, repeat *b.*

c. What word?   (Signal.) *Run.*   Yes, **run.**

d. Return to the ball. Get ready to read the word the fast way.

I'm going to count to five. See if you can remember the word.

e. 1, 2, 3, 4, 5. Get ready.   Move your finger quickly along the arrow.

Run. Yes, **run.** Good reading.

f. Again.   Repeat *e* until firm.

TASK 17   Individual test

Call on different children to do *e* in task 16.

TASK 18   Children read the word in the box the fast way

a. Touch the ball for **in.**

b. You're going to read this word the fast way. I'll move down the arrow and stop under the sounds. But don't say the sounds out loud. Just figure out what you're going to say. Touch under each sound. *Children do not respond.*

c. Return to the ball. (Pause at least three seconds.) Read it the fast way. Get ready. Slash. *In.* Yes, **in.**

TASK 19   Individual test

Call on different children to read the word in task 18 the fast way.

TASK 20   Children read the word in the box the fast way

a. Touch the ball for **fun.**

b. You're going to read this word the fast way. I'll move down the arrow and stop under the sounds. But don't say the sounds out loud. Just figure out what you're going to say. Touch under each sound. *Children do not respond.*

c. Return to the ball. (Pause at least three seconds.) Read it the fast way. Get ready. Slash. *Fun.* Yes, **fun.**

TASK 21   Individual test

Call on different children to read the word in task 20 the fast way.

TASK 22   Children reread the words in the box the fast way.

Repeat tasks 18 and 20.

TASK 22   Individual test

a. Turn back to page 13. I'm going to call on different children to read a whole sentence the fast way.
b. Call on different children to read one of the first three sentences.
Do not clap for each word.

TASK 23   Sentence saying

Good reading. Now, everybody, say all the words in that sentence without looking. (Signal.) *The children repeat the sentence at a normal speaking rate.*

Take-Home 97

SUMMARY OF INDEPENDENT ACTIVITY

TASK 24   Introduction to independent activity

a. Pass out Take-Home 97 to each child.
b. Everybody, you're going to do this take-home on your own.
Tell the children when they will work the items.
Let's go over the things you're going to do.

TASK 25   Sentence copying

a. Hold up side 1 of your take-home and point to the first line in the sentence-copying exercise.
b. Everybody, here's the sentence you're going to write on the lines below.
c. Get ready to read the words in this sentence the fast way.
First word. Check children's responses. Get ready. Clap. *She.*
d. Next word. Check children's responses. Get ready. Clap. *Said.*
e. Repeat *d* for the remaining word.
f. After you finish your take-home, you get to draw a picture about the sentence, **shē said, "I am mē."**

TASK 26   Sound writing

a. Point to the sound-writing exercise. Here are the sounds you're going to write today. I'll touch the sounds. You say them.
b. Touch each sound. *The children respond.*
c. Repeat the series until firm.

TASK 27   Matching

a. Point to the column of words in the Matching Game.
b. Everybody, you're going to follow the lines and write these words.
c. Reading the fast way.
d. Point to the first word. (Pause.) Get ready. (Signal.)
The children respond.
e. Repeat *d* for the remaining words.
f. Repeat *d* and *e* until firm.

TASK 28   Cross-out game

Point to the boxed word in the Cross-out Game. Everybody, here's the word you're going to cross out today. What word? (Signal.)
That. Yes, **that.**

TASK 29   Pair relations

a. Point to the pair-relations exercise on side 2. You're going to circle the picture in each box that shows what the words say.
b. Point to the space at the top of the page. After you finish, remember to draw a picture that shows **shē said, "I am mē."**

END OF LESSON 97

TASK 23   Children read a word beginning with a stop sound (has)

a. Cover **h.** Run your finger under **as.** This part says (pause) **az.**

b. Uncover **h.** Touch the ball for **has.** Rhymes with (pause) **az.**
Get ready. Move quickly along the arrow. *Has.*

c. What word? (Signal.) *Has.* Yes, **has.**

d. Repeat *b* and *c* until firm.

e. Return to the ball. Now you're going to sound out (pause) **has.**
Get ready. Quickly touch **h, a, s** as the children say *haaasss.*

f. What word? (Signal.) *Has.* Yes, **has.** Good reading.

The dog **has** a bone.

g. Repeat *e* and *f* until firm.

TASK 24   Individual test

Call on different children to do *e* and *f* in task 23.

TASK 25   Children read a word beginning with a stop sound (hat)

a. Run your finger under **at.** You're going to sound out this part.
Get ready. Touch **a, t** as the children say *aaat.*

b. Say it fast. (Signal.) *At.* Yes, this part says (pause) **at.**

c. Repeat *a* and *b* until firm.

d. Touch the ball for **hat.** This word rhymes with (pause) **at.**
Get ready. Move quickly along the arrow. *Hat.*

e. What word? (Signal.) *Hat.* Yes, **hat.**

f. Repeat *d* and *e* until firm.

g. Return to the ball. Now you're going to sound out (pause) **hat.**
Get ready. Quickly touch **h, a, t** as the children say *haaat.*

h. What word? (Signal.) *Hat.* Yes, **hat.** Good reading. Put on your **hat.**

i. Repeat *g* and *h* until firm.

TASK 26   Individual test

Call on different children to do *g* and *h* in task 25.

Story 97

Do not clap for any small letters.

TASK 18 Quotation finding

a. Pass out Storybook 1.
b. Open your book to page 13.
c. Hold up your storybook. Underline the third sentence with your finger. **Somebody is saying something in this sentence. Touch the marks that show the words that she is saying.** *(The children touch the quotation marks around **I am not a cat.**)*
d. Underline the fourth sentence with your finger. **Somebody is saying something in this sentence. Touch the marks that show the words that she is saying.** *(The children touch the quotation marks around **I am not a fish.**)*
e. Repeat c and d until firm.

TASK 19 First reading—children read the story and answer questions

Have the children reread any sentences containing words that give them trouble. Keep a list of these words.

a. **You're going to read the story and I'll ask questions.**
b. Clap for the sounds in each word as the children sound out each word one time and tell what word.
c. Present the items below as the children read.

After the children read:	You say:
She said,	**Now we're going to read what she said.**
"I am not a cat."	**What did she say?** (Signal.) *I am not a cat.*
She said,	**Now we're going to read what she said.**
"I am not a fish."	**What did she say?** (Signal.) *I am not a fish.*

d. After the first reading of the story, print on the board the words that the children missed more than one time. Have the children sound out each word one time and tell what word.
e. After the group's responses are firm, call on individual children to read the words.

TASK 20 Second reading—children read the story the fast way and answer questions

a. **Now you're going to read the story the fast way and I'll ask some more questions.**
b. **Remember to stop when you get to a period.**
c. **First word.** Check children's responses. **Get ready.** Clap. *She.*
d. **Next word.** Check children's responses. **Get ready.** Clap. *Can.*
e. Clap for the remaining word in the first sentence. Pause at least three seconds between claps. Pause longer before words that gave the children trouble during the first reading.
f. **Again.** Repeat c through e until firm.
g. Then ask: **What can she do?** (Signal.) *Kick.*
h. **Reading the words in the next sentence the fast way.**
i. **First word.** Check children's responses. **Get ready.** Clap. *She.*
j. Clap for each remaining word in the second sentence. Pause at least three seconds between claps. Pause longer before words that gave the children trouble during the first reading.
k. **Read that sentence again the fast way.** Repeat i and j until firm.
l. Then ask: **What are two things she can do?** (Signal.) *Kick and lick.*
m. Use the procedures in h through k for the remaining sentences in the story. Ask the comprehension questions below as the children read.

After the children read:	You say:
She said, "I am not a cat."	**What did she say?** (Signal.) *I am not a cat.*
She said, "I am not a fish."	**What did she say?** (Signal.) *I am not a fish.*
Is she a man?	**What do you think?** *The children respond.*

TASK 21 Picture comprehension

a. **What do you think she is?** *The children respond.*
b. **Turn the page and look at the picture.**
c. Ask these questions:
   1. **Is she a cat?** *No.*
   2. **Is she a fish?** *No.*
   3. **Is she a man?** *No.*
   4. **Can she kick?** *Yes.*
   5. **Can she lick?** *Yes.*
   6. **What is she?** *A cow.*

Take-Home 68

**TASK 27 First reading—children sound out each word and
tell what word**

a. Pass out Take-Home 68. Do not let the children look at the picture
until task 31.

b. Get ready to read the story. Everybody, touch the first word.
Check children's responses.

c. Get ready. Clap for each sound. *Hēēē.*

d. Again. ·(Pause.) Get ready. Clap for each sound. *Hēēē.*
What word? (Signal.) *He.* Yes, **he.**

e. Next word. Check children's responses. Get ready.
Clap for each sound. *Iiisss.*

f. Again. (Pause.) Get ready. Clap for each sound. *Iiisss.*
What word? (Signal.) *Is.* Yes, **is.**

g. Repeat *e* and *f* for the words **in, thē, sun.**

**TASK 28 Second reading—children sound out each word and
tell what word**

a. Let's read the story again. Everybody, touch the first word.
Check children's responses.

b. Get ready. Clap for each sound. *Hēēē.* What word? (Signal.) *He.*
Yes, **he.**

c. Next word. Check children's responses. Get ready. Clap for each
sound. *Iiisss.* What word? (Signal.) *Is.* Yes, **is.**

d. Repeat *c* for the words **in, thē, sun.**

TASK 29 Individual test

Call on different children to read one word. The child sounds out the
word only one time, then tells what word. The other children are to
point under the sounds that are said.

TASK 30 Teacher and children read the fast way

a. Let's read the fast way. Touch under **thē.** This word is **thē.**
Touch under **sun.** This word is **sun.**

b. Point to **thē.** What are you going to say when I touch this word?
(Signal.) *Thē.*

c. Point to **sun.** What are you going to say when I touch this word?
(Signal.) *Sun.*

d. Repeat *b* and *c* until firm.

e. My turn. Touch under the words as you say: He is in . . . .

f. Your turn. Touch under the words as the children say *the sun.*

g. Repeat *e* and *f* until firm.

TASK 31 Picture comprehension

a. What do you know about the animal you'll see in the picture?
(Signal.) *He is in the sun.*

b. Yes, what do you know about him? (Signal.) *He is in the sun.*

c. Turn your take-home over and look at the picture.

d. Ask these questions:
   1. Where's the sun? *The children respond.* Yes, in the sky.
   2. What's the dog holding? *A fan.*
   3. What do you do with that kind of fan? *The children respond.*
Yes, fan yourself.
   4. What would you do if you were that dog? *The children respond.*

TASK 32 Word finding

a. Turn your take-home back to side 1. Everybody, let's play
Find-the-Words. Look at the words in your story and get ready.

b. One of the words is (pause) **in.** Get ready to touch **in** when I clap.
(Pause three seconds.) Get ready. Clap.
*(The children touch **in.**)*

c. Repeat *b* for these words: **sun, in, is, sun, is, sun, in, is, in,
sun, is, in.**

d. Repeat *b* and *c* until firm.

To correct	For all mistakes, have the children sound out the word and say it fast. Then say: **Remember this word.**

TASK 15   Children read the fast way

a. Get ready to read these words the fast way.
b. Touch the ball for **hē.** (Pause three seconds.) Get ready.   (Signal.) *He.*
c. Touch the ball for **thē.** (Pause three seconds.) Get ready.
(Signal.) *Thē.*

d. Repeat *c* for the remaining words on the page.

TASK 16   Children read the fast way again

a. Get ready to do these words again. Watch where I point.
b. Point to a word. (Pause one second.) Say: Get ready.   (Signal.)
The children respond. Point to the words in this order:
this, hē, that, thē.

c. Repeat *b* until firm.

TASK 17   Individual test

Call on different children to read one word the fast way.

hē

thē

that

this

68

SUMMARY OF INDEPENDENT ACTIVITY

TASK 33   Introduction to independent activity

a. Hold up Take-Home 68.

b. Everybody, you're going to finish this take-home on your own.
Tell the children when they will work the remaining items.
Let's go over the things you're going to do.

TASK 34   Story copying

Point to the dotted words below the story on side 1. You're going to
write the dotted words on this arrow. Then you're going to write
those words on the other arrow.

TASK 35   Pair relations

a. Point to the left column of boxes in the pair-relations exercise.

b. You're going to cross out the boxes in each row that don't say
what these boxes say.

c. Point to the first box. What does this box say?   (Signal.) *t—fff.*

d. Point to the first row. So what are you going to do with every box
in this row that doesn't say **t—fff?**   (Signal.) *Cross it out.*
Yes, cross it out.

e. If the children's responses are not firm, repeat *a* through *d* for
other rows.

TASK 36   Cross-out game

Point to the boxed sounds in the Cross-out Game on side 2.
Everybody, what sound are you going to cross out today?
(Signal.) *uuu.* What sound are you going to circle?   (Signal.) *nnn.*

TASK 37   Matching

a. Point to the first column of words in the Matching Game.

b. Everybody, get ready to read each of the words over here.
Touch the sounds as the children sound out the word.
Then ask: What word?   (Signal.) *The children respond.*

c. Point to the first column. You're going to make lines for every
word over here.

TASK 38   Sound writing

a. Point to the sound-writing exercise. Here are the sounds you're
going to write today. I'll touch the sounds. You say them.

b. Touch each sound. *The children respond.*

c. Repeat the series until firm.

TASK 39   Story picture

Point to the story picture. After you finish your take-home,
you can color the story picture.

END OF LESSON 68

TASK 8   Children sound out the word and tell what word

a. Touch the ball for **hits.**   Sound it out.
b. Get ready.   Touch **h, i, t, s** as the children say *hiiitsss*.
                                  If sounding out is not firm, repeat *b*.
c. What word? (Signal.) *Hits.*   Yes, **hits.**

TASK 9   Children sound out the word and tell what word

a. Touch the ball for **kicks.**   Sound it out.
b. Get ready.   Touch **k, i, c, s** as the children say *kiiicsss*.
                                  If sounding out is not firm, repeat *b*.
c. What word? (Signal.) *Kicks.*   Yes, **kicks.**

TASK 10   Children sound out the word and tell what word

a. Touch the ball for **him.**   Sound it out.
b. Get ready.   Touch **h, i, m** as the children say *hiiimmm*.
                                  If sounding out is not firm, repeat *b*.
c. What word? (Signal.) *Him.*   Yes, **him.**

TASK 11   Children identify, then sound out an irregular word (was)

a. Touch the ball for **was.**   Everybody, you're going to read this
                    word the fast way. (Pause three seconds.)   Get ready.
                  Move your finger quickly along the arrow. *Was.*   Yes, **was.**
b. Now you're going to sound out the word. Get ready.   Quickly touch
                    w, a, s as the children say *wwwaaasss*.
c. Again.   Repeat *b*.
d. How do we say the word? (Signal.) *Was.*   Yes, **was.**
e. Repeat *b* and *d* until firm.

TASK 12   Individual test—Have children do *b* and *d* in task 11.

TASK 13   Children read the words the fast way

a. Now you get to read the words on this page the fast way.
b. Touch the ball for **hits.** (Pause three seconds.)   Get ready.
                        Move your finger quickly along the arrow. *Hits.*
c. Repeat *b* for each word on the page.

TASK 14   Individual test—Have children read one word the fast way.

Do not touch any small letters.

hits

kicₖs

him

was

Lesson 69

g d t c

SOUNDS

TASK 1 Teaching g as in go

a. Point to **g.** **My turn. When I touch it, I'll say it.** (Pause.) Touch **g** for an instant, saying: g. Do not say **guuh.**

b. Point to **g.** **Your turn. When I touch it, you say it.** (Pause.) **Get ready.** Touch **g.** g.

c. **Again.** Touch **g.** g.

d. Repeat c until firm.

TASK 2 Sounds firm-up

a. **Get ready to say the sounds when I touch them.**

b. Alternate touching **g** and **d.** Point to the sound. (Pause one second.) Say: **Get ready.** Touch the sound. *The children respond.*

c. When **g** and **d** are firm, alternate touching **c, d, g,** and **t** until all four sounds are firm.

TASK 3 Individual test

Call on different children to identify **c, d, g,** or **t.**

TASK 4 Teacher introduces cross-out game

a. Use acetate and crayon.

b. **I'll cross out the sounds on this page when you can tell me every sound.**

c. **Remember—when I touch it, you say it.**

d. Go over the sounds until the children can identify all the sounds in order.

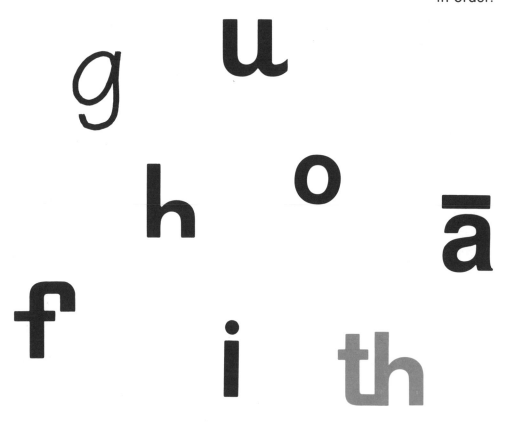

TASK 5 Individual test

Call on different children to identify two or more sounds in task 4.

TASK 6 Teacher crosses out sounds

a. **You told me every sound. Get ready to do it again. This time I'll cross out each sound when you tell me what it is.**

b. Point to each sound. (Pause.) Say: **Get ready.** Touch the sound. *The children respond.* As you cross out the sound, say: **Goodbye, _____ .**

READING VOCABULARY

Do not touch any small letters.

To correct	For all mistakes, have the children sound out the word and say it fast. Then say: **Remember this word.**

TASK 5   Children read the fast way

a. Get ready to read these words the fast way.

b. Touch the ball for **his.** (Pause three seconds.) **Get ready.**
(Signal.) *His.*

c. Touch the ball for **nod.** (Pause three seconds.) **Get ready.**
(Signal.) *Nod.*

d. Repeat *c* for the remaining words on the page.

TASK 6   Children read the fast way again

a. Get ready to do these words again. Watch where I point.

b. Point to a word. (Pause one second.) Say: **Get ready.** (Signal.)
The children respond. Point to the words in this order:
his, nod, licks, nut.

c. Repeat *b* until firm.

TASK 7   Individual test

Call on different children to read one word the fast way.

his

nod

licks

nut

READING VOCABULARY

TASK 7 Children sound out the word, then read it the fast way

a. Touch the ball for **mad.** Sound it out.
b. Get ready. Touch **m, a, d** as the children say *mmmaaad.*
                                 If sounding out is not firm, repeat *b.*
c. What word? (Signal.) *Mad.* Yes, **mad.**
d. Return to the ball. Get ready to read the word the fast way.
         I'm going to count to five. See if you can remember the word.
e. 1, 2, 3, 4, 5. Get ready. Move your finger quickly along the arrow.
                    Mad. Yes, **mad.** Good reading.

f. Again. Repeat *e* until firm.

mad

TASK 8 Individual test

Call on different children to do *e* in task 7.

TASK 9 Children sound out the word, then read it the fast way

a. Touch the ball for **not.** Sound it out.
b. Get ready. Touch **n, o, t** as the children say *nnnooot.*
                                 If sounding out is not firm, repeat *b.*
c. What word? (Signal.) *Not.* Yes, **not.**
d. Return to the ball. Get ready to read the word the fast way.
         I'm going to count to five. See if you can remember the word.
e. 1, 2, 3, 4, 5. Get ready. Move your finger quickly along the arrow.
                    Not. Yes, **not.** Good reading.

f. Again. Repeat *e* until firm.

not

TASK 10 Individual test

Call on different children to do *e* in task 9.

TASK 11 Children sound out the word and tell what word

a. Touch the ball for **nut.** Sound it out.
b. Get ready. Touch **n, u, t** as the children say *nnnuuut.*
                                 If sounding out is not firm, repeat *b.*
c. What word? (Signal.) *Nut.* Yes, **nut.**

nut

Lesson 97

Groups that are firm on Mastery Tests 17 and 18 should skip this lesson and do lesson 98 today.

SOUNDS

TASK 1   Teacher introduces cross-out game

a. Use acetate and crayon.
b. I'll cross out the sounds on this page when you can tell me every sound.

c. Remember—when I touch it, you say it.
d. Go over the sounds until the children can identify all the sounds in order.

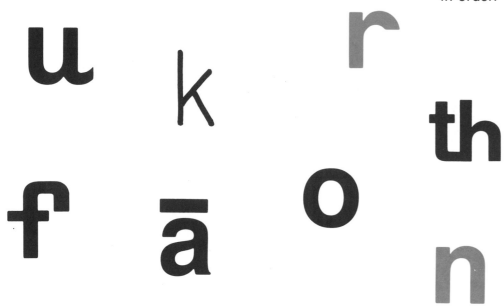

TASK 2   Individual test

Call on different children to identify two or more sounds in task 1.

TASK 3   Teacher crosses out sounds

a. You told me every sound. Get ready to do it again. This time I'll cross out each sound when you tell me what it is.
b. Point to each sound. (Pause.) Say: Get ready. Touch the sound.
The children respond. As you cross out the sound, say:

Goodbye, _____.

TASK 4   Teacher and children play the sounds game

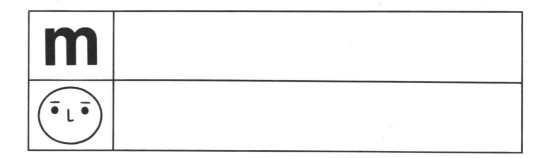

a. Use acetate and crayon. Write the sounds in the symbol box. Keep score in the score box.
b. I'm smart. I bet I can beat you in a game.
c. Here's the rule. When I touch a sound, you say it.
d. Play the game.
Make one symbol at a time in the symbol box. Use the symbols **ē, ā, i,** and **o.**
Make each symbol quickly.
(Pause.) Touch the symbol.
Play the game for about two minutes.
Then ask: Who won? Draw a mouth on the face in the score box.

69

TASK 12   Children sound out the word, then read it the fast way

a. Touch the ball for **us.** Sound it out.
b. Get ready.   Touch **u, s** as the children say *uuusss.*
                     If sounding out is not firm, repeat *b.*
c. What word?   (Signal.) *Us.* Yes, **us.**
d. Return to the ball. Get ready to read the word the fast way.
       I'm going to count to five. See if you can remember the word.
e. 1, 2, 3, 4, 5. Get ready.   Move your finger quickly along the arrow.
                     Us. Yes, **us.** Good reading.

f. Again.   Repeat *e* until firm.

Do not touch any small letters.

TASK 13   Individual test

Call on different children to do *e* in task 12.

TASK 14   Children sound out the word and tell what word

a. Touch the ball for **āte.** Sound it out.
b. Get ready.   Touch **ā, t,** as the children say *āāāt.*
                     If sounding out is not firm, repeat *b.*
c. What word?   (Signal.) *Ate.* Yes, **ate.**

TASK 15   Children sound out the word, then read it the fast way

a. Touch the ball for **mud.** Sound it out.
b. Get ready.   Touch **m, u, d** as the children say *mmmuuud.*
                     If sounding out is not firm, repeat *b.*
c. What word?   (Signal.) *Mud.* Yes, **mud.**
d. Return to the ball. Get ready to read the word the fast way.
       I'm going to count to five. See if you can remember the word.
e. 1, 2, 3, 4, 5. Get ready.   Move your finger quickly along the arrow.
                     Mud. Yes, **mud.** Good reading.

f. Again.   Repeat *e* until firm.

TASK 16   Individual test

Call on different children to do *e* in task 15.

TASK 22   Individual test

a. I'm going to call on different children to read a whole sentence the fast way. Everybody's going to touch the words.
b. First word of the story. Check children's responses. Call on a child to read the first sentence. Do not clap for each word.
c. Call on a child to read the second sentence. Do not clap for each word.

TASK 23   Sentence saying

Good reading. Now, everybody, say all the words in that sentence without looking. (Signal.) *The children repeat the sentence at a normal speaking rate.*

Take-Home 96

SUMMARY OF INDEPENDENT ACTIVITY

TASK 24   Introduction to independent activity

a. Pass out Take-Home 96 to each child.
b. Everybody, you're going to do this take-home on your own. Tell the children when they will work the items. Let's go over the things you're going to do.

TASK 25   Sentence copying

a. Hold up side 1 of your take-home and point to the first line in the sentence-copying exercise.
b. Everybody, here's the sentence you're going to write on the lines below.
c. Get ready to read the words in this sentence the fast way. First word. Check children's responses. Get ready. Clap. *She.*
d. Next word. Check children's responses. Get ready. Clap. *Said.*
e. Repeat *d* for the remaining words.
f. After you finish your take-home, you get to draw a picture about the sentence, **shē said**, "**I ate**."

TASK 26   Sound writing

a. Point to the sound-writing exercise. Here are the sounds you're going to write today. I'll touch the sounds. You say them.
b. Touch each sound. *The children respond.*
c. Repeat the series until firm.

TASK 27   Matching

a. Point to the column of words in the Matching Game.
b. Everybody, you're going to follow the lines and write these words.
c. Reading the fast way.
d. Point to the first word. (Pause.) Get ready. (Signal.) *The children respond.*
e. Repeat *d* for the remaining words.
f. Repeat *d* and *e* until firm.

TASK 28   Cross-out game

Point to the boxed word in the Cross-out Game. Everybody, here's the word you're going to cross out today. What word? (Signal.) *She.* Yes, **she.**

TASK 29   Pair relations

a. Point to the pair-relations exercise on side 2. You're going to circle the picture in each box that shows what the words say.
b. Point to the space at the top of the page After you finish, remember to draw a picture that shows **shē said**, "**I ate**."

END OF LESSON 96

TASK 17   Children sound out the word and tell what word

a. Touch the ball for **fat.**   Sound it out.
b. Get ready. Touch **f, a, t** as the children say *fffaaat.*

If sounding out is not firm, repeat *b.*

c. What word? (Signal.) *Fat.*   Yes, **fat.**

TASK 18   Children read the word in the box the fast way

a. Touch the ball for **us.**
b. You're going to read this word the fast way. I'll move down the arrow and stop under the sounds. But don't say the sounds out loud. Just figure out what you're going to say. Touch under each sound. *Children do not respond.*
c. Return to the ball. (Pause at least three seconds.)   Read it the fast way. Get ready. Slash. *Us.*   Yes, **us.**

TASK 19   Individual test

Call on different children to read the word in task 18 the fast way.

TASK 20   Children read the word in the box the fast way

a. Touch the ball for **not.**
b. You're going to read this word the fast way. I'll move down the arrow and stop under the sounds. But don't say the sounds out loud. Just figure out what you're going to say. Touch under each sound. *Children do not respond.*
c. Return to the ball. (Pause at least three seconds.)   Read it the fast way. Get ready. Slash. *Not.*   Yes, **not.**

TASK 21   Individual test

Call on different children to read the word in task 20 the fast way.

TASK 22   Children reread the words in the box the fast way.

Repeat tasks 18 and 20.

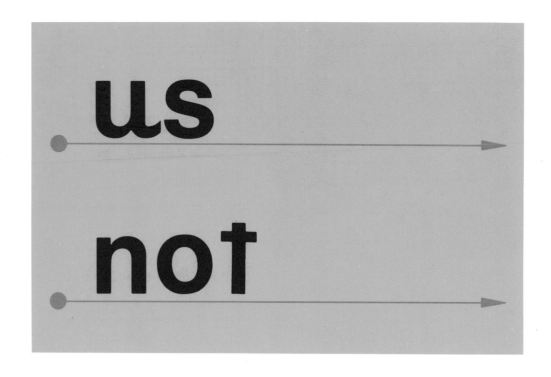

Story 96

Do not clap for any small letters.

TASK 18   Quotation finding

a. Pass out Storybook 1.
b. Open your book to page 11.
c. Point to the quotation marks around the words **I āte a rock** in the second sentence. **These marks show that somebody is saying something. He's saying all the words between these marks.**
d. Point to the quotation marks around **I āte a fish. and now I fēēl sick. These marks show that somebody is saying something. She's saying all the words between these marks.**
e. Point to the quotation marks around **I āte a rock. Everybody, touch these marks in your story.** Check children's responses. **Somebody is saying all the words between those marks.**
f. Point to the quotation marks around I **āte a fish. and now I fēēl sick. Everybody, touch these marks in your story.** Check children's responses. **Somebody is saying all the words between those marks.**
g. Repeat e and f until firm.

TASK 19   First reading—children read the story and answer questions

a. **You're going to read the story and I'll ask questions.**
b. Clap for the sounds in each word as the children sound out each word one time and tell what word. Present the items below as the children read.

After the children read:	You say:
The fish said,	**Now we're going to read what the fish said.**
"I ate a rock."	**What did the fish say?** (Signal.) *I ate a rock.*
The cow said,	**Now we're going to read what the cow said.**
"And now I feel sick."	**What did the cow say?** (Signal.) *I ate a fish. And now I feel sick.*

TASK 20   Second reading—children read the story the fast way and answer questions

a. **You're going to read the story the fast way and I'll ask some more questions.**
b. **Remember to stop when you get to a period.**
c. **First word.** Check children's responses. **Get ready.** Clap. *A.*
d. **Next word.** Check children's responses. **Get ready.** Clap. *Fish.*
e. Clap for the remaining words in the first sentence. Pause at least three seconds between claps. Pause longer before words that gave the children trouble during the first reading.
f. **Again.** Repeat c through e until firm.
g. Then ask: **What did the fish do?** (Signal.) *Ate a rock.*
h. **Reading the words in the next sentence the fast way.**
i. **First word.** Check children's responses. **Get ready.** Clap. *Thē.*
j. Clap for each remaining word in the second sentence. Pause at least three seconds between claps. Pause longer before words that gave the children trouble during the first reading.
k. **Read the sentence again the fast way.** Repeat i and j until firm.
l. Use the procedures in h through k for the remaining sentences in the story. Ask the comprehension questions below as the children read.

After the children read:	You say:
The fish said, "I ate a rock."	**What did the fish say?** (Signal.) *I ate a rock.* **Who ate the rock?** (Signal.) *The fish.*
A cow ate the fish.	**Who ate the fish?** (Signal.) *A cow.*
"And now I feel sick."	**What did the cow say?** (Signal.) *I ate a fish. And now I feel sick.*

TASK 21   Picture comprehension

a. **What do you think you'll see in the picture?** *The children respond.*
b. **Turn the page and look at the picture.**
c. Ask these questions:
   1. **How does that cow feel?** *The children respond.* Sick.
   2. **Why is she sick?** *The children respond.* Because she ate a fish.
   3. **Would you get sick if you ate a fish?** *The children respond.*

TASK 23   Children sound out the word, then read it the fast way

a. Touch the ball for **ant.** Sound it out.
b. Get ready. Touch **a, n, t** as the children say *aaannnt.*
                              If sounding out is not firm, repeat *b.*
c. What word? (Signal.) *Ant.* Yes, **ant.**
d. Return to the ball. Get ready to read the word the fast way.
        I'm going to count to five. See if you can remember the word.
e. 1, 2, 3, 4, 5. Get ready. Move your finger quickly along the arrow.
                              Ant. Yes, **ant.** Good reading.

f. Again. Repeat *e* until firm.

TASK 24   Individual test

Call on different children to do *e* in task 23.

TASK 25   Children read a word beginning with a stop sound (his)

a. Run your finger under **is.** You're going to sound out this part.
                    Get ready. Touch **i, s** as the children say *iiisss.*
b. Say it fast. (Signal.) *Is.* Yes, this part says (pause) **is.**
c. Repeat *a* and *b* until firm.
d. Touch the ball for **his.** This word rhymes with (pause) **is.**
    Get ready. Move quickly along the arrow. *His.*
e. What word? (Signal.) *His.* Yes, **his.**
f. Repeat *d* and *e* until firm.
g. Return to the ball. Now you're going to sound out (pause) **his.**
                Get ready. Quickly touch **h, i, s** as the children say *hiiisss.*
h. What word? (Signal.) *His.* Yes, **his.** Good reading.
i. Repeat *g* and *h* until firm.

TASK 26   Individual test

Call on different children to do *g* and *h* in task 25.

To correct	For all mistakes, have the children sound out the word and say it fast. Then say: **Remember this word.**

TASK 13   Children read the fast way

a. Get ready to read these words the fast way.
b. Touch the ball for **this.** (Pause three seconds.) Get ready.
(Signal.) *This.*
c. Touch the ball for **that.** (Pause three seconds.) Get ready.
(Signal.) *That.*
d. Repeat *c* for **thē.**

TASK 14   Children read the fast way again

a. Get ready to do these words again. Watch where I point.
b. Point to a word. (Pause one second.) Say: Get ready. (Signal.)
The children respond. Point to the words in this order:
thē, that, this.
c. Repeat *b* until firm.

TASK 15   Individual test

Call on different children to read one word in task 14 the fast way.

TASK 16   Children sound out an irregular word (was)

a. Touch the ball for **was. Sound it out.**
b. Get ready. Quickly touch each sound as the children say *wwwaaasss.*

To correct	If the children sound out the word as **wwwuuuzzz**
	1. Say: **You've got to say the sounds I touch.**
	2. Repeat *a* and *b* until firm.

c. Again. Repeat *b* until firm.
d. That's how we <u>sound out</u> the word. Here's how we <u>say</u> the word.
Was. How do we <u>say</u> the word? (Signal.) *Was.*
e. Now you're going to <u>sound out</u> the word. Get ready.
Touch each sound as the children say *wwwaaasss.*
f. Now you're going to <u>say</u> the word. Get ready. (Signal.) *Was.*
g. Repeat *e* and *f* until firm.
h. Yes, this word is **was.** That lady **was** mad at me.

TASK 17   Individual test

Call on different children to do *e* and *f* in task 16.

this

that

thē

was

Take-Home 69

STORY

Do not clap for any small letters.

TASK 27 First reading—children sound out each word and tell what word

a. Pass out Take-Home 69. Do not let the children look at the picture until task 31.

b. Get ready to read the story. Everybody, touch the first word.
Check children's responses.

c. Get ready. Clap for each sound. *Hēēē.*

d. Again. (Pause.) Get ready. Clap for each sound. *Hēēē.*
What word? (Signal.) *He.* Yes, **he.**

e. Next word. Check children's responses. Get ready.
Clap for each sound. *Aāāt.*

f. Again. (Pause.) Get ready. Clap for each sound. *Aāāt.*
What word? (Signal.) *Ate.* Yes, **ate.**

g. Repeat *e* and *f* for the words **a, fat, nut.**

TASK 28 Second reading—children sound out each word and tell what word

a. Let's read the story again. Everybody, touch the first word.
Check children's responses.

b. Get ready. Clap for each sound. *Hēēē.* What word? (Signal.) *He.*
Yes, **he.**

c. Next word. Check children's responses. Get ready. Clap for each
sound. *Aāāt.* What word? (Signal.) *Ate.* Yes, **ate.**

d. Repeat *c* for the words **a, fat, nut.**

TASK 29 Individual test

Call on different children to read one word. The child sounds out the word only one time, then tells what word. The other children are to point under the sounds that are said.

TASK 30 Teacher and children read the fast way

a. Let's read the fast way. Touch under **fat.** This word is **fat.**
Touch under **nut.** This word is **nut.**

b. Point to **fat.** What are you going to say when I touch this word?
(Signal.) *Fat.*

c. Point to **nut.** What are you going to say when I touch this word?
(Signal.) *Nut.*

d. Repeat *b* and *c* until firm.

e. My turn. Touch under the words as you say: He ate a . . . .

f. Your turn. Touch under the words as the children say *fat nut.*

g. Repeat *e* and *f* until firm.

TASK 31 Picture comprehension

a. What do you know about the animal you'll see in the picture?
(Signal.) *He ate a fat nut.*

b. Yes, what do you know about him? (Signal.) *He ate a fat nut.*

c. Turn your take-home over and look at the picture.

d. Ask these questions:
  1. What kind of animal is that? *The children respond.*
  2. How would you like to open up a nut and see him inside?
The children respond.

TASK 32 Word finding

a. Turn your take-home back to side 1. Everybody, let's play
Find-the-Words. Look at the words in your story and get ready.

b. One of the words is (pause) **fat.** Get ready to touch **fat** when I
clap. (Pause three seconds.) Get ready. Clap.
*(The children touch **fat**.)*

c. Repeat *b* for these words: **āte, fat, nut, āte, nut, āte, fat, nut,
fat, āte, nut, fat.**

d. Repeat *b* and *c* until firm.

TASK 7   Children identify, then sound out an irregular word (said)

a. Touch the ball for **said. Everybody, you're going to read this word the fast way.** (Pause three seconds.) **Get ready.** Move your finger quickly along the arrow. *Said.* **Yes, said.**

b. **Now you're going to sound out the word. Get ready.** Quickly touch **s, a, i, d** as the children say *sssaaaiiid*.

c. **Again.** Repeat *b*.

d. **How do we say the word?** (Signal.) *Said.* **Yes, said.**

e. Repeat *b* and *d* until firm.

TASK 8   Individual test

Call on different children to do *b* and *d* in task 7.

TASK 9   Children sound out the word and tell what word

a. Touch the ball for **āte. Sound it out.**

b. **Get ready.** Touch **ā, t** as the children say *āāāt*. If sounding out is not firm, repeat *b*.

c. **What word?** (Signal.) *Ate.* **Yes, ate.**

TASK 10   Children read the fast way

Touch the ball for **lick. Get ready to read this word the fast way.** (Pause three seconds.) **Get ready.** (Signal.) *Lick.*

TASK 11   Children read the words the fast way

a. **Now you get to read the words on this page the fast way.**

b. Touch the ball for **said.** (Pause three seconds.) **Get ready.** Move your finger quickly along the arrow. *Said.*

c. Repeat *b* for each word on the page.

TASK 12   Individual test

Call on different children to read one word the fast way.

Do not touch any small letters.

SUMMARY OF INDEPENDENT ACTIVITY

TASK 33   Introduction to independent activity

a. Hold up Take-Home 69.
b. Everybody, you're going to finish this take-home on your own.
Tell the children when they will work the remaining items.
Let's go over the things you're going to do.

TASK 34   Story copying

Point to the dotted words below the story on side 1. You're going
to write the dotted words on this arrow. Then you're going to write
those words on the other arrow.

TASK 35   Pair relations

a. Point to the left column of boxes in the pair-relations exercise.
b. You're going to cross out the boxes in each row that don't say
what these boxes say.
c. Point to the first box. What does this box say? (Signal.) *āāā—ooo.*
d. Point to the first row. So what are you going to do with every box
in this row that doesn't say *āāā—ooo*? (Signal.) *Cross it out.*
Yes, cross it out.
e. If the children's responses are not firm, repeat *a* through *d* for
other rows.

TASK 36   Cross-out game

Point to the boxed sounds in the Cross-out Game on side 2.
Everybody, what sound are you going to circle today? (Signal.) *t.*
What sound are you going to cross out? (Signal.) *iii.*

TASK 37   Matching

a. Point to the first column of words in the Matching Game.
b. Everybody, get ready to read each of the words over here.
Touch the sounds as the children sound out the word.
Then ask: What word? (Signal.) *The children respond.*
c. Point to the first column. You're going to make lines for every
word over here.

TASK 38   Sound writing

a. Point to the sound-writing exercise. Here are the sounds you're
going to write today. I'll touch the sounds. You say them.
b. Touch each sound. *The children respond.*
c. Repeat the series until firm.

TASK 39   Story picture

Point to the story picture. After you finish your take-home,
you can color the story picture.

END OF LESSON 69

READING VOCABULARY

| To correct | For all mistakes, have the children sound out the word and say it fast. Then say: **Remember this word.** |

TASK 4   Children read the fast way

a. Get ready to read these words the fast way.
b. Touch the ball for **sick.** (Pause three seconds.) Get ready.
(Signal.) *Sick.*
c. Touch the ball for **gāte.** (Pause three seconds.) Get ready.
(Signal.) *Gate.*
d. Repeat *c* for the remaining words on the page.

TASK 5   Children read the fast way again

a. Get ready to do these words again. Watch where I point.
b. Point to a word. (Pause one second.) Say: Get ready. (Signal.)
The children respond. Point to the words in this order:
cow, rock, sick, gāte, fēēl.
c. Repeat *b* until firm.

TASK 6   Individual test

Call on different children to read one word the fast way.

Do not touch any small letters.

sīck

gāte

rŏck

fēēl

cow

g

t

u

d

SOUNDS

TASK 1   Teaching g as in go

a. Point to **g.** My turn. When I touch it, I'll say it. (Pause.) Touch **g** for an instant, saying: g. Do not say **guuh.**

b. Point to **g.** Your turn. When I touch it, you say it. (Pause.) Get ready. Touch **g.** g.

c. Again. Touch **g.** g.

d. Repeat c until firm.

TASK 2   Sounds firm-up

a. Get ready to say the sounds when I touch them.

b. Alternate touching **t** and **g.** Point to the sound. (Pause one second.) Say: Get ready. Touch the sound. *The children respond.*

c. When **t** and **g** are firm, alternate touching **u, d, t,** and **g** until all four sounds are firm.

TASK 3   Individual test

Call on different children to identify **u, d, t,** or **g.**

TASK 4   Sounds firm-up

a. Point to **g.** When I touch the sound, you say it.

b. (Pause.) Get ready. Touch **g.** g.

c. Again. Repeat b until firm.

d. Get ready to say all the sounds when I touch them.

e. Alternate touching **a, i, ā, n, ē, o, g,** and **h** three or four times. Point to the sound. (Pause one second.) Say: Get ready. Touch the sound. *The children respond.*

TASK 5   Individual test

Call on different children to identify one or more sounds in task 4.

Lesson 96

Groups that are firm on Mastery Tests 17 and 18 should skip this lesson and do lesson 98 today.

SOUNDS

TASK 1 Child plays teacher

a. Use acetate and crayon.
b. [Child's name] is going to be the teacher.
c. [He or She] is going to touch the sounds. When [he or she] touches a sound, you say it.
d. The child points to and touches the sounds. You circle any sound that is not firm.
e. After the child has completed the page, present all the circled sounds to the children.

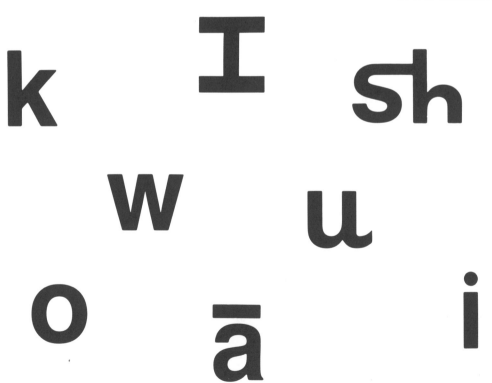

TASK 2 Individual test

Call on different children. If you can say the sound when I call your name, you may cross it out.

TASK 3 Teacher and children play the sounds game

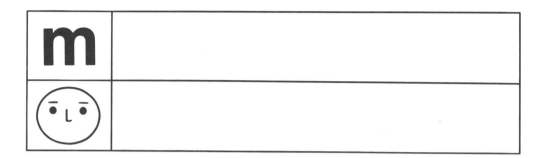

a. Use acetate and crayon. Write the sounds in the symbol box. Keep score in the score box.
b. I'm smart. I bet I can beat you in a game.
c. Here's the rule. When I touch a sound, you say it.
d. Play the game.
Make one symbol at a time in the symbol box. Use the symbols **l, g, c,** and **r.**
Make each symbol quickly. (Pause.) Touch the symbol.
Play the game for about two minutes.
Then ask: Who won? Draw a mouth on the face in the score box.

READING VOCABULARY

TASK 6   Children read a word beginning with a stop sound (has)

a. Cover **h.** Run your finger under **as.** This part says (pause) **az.**

b. Uncover **h.** Touch the ball for **has.** Rhymes with (pause) **az.**
Get ready. Move quickly along the arrow. *Has.*

c. What word? (Signal.) *Has.* Yes, **has.**

d. Repeat *b* and *c* until firm.

e. Return to the ball. Now you're going to sound out (pause) **has.**
Get ready. Quickly touch **h, a, s** as the children say *haaasss.*

f. What word? (Signal.) *Has.* Yes, **has.** Good reading.

g. Repeat *e* and *f* until firm.

has

TASK 7   Individual test

Call on different children to do *e* and *f* in task 6.

TASK 8   Children sound out the word, then read it the fast way

a. Touch the ball for **us.** Sound it out.

b. Get ready. Touch **u, s** as the children say *uuusss.*
If sounding out is not firm, repeat *b.*

c. What word? (Signal.) *Us.* Yes, **us.**

d. Return to the ball. Get ready to read the word the fast way.
I'm going to count to five. See if you can remember the word.

e. 1, 2, 3, 4, 5. Get ready. Move your finger quickly along the arrow.
Us. Yes, **us.** Good reading.

f. Again. Repeat *e* until firm.

us

TASK 9   Individual test

Call on different children to do *e* in task 8.

Mastery Test 18 after lesson 95, before lesson 96

a. **Get ready to read the story.**
b. **First word.** (Pause.) **Get ready.** Clap for the sound as the child sounds out **a** one time.
c. **(test item)** **What word?** (Signal.) *A.*
d. **Next word.** (Pause.) **Get ready.** Clap for each sound as the child sounds out **fish** one time.
e. **(test item)** **What word?** (Signal.) *Fish.*
f. **(8 test items)** Repeat *d* and *e* for the eight remaining words in the story.

Total number of test items: **10**

A group is weak if more than one-third of the children missed two or more words on the test.

WHAT TO DO

If the group is firm on Mastery Test 18 and was firm on Mastery Test 17:

Skip lessons 96 and 97 and present lesson 98 to the group during the next reading period. If more than one child missed two or more words on the test, present the firming procedures specified in the next column to those children.

If the group is firm on Mastery Test 18 but was weak on Mastery Test 17:

Present lesson 96 to the group during the next reading period. If more than one child missed two or more words on the test, present the firming procedures specified below to those children.

If the group is weak on Mastery Test 18:

A. Present these firming procedures to the group during the next reading period. Have the children read the story. Clap for the sounds in each word as the children sound out a word one time and tell what word. Then call on individual children to sound out a word and tell what word. Present each story until the children make no more than two mistakes. Then proceed to the next story.
 1. Story 93.
 2. Story 94.
 3. Story 95.
B. After presenting the above stories, again give Mastery Test 18 individually to members of the group who failed the test.
C. If the group is firm (less than one-third of the total group missed two or more words in the story on the retest), present lesson 96 to the group during the next reading period.
D. If the group is still weak (more than one-third of the total group missed two or more words in the story on the retest), repeat *A* and *B* during the next reading period.

a fish māde a wish.

"I wish I had fēēt."

TASK 10 Children sound out the word, then read it the fast way

a. Touch the ball for **mud.** Sound it out.

b. Get ready. Touch **m, u, d** as the children say *mmmuuud.*

If sounding out is not firm, repeat *b.*

c. What word? (Signal.) *Mud.* Yes, **mud.**

d. Return to the ball. Get ready to read the word the fast way.

I'm going to count to five. See if you can remember the word.

e. 1, 2, 3, 4, 5. Get ready. Move your finger quickly along the arrow.

Mud. Yes, **mud.** Good reading.

f. Again. Repeat *e* until firm.

mud

TASK 11 Individual test

Call on different children to do *e* in task 10.

TASK 12 Children sound out the word, then read it the fast way

a. Touch the ball for **ant.** Sound it out.

b. Get ready. Touch **a, n, t** as the children say *aaannnt.*

If sounding out is not firm, repeat *b.*

c. What word? (Signal.) *Ant.* Yes, **ant.**

d. Return to the ball. Get ready to read the word the fast way.

I'm going to count to five. See if you can remember the word.

e. 1, 2, 3, 4, 5. Get ready. Move your finger quickly along the arrow.

Ant. Yes, **ant.** Good reading.

f. Again. Repeat *e* until firm.

ant

TASK 13 Individual test

Call on different children to do *e* in task 12.

Take-Home 95

SUMMARY OF INDEPENDENT ACTIVITY

TASK 27   Introduction to independent activity

a. Pass out sides 1 and 2 of Take-Home 95 to each child.
b. Everybody, do a good job on your take-home today and I'll give
you a bonus take-home. That is an extra take-home for doing a
good job.

c. Hold up side 1 of your take-home.
You're going to do this take-home on your own.
Tell the children when they will work the items.
Let's go over the things you're going to do.

TASK 28   Sentence copying

a. Point to the first line in the sentence-copying exercise.
b. Everybody, here's the sentence you're going to write on the lines
below.

c. Get ready to read the words in this sentence the fast way.
First word. Check children's responses. Get ready. Clap. *She.*
d. Next word. Check children's responses. Get ready. Clap. *Sat.*
e. Repeat *d* for the remaining words.
f. After you finish your take-home, you get to draw a picture about
the sentence, **shē sat on a hill**.

TASK 29   Sound writing

a. Point to the sound-writing exercise. Here are the sounds you're
going to write today. I'll touch the sounds. You say them.
b. Touch each sound. *The children respond.*
c. Repeat the series until firm.

TASK 30   Matching

a. Point to the column of words in the Matching Game.
b. Everybody, you're going to follow the lines and write these words.
c. Reading the fast way.
d. Point to the first word. (Pause.) Get ready. (Signal.)
The children respond.

e. Repeat *d* for the remaining words.
f. Repeat *d* and *e* until firm.

TASK 31   Cross-out game

Point to the boxed word in the Cross-out Game. Everybody, here's
the word you're going to cross out today. What word? (Signal.)
Is. Yes, **is.**

TASK 32   Pair relations

a. Point to the pair-relations exercise on side 2. You're going to
circle the picture in each box that shows what the words say.
b. Point to the space at the top of the page. After you finish,
remember to draw a picture that shows **shē sat on a hill.**

TASK 33   Bonus take-home

After the children have completed their take-home exercises, give
them sides 3 and 4 of Take-Home 95. Tell them they may keep the
stories and read them.

END OF LESSON 95

Before presenting lesson 96, give Mastery Test 18 to each child.
Do not present lesson 96 to any groups that are not firm on this test.

TASK 14   Children sound out the word, then read it the fast way

a. Touch the ball for **rag.** Sound it out.

b. Get ready. Touch **r, a, g** as the children say *rrraaag.*

If sounding out is not firm, repeat *b.*

c. What word? (Signal.) *Rag.* Yes, **rag.**

d. Return to the ball. Get ready to read the word the fast way. I'm going to count to five. See if you can remember the word.

e. 1, 2, 3, 4, 5. Get ready. Move your finger quickly along the arrow.

Rag. Yes, **rag.** Good reading.

f. Again. Repeat *e* until firm.

TASK 15   Individual test

Call on different children to do *e* in task 14.

TASK 16   Children rhyme with āde

---

a. Point to **māde** and **fāde.** These words rhyme with (pause) **āde.**

b. Touch the ball for **māde.** Sound it out.

c. Get ready. Touch **m, ā, d** as the children say *mmmāāād.*

If sounding out is not firm, repeat *c.*

d. What word? (Signal.) *Made.* Yes, **made.**

e. Return to the ball for **māde.** This word rhymes with (pause) **āde.**

Get ready. Touch **m.** *mmm.* Move your finger quickly along the arrow. *Mmmāde.*

f. What word? (Signal.) *Made.* Yes, **made.**

g. Quickly touch the ball for **fade.** This word rhymes with (pause) **āde.** Get ready. Touch **f.** *fff.* Move your finger quickly along the arrow. *Fffāde.*

h. What word? (Signal.) *Fade.* Yes, **fade.**

Do not touch any small letters.

rag

mād_e

fād_e

TASK 24   Picture comprehension

a. What do you think you'll see in the picture?   *The children respond.*
b. What will the cow be doing?   *The children respond.*
c. Turn the page and look at the picture.
d. Ask these questions:
 1. What's the cow doing?   *The children respond.*
 2. Is the cow having fun?   *The children respond.*
 3. Do you think that cow was sitting on that gate very long?
   The children respond.   No.
 4. Did you ever sit on something hot?   *The children respond.*

TASK 25   Individual test

a. I'm going to call on different children to read a whole sentence the fast way. Everybody's going to touch the words.
b. First word of the story.   Check children's responses. Call on a child to read the first sentence. Do not clap for each word.
c. Call on a child to read the second sentence. Do not clap for each word.

TASK 26   Sentence saying

Good reading. Now, everybody, say all the words in that sentence without looking.   (Signal.) *The children repeat the sentence at a normal speaking rate.*

TASK 17 Children sound out the word, then read it the fast way

a. Touch the ball for **rug**. Sound it out.

b. Get ready. Touch **r, u, g** as the children say *rrruuug*.

If sounding out is not firm, repeat *b*.

c. What word? (Signal.) *Rug*. Yes, **rug**.

d. Return to the ball. Get ready to read the word the fast way.

I'm going to count to five. See if you can remember the word.

e. 1, 2, 3, 4, 5. Get ready. Move your finger quickly along the arrow.

Rug. Yes, **rug**. Good reading.

f. Again. Repeat *e* until firm.

TASK 18 Individual test

Call on different children to do *e* in task 17.

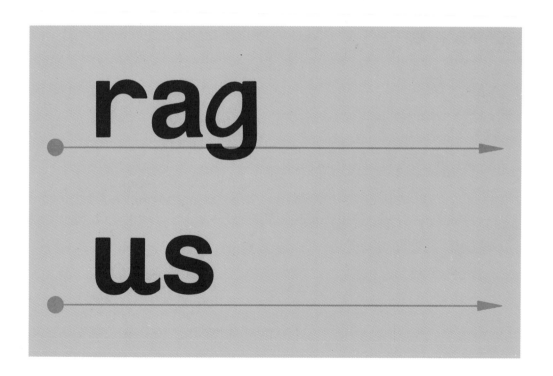

TASK 19 Children read the word in the box the fast way

a. Touch the ball for **rag**. You did this word before.

b. Look at it and get ready to read it the fast way.

c. (Pause at least three seconds.) Get ready. Move your finger
quickly along the arrow. *Rag*. Yes, **rag**. Good reading.

d. Again. Repeat *c* until firm.

TASK 20 Individual test

Call on different children to read the word in task 19 the fast way.

TASK 21 Children read the word in the box the fast way

a. Touch the ball for **us**. You did this word before.

b. Look at it and get ready to read it the fast way.

c. (Pause at least three seconds.) Get ready. Move your finger
quickly along the arrow. *Us*. Yes, **us**. Good reading.

d. Again. Repeat *c* until firm.

TASK 22 Individual test

Call on different children to read the word in task 21 the fast way.

TASK 23 Children reread the words in the box the fast way

Repeat tasks 19 and 21.

Story 95

Do not clap for any small letters.

TASK 21 Quotation finding

a. Pass out Storybook 1.
b. Open your book to page 9.
c. Point to the quotation marks around the words **thē gāte is hot** in the second sentence. These marks show that somebody is saying something. She's saying the words between these marks.
d. Point to the quotation marks around **I hāte hot gātes** in the last sentence. These marks show that somebody is saying something. She's saying all the words between these marks.
e. Point to the quotation marks around **thē gāte is hot.** Everybody, touch these marks in your story. Check children's responses. Somebody is saying the words between those marks.
f. Point to the quotation marks around **I hāte hot gātes.** Everybody, touch these marks in your story. Check children's responses. Somebody is saying all the words between those marks.
g. Repeat e and f until firm.

TASK 22 First reading—children read the story and answer questions

a. You're going to read the story and I'll ask questions.
b. Clap for the sounds in each word as the children sound out each word one time and tell what word. Present the items below as the children read.

After the children read:	You say:
The cow said,	Now we're going to read what the cow said.
"The gate is hot."	What did the cow say? (Signal.) *The gate is hot.*
She said,	Now we're going to read what she said.
"I hate hot gates."	What did she say? (Signal.) *I hate hot gates.*

TASK 23 Second reading—children read the story the fast way and answer questions

a. You're going to read the story the fast way and I'll ask some more questions.
b. Remember to stop when you get to a period.
c. First word. Check children's responses. Get ready. Clap. *Thē.*
d. Next word. Check children's responses. Get ready. Clap. *Cow.*
e. Clap for the remaining words in the first sentence. Pause at least three seconds between claps. Pause longer before words that gave the children trouble during the first reading.
f. Again. Repeat c through e until firm.
g. Then ask: Who sat on the gate? (Signal.) *Thē cow.*
h. Reading the words in the next sentence the fast way.
i. First word. Check children's responses. Get ready. Clap. *Thē.*
j. Clap for each remaining word in the second sentence. Pause at least three seconds between claps. Pause longer before words that gave the children trouble during the first reading.
k. Read that sentence again the fast way. Repeat i and j until firm.
l. Use the procedures in h through k for the remaining sentence in the story. Ask the comprehension questions below as the children read.

After the children read:	You say:
The cow sat on a gate.	Who sat on the gate? (Signal.) *A cow.*
The cow said, "This gate is hot."	What did the cow say? (Signal.) *This gate is hot.*
She said, "I hate hot gates."	What else did the cow say? *I hate hot gates.*

Take-Home 70

until task 28.

STORY

TASK 24   First reading—children sound out each word and tell what word

a. Pass out Take-Home 70. Do not let the children look at the picture until task 28.

b. Get ready to read the story. Everybody, touch the first word.
Check children's responses.

c. Get ready. Clap for each sound. *Hēēē.*

d. Again. (Pause.) Get ready. Clap for each sound. *Hēēē.*
What word? (Signal.) *He.* Yes, he.

e. Next word. Check children's responses. Get ready.
Clap for each sound. *Haaad.*

f. Again. (Pause.) Get ready. Clap for each sound. *Haaad.*
What word? (Signal.) *Had.* Yes, had.

g. Repeat *e* and *f* for the remaining words in the story.

TASK 25   Second reading—children sound out each word and tell what word

a. Let's read the story again. Everybody, touch the first word.
Check children's responses.

b. Get ready. Clap for each sound. *Hēēē.* What word? (Signal.) *He.*
Yes, he.

c. Next word. Check children's responses. Get ready. Clap for each sound. *Haaad.* What word? (Signal.) *Had.* Yes, had.

d. Repeat *c* for the remaining words in the story.

TASK 26   Individual test

Call on different children to read one word. The child sounds out the word only one time, then tells what word. The other children are to point under the sounds that are said.

TASK 27   Teacher and children read the fast way

a. Let's read the fast way. Touch under **his.** This word is **his.**
Touch under **hut.** This word is **hut.**

b. Point to **his.** What are you going to say when I touch this word?
(Signal.) *His.*

c. Point to **hut.** What are you going to say when I touch this word?
(Signal.) *Hut.*

d. Repeat *b* and *c* until firm.

e. My turn. Touch under the words as you say: He had a hut.
He had a nut in . . . .

f. Your turn. Touch under the words as the children say *his hut.*

g. Repeat *e* and *f* until firm.

TASK 28   Picture comprehension

a. The story tells us that he had a hut and . . . . (Signal.)
He had a nut in his hut.

b. Yes, he had a hut and . . . . (Signal.) *He had a nut in his hut.*

c. Turn your take-home over and look at the picture.

d. Ask these questions:
1. Where is he? *The children respond.* Yes, in a hut.
2. What is he doing in the hut? *The children respond.* Holding a nut.
3. Does he look happy? *The children respond.*
4. Did you ever eat a nut? *The children respond.*

TASK 29   Word finding

a. Turn your take-home back to side 1. Everybody, let's play
Find-the-Words. Look at the words in your story and get ready.

b. One of the words is (pause) **a.** Get ready to touch **a** when I clap.
(Pause three seconds.) Get ready. Clap.
*(The children touch **a**.)*

c. Repeat *b* for these words: **his, a, hē, a, his, hē, a, hē, his, a, hē, his.**

d. Repeat *b* and *c* until firm.

After you read the words on this page, you'll get to read the words the fast way.

Do not touch any small letters.

TASK 16 Children sound out the word and tell what word

a. Touch the ball for **gāte.** Sound it out.
b. Get ready. Touch **g, ā, t** as the children say *gāāāt*.
                    If sounding out is not firm, repeat *b*.
c. What word? (Signal.) *Gate.* Yes, **gate.**

TASK 17 Children sound out an irregular word (was)

a. Touch the ball for **was.** Sound it out.
b. Get ready. Quickly touch each sound as the children say *wwwaaasss*.

To correct	If the children sound out the word as **wwwuuuzzz**
	1. Say: You've got to say the sounds I touch.
	2. Repeat *a* and *b* until firm.

c. Again. Repeat *b* until firm.
d. That's how we <u>sound out</u> the word. Here's how we <u>say</u> the word.
                    Was. How do we <u>say</u> the word? (Signal.) *Was.*
e. Now you're going to <u>sound out</u> the word. Get ready.
                    Touch each sound as the children say *wwwaaasss*.
f. Now you're going to say the word. Get ready. (Signal.) *Was.*
g. Repeat *e* and *f* until firm.
h. Yes, this word is **was.** When I gave him five dollars, he **was** happy.

TASK 18 Individual test

Call on different children to do *e* and *f* in task 17.

TASK 19 Children read the words the fast way

a. Now you get to read the words on this page the fast way.
b. Touch the ball for **gāte.** (Pause three seconds.) Get ready.
                    Move your finger quickly along the arrow. *Gate.*
c. Repeat *b* for **was.**

TASK 20 Individual test

Call on different children to read one word the fast way.

70

PAIR RELATIONS
The children will need pencils.

TASK 30   Children cross out the incorrect boxes

---

a. Hold up Take-Home 70. Point to the first box in the pair-relations exercise on side 2.

b. Everybody, this word is **rock**. What word? (Signal.) *Rock.*
The word in the box is **rock** and the picture shows a **rock**.
If the children don't object, say: I fooled you.
This picture is not a **rock**; it's a woman.

c. This box is wrong because the word doesn't tell about the picture.
The word is **rock**, but the picture is not a **rock**. So you'll have to cross out this box. Do it.   Check children's responses.

d. Point to the second box. What's the word in this box? (Signal.)
Rock. Yes, **rock**.

e. What does this picture show? (Signal.) *A woman.* The picture does not show a **rock**. So this box is wrong.
Are you going to cross it out? (Signal.) *Yes.*
Do it.   Check children's responses.

f. Point to the third box. What's the word in this box? (Signal.)
Rock. Yes, **rock**.

g. What does this picture show? (Signal.) *A rock.*
So this box is right. You won't cross it out.

h. You will do the other rows of boxes later.

SUMMARY OF INDEPENDENT ACTIVITY

TASK 31   Introduction to independent activity

Everybody, you're going to finish this take-home on your own.
Tell the children when they will work the remaining items.
Let's go over the things you're going to do.

TASK 32   Story copying

Point to the dotted words below the story on side 1. You're going to write the dotted words on this arrow. Then you're going to write those words on the other arrows.

TASK 33   Matching

a. Point to the first column of words in the Matching Game.
b. Everybody, get ready to read each of the words over here.
Touch the sounds as the children sound out the word.
Then ask: What word? (Signal.) *The children respond.*
c. Point to the first column. You're going to make lines for every word over here.

TASK 34   Cross-out game

Point to the boxed sounds in the Cross-out Game. Everybody, what sound are you going to cross out today? (Signal.) *uuu.*
What sound are you going to circle? (Signal.) *h.*

TASK 35   Sound writing

a. Point to the sound-writing exercise on side 2. Here are the sounds you're going to write today. I'll touch the sounds. You say them.
b. Touch each sound. *The children respond.*
c. Repeat the series until firm.

TASK 36   Pair relations

Point to the pair-relations exercise. Everybody, remember the rule.
If the picture doesn't show what the word says, you cross out the box.

TASK 37   Story picture

Point to the story picture. After you finish your take-home, you can color the story picture.

END OF LESSON 70

Before presenting lesson 71, give Mastery Test 13 to each child.
Do not present lesson 71 to any groups that are not firm on this test.

After you read the words on this page, you'll get to read the words the fast way.

Do not touch any small letters.

TASK 11 **Children rhyme with late**

a. Touch the ball for **late.** Sound it out.
b. Get ready. Touch **l, ā, t** as the children say *lllāāāt.*
> If sounding out is not firm, repeat *b.*
c. What word? (Signal.) *Late.* Yes, **late.**
d. Quickly touch the ball for **hāte.** This word rhymes with (pause) **late.** Get ready. Touch **h.** *h.* Move your finger quickly along the arrow. *Hate.*
e. What word? (Signal.) *Hate.* Yes, **hate.**

lāte

TASK 12 **Children identify, then sound out an irregular word (said)**

a. Touch the ball for **said.** Everybody, you're going to read this word the fast way. (Pause three seconds.) Get ready. Move your finger quickly along the arrow. *Said.* Yes, **said.**
b. Now you're going to sound out the word. Get ready. Quickly touch **s, a, i, d** as the children say *sssaaaiiid.*
c. Again. Repeat *b.*
d. How do we say the word? (Signal.) *Said.* Yes, **said.**
e. Repeat *b* and *d* until firm.

hāte

TASK 13 **Individual test**

Call on different children to do *b* and *d* in task 12.

said

TASK 14 **Children read the words the fast way**

a. Now you get to read the words on this page the fast way.
b. Touch the ball for **lāte.** (Pause three seconds.) Get ready. Move your finger quickly along the arrow. *Late.*
c. Repeat *b* for each word on the page.

TASK 15 **Individual test**

Call on different children to read one word the fast way.

Mastery Test 13 after lesson 70, before lesson 71

a. When I touch the sound, you say it.
b. (test item) Point to ā. Get ready. Touch ā. *āāā.*
c. (test item) Point to h. Get ready. Touch h. *h.*
d. (test item) Point to u. Get ready. Touch u. *uuu.*
e. (test item) Point to a. Get ready. Touch a. *aaa.*
f. (test item) Point to i. Get ready. Touch i. *iii.*

Total number of test items: **5**

A group is weak if more than one-third of the children missed any of the items on the test.

ā

h

u

a

i

WHAT TO DO

If the group is firm on Mastery Test 13 and was firm on Mastery Test 12:

Present lessons 71 and 72, and then skip lesson 73. If more than one child missed any of the items on the test, present the firming procedures specified below to those children.

If the group is firm on Mastery Test 13 but was weak on Mastery Test 12:

Present lesson 71 to the group during the next reading period. If more than one child missed any of the items on the test, present the firming procedures specified below to those children.

If the group is weak on Mastery Test 13:

A. Present these firming procedures to the group during the next reading period.
   1. Lesson 68, Sounds, page 71, tasks 5, 6.
   2. Lesson 68, Reading Vocabulary, page 73, tasks 12 through 15.
   3. Lesson 69, Reading Vocabulary, page 79, tasks 7 through 11.
   4. Lesson 70, Sounds, page 85, tasks 4, 5.
B. After presenting the above tasks, again give Mastery Test 13 individually to members of the group who failed the test.
C. If the group is firm (less than one-third of the total group missed any items on the retest), present lesson 71 to the group during the next reading period.
D. If the group is still weak (more than one-third of the total group missed any items on the retest), repeat *A* and *B* during the next reading period.

READING VOCABULARY

After you read the words on this page, you'll get to read the words the fast way.

Do not touch any small letters.

gāteS

TASK 5   Children sound out the word and tell what word

a. Touch the ball for **gāteS.** Sound it out.
b. Get ready. Touch **g, ā, t, s** as the children say *gāāātsss*.
            If sounding out is not firm, repeat *b*.
c. What word? (Signal.) *Gates*. Yes, **gates**.

siCk

TASK 6   Children sound out the word and tell what word

a. Touch the ball for **sick.** Sound it out.
b. Get ready. Touch **s, i, c** as the children say *sssiiic*.
            If sounding out is not firm, repeat *b*.
c. What word? (Signal.) *Sick*. Yes, **sick**.

fēēl

TASK 7   Children sound out the word and tell what word

a. Touch the ball for **fēēl.** Sound it out.
b. Get ready. Touch **f,** between the **ē**'s, **l** as the children say *fffēēēlll*.
            If sounding out is not firm, repeat *b*.
c. What word? (Signal.) *Feel*. Yes, **feel**.

cow

TASK 8   Children sound out the word and tell what word

a. Touch the ball for **cow.** Sound it out.
b. Get ready. Touch **c, o, w** as the children say *cooowww*.
            If sounding out is not firm, repeat *b*.
c. What word? (Signal.) *Cow*. Yes, **cow**.

TASK 9   Children read the words the fast way

a. Now you get to read the words on this page the fast way.
b. Touch the ball for **gates.** (Pause three seconds.) Get ready.
            Move your finger quickly along the arrow. *Gates*.
c. Repeat *b* for each word on the page.

TASK 10   Individual test

Call on different children to read one word the fast way.

Lesson 71

SOUNDS

TASK 1   Teacher and children play the sounds game

a. Use acetate and crayon. Write the
   sounds in the symbol box.
   Keep score in the score box.
b. **I'm smart. I bet I can beat you
   in a game.**
c. **Here's the rule. When I touch
   a sound, you say it.**
d. Play the game.
   Make one symbol at a time in the
   symbol box. Use the symbols
   m, u, i, a, s, and **r.**
   Make each symbol quickly.
   (Pause.) Touch the symbol.
   Play the game for about two
   minutes.
   Then ask: **Who won?** Draw a
   mouth on the face in the score
   box.

TASK 2   Child plays teacher

a. Use acetate and crayon.
b. [Child's name] is going to be the teacher.
c. [He or She] is going to touch the sounds. When [he or she]
   touches a sound, you say it.
d. The child points to and touches the sounds. You circle any sound
   that is not firm.
e. After the child has completed the page, present all the circled sounds
   to the children.

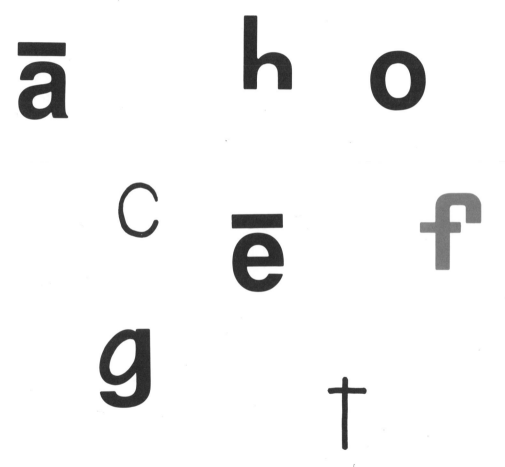

TASK 3   Individual test

Call on different children. **If you can say the sound when I call your
name, you may cross it out.**

Lesson 95

w

u

I

I

l

sh

i

k

n

a

h

o

ē

th

g

d

ā

SOUNDS

TASK 1   Child plays teacher

a. Use acetate and crayon.
b. [Child's name] is going to be the teacher.
c. [He or She] is going to touch the sounds. When [he or she] touches a sound, you say it.
d. The child points to and touches the sounds. You circle any sound that is not firm.
e. After the child has completed the page, present all the circled sounds to the children.

TASK 2   Individual test

Call on different children.
If you can say the sound when I call your name, you may cross it out.

TASK 3   Sounds firm-up

a. Point to **w.** When I touch the sound, you say it.
b. (Pause.) Get ready. Touch **w.** *www*.
c. Again. Repeat *b* until firm.
d. Get ready to say all the sounds when I touch them.
e. Alternate touching **n, u, sh, k, w, h, o,** and **ē** three or four times.
Point to the sound. (Pause one second.) Say: Get ready.
Touch the sound. *The children respond.*

TASK 4   Individual test

Call on different children to identify one or more sounds in task 3.

READING VOCABULARY

TASK 4   Children sound out the word, then read it the fast way

a. Touch the ball for **us**. Sound it out.

b. Get ready. Touch **u, s** as the children say *uuusss*.

If sounding out is not firm, repeat *b*.

c. What word? (Signal.) *Us*. Yes, **us**.

d. Return to the ball. Get ready to read the word the fast way.

I'm going to count to five. See if you can remember the word.

e. 1, 2, 3, 4, 5. Get ready. Move your finger quickly along the arrow.

Us. Yes, **us**. Good reading.

f. Again. Repeat *e* until firm.

TASK 5   Children sound out the word, then read it the fast way

a. Touch the ball for **fēēt**. Sound it out.

b. Get ready. Touch **f,** between the **e**'s, **t** as the children say *fffēēēt*.

If sounding out is not firm, repeat *b*.

c. What word? (Signal.) *Feet*. Yes, **feet**.

d. Return to the ball. Get ready to read the word the fast way.

I'm going to count to five. See if you can remember the word.

e. 1, 2, 3, 4, 5. Get ready. Move your finger quickly along the arrow.

Feet. Yes, **feet**. Good reading.

f. Again. Repeat *e* until firm.

TASK 6   Children sound out the word and tell what word

a. Touch the ball for **dot**. Sound it out.

b. Get ready. Touch **d, o, t** as the children say *dooot*.

c. Again. Repeat *b* until firm.

d. Yes, what word? (Signal.) *Dot*.

TASK 7   Children read a word beginning with a stop sound (hē)

a. Point under **ē**. What's this sound? (Signal.) *ēēē*.

b. Touch the ball for **he**. This word rhymes with **ēē**.
Get ready. Move quickly along the arrow. *Hē*.

c. What word? (Signal.) *He*. Yes, **he**.

d. Again. Repeat *b* and *c* until firm.

e. Return to the ball. Sound it out. Remember—say the sounds when
I touch them. Get ready. Quickly touch **h, ē** as the children say
hēēē.

f. What word? (Signal.) *He*. Yes, **he**.
Good reading. **He** is my friend.

g. Repeat *e* and *f* until firm.

us

fēēt

dot

hē

Take-Home 94

SUMMARY OF INDEPENDENT ACTIVITY

TASK 30 Introduction to independent activity

a. Pass out Take-Home 94 to each child.
b. Everybody, you're going to do this take-home on your own.
Tell the children when they will work the items.
Let's go over the things you're going to do.

TASK 31 Sentence copying

a. Hold up side 1 of your take-home and point to the first line in the
sentence-copying exercise.
b. Everybody, here's the sentence you're going to write on the lines
below.
c. Get ready to read the words in this sentence the fast way.
First word. Check children's responses. Get ready. Clap. *The̅*.
d. Next word. Check children's responses. Get ready. Clap. *Fish*.
e. Repeat *d* for the remaining words.
f. After you finish your take-home, you get to draw a picture about
the sentence, **the̅ fish had fun**.

TASK 32 Sound writing

a. Point to the sound-writing exercise. Here are the sounds you're
going to write today. I'll touch the sounds. You say them.
b. Touch each sound. *The children respond.*
c. Repeat the series until firm.

TASK 33 Matching

a. Point to the column of words in the Matching Game.
b. Everybody, you're going to follow the lines and write these words.
c. Reading the fast way.
d. Point to the first word. (Pause.) Get ready. (Signal.)
The children respond.
e. Repeat *d* for the remaining words.
f. Repeat *d* and *e* until firm.

TASK 34 Cross-out game

Point to the boxed word in the Cross-out Game. Everybody, here's
the word you're going to cross out today. What word? (Signal.)
This. Yes, **this**.

TASK 35 Pair relations

a. Point to the pair-relations exercise on side 2. You're going to
circle the picture in each box that shows what the words say.
b. Point to the space at the top of the page. After you finish,
remember to draw a picture that shows **the̅ fish had fun**.

END OF LESSON 94

TASK 8   Children sound out the word, then read it the fast way

a. Touch the ball for **mud.** Sound it out.

b. Get ready. Touch **m, u, d** as the children say *mmmuuud.*

If sounding out is not firm, repeat *b.*

c. What word? (Signal.) *Mud.* Yes, **mud.**

d. Return to the ball. Get ready to read the word the fast way.

I'm going to count to five. See if you can remember the word.

e. 1, 2, 3, 4, 5. Get ready. Move your finger quickly along the arrow.

Mud. Yes, **mud.** Good reading.

f. Again. Repeat *e* until firm.

TASK 9   Individual test

Call on different children to do *e* in task 8.

mud

TASK 10   Children sound out the word, then read it the fast way

a. Touch the ball for **in.** Sound it out.

b. Get ready. Touch **i, n** as the children say *iiinnn.*

If sounding out is not firm, repeat *b.*

c. What word? (Signal.) *In.* Yes, **in.**

d. Return to the ball. Get ready to read the word the fast way.

I'm going to count to five. See if you can remember the word.

e. 1, 2, 3, 4, 5. Get ready. Move your finger quickly along the arrow.

In. Yes, **in.** Good reading.

f. Again. Repeat *e* until firm.

TASK 11   Individual test

Call on different children to do *e* in task 10.

in

TASK 12   Children rhyme with at

a. Touch the ball for **at.** Sound it out.

b. Get ready. Touch **a, t** as the children say *aaat.*

If sounding out is not firm, repeat *b.*

c. What word? (Signal.) *At.* Yes, **at.**

d. Quickly touch the ball for **sat.** This word rhymes with (pause) **at.**

Get ready. Touch **s.** *sss.* Move your finger quickly along the arrow.

Sssat.

e. What word? (Signal.) *Sat.* Yes, **sat.**

at

sat

TASK 27 Picture comprehension

a. What do you think you'll see in the picture? *The children respond.*

b. Turn the page and look at the picture.

c. Ask these questions:
  1. What's the little fish doing? *The children respond.*

    He's sitting on a fat fish.
  2. Which fish is Mom? *The children respond.*
  3. What would you do if a little fish sat on you?

    The children respond.

TASK 28 Individual test

a. I'm going to call on different children to read a whole sentence the fast way. Everybody's going to touch the words.

b. First word of the story. Check children's responses. Call on a child to read the first sentence. Do not clap for each word.

c. Call on a child to read the second sentence. Do not clap for each word.

TASK 29 Sentence saying

Good reading. Now, everybody, say all the words in that sentence without looking. (Signal.) *The children repeat the sentence at a normal speaking rate.*

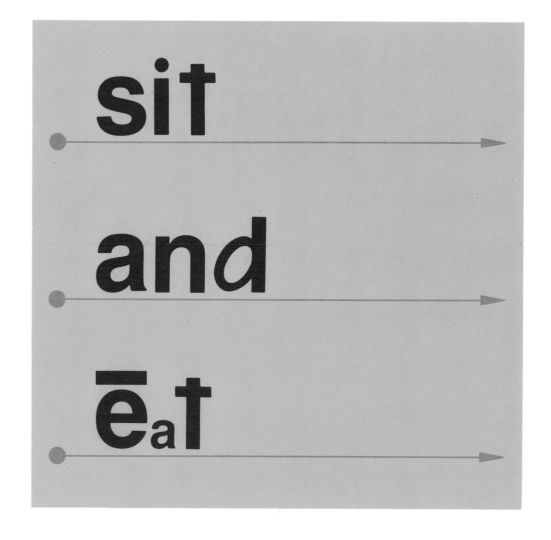

71

After you read the words on this page, you'll get to read the words in the box the fast way.

Do not touch any small letters.

To correct	For all mistakes, have the children sound out the word and say it fast. Then say: **Remember this word.**

TASK 13   Children sound out the word and tell what word

a. Touch the ball for **sit.** Sound it out.

b. Get ready. Touch **s, i, t** as the children say *sssiiit.*

If sounding out is not firm, repeat *b.*

c. What word? (Signal.) *Sit.* Yes, **sit.**

TASK 14   Children sound out the word and tell what word

a. Touch the ball for **and.** Sound it out.

b. Get ready. Touch **a, n, d** as the children say *aaannnd.*

If sounding out is not firm, repeat *b.*

c. What word? (Signal.) *And.* Yes, **and.**

TASK 15   Children sound out the word and tell what word

a. Touch the ball for **ēat.** Sound it out.

b. Get ready. Touch **ē, t** as the children say *ēēēt.*

If sounding out is not firm, repeat *b.*

c. What word? (Signal.) *Eat.* Yes, **eat.**

TASK 16   Children read the words in the box the fast way

a. Now you're going to read the words in the box the fast way.

b. Touch the ball for **sit.** (Pause three seconds.) Get ready.

Move your finger quickly along the arrow. *Sit.*

c. Repeat *b* for the words **and** and **ēat.**

d. Present the series **sit, and, ēat** at least two times.

TASK 17   Individual test

Call on different children to read one word in the box the fast way.

Story 94

Do not clap for any small letters.

TASK 24 Quotation finding

a. Pass out Storybook 1.
b. **Open your book to page 7.**
c. Point to the quotation marks around the word **wow** in the second sentence. **These marks show that somebody is saying something. He's saying the word between these marks.**
d. Point to the quotation marks around **that fat fish is mom** in the last sentence. **These marks show that somebody is saying something. He's saying all the words between these marks.**
e. Point to the quotation marks around **wow. Everybody, touch these marks in your story.** Check children's responses. **Somebody is saying the word between those marks.**
f. Point to the quotation marks around **that fat fish is mom. Everybody, touch these marks in your story.** Check children's responses. **Somebody is saying all the words between those marks.**
g. Repeat e and f until firm.

TASK 25 First reading—children read the story and answer questions

a. **You're going to read the story and I'll ask questions.**
b. Clap for the sounds in each word as the children sound out each word one time and tell what word. Present the items below as the children read.

After the children read:	You say:
The little fish said,	**Now we're going to read what he said.**
"Wow."	**What did the little fish say?** (Signal.) *Wow.*
The little fish said,	**Now we're going to read what he said.**
"That fat fish is Mom."	**What did he say?** (Signal.) *That fat fish is Mom.*

TASK 26 Second reading—children read the story the fast way and answer questions

a. **You're going to read the story the fast way and I'll ask some more questions.**
b. **Remember to stop when you get to a period.**
c. **First word.** Check children's responses. **Get ready.** Clap. *A.*
d. **Next word.** Check children's responses. **Get ready.** Clap. *Little.*
e. Clap for the remaining words in the first sentence. Pause at least three seconds between claps. Pause longer before words that gave the children trouble during the first reading.
f. **Again.** Repeat c through e until firm.
g. Then ask: **Who sat on who?** (Signal.) *A little fish sat on a fat fish.*
h. **Reading the words in the next sentence the fast way.**
i. **First word.** Check children's responses. **Get ready.** Clap. *Thē.*
j. Clap for each remaining word in the second sentence. Pause at least three seconds between claps. Pause longer before words that gave the children trouble during the first reading.
k. **Read that sentence again the fast way.** Repeat i and j until firm.
l. Use the procedures in h through k for the remaining sentences in the story. Ask the comprehension questions below as the children read.

After the children read:	You say:
A little fish sat on a fat fish.	**Who sat on who?** (Signal.) *A little fish sat on a fat fish.*
The little fish said, "Wow."	**What did he say?** (Signal.) *Wow.*
The little fish did not hate the fat fish.	**Did the little fish hate the fat fish?** (Signal.) *No.*
The little fish said, "That fat fish is Mom."	**What did he say?** (Signal.) *That fat fish is Mom.* **Who said, "That fat fish is Mom"?** (Signal.) *The little fish.*

Take-Home 71

STORY

TASK 18 · First reading—children sound out each word and tell what word

a. Pass out Take-Home 71. Do not let the children look at the picture until task 22.

b. Get ready to read the story. Everybody, touch the first word. Check children's responses.

c. Get ready. Clap for each sound. *Thththēēē.*

d. Again. (Pause.) Get ready. Clap for each sound. *Thththēēē.* What word? (Signal.) *Thē.* Yes, **thē.**

e. Next word. Check children's responses. Get ready. Clap for each sound. *Sssuuunnn.*

f. Again. (Pause.) Get ready. Clap for each sound. *Sssuuunnn.* What word? (Signal.) *Sun.* Yes, **sun.**

g. Repeat **e** and **f** for the remaining words in the story.

TASK 19 Second reading—children sound out each word and tell what word

a. Let's read the story again. Everybody, touch the first word. Check children's responses.

b. Get ready. Clap for each sound. *Thththēēē.* What word? (Signal.) *Thē.* Yes, **thē.**

c. Next word. Check children's responses. Get ready. Clap for each sound. *Sssuuunnn.* What word? (Signal.) *Sun.* Yes, **sun.**

d. Repeat *c* for the remaining words in the story.

TASK 20 Individual test

Call on different children to read one word. The child sounds out the word only one time, then tells what word. The other children are to point under the sounds that are said.

TASK 21 Teacher and children read the fast way

a. Let's read the fast way. Touch under **at.** This word is **at.** Touch under **us.** This word is **us.**

b. Point to **at.** What are you going to say when I touch this word? (Signal.) *At.*

c. Point to **us.** What are you going to say when I touch this word? (Signal.) *Us.*

d. Repeat *b* and *c* until firm.

e. My turn. Touch under the words as you say: Thē sun is hot. A man ran a fan . . . .

f. Your turn. Touch under the words as the children say *at us.*

g. Repeat *e* and *f* until firm.

TASK 22 Picture comprehension

a. The story tells us that the sun is hot and . . . . (Signal.) *A man ran a fan at us.*

b. Yes, the sun is hot and . . . . (Signal.) *A man ran a fan at us.*

c. Turn your take-home over and look at the picture.

d. Ask these questions:
   1. What is the man doing? *The children respond.* He's running a fan at the girl and her kitten.
   2. Where is the wind coming from? *The children respond.* Yes, from the fan.
   3. Did you ever stand in front of a fan? *The children respond.*

TASK 23 Word finding

a. Turn your take-home back to side 1. Everybody, let's play Find-the-Words. Look at the words in your story and get ready.

b. One of the words is (pause) **man.** Get ready to touch **man** when I clap. (Pause three seconds.) Get ready. Clap. *(The children touch **man**.)*

c. Repeat *b* for these words: **us, ran, us, man, ran, us, man, us, man, ran, man, ran.**

d. Repeat *b* and *c* until firm.

After you read the words on this page, you'll get to read the words the fast way.

TASK 18   Children sound out the word and tell what word

a. Touch the ball for **wish.** Sound it out.
b. Get ready.   Touch **w, i, sh** as the children say *wwwiiishshsh*.
If sounding out is not firm, repeat *b*.
c. What word?   (Signal.) *Wish.* Yes, **wish.**

TASK 19   Children sound out the word and tell what word

Repeat the procedures in task 18 for **now.**

TASK 20   Children sound out an irregular word (was)

a. Touch the ball for **was.** Sound it out.
b. Get ready.   Quickly touch each sound as the children say *wwwaaasss*.

To correct	If the children sound out the word as **wwwuuuzzz**
	1. Say: You've got to say the sounds I touch.
	2. Repeat *a* and *b* until firm.

c. Again.   Repeat *b* until firm.
d. That's how we sound out the word. Here's how we say the word.
Was. How do we say the word?   (Signal.) *Was.*
e. Now you're going to sound out the word. Get ready.
Touch each sound as the children say *wwwaaasss*.
f. Now you're going to say the word. Get ready.   (Signal.) *Was.*
g. Repeat *e* and *f* until firm.
h. Yes, this word is **was.** That **was** good reading.

TASK 21   Individual test

Call on different children to do *e* and *f* in task 20.

TASK 22   Children read the words the fast way

a. Now you get to read the words on this page the fast way.
b. Touch the ball for **wish.** (Pause three seconds.) Get ready.
Move your finger quickly along the arrow. *Wish.*
c. Repeat *b* for each word on the page.

TASK 23   Individual test

Call on different children to read one word the fast way.

wish

now

was

PAIR RELATIONS

The children will need pencils.

TASK 24   Children cross out the incorrect boxes

a. Hold up Take-Home 71. Point to the first box in the pair-relations exercise on side 2.

b. Everybody, this word is **sack**. What word?   (Signal.) *Sack.*
The word in the box is **sack** and the picture shows a **sack**.
If the children don't object, say: I fooled you.
This picture is not a **sack**; it's a ball.

c. This box is wrong because the word doesn't tell about the picture.
The word is **sack**, but the picture is not a **sack**. So you'll have to cross out this box. Do it.   Check children's responses.

d. Point to the second box. What's the word in this box?   (Signal.)
Sack. Yes, **sack**.

e. What does this picture show?   (Signal.) *A sack.* So this box is right. You won't cross it out.

f. Point to the third box. What's the word in this box?   (Signal.)
Sack. Yes, **sack**.

g. What does this picture show?   (Signal.) *A wagon.* The picture does not show a **sack**. So this box is wrong.
Are you going to cross it out?   (Signal.) *Yes.*
Do it.   Check children's responses.

h. You will do the other rows of boxes later.

SUMMARY OF INDEPENDENT ACTIVITY

TASK 25   Introduction to independent activity

Everybody, you're going to finish this take-home on your own.
Tell the children when they will work the remaining items.
Let's go over the things you're going to do.

TASK 26   Story copying

Point to the dotted words below the story on side 1. You're going to write the dotted words on this arrow. Then you're going to write those words on the other arrows.

TASK 27   Matching

a. Point to the first column of words in the Matching Game.

b. Everybody, get ready to read each of the words over here.
Touch the sounds as the children sound out the word.
Then ask: What word?   (Signal.) *The children respond.*

c. Point to the first column. You're going to make lines for every word over here.

TASK 28   Cross-out game

Point to the boxed sounds in the Cross-out Game. Everybody, what sound are you going to circle today?   (Signal.) *iii.*
What sound are you going to cross out?   (Signal.) *t.*

TASK 29   Sound writing

a. Point to the sound-writing exercise on side 2. Here are the sounds you're going to write today. I'll touch the sounds. You say them.

b. Touch each sound. *The children respond.*

c. Repeat the series until firm.

TASK 30   Pair relations

Point to the pair-relations exercise. Everybody, remember the rule.
If the picture doesn't show what the word says, you cross out the box.

TASK 31   Story picture

Point to the story picture. After you finish your take-home, you can color the story picture.

END OF LESSON 71

After you read the words on this page, you'll get to read the words the fast way.

TASK 13   Children sound out the word and tell what word

a. Touch the ball for **mom.** Sound it out.
b. Get ready.   Touch **m, o, m** as the children say *mmmooommm*.
                                    If sounding out is not firm, repeat *b*.
c. What word?   (Signal.) *Mom.* Yes, **mom.**

mom

TASK 14   Children sound out the word and tell what word

a. Touch the ball for **win.** Sound it out.
b. Get ready.   Touch **w, i, n** as the children say *wwwiiinnn*.
                                    If sounding out is not firm, repeat *b*.
c. What word?   (Signal.) *Win.* Yes, **win.**

win

TASK 15   Children sound out the word and tell what word

a. Touch the ball for **got.** Sound it out.
b. Get ready.   Touch **g, o, t** as the children say *gooot*.
                                    If sounding out is not firm, repeat *b*.
c. What word?   (Signal.) *Got.* Yes, **got.**

got

TASK 16   Children read the words the fast way

a. Now you get to read the words on this page the fast way.
b. Touch the ball for **mom.** (Pause three seconds.) Get ready.
                Move your finger quickly along the arrow. *Mom.*
c. Repeat *b* for each word on the page.

TASK 17   Individual test

Call on different children to read one word the fast way.

l

g

r

u

g

SOUNDS

TASK 1   Teaching l as in late

a. Point to **l**. Here's a new sound.
b. My turn. (Pause.) Touch **l** and
say: lll.
c. Again. Touch **l** for a longer time.
lllll. Lift your finger.
d. Point to **l**. Your turn. When I
touch it, you say it. (Pause.)
Get ready. Touch **l**. lll.
Lift your finger.
e. Again. Touch **l**. llllll.
Lift your finger.
f. Repeat *e* until firm.

TASK 2   Individual test

Call on different children to identify **l**.

TASK 3   Sounds firm-up

a. Get ready to say the sounds
when I touch them.
b. Alternate touching **l** and **r**. Point
to the sound. (Pause one second.)
Say: Get ready. Touch the
sound. *The children respond.*
c. When **l** and **r** are firm, alternate
touching **l, u, r,** and **g** until all
four sounds are firm.

l

s

u

g

i

o

ā   h

TASK 5   Sounds firm-up

a. Point to **l**. When I touch the sound, you say it.
b. (Pause.) Get ready. Touch **l**. lll.
c. Again. Repeat *b* until firm.
d. Get ready to say all the sounds when I touch them.
e. Alternate touching **g, s, u, l, i, o, ā,** and **h** three or four times.
Point to the sound. (Pause one second.) Say: Get ready.
Touch the sound. *The children respond.*

TASK 4   Individual test

Call on different children to identify **l, u, r,** or **g**.

TASK 6   Individual test

Call on different children to identify one or more sounds in task 5.

READING VOCABULARY

After you read the words on this page, you'll get to read the words the fast way.

Do not touch any small letters.

TASK 7   Children sound out the word and tell what word

a. Touch the ball for **lāte.** Sound it out.
b. Get ready. Touch **l, ā, t** as the children say *lllāāāt.*
If sounding out is not firm, repeat b.
c. What word? (Signal.) *Late.* Yes, **late.**

lāte

TASK 8   Children sound out the word and tell what word

a. Touch the ball for **shot.** Sound it out.
b. Get ready. Touch **sh, o, t** as the children say *shshshooot.*
If sounding out is not firm, repeat b.
c. What word? (Signal.) *Shot.* Yes, **shot.**

shot

TASK 9   Children sound out the word and tell what word

a. Touch the ball for **shut.** Sound it out.
b. Get ready. Touch **sh, u, t** as the children say *shshshuuut.*
If sounding out is not firm, repeat b.
c. What word? (Signal.) *Shut.* Yes, **shut.**

shut

TASK 10   Children sound out the word and tell what word

a. Touch the ball for **hāte.** Sound it out.
b. Get ready. Touch **h, ā, t** as the children say *hāāāt.*
If sounding out is not firm, repeat b.
c. What word? (Signal.) *Hate.* Yes, **hate.**

hāte

TASK 11   Children read the words the fast way

a. Now you get to read the words on this page the fast way.
b. Touch the ball for **lāte.** (Pause three seconds.) Get ready.
Move your finger quickly along the arrow. Late.
c. Repeat *b* for each word on the page.

TASK 12   Individual test

Call on different children to read one word the fast way.

READING VOCABULARY

TASK 7 Children sound out the word, then read it the fast way

a. Touch the ball for **nut.** Sound it out.
b. Get ready. Touch **n, u, t** as the children say *nnnuuut.*
                              If sounding out is not firm, repeat *b.*
c. What word? (Signal.) *Nut.* Yes, **nut.**
d. Return to the ball. Get ready to read the word the fast way.
         I'm going to count to five. See if you can remember the word.
e. 1, 2, 3, 4, 5. Get ready. Move your finger quickly along the arrow.
                              Nut. Yes, **nut.** Good reading.

f. Again. Repeat *e* until firm.

nut

TASK 8 Individual test

Call on different children to do *e* in task 7.

TASK 9 Children sound out the word, then read it the fast way

a. Touch the ball for **at.** Sound it out.
b. Get ready. Touch **a, t** as the children say *aaat.*
                              If sounding out is not firm, repeat *b.*
c. What word? (Signal.) *At.* Yes, **at.**
d. Return to the ball. Get ready to read the word the fast way.
         I'm going to count to five. See if you can remember the word.
e. 1, 2, 3, 4, 5. Get ready. Move your finger quickly along the arrow.
                              At. Yes, **at.** Good reading.

f. Again. Repeat *e* until firm.

at

TASK 10 Individual test

Call on different children to do *e* in task 9.

Lesson 94

k

t

c

SOUNDS

TASK 1 Teaching k as in kick

a. Point to **k**: My turn. When I touch it, I'll say it. (Pause.) Touch **k** for an instant, saying: k. Do not say **kuuh** or **kiih.**

b. Point to **k.** Your turn. When I touch it, you say it. (Pause.) Get ready. Touch **k.** *k.*

c. Again. Touch **k.** *k.*

d. Repeat *c* until firm.

TASK 2 Sounds firm-up

a. Get ready to say the sounds when I touch them.

b. Alternate touching **t** and **k**. Point to the sound. (Pause one second.) Say: Get ready. Touch the sound. *The children respond.*

c. When **t** and **k** are firm, alternate touching **k, h, c,** and **t** until all four sounds are firm.

TASK 3 Individual test

Call on different children to identify **k, h, c,** or **t.**

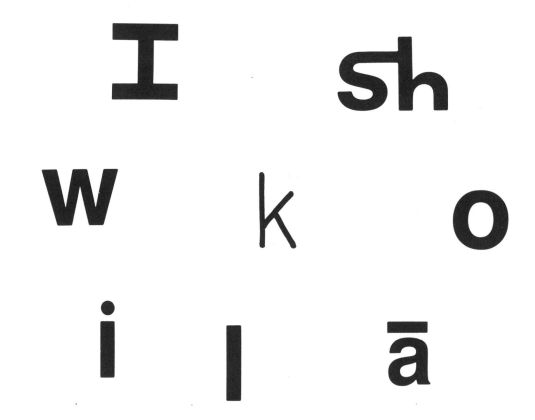

TASK 4 Teacher introduces cross-out game

a. Use acetate and crayon.

b. I'll cross out the sounds on this page when you can tell me every sound.

c. Remember—when I touch it, you say it.

d. Go over the sounds until the children can identify all the sounds in order.

TASK 5 Individual test

Call on different children to identify two or more sounds in task 4.

TASK 6 Teacher crosses out sounds

a. You told me every sound. Get ready to do it again. This time I'll cross out each sound when you tell me what it is.

b. Point to each sound. (Pause.) Say: Get ready. Touch the sound. *The children respond.* As you cross out the sound, say: Goodbye, _____.

TASK 11   Children sound out the word, then read it the fast way

a. Touch the ball for **in.** Sound it out.

b. Get ready.   Touch **i, n** as the children say *iiinnn.*

If sounding out is not firm, repeat *b.*

c. What word?   (Signal.) *In.* Yes, **in.**

d. Return to the ball.   Get ready to read the word the fast way.
I'm going to count to five. See if you can remember the word.

e. 1, 2, 3, 4, 5. Get ready.   Move your finger quickly along the arrow.
In. Yes, **in.** Good reading.

f. Again.   Repeat *e* until firm.

Do not touch any small letters.

TASK 12   Individual test

Call on different children to do *e* in task 11.

TASK 13   Children sound out the word, then read it the fast way

a. Touch the ball for **āte.** Sound it out.

b. Get ready.   Touch **ā, t** as the children say *āāāt.*

If sounding out is not firm, repeat *b.*

c. What word?   (Signal.) *Ate.* Yes, **ate.**

d. Return to the ball.   Get ready to read the word the fast way.
I'm going to count to five. See if you can remember the word.

e. 1, 2, 3, 4, 5. Get ready.   Move your finger quickly along the arrow.
Ate. Yes, **ate.** Good reading.

f. Again.   Repeat *e* until firm.

TASK 14   Individual test

Call on different children to do *e* in task 13.

SUMMARY OF INDEPENDENT ACTIVITY

TASK 30   Introduction to independent activity

a. Hold up Take-Home 93.
b. Everybody, you're going to finish this take-home on your own.
Tell the children when they will work the remaining items.
Let's go over the things you're going to do.

TASK 31   Sentence copying

Point to the first line in the sentence-copying exercise on side 1.
Remember—you're going to write this sentence on the arrows below.

TASK 32   Sound writing

a. Point to the sound-writing exercise. Here are the sounds you're
going to write today. I'll touch the sounds. You say them.
b. Touch each sound. *The children respond.*
c. Repeat the series until firm.

TASK 33   Matching

a. Point to the column of words in the Matching Game.
b. Everybody, you're going to follow the lines and write these words.
c. Reading the fast way.
d. Point to the first word. (Pause.) Get ready.   (Signal.)
The children respond.
e. Repeat *d* for the remaining words.
f. Repeat *d* and *e* until firm.

TASK 34   Cross-out game

Point to the boxed word in the Cross-out Game. Everybody, here's
the word you're going to cross out today. What word?   (Signal.)
We. Yes, **we.**

TASK 35   Pair relations

a. Point to the pair-relations exercise on side 2. You're going to
circle the picture in each box that shows what the words say.
b. Point to the space at the top of the page. After you finish,
remember to draw a picture that shows **thē cat has fun**.

END OF LESSON 93

TASK 15   Children sound out the word, then read it the fast way

a. Touch the ball for **hē.** Sound it out.
b. Get ready. Touch **h, ē** as the children say *hēēē.*
If sounding out is not firm, repeat *b.*
c. What word? (Signal.) *He.* Yes, **he.**
d. Return to the ball. Get ready to read the word the fast way.
I'm going to count to five. See if you can remember the word.
e. 1, 2, 3, 4, 5. Get ready. Move your finger quickly along the arrow.
He. Yes, **he.** Good reading.
f. Again. Repeat *e* until firm.

TASK 16   Individual test

Call on different children to do *e* in task 15.

TASK 17   Children read a word beginning with a stop sound (has)

a. Cover **h.** Run your finger under **as.** This part says (pause) **az.**
b. Uncover **h.** Touch the ball for **has.** Rhymes with (pause) **az.**
   Get ready. Move quickly along the arrow. *Has.*
c. What word? (Signal.) *Has.* Yes, **has.**
d. Repeat *b* and *c* until firm.
e. Return to the ball. Now you're going to sound out (pause) **has.**
Get ready. Quickly touch **h, a, s** as the children say *haaasss.*
f. What word? (Signal.) *Has.* Yes, **has.** Good reading. My mother **has**
a new car.
g. Repeat *e* and *f* until firm.

TASK 18   Individual test

Call on different children to do *e* and *f* in task 17.

TASK 27   Individual test

a. Everybody, finger on the ball of the top line.
                    Check children's responses.
b. We're going to have different children read the fast way.
                    Everybody's going to touch the words.
c. First word.   Check children's responses. Call on a child. Clap.
                    The child responds.
d. Next word.   Check children's responses. Call on a child. Clap.
                    The child responds.
e. Repeat *d* for the remaining words in the first sentence.

TASK 28   Sentence saying

Good reading. Now, everybody, say all the words in that sentence
        without looking.   (Signal.) *The children repeat the sentence
                    at a normal speaking rate.*

Take-Home 93

SENTENCE COPYING

TASK 29   Children read the sentence they will copy

a. Pass out Take-Home 93 to each child.
b. Hold up side 1 of your take-home. Point to the first sentence,
                    thē cat has fun.
c. Here's the sentence you're going to write on the lines below.
                    Everybody, touch this sentence on your take-home.
                    Check children's responses.
d. Get ready to read the words in this sentence the fast way.
                    First word.   Check children's responses. (Pause.) Get ready.
                    Clap for each word as the children read: *Thē cat has fun.*
e. Have the children reread the sentence at least once.
f. Point to the dotted words on the second arrow. You're going to
                    write the dotted words on this arrow. Then you're
                    going to write those words on the other arrows.
g. After you finish your take-home, you get to draw a picture about
                    the sentence, **thē cat has fun.**
h. Turn your take-home over.   Point to the space at the top of the page.
                    Here's where you are going to draw your picture.
i. What are you going to draw?   (Signal.) *The children respond.*
                    Yes, a picture that shows **thē cat has fun.**
j. Repeat *i* until firm.
k. You will write the sentences and draw the picture later.
                    Now turn your take-home back to side 1.

After you read the words on this page, you'll get to read the words in the box the fast way.

To correct	For all mistakes, have the children sound out the word and say it fast. Then say: **Remember this word.**

TASK 19   Children sound out the word and tell what word

a. Touch the ball for **ant.** Sound it out.

b. Get ready. Touch **a, n, t** as the children say *aaannnt.*

If sounding out is not firm, repeat *b.*

c. What word? (Signal.) *Ant.* Yes, **ant.**

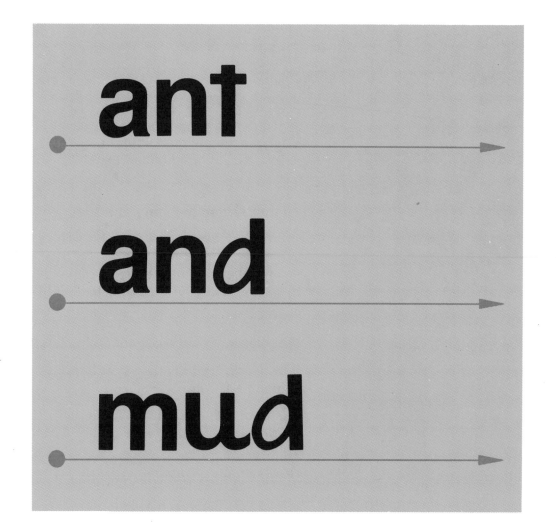

TASK 20   Children sound out the word and tell what word

a. Touch the ball for **and.** Sound it out.

b. Get ready. Touch **a, n, d** as the children say *aaannnd.*

If sounding out is not firm, repeat *b.*

c. What word? (Signal.) *And.* Yes, **and.**

TASK 21   Children sound out the word and tell what word

a. Touch the ball for **mud.** Sound it out.

b. Get ready. Touch **m, u, d** as the children say *mmmuuud.*

If sounding out is not firm, repeat *b.*

c. What word? (Signal.) *Mud.* Yes, **mud.**

TASK 22   Children read the words in the box the fast way

a. Now you're going to read the words in the box the fast way.

b. Touch the ball for **ant.** (Pause three seconds.) Get ready.

Move your finger quickly along the arrow. *Ant.*

c. Repeat *b* for the words **and** and **mud.**

d. Present the series **ant, and, mud** at least two times.

TASK 23   Individual test

Call on different children to read one word in the box the fast way.

Story 93

Do not clap for any small letters.

TASK 23   First reading—children sound out each word and tell what word

a. Pass out Storybook 1.

b. There are stories in this book. We're going to read one of them now.

c. Open your book to page 5 and get ready to read.

Check children's responses.

d. Clap for the sounds in each word as the children sound out each word one time and tell what word.

TASK 24   Second reading—children reread the story and answer questions

a. This time you'll read the story and I'll ask questions.

b. Repeat *d* in task 23. Ask the comprehension questions below as the children read.

After the children read:	You say:
He has a fat cat.	Who has a fat cat? (Signal.) *He does.*
He has fun with his fat cat.	What does he do with the fat cat? (Signal.) *Has fun.*
His Mom has a little cat.	What does his Mom have? (Signal.) *A little cat.*
She has fun with the little cat.	What does she do? (Signal.) *She has fun with the little cat.*
The little cat has fun in the sand.	Which cat has fun? (Signal.) *The little cat.* Where does he have fun? (Signal.) *In the sand.*

TASK 25   Picture comprehension

a. What do you think you'll see in the picture? *The children respond.*

b. Turn the page and look at the picture.

c. Ask these questions:

1. Who has the fat cat? *The boy.*
2. Who has the little cat? *His Mom.*
3. What are those cats doing? *The children respond.*

They're playing.

4. What would you do if you had a fat cat? *The children respond.*

TASK 26   Children read the story the fast way

a. Turn back to page 5. Everybody, touch the first word of the story.

Check children's responses.

b. Move along the line until you come to a period.

Check children's responses.

c. Again. Repeat *a* and *b* until firm.

d. Now you're going to read the words in that sentence the fast way.

e. First word. Check children's responses. Get ready. Clap. *He.*

f. Next word. Check children's responses. Get ready. Clap. *Has.*

g. Repeat *f* for the remaining words in the first sentence.

h. After the children read **cat,** say: Stop. That's the end of the first sentence.

i. Have the children reread the first sentence until firm.

j. Reading the words in the next sentence the fast way.

k. First word. Check children's responses. Get ready. Clap. *He.*

l. Clap for each remaining word in the second sentence. Pause at least three seconds between claps. Pause longer before words that gave the children trouble during the first reading.

m. Read that sentence again the fast way. Repeat *k* and *l* until firm.

n. Use the procedures in *j* through *m* for the remaining sentences in the story.

Take-Home 72

STORY

TASK 24 First reading—children sound out each word and tell what word

a. Pass out Take-Home 72. Do not let the children look at the picture
until task 28.

b. Get ready to read the story. Everybody, touch the first word.
Check children's responses.

c. Get ready. Clap for each sound. *Hēēē.*

d. Again. (Pause.) Get ready. Clap for each sound. *Hēēē.*
What word? (Signal.) *He.* Yes, **he.**

e. Next word. Check children's responses. Get ready.
Clap for each sound. *Haaasss.*

f. Again. (Pause.) Get ready. Clap for each sound. *Haaasss.*
What word? (Signal.) *Has.* Yes, **has.**

g. Repeat *e* and *f* for the remaining words in the story.

TASK 25 Second reading—children sound out each word and tell what word

a. Let's read the story again. Everybody, touch the first word.
Check children's responses.

b. Get ready. Clap for each sound. *Hēēē.* What word? (Signal.)
He. Yes, **he.**

c. Next word. Check children's responses. Get ready. Clap for each
sound. *Haaasss.* What word? (Signal.) *Has.* Yes, **has.**

d. Repeat *c* for the remaining words in the story.

TASK 26 Individual test

Call on different children to read one word. The child sounds out the
word only one time, then tells what word. The other children are to
point under the sounds that are said.

TASK 27 Teacher and children read the fast way

a. Let's read the fast way. Touch under **his.** This word is **his.**
Touch under **hut.** This word is **hut.**

b. Point to **his.** What are you going to say when I touch this word?
(Signal.) *His.*

c. Point to **hut.** What are you going to say when I touch this word?
(Signal.) *Hut.*

d. Repeat *b* and *c* until firm.

e. My turn. Touch under the words as you say: He has a rug. That
rug is in . . . .

f. Your turn. Touch under the words as the children say *his hut.*

g. Repeat *e* and *f* until firm.

TASK 28 Picture comprehension

a. In the picture, you'll see that he has . . . . (Signal.) *A rug.*

b. And that rug is . . . . (Signal.) *In his hut.*

c. Yes, he has . . . . (Signal.) *A rug.*

d. And that rug is . . . . (Signal.) *In his hut.*

e. Turn your take-home over and look at the picture.

f. Ask these questions:
  1. Where is the rug? *The children respond.* In the hut.
  2. What is sitting on the rug? *The children respond.*
  A boy and a tiger.
  3. Would you sit in that hut with a tiger? *The children respond.*

TASK 29 Word finding

a. Turn your take-home back to side 1. Everybody, let's play
Find-the-Words. Look at the words in your story and get ready.

b. One of the words is (pause) **his.** Get ready to touch **his** when I
clap. (Pause three seconds.) Get ready. Clap.
*(The children touch **his.**)*

c. Repeat *b* for these words: **that, has, his, that, has, his, that, his,**
has, that, has, his.

d. Repeat *b* and *c* until firm.

After you read the words on this page, you'll get to read the words the fast way.

wish

TASK 18   Children sound out the word and tell what word

a. Touch the ball for **wish.** Sound it out.
b. Get ready. Touch **w, i, sh** as the children say *wwwiiishshsh*.
If sounding out is not firm, repeat *b*.
c. What word? (Signal.) *Wish.* Yes, **wish.**

said

TASK 19   Children identify, then sound out an irregular word (said)

a. Touch the ball for **said.** Everybody, you're going to read this word the fast way. (Pause three seconds.) Get ready. Move your finger quickly along the arrow. *Said.* Yes, **said.**
b. Now you're going to sound out the word. Get ready. Quickly touch **s, a, i, d** as the children say *sssaaaiiid*.
c. Again. Repeat *b*.
d. How do we say the word? (Signal.) *Said.* Yes, **said.**
e. Repeat *b* and *d* until firm.

TASK 20   Individual test

Call on different children to do *b* and *d* in task 19.

TASK 21   Children read the words the fast way

a. Now you get to read the words on this page the fast way.
b. Touch the ball for **wish.** (Pause three seconds.) Get ready. Move your finger quickly along the arrow. *Wish.*
c. Repeat *b* for **said.**

TASK 22   Individual test

Call on different children to read one word the fast way.

PAIR RELATIONS

The children will need pencils.

TASK 30　Children cross out the incorrect boxes

a. Hold up Take-Home 72. Point to the first box in the pair-relations exercise on side 2.

b. Everybody, this word is **nut**. What word? (Signal.) *Nut.*
The word in the box is **nut** and the picture shows a **nut**.
If the children don't object, say: I fooled you.
This picture is not a **nut**; it's an apple.

c. This box is wrong because the word doesn't tell about the picture.
The word is **nut**, but the picture is not a **nut**. So you'll have to cross out this box. Do it. Check children's responses.

d. Point to the second box. What's the word in this box? (Signal.)
Nut. Yes, **nut**.

e. What does this picture show? (Signal.) *A house.* The picture does not show a **nut**. So this box is wrong.
Are you going to cross it out? (Signal.) *Yes.*
Do it. Check children's responses.

f. Point to the third box. What's the word in this box? (Signal.)
Nut. Yes, **nut**.

g. What does this picture show? (Signal.) *A nut.* So this box is right.
You won't cross it out.

h. You will do the other rows of boxes later.

SUMMARY OF INDEPENDENT ACTIVITY

TASK 31　Introduction to independent activity

Everybody, you're going to finish this take-home on your own.
Tell the children when they will work the remaining items.
Let's go over the things you're going to do.

TASK 32　Story copying

Point to the dotted words below the story on side 1. You're going to write the dotted words on this arrow. Then you're going to write those words on the other arrows.

TASK 33　Matching

a. Point to the first column of words in the Matching Game.

b. Everybody, get ready to read each of the words over here.
Touch the sounds as the children sound out the word.
Then ask: What word? (Signal.) *The children respond.*

c. Point to the first column. You're going to make lines for every word over here.

TASK 34　Cross-out game

Point to the boxed sounds in the Cross-out Game. Everybody, what sound are you going to cross out today? (Signal.) *g.*
What sound are you going to circle? (Signal.) *d.*

TASK 35　Sound writing

a. Point to the sound-writing exercise on side 2. Here are the sounds you're going to write today. I'll touch the sounds. You say them.

b. Touch each sound. *The children respond.*

c. Repeat the series until firm.

TASK 36　Pair relations

Point to the pair-relations exercise. Everybody, remember the rule.
If the picture doesn't show what the word says, you cross out the box.

TASK 37　Story picture

Point to the story picture. After you finish your take-home, you can color the story picture.

END OF LESSON 72

After you read the words on this page, you'll get to read the words the fast way.

TASK 13 Children sound out the word and tell what word

a. Touch the ball for **sand.** Sound it out.
b. Get ready. Touch **s, a, n, d** as the children say *sssaaannnd*.
    If sounding out is not firm, repeat *b*.
c. What word? (Signal.) *Sand.* Yes, **sand.**

sand

TASK 14 Children sound out the word and tell what word

a. Touch the ball for **how.** Sound it out.
b. Get ready. Touch **h, o, w** as the children say *hooowww*.
    If sounding out is not firm, repeat *b*.
c. What word? (Signal.) *How.* Yes, **how.**

how

TASK 15 Children sound out the word and tell what word

a. Touch the ball for **now.** Sound it out.
b. Get ready. Touch **n, o, w** as the children say *nnnooowww*.
    If sounding out is not firm, repeat *b*.
c. What word? (Signal.) *Now.* Yes, **now.**

now

TASK 16 Children sound out the word and tell what word

a. Touch the ball for **mom.** Sound it out.
b. Get ready. Touch **m, o, m** as the children say *mmmooommm*.
c. What word? (Signal.) *Mom.* Yes, **mom.**

mom

TASK 17 Children read the words the fast way

a. Now you get to read the words on this page the fast way.
b. Touch the ball for **sand.** (Pause three seconds.) Get ready.
    Move your finger quickly along the arrow. *Sand.*
c. Repeat *b* for each word on the page.

Individual test

Call on different children to read one word the fast way.

Lesson 73

Groups that are firm on Mastery Tests 12 and 13 should skip this lesson and do lesson 74 today.

l

u

o

i

SOUNDS

TASK 1   Teaching l as in **late**

a. Point to l. **My turn.** (Pause.) Touch l and say: *lll.*
b. Point to l. **Your turn. When I touch it, you say it.** (Pause.) **Get ready.** Touch l. *lll.* Lift your finger.
c. **Again.** Touch l. *llll.* Lift your finger.
d. Repeat *c* until firm.

TASK 2   Sounds firm-up

a. **Get ready to say the sounds when I touch them.**
b. Alternate touching **u** and **l**. Point to the sound. (Pause one second.) Say: **Get ready.** Touch the sound. *The children respond.*
c. When **u** and **l** are firm, alternate touching **i, u, o,** and **l** until all four sounds are firm.

TASK 3   Individual test

Call on different children to identify **i, u, o,** or **l.**

l   h   c

i   g

ā   n

o

TASK 4   Sounds firm-up

a. Point to l. **When I touch the sound, you say it.**
b. (Pause.) **Get ready.** Touch l. *lll.*
c. **Again.** Repeat *b* until firm.
d. **Get ready to say all the sounds when I touch them.**
e. Alternate touching **ā, h, c, i, g, l, o,** and **n** three or four times.
   Point to the sound. (Pause one second.) Say: **Get ready.**
   Touch the sound. *The children respond.*

TASK 5   Individual test

Call on different children to identify one or more sounds in task 4.

READING VOCABULARY

After you read the words on this page, you'll get to read the words the fast way.

TASK 7   Children sound out the word and tell what word

a. Touch the ball for **cow**. Sound it out.
b. Get ready. Touch **c, o, w** as the children say *cooowww*.
                          If sounding out is not firm, repeat *b*.
c. What word? (Signal.) *Cow*. Yes, **cow**.

TASK 8   Children sound out the word and tell what word

a. Touch the ball for **this**. Sound it out.
b. Get ready. Touch **th, i, s** as the children say *thththiiiisss*.
                          If sounding out is not firm, repeat *b*.
c. What word? (Signal.) *This*. Yes, **this**.

TASK 9   Children sound out the word and tell what word

a. Touch the ball for **that**. Sound it out.
b. Get ready. Touch **th, a, t** as the children say *thththaaat*.
                          If sounding out is not firm, repeat *b*.
c. What word? (Signal.) *That*. Yes, **that**.

TASK 10   Children sound out the word and tell what word

a. Touch the ball for **will**. Sound it out.
b. Get ready. Touch **w, i,** between the l's as the children say *wwwiiilll*.
                          If sounding out is not firm, repeat *b*.
c. What word? (Signal.) *Will*. Yes, **will**.

TASK 11   Children read the words the fast way

a. Now you get to read the words on this page the fast way.
b. Touch the ball for **cow**. (Pause three seconds.) Get ready.
                          Move your finger quickly along the arrow. *Cow*.
c. Repeat *b* for each word on the page.

TASK 12   Individual test

Call on different children to read one word the fast way.

cow

this

that

will

READING VOCABULARY

Do not touch any small letters.

TASK 6   Children sound out the word, then read it the fast way

a. Touch the ball for **that.** Sound it out.
b. Get ready. Touch **th, a, t** as the children say *thththaaat.*
　　　　　　　　　　　　If sounding out is not firm, repeat *b.*
c. What word? (Signal.) *That.* Yes, **that.**
d. Return to the ball. Get ready to read the word the fast way.
　　　I'm going to count to five. See if you can remember the word.
e. 1, 2, 3, 4, 5. Get ready. Move your finger quickly along the arrow.
　　　　　　　　　　　That. Yes, **that.** Good reading.

f. Again. Repeat *e* until firm.

TASK 7   Individual test

Call on different children to do *e* in task 6.

TASK 8   Children sound out the word, then read it the fast way

Repeat the procedures in task 6 for **mēan.**

TASK 9   Individual test

Call on different children to do *e* in task 6 for **mēan.**

TASK 10   Children read a word beginning with a stop sound (hat)

a. Run your finger under **at.** You're going to sound out this part.
　　　　　　　　　　Get ready. Touch **a, t** as the children say *aaat.*
b. Say it fast. (Signal.) *At.* Yes, this part says (pause) **at.**
c. Repeat *a* and *b* until firm.
d. Touch the ball for **hat.** This word rhymes with (pause) **at.**
　　Get ready. Move quickly along the arrow. *Hat.*
e. What word? (Signal.) *Hat.* Yes, **hat.**
f. Repeat *d* and *e* until firm.
g. Return to the ball. Now you're going to sound out (pause) **hat.**
　　　　　Get ready. Quickly touch **h, a, t** as the children say *ḣaaat.*
h. What word? (Signal.) *Hat.* Yes, **hat.** Good reading. Where is your
　　　　　　　　　　　　　　　　　　　　　hat?

i. Repeat *g* and *h* until firm.

TASK 11   Individual test

Call on different children to do *g* and *h* in task 10.

that

mēan

hat

Lesson 93

k

c

t

g

SOUNDS

TASK 1   Teaching **k** as in **kick**

a. Point to **k**. **My turn. When I touch it, I'll say it.** (Pause.) Touch **k** for an instant, saying: *k.* Do not say **kuuh** or **kiih.**

b. Point to **k**. **Your turn. When I touch it, you say it.** (Pause.) **Get ready.** Touch **k**. *k.*

c. **Again:** Touch **k**. *k.*

d. Repeat *c* until firm.

TASK 2   Sounds firm-up

a. **Get ready to say the sounds when I touch them.**

b. Alternate touching **c** and **k**. Point to the sound. (Pause one second.) Say: **Get ready.** Touch the sound. *The children respond.*

c. When **c** and **k** are firm, alternate touching **c, t, k,** and **g** until all four sounds are firm.

TASK 3   Individual test

Call on different children to identify **c, t, k,** or **g.**

TASK 4   Teacher introduces cross-out game

a. Use acetate and crayon.

b. **I'll cross out the sounds on this page when you can tell me every sound.**

c. **Remember—when I touch it, you say it.**

d. Go over the sounds until the children can identify all the sounds in order.

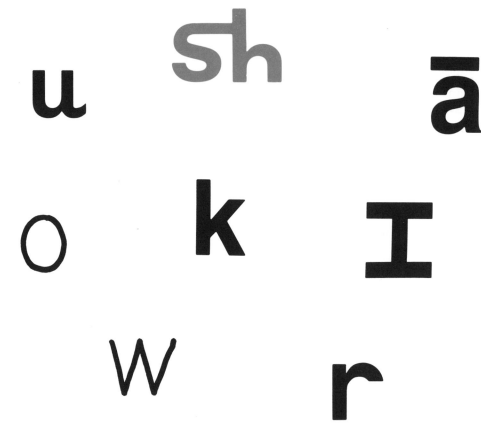

TASK 5   Individual test

Call on different children to identify two or more sounds in task 4.

TASK 6   Teacher crosses out sounds

a. **You told me every sound. Get ready to do it again. This time I'll cross out each sound when you tell me what it is.**

b. Point to each sound. (Pause.) Say: **Get ready.** Touch the sound. *The children respond.* As you cross out the sound, say: **Goodbye, _____ .**

TASK 12 Children sound out the word, then read it the fast way

a. Touch the ball for **fat.** Sound it out.
b. Get ready. Touch **f, a, t** as the children say *fffaaat.*
                    If sounding out is not firm, repeat *b.*
c. What word? (Signal.) *Fat.* Yes, **fat.**
d. Return to the ball. Get ready to read the word the fast way.
          I'm going to count to five. See if you can remember the word.
e. 1, 2, 3, 4, 5. Get ready. Move your finger quickly along the arrow.
                              Fat. Yes, **fat.** Good reading.
f. Again. Repeat *e* until firm.

TASK 13 Individual test

Call on different children to do *e* in task 12.

TASK 14 Children rhyme with āme

a. Touch the ball for **āme.** Sound it out.
b. Get ready. Touch **ā, m** as the children say *āāāmmm.*
      If sounding out is not firm, repeat *b.*
c. What word? (Signal.) *Ame.* Yes, **ame.**
d. Quickly touch the ball for **cāme.** This word rhymes with (pause)
      āme.
      Get ready. Move your finger quickly along the arrow. *Came.*
e. What word? (Signal.) *Came.* Yes, **came.** I **came** home late.

TASK 15 Children sound out the word and tell what word

a. Touch the ball for **cāme.** Sound it out.
b. Get ready. Touch **c, ā, m** as the children say *cāāāmmm.*
c. Again. Repeat *b* until firm.
d. Yes, what word? (Signal.) *Came.*

Do not touch any small letters.

fat

āme

cāme

MATCHING

The children will need pencils.

TASK 29 Children follow the line and write the matching word

a. Point to the column of words in the matching exercise on side 1.

b. The lines show where the words are that match. But words are missing. Everybody, you're going to touch the word **is**. (Pause four seconds.) Get ready. (Signal.) Check children's responses.

c. Follow the dotted line to where the other word **is** should be. (Signal.) Check children's responses.

d. Where's the word **is**? It's missing. You're going to have to write it in. Everybody, take your pencil and write the word **is** where it should be. Check children's responses.

e. Everybody, you're going to touch the word **feet**. (Pause four seconds.) Get ready. (Signal.) Check children's responses.

f. Follow the dotted line to where the other word **feet** should be. Check children's responses.

g. Where is the word **feet**? (Signal.) *It's missing.* You're going to have to write it in. Everybody, take your pencil and write the word **feet** where it should be. Check children's responses.

h. You'll write the rest of the words later. Remember to follow the lines.

SUMMARY OF INDEPENDENT ACTIVITY

TASK 30 Introduction to independent activity

a. Hold up Take-Home 92

b. Everybody, you're going to finish this take-home on your own. Tell the children when they will work the remaining items. Let's go over the things you're going to do.

TASK 31 Sentence copying

Point to the first line in the sentence-copying exercise on side 1. Remember—you're going to write this sentence on the arrows below.

TASK 32 Sound writing

a. Point to the sound-writing exercise. Here are the sounds you're going to write today. I'll touch the sounds. You say them.

b. Touch each sound. *The children respond.*

c. Repeat the series until firm.

TASK 33 Matching

Point to the column of words in the Matching Game. Remember—you're going to follow the lines and write these words.

TASK 34 Cross-out game

Point to the boxed word in the Cross-out Game. Everybody, here's the word you're going to cross out today. What word? (Signal.) *Sack.* Yes, **sack**.

TASK 35 Pair relations

a. Point to the pair-relations exercise on side 2. You're going to circle the picture in each box that shows what the words say.

b. Point to the space at the top of the page. After you finish, remember to draw a picture that shows **I wish I had sand**.

END OF LESSON 92

After you read the words on this page, you'll get to read the words in the box the fast way.

To correct	For all mistakes, have the children sound out the word and say it fast. Then say: **Remember this word.**

TASK 16   Children sound out the word and tell what word

a. Touch the ball for **fig.** **Sound it out.**
b. **Get ready.**   Touch **f, i, g** as the children say *fffiiig.*
If sounding out is not firm, repeat *b.*
c. **What word?**   (Signal.) *Fig.* **Yes, fig.**

TASK 17   Children sound out the word and tell what word

a. Touch the ball for **rat.** **Sound it out.**
b. **Get ready.**   Touch **r, a, t** as the children say *rrraaat.*
If sounding out is not firm, repeat *b.*
c. **What word?**   (Signal.) *Rat.* **Yes, rat.**

TASK 18   Children read the words in the box the fast way

a. Now you're going to read the words in the box the fast way.
b. Touch the ball for **fig.** (Pause three seconds.) **Get ready.**
Move your finger quickly along the arrow. *Fig.*
c. Repeat *b* for **rat.**
d. Present the series **fig, rat** at least two times.

TASK 19   Individual test

Call on different children to read one word in the box the fast way.

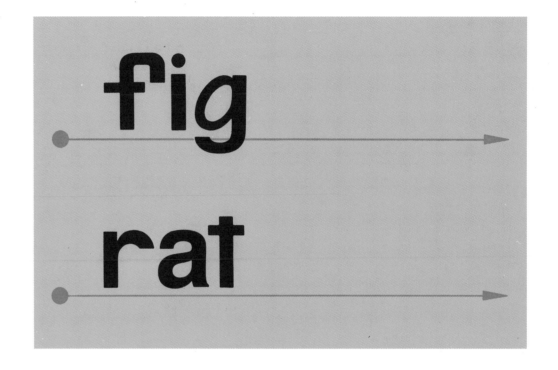

TASK 26 Individual test

a. Everybody, finger on the ball of the top line.
Check children's responses.

b. We're going to have different children read the fast way.
Everybody's going to touch the words.

c. First word. Check children's responses. Call on a child. Clap.
The child responds.

d. Next word. Check children's responses. Call on a child. Clap.
The child responds.

e. Repeat *d* for the remaining words in the first sentence.

TASK 27 Sentence saying

Good reading. Now, everybody, say all the words in that sentence
without looking. (Signal.) *The children repeat the sentence*
at a normal speaking rate.

Take-Home 92

SENTENCE COPYING

TASK 28 Children read the sentence they will copy

a. Pass out Take-Home 92 to each child.

b. Hold up side 1 of your take-home. Point to the first sentence,
I wish I had sand.

c. Here's the sentence you're going to write on the lines below.
Everybody, touch this sentence on your take-home.
Check children's responses.

d. Get ready to read the words in this sentence the fast way.
First word. Check children's responses. (Pause.) Get ready.
Clap for each word as the children read: *I wish I had sand.*

e. Have the children reread the sentence at least once.

f. Point to the dotted words on the second arrow. You're going to
write the dotted words on this arrow. Then you're
going to write those words on the other arrows.

g. After you finish your take-home, you get to draw a picture about
the sentence, **I wish I had sand.**

h. Turn your take-home over. Point to the space at the top of the page.
Here's where you are going to draw your picture.

i. What are you going to draw? (Signal.) *The children respond.*
Yes, a picture that shows **I wish I had sand.**

j. Repeat *i* until firm.

k. You will write the sentences and draw the picture later.
Now turn your take-home back to side 1.

Take-Home 73

STORY
Do not clap for any small letters.

TASK 20 First reading—children sound out each word and tell what word

a. Pass out Take-Home 73. Do not let the children look at the picture until task 24.

b. Get ready to read the story. Everybody, touch the first word.
Check children's responses.

c. Get ready. Clap for each sound. *Hēēē.*

d. Again. (Pause.) Get ready. Clap for each sound. *Hēēē.*
What word? (Signal.) *He.* Yes, **he.**

e. Next word. Check children's responses. Get ready.
Clap for each sound. *Iiisss.*

f. Again. (Pause.) Get ready. Clap for each sound. *Iiisss.*
What word? (Signal.) *Is.* Yes, **is.**

g. Repeat *e* and *f* for the remaining words in the story.

TASK 21 Second reading—children sound out each word and tell what word

a. Let's read the story again. Everybody, touch the first word.
Check children's responses.

b. Get ready. Clap for each sound. *Hēēē.* What word? (Signal.) *He.*
Yes, **he.**

c. Next word. Check children's responses. Get ready. Clap for each sound. *Iiisss.* What word? (Signal.) *Is.* Yes, **is.**

d. Repeat *c* for the remaining words in the story.

TASK 22 Individual test

Call on different children to read one word. The child sounds out the word only one time, then tells what word. The other children are to point under the sounds that are said.

TASK 23 Teacher and children read the fast way

a. Let's read the fast way. Touch under **his.** This word is **his.**
Touch under **fēēt.** This word is **feet.**

b. Point to **his.** What are you going to say when I touch this word?
(Signal.) *His.*

c. Point to **fēēt.** What are you going to say when I touch this word?
(Signal.) *Feet.*

d. Repeat *b* and *c* until firm.

e. My turn. Touch under the words as you say: He is an ant.
He has a sock on . . . .

f. Your turn. Touch under the words as the children say *his feet.*

g. Repeat *e* and *f* until firm.

TASK 24 Picture comprehension

a. You'll see a picture that shows that he is . . . . (Signal.) *An ant.*

b. And he has . . . . (Signal.) *A sock on his feet.*

c. Yes, he is . . . . (Signal.) *An ant.*

d. And he has . . . . (Signal.) *A sock on his feet.*

e. Turn your take-home over and look at the picture.

f. Ask these questions:
1. How many socks is that ant wearing? *The children respond.*
Yes, one.
2. Does that sock fit? *The children respond.*
3. Couldn't you dress faster if you could wear one big sock like that? *The children respond.*

TASK 25 Word finding

a. Turn your take-home back to side 1. Everybody, let's play Find-the-Words. Look at the words in your story and get ready.

b. One of the words is (pause) **ant.** Get ready to touch **ant** when I clap. (Pause three seconds.) Get ready. Clap.
(The children touch ant.)

c. Repeat *b* for these words: **an, on, ant, an, on, an, ant, an, ant, on, ant, on.**

d. Repeat *b* and *c* until firm.

Story 92

Do not clap for any small letters.

TASK 22   First reading—children sound out each word and tell what word

a. Pass out Storybook 1.
b. There are stories in this book. We're going to read one of them now.
c. Open your book to page 3 and get ready to read.
                                         Check children's responses.
d. Clap for the sounds in each word as the children sound out each word one time and tell what word.

TASK 23   Second reading—children reread the story and answer questions

a. This time you'll read the story and I'll ask questions.
b. Repeat d in task 22. Ask the comprehension questions below as the children read.

After the children read:	You say:
I wish I had sand.	What did I wish for? (Signal.) *Sand.*
I wish I had a rake.	What did I wish for? (Signal.) *A rake.*
I wish I had a fish.	What did I wish for? (Signal.) *A fish.*
I wish I had a lake.	What did I wish for? (Signal.) *A lake.* Name everything I wished for. (Signal.) *Sand, a rake, a fish, and a lake.*

TASK 24   Picture comprehension

a. What do you think you'll see in the picture? The children respond.
b. Turn the page and look at the picture.
c. Ask these questions:
   1. Did she get her wish? *Yes.*
   2. Where's the rake? *The children respond.*
   3. Where's the fish? *The children respond.*
   4. Where's the sand? *The children respond.*
   5. Where's the lake? *The children respond.*
   6. What's she doing with that rake? *The children respond.*
   7. What would you do if you had a lake? *The children respond.*

TASK 25   Children read the story the fast way

a. Turn back to page 3. Everybody, touch the first word of the story.
                                         Check children's responses.
b. Move along the line until you come to a period.
                                         Check children's responses.
c. Again. Repeat a and b until firm.
d. Now you're going to read the words in that sentence the fast way.
e. First word. Check children's responses. Get ready. Clap. *I.*
f. Next word. Check children's responses. Get ready. Clap. *Wish.*
g. Repeat f for the remaining words in the first sentence.
h. After the children read **sand**, say: Stop. That's the end of the first sentence.
i. Have the children reread the first sentence until firm.
j. Reading the words in the next sentence the fast way.
k. First word. Check children's responses. Get ready. Clap. *I.*
l. Clap for each remaining word in the second sentence. Pause at least three seconds between claps. Pause longer before words that gave the children trouble during the first reading.
m. Read that sentence again the fast way. Repeat k and l until firm.
n. Use the procedures in j through m for the remaining sentences in the story.

73

SUMMARY OF INDEPENDENT ACTIVITY

TASK 26   Introduction to independent activity

a. Hold up Take-Home 73.
b. Everybody, you're going to finish this take-home on your own.
Tell the children when they will work the remaining items.
Let's go over the things you're going to do.

TASK 27   Story copying

Point to the dotted words below the story on side 1. You're going to
write the dotted words on this arrow. Then you're going to write
those words on the other arrows.

TASK 28   Matching

a. Point to the first column of words in the Matching Game.
b. Everybody, get ready to read each of the words over here.
Touch the sounds as the children sound out the word.
Then ask: What word? (Signal.) *The children respond.*
c. Point to the first column. You're going to make lines for every
word over here.

TASK 29   Cross-out game

Point to the boxed sounds in the Cross-out Game. Everybody, what
sound are you going to circle today? (Signal.) *nnn.*
What sound are you going to cross out? (Signal.) *h.*

TASK 30   Sound writing

a. Point to the sound-writing exercise on side 2. Here are the sounds
you're going to write today. I'll touch the sounds. You say them.
b. Touch each sound. *The children respond.*
c. Repeat the series until firm.

TASK 31   Pair relations

---

a. Point to the pair-relations exercise.
b. Everybody, remember the rule. If the picture doesn't show what
the word says, you cross out the box.
c. Point to the first box. This word is **man**. What word? (Signal.) *Man.*
Everybody, does the picture show a man? (Signal.) *No.*
Are you going to cross it out? (Signal.) *Yes.*
d. If the children's responses are not firm, repeat *c* with one or
more boxes.

TASK 32   Story picture

Point to the story picture. After you finish your take-home,
you can color the story picture.

END OF LESSON 73

After you read the words on this page, you'll get to read the words the fast way.

Do not touch any small letters.

TASK 18   Children rhyme with nāmes

a. Touch the ball for **nāmes.** Sound it out.
b. Get ready. Touch **n, ā, m, s** as the children say *nnnāāāmmmsss.*
                    If sounding out is not firm, repeat *b.*
c. What word? (Signal.) *Names.* Yes, **names.**
d. Quickly touch the ball for **gāmes.** This word rhymes with (pause)
            names. Get ready. Touch **g.** *g.* Move your finger quickly along
                                the arrow. *Games.*
e. What word? (Signal.) *Games.* Yes, **games.**

TASK 19   Children sound out the word and tell what word

a. Touch the ball for **hot.** Sound it out.
b. Get ready. Touch **h, o, t** as the children say *hooot.*
                        If sounding out is not firm, repeat *b.*
c. What word? (Signal.) *Hot.* Yes, **hot.**

TASK 20   Children read the words the fast way

a. Now you get to read the words on this page the fast way.
b. Touch the ball for **nāmes.** (Pause three seconds.) Get ready.
                Move your finger quickly along the arrow. *Names.*
c. Repeat *b* for each word on the page.

TASK 21   Individual test

Call on different children to read one word the fast way.

nāmes

gāmes

hot

Lesson 74

l

g

u

r

SOUNDS

TASK 1   Teaching l as in **late**

a. Point to l. **My turn.** (Pause.) Touch l and say: lll.

b. Point to l. **Your turn. When I touch it, you say it.** (Pause.) **Get ready.** Touch l. *lll.* Lift your finger.

c. **Again.** Touch l. *llll.* Lift your finger.

d. Repeat *c* until firm.

TASK 2   Sounds firm-up

a. **Get ready to say the sounds when I touch them.**

b. Alternate touching **g** and **l**. Point to the sound. (Pause one second.) Say: **Get ready.** Touch the sound. *The children respond.*

c. When **g** and **l** are firm, alternate touching **u, l, g,** and **r** until all four sounds are firm.

TASK 3   Individual test

Call on different children to identify **u, l, g,** or **r.**

TASK 4   Teacher introduces cross-out game

a. Use acetate and crayon.

b. **I'll cross out the sounds on this page when you can tell me every sound.**

c. **Remember—when I touch it, you say it.**

d. Go over the sounds until the children can identify all the sounds in order.

h   t   i

f   l   ē   ā

o

TASK 5   Individual test

Call on different children to identify two or more sounds in task 4.

TASK 6   Teacher crosses out sounds

a. **You told me every sound. Get ready to do it again. This time I'll cross out each sound when you tell me what it is.**

b. Point to each sound. (Pause.) Say: **Get ready.** Touch the sound. *The children respond.* As you cross out the sound, say: **Goodbye, _____ .**

After you read the words on this page, you'll get to read the words the fast way.

Do not touch any small letters.

TASK 13   Children sound out the word and tell what word

a. Touch the ball for **hāte.**   Sound it out.
b. Get ready.   Touch **h, ā, t** as the children say *hāāāt.*

If sounding out is not firm, repeat *b*.

c. What word? (Signal.) *Hate.*   Yes, **hate.**

TASK 14   Children sound out the word and tell what word

a. Touch the ball for **digs.**   Sound it out.
b. Get ready.   Touch **d, i, g, s** as the children say *diiigsss.*

If sounding out is not firm, repeat *b*.

c. What word? (Signal.) *Digs.*   Yes, **digs.**

TASK 15   Children sound out the word and tell what word

a. Touch the ball for **little.**   Sound it out.
b. Get ready.   Touch **l, i,** between the **t**'s, **l** as the children say

llliiitlll. If sounding out is not firm, repeat *b*.

c. What word? (Signal.) *Little.*   Yes, **little.**

TASK 16   Children read the words the fast way

a. Now you get to read the words on this page the fast way.
b. Touch the ball for **hāte.** (Pause three seconds.)   Get ready.

Move your finger quickly along the arrow. *Hāte.*

c. Repeat *b* for each word on the page.

TASK 17   Individual test

Call on different children to read one word the fast way.

hāt_e

digs

littl_e

74

READING VOCABULARY

TASK 7   Children read a word beginning with a stop sound (hot)

a. Run your finger under **ot.** You're going to sound out this part.
Get ready.   Touch **o, t** as the children say *ooot.*
b. Say it fast.   (Signal.) *Ot.* Yes, this part says   (pause) **ot.**
c. Repeat *a* and *b* until firm.
d. Touch the ball for **hot.** This word rhymes with   (pause) **ot.**
Get ready.   Move quickly along the arrow. *Hot.*
e. What word?   (Signal.) *Hot.* Yes, **hot.**
f. Repeat *d* and *e* until firm.
g. Return to the ball. Now you're going to sound out   (pause) **hot.**
Get ready.   Quickly touch **h, o, t** as the children say *hooot.*
h. What word?   (Signal.) *Hot.* Yes, **hot.** Good reading. The water
is **hot.**

i. Repeat *g* and *h* until firm.

TASK 8   Individual test

Call on different children to do *g* and *h* in task 7.

TASK 9   Children read a word beginning with a stop sound (his)

a. Run your finger under **is.** You're going to sound out this part.
Get ready.   Touch **i, s** as the children say *iiisss.*
b. Say it fast.   (Signal.) *Is.* Yes, this part says   (pause) **is.**
c. Repeat *a* and *b* until firm.
d. Touch the ball for **his.** This word rhymes with   (pause) **is.**
Get ready.   Move quickly along the arrow. *His.*
e. What word?   (Signal.) *His.* Yes, **his.**
f. Repeat *d* and *e* until firm.
g. Return to the ball. Now you're going to sound out   (pause) **his.**
Get ready.   Quickly touch **h, i, s** as the children say *hiiisss.*
h. What word?   (Signal.) *His.* Yes, **his.** Good reading.
His sister is pretty.

i. Repeat *g* and *h* until firm.

TASK 10   Individual test

Call on different children to do *g* and *h* in task 9.

READING VOCABULARY

After you read the words on this page, you'll get to read the words the fast way.

TASK 7   Children identify, then sound out an irregular word (said)

a. Touch the ball for **said.** Everybody, you're going to read this word the fast way. (Pause three seconds.) Get ready. Move your finger quickly along the arrow. *Said.* Yes, **said**.

b. Now you're going to sound out the word. Get ready. Quickly touch **s, a, i, d** as the children say *sssaaaiiid*.

c. Again. Repeat *b*.

d. How do we say the word? (Signal.) *Said.* Yes, **said**.

e. Repeat *b* and *d* until firm.

TASK 8   Individual test

Call on different children to do *b* and *d* in task 7.

TASK 9   Children sound out the word and tell what word

a. Touch the ball for **now.** Sound it out.

b. Get ready. Touch **n, o, w** as the children say *nnnooowww*. If sounding out is not firm, repeat *b*.

c. What word? (Signal.) *Now.* Yes, **now**.

TASK 10   Children sound out the word and tell what word

a. Touch the ball for **rigs.** Sound it out.

b. Get ready. Touch **r, i, g, s** as the children say *rrriiigsss*. If sounding out is not firm, repeat *b*.

c. What word? (Signal.) *Rigs.* Yes, **rigs**.

TASK 11   Children read the words the fast way

a. Now you get to read the words on this page the fast way.

b. Touch the ball for **said.** (Pause three seconds.) Get ready. Move your finger quickly along the arrow. *Said.*

c. Repeat *b* for each word on the page.

TASK 12   Individual test

Call on different children to read one word the fast way.

After you read the words on this page, you'll get to read the words in the box the fast way.

Do not touch any small letters.

To correct	For all mistakes, have the children sound out the word and say it fast. Then say: **Remember this word.**

TASK 11   Children sound out the word and tell what word

a. Touch the ball for **rug.** Sound it out.
b. Get ready.   Touch **r, u, g** as the children say *rrruuug.*
                    If sounding out is not firm, repeat *b.*
c. What word?   (Signal.) *Rug.* Yes, **rug.**

TASK 12   Children sound out the word and tell what word

a. Touch the ball for **sick.** Sound it out.
b. Get ready.   Touch **s, i, c** as the children say *sssiiic.*
                    If sounding out is not firm, repeat *b.*
c. What word?   (Signal.) *Sick.* Yes, **sick.**

TASK 13   Children sound out the word and tell what word

a. Touch the ball for **and.** Sound it out.
b. Get ready.   Touch **a, n, d** as the children say *aaannnd.*
                    If sounding out is not firm, repeat *b.*
c. What word?   (Signal.) *And.* Yes, **and.**

TASK 14   Children read the words in the box the fast way

a. Now you're going to read the words in the box the fast way.
b. Touch the ball for **rug.** (Pause three seconds.) Get ready.
                    Move your finger quickly along the arrow. *Rug.*
c. Repeat *b* for the words **sick** and **and.**
d. Present the series **rug, sick, and** at least two times.

TASK 15   Individual test

Call on different children to read one word in the box the fast way.

k

g

c

I

k

sh

u

i

w

l ē a

SOUNDS

TASK 1 Teaching k as in kick

a. Point to **k**. Here's a new sound. It's a quick sound.
b. My turn. (Pause.)
Touch **k** for an instant, saying: k.
Do not say **kuuh** or **kiih.**
c. Again. Touch **k** and say: k.
d. Point to **k**. Your turn. When I touch it, you say it. (Pause.) Get ready. Touch **k.** *k.*
e. Again. Touch **k.** *k.*
f. Repeat e until firm.

TASK 2 Individual test

Call on different children to identify **k.**

TASK 3 Sounds firm-up

a. Get ready to say the sounds when I touch them.
b. Alternate touching **k** and **g**. Point to the sound. (Pause one second.) Say: Get ready. Touch the sound. *The children respond.*
c. When **k** and **g** are firm, alternate touching **k, c, g,** and **I** until all four sounds are firm.

TASK 5 Sounds firm-up

a. Point to **k**. When I touch the sound, you say it.
b. (Pause.) Get ready. Touch **k.** *k.*
c. Again. Repeat b until firm.
d. Get ready to say all the sounds when I touch them.
e. Alternate touching **w, u, sh, i, k, l, ē,** and **a** three or four times.
Point to the sound. (Pause one second.) Say: Get ready.
Touch the sound. *The children respond.*

TASK 4 Individual test

Call on different children to identify **k, c, g,** or **I.**

TASK 6 Individual test

Call on different children to identify one or more sounds in task 5.

TASK 16   Children sound out the word, then read it the fast way

a. Touch the ball for **mēat.** Sound it out.
b. Get ready. Touch **m, ē, t** as the children say *mmmēēēt.*
 If sounding out is not firm, repeat *b.*
c. What word? (Signal.) *Meat.* Yes, **meat.**
d. Return to the ball. Get ready to read the word the fast way.
 I'm going to count to five. See if you can remember the word.
e. 1, 2, 3, 4, 5. Get ready. Move your finger quickly along the arrow.
 Meat. Yes, **meat.** Good reading.
f . Again. Repeat *e* until firm.

TASK 17   Children sound out the word, then read it the fast way

Repeat the procedures in task 16 for **mēan.**

TASK 18   Children sound out the word, then read it the fast way

Repeat the procedures in task 16 for **lāte.**

TASK 19   Individual test

Call on different children to do task 16, 17, or 18.

TASK 20   Children rhyme with an

a. Touch the ball for **an.** Sound it out.
b. Get ready. Touch **a, n** as the children say *aaannn.*
 If sounding out is not firm, repeat *b.*
c. What word? (Signal.) *An.* Yes, **an.**
d. Quickly touch the ball for **tan.** This word rhymes with (pause) **an.**
 Get ready. Move your finger quickly along the arrow. *Tan.*
e. What word? (Signal.) *Tan.* Yes, **tan.**

TASK 21   Children sound out the word and tell what word

a. Touch the ball for **tan.** Sound it out.
b. Get ready. Touch **t, a, n** as the children say *taaannn.*
c. Again. Repeat *b* until firm.
d. Yes, what word? (Signal.) *Tan.*

Do not touch any small letters.

mēat

mēan

lāte

an

tan

SUMMARY OF INDEPENDENT ACTIVITY

TASK 25   Introduction to independent activity

a. Hold up Take-Home 91.
b. Everybody, you're going to finish this take-home on your own.
Tell the children when they will work the remaining items.
Let's go over the things you're going to do.

TASK 26   Sentence copying

Point to the first line in the sentence-copying exercise on side 1.
Remember—you're going to write this sentence on the arrows below.

TASK 27   Sound writing

a. Point to the sound-writing exercise. Here are the sounds you're
going to write today. I'll touch the sounds. You say them.
b. Touch each sound. *The children respond.*
c. Repeat the series until firm.

TASK 28   Matching

Point to the column of words in the Matching Game.
Remember—you're going to follow the lines and write these words.

TASK 29   Cross-out game

Point to the boxed word in the Cross-out Game. Everybody, here's
the word you're going to cross out today. What word? (Signal.)
Sit. Yes, **sit**.

TASK 30   Pair relations

a. Point to the pair-relations exercise on side 2. You're going to
circle the picture in each box that shows what the words say.
b. Point to the space at the top of the page. After you finish,
remember to draw a picture that shows **now I will run**.

END OF LESSON 91

Take-Home 74

STORY

Do not clap for any small letters.

TASK 22 First reading—children sound out each word and tell what word

a. Pass out Take-Home 74. Do not let the children look at the picture until task 26.

b. Get ready to read the story. Everybody, touch the first word.
Check children's responses.

c. Get ready. Clap for each sound. *Hēēē.*

d. Again. (Pause.) Get ready. Clap for each sound. *Hēēē.*
What word? (Signal.) *He.* Yes, **he.**

e. Next word. Check children's responses. Get ready.
Clap for each sound *Haaasss.*

f. Again. (Pause.) Get ready. Clap for each sound. *Haaasss.*
What word? (Signal.) *Has.* Yes, **has.**

g. Repeat *e* and *f* for the remaining words in the story.

TASK 23 Second reading—children sound out each word and tell what word

a. Let's read the story again. Everybody, touch the first word.
Check children's responses.

b. Get ready. Clap for each sound. *Hēēē.* What word? (Signal.)
He. Yes, **he.**

c. Next word. Check children's responses. Get ready. Clap for each
sound. *Haaasss.* What word? (Signal.) *Has.* Yes, **has.**

d. Repeat *c* for the remaining words in the story.

TASK 24 Individual test

Call on different children to read one word. The child sounds out the
word only one time, then tells what word. The other children are to
point under the sounds that are said.

TASK 25 Teacher and children read the fast way

a. Let's read the fast way. Touch under **fat**. This word is **fat**.
Touch under **sēēd**. This word is **seed**.

b. Point to **fat**. What are you going to say when I touch this word?
(Signal.) *Fat.*

c. Point to **sēēd**. What are you going to say when I touch this word?
(Signal.) *Seed.*

d. Repeat *b* and *c* until firm.

e. My turn. Touch under the words as you say: He has an ant.
That ant ate a . . . .

f. Your turn. Touch under the words as the children say *fat seed.*

g. Repeat *e* and *f* until firm.

TASK 26 Picture comprehension

a. The picture you will see shows that he has . . . . (Signal.) *An ant.*

b. And that ant ate . . . . (Signal.) *A fat seed.*

c. Yes, the picture you will see shows that he has . . . . (Signal.)
An ant.

d. And that ant ate . . . . (Signal.) *A fat seed.*

e. Turn your take-home over and look at the picture.

f. Ask these questions:
  1. Who is eating? *The children respond.* Yes, an ant.
  2. What is that ant eating? *The children respond.*
He's eating a seed.
  3. How would you like to have that ant on your table?
The children respond.

TASK 27 Word finding

a. Turn your take-home back to side 1. Everybody, let's play
Find-the-Words. Look at the words in your story and get ready.

b. One of the words is (pause) **has**. Get ready to touch **has** when I
clap. (Pause three seconds.) Get ready. Clap.
*(The children touch **has**.)*

c. Repeat *b* for these words: **an, has, a, an, has, a, an, a, has, an, a.**

d. Repeat *b* and *c* until firm.

Take-Home 91

SENTENCE COPYING

TASK 23 Children read the sentence they will copy

a. Pass out Take-Home 91 to each child.

b. Hold up side 1 of your take-home. Point to the first sentence, **now I will run.**

c. Here's the sentence you're going to write on the lines below. Everybody, touch this sentence on your take-home. Check children's responses.

d. Get ready to read the words in this sentence the fast way. First word. Check children's responses. (Pause.) Get ready. Clap for each word as the children read: *Now I will run.*

e. Have the children reread the sentence at least once.

f. Point to the dotted words on the second arrow. You're going to write the dotted words on this arrow. Then you're going to write those words on the other arrows.

g. After you finish your take-home, you get to draw a picture about the sentence, **now I will run.**

h. Turn your take-home over. Point to the space at the top of the page. Here's where you are going to draw your picture.

i. What are you going to draw? (Signal.) *The children respond.* Yes, a picture that shows **now I will run.**

j. Repeat *i* until firm.

k. You will write the sentences and draw the picture later. Now turn your take-home back to side 1.

MATCHING
The children will need pencils.

TASK 24 Children follow the line and write the matching word

a. Point to the column of words in the matching exercise on side 1.

b. The lines show where the words are that match. But words are missing. Everybody, you're going to touch the word **hat**. (Pause four seconds.) Get ready. (Signal.) Check children's responses.

c. Follow the dotted line to where the other word **hat** should be. (Signal.) Check children's responses.

d. Where's the word **hat**? It's missing. You're going to have to write it in. Everybody, take your pencil and write the word **hat** where it should be. Check children's responses.

e. Everybody, you're going to touch the word **rag**. (Pause four seconds.) Get ready. (Signal.) Check children's responses.

f. Follow the dotted line to where the other word **rag** should be. Check children's responses.

g. Where is the word **rag**? (Signal.) *It's missing.* You're going to have to write it in. Everybody, take your pencil and write the word **rag** where it should be. Check children's responses.

h. You'll write the rest of the words later. Remember to follow the lines.

SUMMARY OF INDEPENDENT ACTIVITY

TASK 28   Introduction to independent activity

a. Hold up Take-Home 74.
b. **Everybody, you're going to finish this take-home on your own.**
Tell the children when they will work the remaining items.
Let's go over the things you're going to do.

TASK 29   Story copying

Point to the dotted words below the story on side 1.   **You're going to write the dotted words on this arrow. Then you're going to write those words on the other arrows.**

TASK 30   Matching

a. Point to the first column of words in the Matching Game.
b. **Everybody, get ready to read each of the words over here.**
Touch the sounds as the children sound out the word.
Then ask: **What word?**   (Signal.) *The children respond.*
c. Point to the first column.   **You're going to make lines for every word over here.**

TASK 31   Cross-out game

Point to the boxed sounds in the Cross-out Game.   **Everybody, what sound are you going to cross out today?**   (Signal.) *d.*
What sound are you going to circle?   (Signal.) *g.*

TASK 32   Sound writing

a. Point to the sound-writing exercise on side 2.   **Here are the sounds you're going to write today. I'll touch the sounds. You say them.**
b. Touch each sound. *The children respond.*
c. Repeat the series until firm.

TASK 33   Pair relations

a. Point to the pair-relations exercise.
b. **Everybody, remember the rule. If the picture doesn't show what the word says, you cross out the box.**
c. Point to the first box.   **This word is sad. What word?**   (Signal.) *Sad.*
Everybody, does the picture show someone who is sad?   (Signal.)
Yes.   **Are you going to cross it out?**   (Signal.) *No.*
d. If the children's responses are not firm, repeat c with one or more boxes.

TASK 34   Story picture

Point to the story picture.   **After you finish your take-home, you can color the story picture.**

END OF LESSON 74

Story 91

Do not clap for any small letters.

TASK 17 First reading—children sound out each word and tell what word

a. Pass out Storybook 1.
b. There are stories in this book. We're going to read one of them now.
c. Open your book to page 1 and get ready to read.
Check children's responses.

d. Clap for the sounds in each word as the children sound out each word one time and tell what word.

TASK 18 Second reading—children reread the story and answer questions

a. This time you'll read the story and I'll ask questions.
b. Repeat *d* in task 17. Ask the comprehension questions below as the children read.

After the children read:	You say:
I am late.	Who is late? (Signal.) *I am.*
I ate ham on a hill.	What did I do? (Signal.) *Ate ham on a hill.*
And now I am late.	What's wrong? (Signal.) *I am late.* Why am I late? (Signal.) *I ate ham on a hill.*
I will run.	What am I going to do? (Signal.) *Run.*

TASK 19 Picture comprehension

a. What do you think you'll see in the picture? *The children respond.*
b. Turn the page and look at the picture.
c. Ask these questions:
  1. What is he doing? *The children respond.*
He's running down the hill.

  2. What do you think he's late for? *The children respond.*
  3. Were you ever late? *The children respond.*

TASK 20 Children read the story the fast way

a. Turn back to page 1. Everybody, touch the first word of the story.
Check children's responses.

b. Move along the line until you come to a period.
Check children's responses.

c. Again. Repeat *a* and *b* until firm.
d. Now you're going to read the words in that sentence the fast way.
e. First word. Check children's responses. Get ready. Clap. *I.*
f. Next word. Check children's responses. Get ready. Clap. *Am.*
g. Repeat *f* for the remaining word in the first sentence.
h. After the children read **late,** say: Stop. That's the end of the first sentence.

i. Have the children reread the first sentence until firm.
j. Reading the words in the next sentence the fast way.
k. First word. Check children's responses. Get ready. Clap. *I.*
l. Clap for each remaining word in the second sentence. Pause at least three seconds between claps. Pause longer before words that gave the children trouble during the first reading.
m. Read that sentence again the fast way. Repeat *k* and *l* until firm.
n. Use the procedures in *j* through *m* for the remaining sentences in the story.

TASK 21 Individual test

a. Everybody, finger on the ball of the top line.
Check children's responses.

b. We're going to have different children read the fast way.
Everybody's going to touch the words.

c. First word. Check children's responses. Call on a child. Clap.
The child responds.

d. Next word. Check children's responses. Call on a child. Clap.
The child responds.

e. Repeat *d* for the remaining word in the first sentence.

TASK 22 Sentence saying

Good reading. Now, everybody, say all the words in that sentence without looking. (Signal.) *The children repeat the sentence at a normal speaking rate.*

Lesson 75

SOUNDS

TASK 1 Teacher and children play the sounds game

m	

a. Use acetate and crayon. Write the
   sounds in the symbol box.
   Keep score in the score box.
b. I'm smart. I bet I can beat you in
   a game.
c. Here's the rule. When I touch
   a sound, you say it.
d. Play the game.
   Make one symbol at a time in the
   symbol box. Use the symbols
   i, c, n, t, and **s.**
   Make each symbol quickly.
   (Pause.) Touch the symbol.
   Play the game for about two
   minutes.
   Then ask: Who won? Draw a
   mouth on the face in the score
   box.

TASK 2 Child plays teacher

a. Use acetate and crayon.
b. [Child's name] is going to be the
   teacher.
c. [He or She] is going to touch
   the sounds. When [he or she]
   touches a sound, you say it.
d. The child points to and touches
   the sounds. You circle any sound
   that is not firm.
e. After the child has completed the
   page, present all the circled
   sounds to the children.

TASK 3 Individual test

Call on different children. If you
can say the sound when I call your
name, you may cross it out.

u

g

o

th

ē

h   a   l

After you read the words on this page, you'll get to read the words the fast way.

Do not touch any small letters.

TASK 9   Children sound out the word and tell what word

a. Touch the ball for **dish.** Sound it out.
b. Get ready.   Touch **d, i, sh** as the children say *diiishshsh*.

If sounding out is not firm, repeat *b*.

c. What word?   (Signal.) *Dish*.   Yes, **dish**.

TASK 10   Children sound out the word and tell what word

Repeat the procedures in task 9 for **will.**

TASK 11   Children sound out the word and tell what word

Repeat the procedures in task 9 for **now.**

TASK 12   Children sound out the word and tell what word

Repeat the procedures in task 9 for **licks.**

TASK 13   Children sound out an irregular word (said)

a. Touch the ball for **said.** Sound it out.
b. Get ready.   Quickly touch each sound as the children say *sssaaaiiid*.
c. Again.   Repeat *b* until firm.
d. That's how we <u>sound out</u> the word. Here's how we <u>say</u> the word.
                      Said. How do we <u>say</u> the word?   (Signal.) *Said*.
e. Now you're going to <u>sound out</u> the word. Get ready.
                      <u>Touch</u> each sound as the children say *sssaaaiiid*.
f. Now you're going to say the word. Get ready.   (Signal.) *Said*.
g. Repeat *e* and *f* until firm.
h. Yes, this word is **said**. The boy **said**, "You are my friend."

TASK 14   Individual test—Have children do *e* and *f* in task 13.

TASK 15   Children read the words the fast way

Have the children read the words on this page the fast way.

TASK 16   Individual test—Have children read one word the fast way.

dish

will

now

licₖs

said

READING VOCABULARY

Do not touch any small letters.

TASK 4   Children sound out the word, then read it the fast way

a. Touch the ball for **sand.** Sound it out.
b. Get ready.   Touch **s, a, n, d** as the children say *sssaaannnd.*
                        If sounding out is not firm, repeat *b.*
c. What word?   (Signal.) *Sand.* Yes, **sand.**
d. Return to the ball. Get ready to read the word the fast way.
        I'm going to count to five. See if you can remember the word.
e. 1, 2, 3, 4, 5. Get ready.   Move your finger quickly along the arrow.
                        Sand. Yes, **sand.** Good reading.

f. Again.   Repeat *e* until firm.

TASK 5   Individual test

Call on different children to do *e* in task 4.

TASK 6   Children sound out the word, then read it the fast way

a. Touch the ball for **lāte.** Sound it out.
b. Get ready.   Touch **l, ā, t** as the children say *lllāāāt.*
                        If sounding out is not firm, repeat *b.*
c. What word?   (Signal.) *Late.* Yes, **late.**
d. Return to the ball. Get ready to read the word the fast way.
        I'm going to count to five. See if you can remember the word.
e. 1, 2, 3, 4, 5. Get ready.   Move your finger quickly along the arrow.
                        Late. Yes, **late.** Good reading.

f. Again.   Repeat *e* until firm.

TASK 7   Individual test

Call on different children to do *e* in task 6.

TASK 8   Children sound out the word, then read it the fast way

Repeat the procedures in task 6 for **rain.**

TASK 9   Individual test

Call on different children to do *e* in task 6 for **rain.**

READING VOCABULARY

After you read the words on this page, you'll get to read the words the fast way.

Do not touch any small letters.

ēₐrs

tēₐrs

wish

win

TASK 4   Children rhyme with ēars

a. Touch the ball for **ēars.** Sound it out.
b. Get ready. Touch **ē, r, s** as the children say *ēēērrrsss.*
　　　　　　　　If sounding out is not firm, repeat *b.*
c. What word? (Signal.) *Ears.* Yes, **ears.**
d. Quickly touch the ball for **tēars.** This word rhymes with (pause)
　　　　ears. Get ready. Touch **t.** *t.* Move your finger quickly along
　　　　　　　　　　　　　　the arrow. *Tears.*

e. What word? (Signal.) *Tears.* Yes, **tears.**

TASK 5 Children sound out the word and tell what word

a. Touch the ball for **wish.** Sound it out.
b. Get ready. Touch **w, i, sh** as the children say *wwwiiishshsh.*
　　　　　　　　If sounding out is not firm, repeat *b.*
c. What word? (Signal.) *Wish.* Yes, **wish.**

TASK 6   Children sound out the word and tell what word

a. Touch the ball for **win.** Sound it out.
b. Get ready. Touch **w, i, n** as the children say *wwwiiinnn.*
　　　　　　　　If sounding out is not firm, repeat *b.*
c. What word? (Signal.) *Win.* Yes, **win.**

TASK 7   Children read the words the fast way

a. Now you get to read the words on this page the fast way.
b. Touch the ball for **ēars.** (Pause three seconds.) Get ready.
　　　　Move your finger quickly along the arrow. *Ears.* Yes, **ears.**
c. Repeat *b* for each word on the page.

TASK 8   Individual test

Call on different children to read one word the fast way.

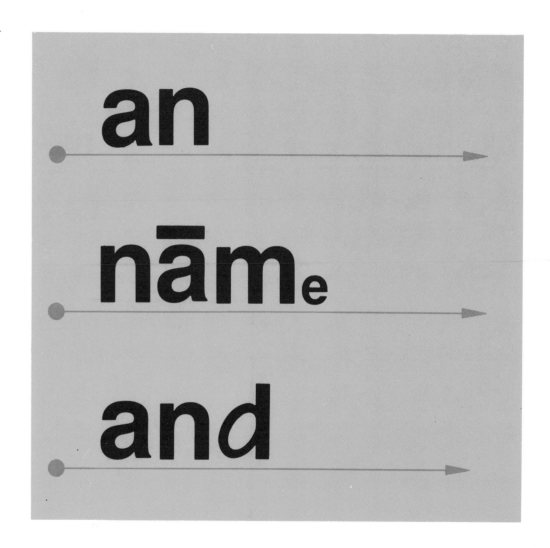

After you read the words on this page, you'll get to read the words in the box the fast way.

Do not touch any small letters.

To correct	For all mistakes, have the children sound out the word and say it fast. Then say: **Remember this word.**

TASK 10   Children sound out the word and tell what word

a. Touch the ball for **an.** Sound it out.
b. Get ready.   Touch **a, n** as the children say *aaannn.*
                              If sounding out is not firm, repeat *b.*
c. What word?   (Signal.) *An.* Yes, **an.**

TASK 11   Children sound out the word and tell what word

a. Touch the ball for **nāme.** Sound it out.
b. Get ready.   Touch **n, ā, m** as the children say *nnnāāāmmm.*
                              If sounding out is not firm, repeat *b.*
c. What word?   (Signal.) *Name.* Yes, **name.**

TASK 12   Children sound out the word and tell what word

a. Touch the ball for **and.** Sound it out.
b. Get ready.   Touch **a, n, d** as the children say *aaannnd.*
                              If sounding out is not firm, repeat *b.*
c. What word?   (Signal.) *And.* Yes, **and.**

TASK 13   Children read the words in the box the fast way

a. Now you're going to read the words in the box the fast way.
b. Touch the ball for **an.** (Pause three seconds.) Get ready.
                              Move your finger quickly along the arrow. *An.*
c. Repeat *b* for the words **nāme** and **and.**
d. Present the series **an, nāme, and** at least two times.

TASK 14   Individual test

Call on different children to read one word in the box the fast way.

Lesson 91

Groups that are firm on Mastery Tests 16 and 17 should skip this lesson and do lesson 92 today.

SOUNDS

TASK 1 Teacher and children play the sounds game

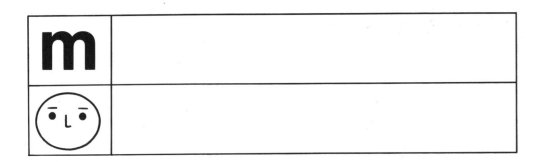

a. Use acetate and crayon. Write the sounds in the symbol box. Keep score in the score box.
b. I'm smart. I bet I can beat you in a game.
c. Here's the rule. When I touch a sound, you say it.
d. Play the game.
Make one symbol at a time in the symbol box. Use the symbols **g, d, u,** and **ā.**
Make each symbol quickly. (Pause.) Touch the symbol.
Play the game for about two minutes.
Then ask: **Who won?** Draw a mouth on the face in the score box.

TASK 2 Child plays teacher

a. Use acetate and crayon.
b. [Child's name] is going to be the teacher.
c. [He or She] is going to touch the sounds. When [he or she] touches a sound, you say it.
d. The child points to and touches the sounds. You circle any sound that is not firm.
e. After the child has completed the page, present all the circled sounds to the children.

TASK 3 Individual test

Call on different children. If you can say the sound when I call your name, you may cross it out.

TASK 15 Children rhyme with sick

a. Touch the ball for **sick.** Sound it out.
b. Get ready. Touch **s, i, c** as the children say *sssiiic.*
　　　　　　　　　　　　If sounding out is not firm, repeat *b.*
c. What word? (Signal.) *Sick.* Yes, **sick.**
d. Quickly touch the ball for **lick.** This word rhymes with (pause) **sick.**
　Get ready. Touch **l.** *lll.* Move quickly along the arrow. *Lllick.*
e. What word? (Signal.) *Lick.* Yes, **lick.**

TASK 16 Children read a word beginning with a stop sound (hāte)

a. Run your finger under **āte.** You're going to sound out this part.
　　　　　　　　　　Get ready. Touch **ā, t** as the children say *āāāt.*
b. Say it fast. (Signal.) *Ate.* Yes, this part says (pause) **ate.**
c. Repeat *a* and *b* until firm.
d. Touch the ball for **hāte.** This word rhymes with (pause) **āāt.**
　　　　　　　　Get ready. Move quickly along the arrow. *Hate.*
e. What word? (Signal.) *Hate.* Yes, **hate.**
f. Repeat *d* and *e* until firm.
g. Return to the ball. Now you're going to sound out (pause) **hate.**
　　　　　Get ready. Quickly touch **h, ā, t** as the children say *hāāāt.*
h. What word? (Signal.) *Hate.* Yes, **hate.** Good reading.
　Do you **hate** monsters?
i. Repeat *g* and *h* until firm.

TASK 17 Children read a word beginning with a stop sound (cāme)

Repeat the procedures in task 16 for **cāme.**

TASK 18 Children read the words the fast way

---

a. Now you get to read these words the fast way.
b. Touch the ball for **lick.** (Pause three seconds.) Get ready.
　　　　　　　　Move your finger quickly along the arrow. *Lick.*
c. Repeat *b* for **sick, hāte,** and **cāme.**
d. Have the children sound out the words they had difficulty identifying.

TASK 19 Individual test

Call on different children to read one word the fast way.

Do not touch any small letters.

sick

lick

hāte

cāme

Mastery Test 17 after lesson 90, before lesson 91

a. When I touch the sound, you say it.
b. **(test item)** Point to **w.** Get ready. Touch **w.** *www.*
c. **(test item)** Point to **g.** Get ready. Touch **g.** *g.*
d. **(test item)** Point to **sh.** Get ready. Touch **sh.** *shshsh.*
e. **(test item)** Point to **l.** Get ready. Touch **l.** *lll.*
f. **(test item)** Point to **o.** Get ready. Touch **o.** *ooo.*

Total number of test items: **5**

A group is weak if more than one-third of the children missed any of the items on the test.

w

g

sh

l

o

WHAT TO DO

If the group is firm on Mastery Test 17 and was firm on Mastery Test 16:

Skip lesson 91 and present lesson 92 to the group during the next reading period. If more than one child missed any of the items on the test, present the firming procedures specified below to those children.

If the group is firm on Mastery Test 17 but was weak on Mastery Test 16:

Present lesson 91 to the group during the next reading period. If more than one child missed any of the items on the test, present the firming procedures specified below to those children.

If the group is weak on Mastery Test 17:

A. Present these firming procedures to the group during the next reading period.
  1. Lesson 88, Sounds, page 200, tasks 5, 6.
  2. Lesson 88, Reading Vocabulary, page 201, tasks 7 through 13.
  3. Lesson 89, Reading Vocabulary, page 207, tasks 6 through 11.
  4. Lesson 89, Sounds, page 206, tasks 4, 5.
B. After presenting the above tasks, again give Mastery Test 17 individually to members of the group who failed the test.
C. If the group is firm (less than one-third of the total group missed any items on the retest), present lesson 91 to the group during the next reading period.
D. If the group is still weak (more than one-third of the total group missed any items on the retest), repeat A and B during the next reading period.

Take-Home 75

STORY
Do not clap for any small letters.

TASK 20 First reading—children sound out each word and tell what word

---

a. Pass out Take-Home 75. Do not let the children look at the picture
until task 22.

b. Get ready to read the story. First word. Check children's responses.

c. Get ready. Clap for each sound. *Hēēē.* What word? (Signal.) *He.*
Yes, **he.**

d. Next word. Check children's responses.

e. Get ready. Clap for each sound. *Aāāt.* What word? (Signal.) *Ate.*
Yes, **ate.**

f. Repeat d and e for the remaining words in the story.

TASK 21 Second reading—children reread the story and answer questions

---

a. This time you'll read the story and I'll ask questions.
Back to the first word. Check children's responses.

b. Repeat c through f in task 20. Ask the comprehension questions
below as the children read.

After the children read:	You say:
He ate a fig.	What did he eat? (Signal.) *A fig.*
And he is sick.	How does he feel? (Signal.) *Sick.* Why? (Signal.) *Because he ate a fig.*
To correct	If the children do not give acceptable answers, have them reread the sentence that answers the question. Then ask the question again.

TASK 22 Picture comprehension

a. What do you think you are going to see in the picture?
The children respond.

b. Turn your take-home over and look at the picture.

c. Ask these questions:
 1. Is he eating a fig? *The children respond.* No.
 2. Why is he sick? *The children respond.* He ate a fig.
 3. What is that thing in his mouth? *The children respond.*
A thermometer.
 4. What's the doctor going to do to make him feel better?
The children respond.

TASK 23 Word finding

a. Turn your take-home back to side 1. Everybody, look at the words
in the top line. One of the words is **he.**

b. Get ready to touch **he** when I clap. (Pause three seconds.)
Get ready. Clap. *(The children touch* **hē.***)*

c. Repeat b for these words: **fig, hē, āte, fig, āte, fig, hē, āte, hē,
fig, āte.**

TASK 24 Children read the first sentence the fast way

---

a. Everybody, now you're going to read part of the story the fast way.
Finger on the ball of the top line. Check children's responses.

b. Move your finger under the sounds of the first word and figure out
the sounds you're going to say. Don't say the sounds out loud.
Just figure out what you're going to say. Check children's
responses. Prompt children who don't touch under the sounds.
(Pause five seconds.) Read the word the fast way. Get ready.
Clap. Say **he** with the children. *He.*

c. Next word. Move your finger under the sounds and figure out the
sounds. Check children's responses. (Pause five seconds.) Read
the word the fast way. Get ready. Clap. Say **ate** with the children.
Ate.

d. Repeat c for the words **a, fig.**

TURN THE PAGE FOR THE REST OF TASK 24.

SUMMARY OF INDEPENDENT ACTIVITY

TASK 26   Introduction to independent activity

a. Hold up Take-Home 90.
b. Everybody, you're going to finish this take-home on your own.
Tell the children when they will work the remaining items.
Let's go over the things you're going to do.

TASK 27   Story copying

Point to the dotted words below the story on side 1. You're going to write the dotted words on this arrow. Then you're going to write those words on the other arrows.

TASK 28   Cross-out game

Point to the boxed word in the Cross-out Game. Everybody, here's the word you're going to cross out today. What word? (Signal.) *She*. Yes, **she**.

TASK 29   Matching

a. Point to the first column of words in the Matching Game.
b. Everybody, get ready to read each of the words over here.
Reading the fast way.
c. Point to the first word. Get ready. (Signal.) *The children respond.*
d. Repeat *c* for the remaining words.
e. Point to the first column. You're going to make lines for every word over here.

TASK 30   Sound writing

a. Point to the sound-writing exercise on side 2. Here are the sounds you're going to write today. I'll touch the sounds. You say them.
b. Touch each sound. *The children respond.*
c. Repeat the series until firm.

TASK 31   Pair relations

a. Point to the word **rag** in the first row of the pair-relations exercise.
b. Everybody, touch this box on your take-home.
Check children's responses.
c. Get ready to tell me this word. (Pause.) What word? (Signal.) *Rag*.
d. You're going to circle the picture that shows a (pause) **rag**. Do it.
Check children's responses.
e. Point to the other boxes. Remember—you're going to circle the picture in each box that shows what the words say.

TASK 32   Story picture

Point to the story picture. After you finish your take-home, you can color the story picture.

END OF LESSON 90

Before presenting lesson 91, give Mastery Test 17 to each child.
Do not present lesson 91 to any groups that are not firm on this test.

e. **Let's read the words the fast way again. Everybody, finger on the ball of the top line.** Check children's responses. **Figure out the first word and get ready to read it the fast way. Say the sounds to yourself.** (Pause five seconds.) **What word?** Clap. *He.* **Yes, he.**

f. **Figure out the next word. Say the sounds to yourself.** (Pause five seconds.) **What word?** Clap. *Ate.* **Yes, ate.**

g. Repeat *f* for the words **a, fig.**

TASK 25   Individual test

a. **Everybody, finger on the ball of the top line.**
Check children's responses.

b. **We're going to have different children read. Everybody's going to touch the words.**

c. **Everybody, touch the first word.** Check children's responses.

d. Call on a child. **Reading the fast way. Get ready.** Clap. *He.*

e. **Next word.** Check children's responses.

f. **Everybody reading. Get ready.** Clap. *Ate.*

g. **Next word.** Check children's responses.

h. Call on a child. **Get ready.** Clap. *A.*

i. Repeat *e* and *f* for **fig.**

SUMMARY OF INDEPENDENT ACTIVITY

TASK 26   Introduction to independent activity

a. Hold up Take-Home 75.

b. **Everybody, you're going to finish this take-home on your own.** Tell the children when they will work the remaining items. **Let's go over the things you're going to do.**

TASK 27   Story copying

Point to the dotted words below the story on side 1. **You're going to write the dotted words on this arrow. Then you're going to write those words on the other arrows.**

TASK 28   Matching

a. Point to the first column of words in the Matching Game.

b. **Everybody, get ready to read each of the words over here.** Touch the sounds as the children sound out the word. Then ask: **What word?** (Signal.) *The children respond.*

c. Point to the first column. **You're going to make lines for every word over here.**

TASK 29   Cross-out game

Point to the boxed sounds in the Cross-out Game. **Everybody, what sound are you going to circle today?** (Signal.) *āāā.* **What sound are you going to cross out?** (Signal.) *lll.*

TASK 30   Sound writing

a. Point to the sound-writing exercise on side 2. **Here are the sounds you're going to write today. I'll touch the sounds. You say them.**

b. Touch each sound. *The children respond.*

c. Repeat the series until firm.

TASK 31   Pair relations

a. Point to the pair-relations exercise.

b. **Everybody, remember the rule. If the picture doesn't show what the word says, you cross out the box.**

c. Point to the first box. **This word is sick. What word?** (Signal.) *Sick.* **Everybody, does the picture show someone who is sick?** (Signal.) *No.* **Are you going to cross it out?** (Signal.) *Yes.*

d. If the children's responses are not firm, repeat *c* with one or more boxes.

TASK 32   Story picture

Point to the story picture. **After you finish your take-home, you can color the story picture.**

END OF LESSON 75

Before presenting lesson 76, give Mastery Test 14 to each child.
Do not present lesson 76 to any groups that are not firm on this test.

TASK 22   Children read the first sentence the fast way

a. Everybody, get ready to read all the words in the first sentence the fast way.

b. Touch the first word. Check children's responses.
(Pause three seconds.) Get ready. Clap. *A.*

c. Next word. Check children's responses. (Pause three seconds.)
Get ready. Clap. *Fish.*

d. Repeat *c* for the words **made, a, wish.**

e. After the children read **wish,** say: Stop. That's the end of the sentence.

f. Let's read that sentence again, the fast way.

g. First word. Check children's responses. Get ready. Clap. *A.*

h. Next word. Check children's responses. Get ready. Clap. *Fish.*

i. Repeat *h* for the words **made, a, wish.**

j. After the children read **wish,** say: Stop. You've read the first sentence.

TASK 23   Children read the second sentence the fast way

a. Everybody, put your finger on the period after **wish.**
Check children's responses.

b. Now move along the arrows until you find the next period.
Check children's responses.

c. Repeat *a* and *b* until firm.

d. Put your finger on the period after **wish.**
Check children's responses.

e. Get ready to read all the words until we come to the next period.

f. Starting with the first word after **wish.** Check children's responses.
(Pause three seconds.) Get ready. Clap. *I.*

g. Next word. Check children's responses. (Pause three seconds.)
Get ready. Clap. *Wish.*

h. Repeat *g* for the remaining words in the second sentence.

i. After the children read **feet,** say: Stop. You've read the sentence.

j. Let's read it again. Go back to the period after **wish.**
Check children's responses.
Get ready to read all the words in the sentence.

k. First word. Check children's responses. Get ready. Clap. *I.*

l. Next word. Check children's responses. Get ready. Clap. *Wish.*

m. Repeat *l* for the remaining words in the second sentence.

TASK 24   Individual test

a. Everybody, finger on the ball of the top line.
Check children's responses.

b. We're going to have different children read the fast way.
Everybody's going to touch the words.

c. First word. Check children's responses. Call on a child. Clap.
The child responds.

d. Next word. Check children's responses. Call on a child.
Clap. *The child responds.*

e. Repeat *d* for the remaining words in the first sentence.

TASK 25   Sentence saying

Good reading. Now, everybody, say all the words in that sentence without looking. (Signal.) *The children repeat the sentence at a normal speaking rate.*

Mastery Test 14 after lesson 75, before lesson 76

a. Touch the first word. *(The child responds.)* Get ready. Clap for each sound. *Hēēē.*
b. Again. (Pause.) Get ready. Clap for each sound. *Hēēē.*
c. **(test item)** What word? (Signal.) *He.*
d. Next word. *(The child responds.)* Get ready. Clap for each sound. *Iiisss.*
e. Again. (Pause.) Get ready. Clap for each sound. *Iiisss.*
f. **(test item)** What word? (Signal.) *Is.*
g. Next word. *(The child responds.)* Get ready. Clap for each sound. *Sssiiic.*
h. Again. (Pause.) Get ready. Clap for each sound. *Sssiiic.*
i. **(test item)** What word? (Signal.) *Sick.*
j. Next word. *(The child responds.)* Get ready. Clap for each sound. *Aaannnd.*
k. Again. (Pause.) Get ready. Clap for each sound. *Aaannnd.*
l. **(test item)** What word? (Signal.) *And.*
m. Next word. *(The child responds.)* Get ready. Clap for each sound. *Sssaaad.*
n. Again. (Pause.) Get ready. Clap for each sound. *Sssaaad.*
o. **(test item)** What word? (Signal.) *Sad.*

Total number of test items: **5**

A group is weak if more than one-third of the children missed any of the items on the test.

hē ▪ is ▪ sicₖ
anₐ▪ saₐ.

WHAT TO DO

If the group is firm on Mastery Test 14 and was firm on Mastery Test 13:

Present lesson 76, skip lesson 77, present lesson 78, and skip lesson 79. If more than one child missed any of the items on the test, present the firming procedures specified below to those children.

If the group is firm on Mastery Test 14 but was weak on Mastery Test 13:

Present lesson 76 to the group during the next reading period. If more than one child missed any of the items on the test present the firming procedures specified below to those children.

If the group is weak on Mastery Test 14:

A. Present these firming procedures to the group during the next reading period. Present each story until the children can read it without making a mistake. Then proceed to the next story.
   1. Lesson 73, Story, page 110, tasks 20, 21, 22.
   2. Lesson 74, Story, page 116, tasks 22, 23, 24.
   3. Lesson 75, Story, page 122. Present task 20 two times. Then call on individual children to sound out a word and tell what word.
   Duplicate stories for lessons 73, 74, and 75 are provided in the Teacher's Guide. You may reproduce these stories for use in presenting the firming procedures.
B. After presenting the above tasks, again give Mastery Test 14 individually to members of the group who failed the test.
C. If the group is firm (less than one-third of the total group missed any items on the retest), present lesson 76 to the group during the next reading period.
D. If the group is still weak (more than one-third of the total group missed any items on the retest), repeat *A* and *B* during the next reading period.

Take-Home 90

STORY
Do not clap for any small letters.

TASK 18 **First reading—children sound out each word and tell what word**

a. Pass out Take-Home 90. Do not let the children look at the picture

until task 20.

b. Get ready to read the story.

c. First word. (Pause.) Get ready. Clap. *Aaa.*

What word? (Signal.) *A.* Yes, **a.**

d. Next word. (Pause.) Get ready. Clap for each sound. *Fffiiishshsh.*

What word? (Signal.) *Fish.* Yes, **fish.**

e. Repeat *d* for the remaining words in the story.

TASK 19 **Second reading—children reread the story and answer questions**

a. This time you'll read the story and I'll ask questions.

b. Repeat *c* through *e* in task 18. Ask the comprehension questions

below as the children read.

After the children read:	You say:
A fish made a wish.	What did the fish do? (Signal.) *Made a wish.*
I wish I had feet.	What did that fish say? (Signal.) *I wish I had feet.*
I wish I had a tail.	The fish wanted feet and what else? (Signal.) *A tail.*
I wish I had a hat.	The fish wanted feet and a tail and what else? (Signal.) *A hat.*
I wish I had a dish.	Name everything the fish wished for. (Signal.) *Feet, tail, hat, and dish.*

TASK 20 **Picture comprehension**

a. What do you think you'll see in the picture? *The children respond.*

b. Turn your take-home over and look at the picture.

c. Show me what the fish is wishing for. *(The children respond.)*

d. Ask these questions:

1. What is the fish wishing for? *The children respond.*

She's wishing for feet, a tail, a hat, and a dish.

2. What would you wish for if you were a fish?

The children respond.

TASK 21 **Period finding**

a. Turn your take-home back to side 1. Everybody, we're going to

read all the words in the first sentence the fast way.

b. Point to the first word. The first <u>sentence</u> begins here and goes

all the way to a little dot called a period. So I just go along

the arrow until I find a period.

c. Touch **a.** Have I come to a period yet? (Signal.) *No.*

Touch **fish.** Have I come to a period yet? (Signal.) *No.*

Touch **māde.** Have I come to a period yet? (Signal.) *No.*

Touch **a.** Have I come to a period yet? (Signal.) *No.*

Touch **wish.** Have I come to a period yet? (Signal.) *Yes.*

d. Again. Repeat *b* and *c* until firm.

e. Everybody, put your finger on the ball of the top line.

Check children's responses.

f. Get ready to find the period for the first sentence. Go along

the arrow until you find that period. Check children's responses.

Lesson 76

w

r

l

u

SOUNDS

TASK 1 Teaching w as in we

a. Point to **w**. Here's a new sound.
b. My turn. (Pause.) Touch **w** and say: www.
c. Again. Touch **w** for a longer time. wwwww. Lift your finger.
d. Point to **w**. Your turn. When I touch it, you say it. (Pause.) Get ready. Touch **w**. *www*. Lift your finger.
e. Again. Touch **w**. *wwwwww*. Lift your finger.
f. Repeat e until firm.

TASK 2 Individual test

Call on different children to identify **w**.

TASK 3 Sounds firm-up

a. Get ready to say the sounds when I touch them.
b. Alternate touching **r** and **w**. Point to the sound. (Pause one second.) Say: Get ready. Touch the sound. *The children respond.*
c. When **r** and **w** are firm, alternate touching **w**, **l**, **r**, and **u** until all four sounds are firm.

TASK 4 Individual test

Call on different children to identify **w**, **l**, **r**, or **u**.

TASK 5 Sounds firm-up

a. Point to **w**. When I touch the sound, you say it.
b. (Pause.) Get ready. Touch **w**. *www*.
c. Again. Repeat b until firm.
d. Get ready to say all the sounds when I touch them.
e. Alternate touching **i, g, ā, o, ē, h, f,** and **w** three or four times.
Point to the sound. (Pause one second.) Say: Get ready. Touch the sound. *The children respond.*

TASK 6 Individual test

Call on different children to identify one or more sounds in task 5.

After you read the words on this page, you'll get to read the words the fast way.

Do not touch any small letters.

with

TASK 12   Children sound out the word and tell what word

a. Touch the ball for **with.** Sound it out.
b. Get ready. Touch **w, i, th** as the children say *wwwiiiththth*.
                              If sounding out is not firm, repeat *b*.
c. What word? (Signal.) *With*. Yes, **with.**

TASK 13   Children sound out the word and tell what word

Repeat the procedures in task 12 for **sacks.**

sac_ks

TASK 14   Children sound out an irregular word (said)

a. Touch the ball for **said.** Sound it out.
b. Get ready. Quickly touch each sound as the children say *sssaaaiiid*.
c. Again. Repeat *b* until firm.
d. That's how we <u>sound out</u> the word. Here's how we <u>say</u> the word.
                    Said. How do we <u>say</u> the word? (Signal.) *Said*.
e. Now you're going to <u>sound out</u> the word. Get ready.
                    Touch each sound as the children say *sssaaaiiid*.
f. Now you're going to say the word. Get ready. (Signal.) *Said*.
g. Repeat *e* and *f* until firm.
h. Yes, this word is **said**. The fish **said**, "Wow."

said

TASK 15   Individual test

Call on different children to do *e* and *f* in task 14.

TASK 16   Children read the words the fast way.

a. Now you get to read the words on this page the fast way.
b. Touch the ball for **with.** (Pause three seconds.) Get ready.
                    Move your finger quickly along the arrow. *With*.
c. Repeat *b* for each word on the page.

TASK 17   Individual test—Have children read one word the fast way.

READING VOCABULARY

TASK 7   Children read a word beginning with a stop sound (hand)

a. Run your finger under **and.** You're going to sound out this part.
Get ready. Touch **a, n, d** as the children say *aaannnd.*
b. Say it fast. (Signal.) *And.* Yes, this part says (pause) **and.**
c. Repeat *a* and *b* until firm.
d. Touch the ball for **hand.** This word rhymes with (pause) **and.**
Get ready. Move quickly along the arrow. *Hand.*
e. What word? (Signal.) *Hand.* Yes, **hand.**
f. Repeat *d* and *e* until firm.
g. Return to the ball. Now you're going to sound out (pause) **hand.**
Get ready. Quickly touch **h, a, n, d** as the children say *haaannnd.*
h. What word? (Signal.) *Hand.* Yes, **hand.** Good reading.
Look at my **hand.**

i. Repeat *g* and *h* until firm.

TASK 8   Individual test

Call on different children to do *g* and *h* in task 7.

TASK 9   Children sound out the word, then read it the fast way

a. Touch the ball for **lock.** Sound it out.
b. Get ready. Touch **l, o, c** as the children say *llloooc.*
If sounding out is not firm, repeat *b.*
c. What word? (Signal.) *Lock.* Yes, **lock.**
d. Return to the ball. Get ready to read the word the fast way.
I'm going to count to five. See if you can remember the word.
e. 1, 2, 3, 4, 5. Get ready. Move your finger quickly along the arrow.
Lock. Yes, **lock.** Good reading.

f. Again. Repeat *e* until firm.

Individual test

Call on different children to do *e* in task 9.

TASK 10   Children read a word beginning with a stop sound (has)

a. Cover **h.** Run your finger under **as.** This part says (pause) **az.**
b. Uncover **h.** Touch the ball for **has.** Rhymes with (pause) **az.**
Get ready. Move quickly along the arrow. *Has.*
c. What word? (Signal.) *Has.* Yes, **has.**
d. Repeat *b* and *c* until firm.
e. Return to the ball. Now you're going to sound out (pause) **has.**
Get ready. Quickly touch **h, a, s** as the children say *haaasss.*
f. What word? (Signal.) *Has.* Yes, **has.** Good reading. She **has**
money.
g. Repeat *e* and *f* until firm.

Individual test

Call on different children to do *e* and *f* in task 10.

hand

lock

has

READING VOCABULARY

After you read the words on this page, you'll get to read the words the fast way.

Do not touch any small letters

TASK 7   Children sound out the word and tell what word

a. Touch the ball for **shē**. Sound it out.
b. Get ready.   Touch **sh, ē** as the children say *shshshēēē*.
　　　　　　　　　If sounding out is not firm, repeat *b*.
c. What word?   (Signal.) *She*. Yes, **she**.

shē

TASK 8   Children sound out the word and tell what word

a. Touch the ball for **shut**. Sound it out.
b. Get ready.   Touch **sh, u, t** as the children say *shshshuuut*.
　　　　　　　　　If sounding out is not firm, repeat *b*.
c. What word?   (Signal.) *Shut*. Yes, **shut**.

shut

TASK 9   Children sound out the word and tell what word

a. Touch the ball for **tacks**. Sound it out.
b. Get ready.   Touch **t, a, c, s** as the children say *taaacsss*.
　　　　　　　　　If sounding out is not firm, repeat *b*.
c. What word?   (Signal.) *Tacks*. Yes, **tacks**.

tacks

TASK 10   Children read the words the fast way

a. Now you get to read the words on this page the fast way.
b. Touch the ball for **shē**. (Pause three seconds.) Get ready.
　　　　　　　　Move your finger quickly along the arrow. *She*.
c. Repeat *b* for each word on the page.

TASK 11   Individual test

Call on different children to read one word the fast way.

TASK 11   Children sound out the word, then read it the fast way

a. Touch the ball for **sack.** Sound it out.
b. Get ready.   Touch **s, a, c** as the children say *sssaaac.*
                  If sounding out is not firm, repeat *b.*
c. What word?   (Signal.) *Sack.* Yes, **sack.**
d. Return to the ball.   Get ready to read the word the fast way.
      I'm going to count to five. See if you can remember the word.
e. 1, 2, 3, 4, 5. Get ready.   Move your finger quickly along the arrow.
               Sack. Yes, **sack.** Good reading.

f. Again.   Repeat *e* until firm.

TASK 12   Individual test

Call on different children to do *e* in task 11.

TASK 13   Children sound out the word, then read it the fast way

a. Touch the ball for **and.** Sound it out.
b. Get ready.   Touch **a, n, d** as the children say *aaannnd.*
                 If sounding out is not firm, repeat *b.*
c. What word?   (Signal.) *And.* Yes, **and.**
d. Return to the ball.   Get ready to read the word the fast way.
      I'm going to count to five. See if you can remember the word.
e. 1, 2, 3, 4, 5. Get ready.   Move your finger quickly along the arrow.
            And. Yes, **and.** Good reading.

f. Again.   Repeat *e* until firm.

TASK 14   Individual test

Call on different children to do *e* in task 13.

TASK 15   Children rhyme with sand

a. Touch the ball for **sand.** Sound it out.
b. Get ready.   Touch **s, a, n, d** as the children say *sssaaannnd.*
                 If sounding out is not firm, repeat *b.*
c. What word?   (Signal.) *Sand.* Yes, **sand.**
d. Quickly touch the ball for **land.** This word rhymes with (pause)
     sand. Get ready.   Touch **l.** *lll.* Move your finger quickly along
                the arrow. *Llland.*
e. What word?   (Signal.) *Land.* Yes, **land.**

Do not touch any small letters.

sack

and

sand

land

Lesson 90

I

t

i

l

SOUNDS

TASK 1 Teaching I as in Ice

a. Point to **I**. **My turn.** (Pause.)
Touch **I** and say: III.
b. Point to **I**. **Your turn. When
I touch it, you say it.** (Pause.)
Get ready. Touch **I**. *III.*
Lift your finger.
c. **Again.** Touch **I**. *III.*
Lift your finger.
d. Repeat *c* until firm.

TASK 2 Sounds firm-up

a. **Get ready to say the sounds
when I touch them.**
b. Alternate touching **I** and **t**. Point
to the sound. (Pause one second.)
Say: **Get ready.** Touch the
sound. *The children respond.*
c. When **I** and **t** are firm, alternate
Touching **t, i, I,** and **I** until all
four sounds are firm.

TASK 3 Individual test

Call on different children to identify **t, i, I,** or **I**.

TASK 4 Teacher introduces cross-out game

a. Use acetate and crayon.
b. **I'll cross out the sounds on this page when you can tell me every
sound.**
c. **Remember—when I touch it, you say it.**
d. Go over the sounds until the children can identify all the sounds
in order.

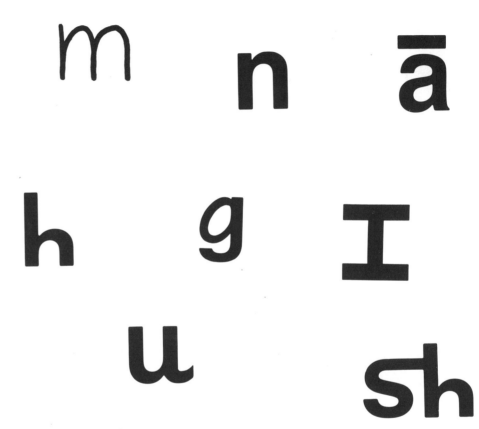

TASK 5 Individual test

Call on different children to identify two or more sounds in task 4.

TASK 6 Teacher crosses out sounds

a. **You told me every sound. Get ready to do it again. This time I'll
cross out each sound when you tell me what it is.**
b. Point to each sound. (Pause.) Say: **Get ready.** Touch the sound.
The children respond. As you cross out the sound, say:
Goodbye, _____.

After you read the words on this page, you'll get to read the words in the box the fast way.

Do not touch any small letters.

To correct	For all mistakes, have the children sound out the word and say it fast. Then say: **Remember this word.**

TASK 16   Children sound out the word and tell what word

a. Touch the ball for **rag.** Sound it out.
b. Get ready. Touch **r, a, g** as the children say *rrraaag.*
　　　　　　　　　If sounding out is not firm, repeat *b.*
c. What word? (Signal.) *Rag.* Yes, **rag.**

TASK 17   Children sound out the word and tell what word

a. Touch the ball for **lāte.** Sound it out.
b. Get ready. Touch **l, ā, t** as the children say *lllāāāt.*
　　　　　　　　　If sounding out is not firm, repeat *b.*
c. What word? (Signal.) *Late.* Yes, **late.**

TASK 18   Children sound out the word and tell what word

a. Touch the ball for **rāin.** Sound it out.
b. Get ready. Touch **r, ā, n** as the children say *rrrāāānnn.*
　　　　　　　　　If sounding out is not firm, repeat *b.*
c. What word? (Signal.) *Rain.* Yes, **rāin.**

TASK 19   Children read the words in the box the fast way

a. Now you're going to read the words in the box the fast way.
b. Touch the ball for **rag.** (Pause three seconds.) Get ready.
　　　　　　　　Move your finger quickly along the arrow. *Rag.*
c. Repeat *b* for the words **lāte** and **rāin.**
d. Present the series **rag, lāte, rāin** at least two times.

TASK 20   Individual test

Call on different children to read one word in the box the fast way.

SUMMARY OF INDEPENDENT ACTIVITY

TASK 25   Introduction to independent activity

a. Hold up Take-Home 89.
b. Everybody, you're going to finish this take-home on your own.
Tell the children when they will work the remaining items.
Let's go over the things you're going to do.

TASK 26   Story copying

Point to the dotted words below the story on side 1. You're going
to write the dotted words on this arrow. Then you're going to write
those words on the other arrows.

TASK 27   Cross-out game

Point to the boxed words in the Cross-out Game. Everybody, here's
the word you're going to cross out today. What word? (Signal.)
Sat. Yes, **sat**.

TASK 28   Matching

a. Point to the first column of words in the Matching Game.
b. Everybody, get ready to read each of the words over here.
Reading the fast way.
c. Point to the first word. Get ready. (Signal.) *The children respond.*
d. Repeat *c* for the remaining words.
e. Point to the first column. You're going to make lines for every
word over here.

TASK 29   Sound writing

a. Point to the sound-writing exercise on side 2. Here are the sounds
you're going to write today. I'll touch the sounds. You say them.
b. Touch each sound. *The children respond.*
c. Repeat the series until firm.

TASK 30   Pair relations

a. Point to the word **sack** in the first row of the pair-relations exercise.
b. Everybody, touch this box on your take-home.
Check children's responses.
c. Get ready to tell me this word. (Pause.) What word? (Signal.) *Sack*.
d. You're going to circle the picture that shows a (pause) **sack**. Do it.
Check children's responses.
e. Point to the other boxes. Remember—you're going to circle the
picture in each box that shows what the words say.

TASK 31   Story picture

Point to the story picture. After you finish your take-home,
you can color the story picture.

END OF LESSON 89

Take-Home 76

STORY
Do not clap for any small letters.

TASK 21 **First reading—children sound out each word and
tell what word**

a. Pass out Take-Home 76. Do not let the children look at the picture
until task 23.
b. Get ready to read the story. First word. Check children's responses.
c. Get ready. Clap for each sound. *Hēēē.* What word? (Signal.) *He.*
Yes, he.

d. Next word. Check children's responses.
e. Get ready. Clap for each sound. *Haaasss.* What word? (Signal.)
Has. **Yes, has.**

f. Repeat *d* and *e* for the remaining words in the story.

TASK 22 **Second reading—children reread the story and
answer questions**

a. This time you'll read the story and I'll ask questions.
Back to the first word. Check children's responses.
b. Repeat *c* through *f* in task 21. Ask the comprehension questions
below as the children read.

After the children read:	You say:
He has a sack.	What does he have? (Signal.) *A sack.*
He has a fan	He has a sack and what else? (Signal.) *A fan.*
and a rat	Can you name all the things he has? (Signal.) *A sack, a fan, and a rat.*
and a rag.	Can you name all the things he has? (Signal.) *A sack, a fan, a rat, and a rag.*
To correct	If the children do not give acceptable answers, have them reread the sentence that answers the question. Then ask the question again.

TASK 23 **Picture comprehension**

a. Name some of the things you think you'll see in the picture.
A sack, a fan, a rat, and a rag.
b. Turn your take-home over and look at the picture.
c. Show me what he has.
  1. Show me the sack. *(The children respond.)*
  2. Show me the fan. *(The children respond.)*
  3. Show me the rat. *(The children respond.)*
  4. Show me the rag. *(The children respond.)*
d. Ask these questions:
  1. What's wrong with his sack? *The children respond.* It's torn.
  2. Does he look like he's having fun? *The children respond.* No.

TASK 24 **Word finding**

a. Turn your take-home back to side 1. Everybody, look at the words
in the top line. One of the words is **a.**
b. Get ready to touch **a** when I clap. (Pause three seconds.)
Get ready. Clap. *(The children touch **a.**)*
c. Repeat *b* for these words: **has, sack, a, has, a, has, sack, a, sack,
has, sack, a.**

TASK 25 **Children read the first sentence the fast way**

a. Everybody, now you're going to read part of the story the fast way.
Finger on the ball of the top line. Check children's responses.
b. Move your finger under the sounds of the first word and figure out
the sounds you're going to say. Don't say the sounds out loud.
Just figure out what you're going to say. Check children's
responses. Prompt children who don't touch under the sounds.
(Pause five seconds.) Read the word the fast way. Get ready.
Clap. Say **he** with the children. *He.*
c. Next word. Move your finger under the sounds and figure out the
sounds. Check children's responses. (Pause five seconds.) Read
the word the fast way. Get ready. Clap. Say **has** with the children.
Has.
d. Repeat *c* for the words **a, sack.**

TURN THE PAGE FOR THE REST OF TASK 25.

TASK 21 Children read the first sentence the fast way

a. Everybody, get ready to read all the words in the first sentence the fast way.

b. Touch the first word. Check children's responses. (Pause three seconds.) Get ready. Clap. *Thē*.

c. Next word. Check children's responses. (Pause three seconds.) Get ready. Clap. *Sand*.

d. Repeat *c* for the words **is, hot.**

e. After the children read **hot,** say: Stop. That's the end of the sentence.

f. Let's read that sentence again, the fast way.

g. First word. Check children's responses. Get ready. Clap. *Thē*.

h. Next word. Check children's responses. Get ready. Clap. *Sand*.

i. Repeat *h* for the words **is, hot.**

j. After the children read **hot,** say: Stop: You've read the first sentence.

TASK 22 Children read the second sentence the fast way

a. Everybody, put your finger on the period after **hot**. Check children's responses.

b. Now move along the arrows until you find the next period. Check children's responses.

c. Repeat *a* and *b* until firm.

d. Go back to the first period. Check children's responses.

e. Get ready to read all the words until we come to the next period.

f. Starting with the first word after **hot**. Check children's responses. (Pause three seconds.) Get ready. Clap. *His*.

g. Next word. Check children's responses. (Pause three seconds.) Get ready. Clap. *Feet*.

h. Repeat *g* for the remaining words in the second sentence.

i. After the children read **hot,** say: Stop. You've read the sentence.

j. Let's read it again. Go back to the period after the word **hot** on the top line. Check children's responses. Get ready to read all the words in the sentence.

k. First word. Check children's responses. Get ready. Clap. *His*.

l. Next word. Check children's responses. Get ready. Clap. *Feet*.

m. Repeat *l* for the remaining words in the second sentence.

TASK 23 Individual test

a. Everybody, finger on the ball of the top line. Check children's responses.

b. We're going to have different children read the fast way. Everybody's going to touch the words.

c. First word. Check children's responses. Call on a child. Clap. *The child responds.*

d. Next word. Check children's responses. Call on a child. Clap. *The child responds.*

e. Repeat *d* for the remaining words in the first sentence.

TASK 24 Sentence saying

Good reading. Now, everybody, say all the words in that sentence without looking. (Signal.) *The children repeat the sentence at a normal speaking rate.*

e. Let's read the words the fast way again. Everybody, finger on the ball of the top line. Check children's responses. Figure out the first word and get ready to read it the fast way. Say the sounds to yourself. (Pause five seconds.) What word? Clap. *He.* Yes, **he.**

f. Figure out the next word. Say the sounds to yourself. (Pause five seconds.) What word? Clap. *Has.* Yes, **has.**

g. Repeat *f* for the words **a, sack.**

TASK 26 Individual test

a. Everybody, finger on the ball of the top line.
Check children's responses.

b. We're going to have different children read. Everybody's going to touch the words.

c. Everybody, touch the first word. Check children's responses.

d. Call on a child. Reading the fast way. Get ready. Clap. *He.*

e. Next word. Check children's responses.

f. Everybody reading. Get ready. Clap. *Has.*

g. Next word. Check children's responses.

h. Call on a child. Get ready. Clap. *A.*

i. Repeat *e* and *f* for **sack.**

SUMMARY OF INDEPENDENT ACTIVITY

TASK 27 Introduction to independent activity

a. Hold up Take-Home 76.

b. Everybody, you're going to finish this take-home on your own. Tell the children when they will work the remaining items. Let's go over the things you're going to do.

TASK 28 Story copying

Point to the dotted words below the story on side 1. You're going to write the dotted words on this arrow. Then you're going to write those words on the other arrows.

TASK 29 Matching

a. Point to the first column of words in the Matching Game.

b. Everybody, get ready to read each of the words over here. Touch the sounds as the children sound out the word. Then ask: What word? (Signal.) *The children respond.*

c. Point to the first column. You're going to make lines for every word over here.

TASK 30 Cross-out game

Point to the boxed sounds in the Cross-out Game. Everybody, what sound are you going to cross out today? (Signal.) *ooo.* What sound are you going to circle? (Signal.) *c.*

TASK 31 Sound writing

a. Point to the sound-writing exercise on side 2. Here are the sounds you're going to write today. I'll touch the sounds. You say them.

b. Touch each sound. *The children respond.*

c. Repeat the series until firm.

TASK 32 Pair relations

a. Point to the pair-relations exercise.

b. Everybody, remember the rule. If the picture doesn't show what the word says, you cross out the box.

c. Point to the first box. This word is **mad**. What word? (Signal.) *Mad.* Everybody, does the picture show someone who is **mad**? (Signal.) *No.* Are you going to cross it out? (Signal.) *Yes.*

d. If the children's responses are not firm, repeat *c* with one or more boxes.

TASK 33 Story picture

Point to the story picture. After you finish your take-home, you can color the story picture.

END OF LESSON 76

Take-Home 89

STORY

TASK 17 First reading—children sound out each word and tell what word

a. Pass out Take-Home 89. Do not let the children look at the picture
until task 19.

b. Get ready to read the story.
c. First word. (Pause.) Get ready. Clap for each sound. *Thththēēē.*
What word? (Signal.) *Thē.* Yes, **thē**.
d. Next word. (Pause.) Get ready. Clap for each sound. *Sssaaannnd.*
What word? (Signal.) *Sand.* Yes, **sand**.
e. Repeat *d* for the remaining words in the story.

TASK 18 Second reading—children reread the story and answer questions

a. This time you'll read the story and I'll ask questions.
b. Repeat *c* through *e* in task 17. Ask the comprehension questions
below as the children read.

After the children read:	You say:
The sand is hot.	Tell me about the sand. (Signal.) *It's hot.*
His feet got hot.	What happened to his feet? (Signal.) *His feet got hot.* Why did they get hot? (Signal.) *Because the sand is hot.*
His hat is not hot.	Tell me about his hat. (Signal.) *It's not hot.*

TASK 19 Picture comprehension

a. What do you think you'll see in the picture? *The children respond.*
b. You'll see somebody. Where will he be? *The children respond.*
c. What will he be wearing? *A hat.*
d. Turn your take-home over and look at the picture.
e. Ask these questions:
  1. Where is the boy? *The children respond.* He's at the beach.
  2. Why is he jumping around? *The children respond.*
The sand is hot.
  3. Is his hat hot? *The children respond.* No.
  4. What would you do if you were trying to walk on hot sand with
no shoes? *The children respond.*

TASK 20 Period finding

a. Turn your take-home back to side 1. Everybody, we're going to
read all the words in the first sentence the fast way.
b. Point to the first word. The first <u>sentence</u> begins here and goes
all the way to a little dot called a period. So I just go along
the arrow until I find a period.
c. Touch **thē**. Have I come to a period yet? (Signal.) *No.*
Touch **sand**. Have I come to a period yet? (Signal.) *No.*
Touch **is**. Have I come to a period yet? (Signal.) *No.*
Touch **hot**. Have I come to a period yet? (Signal.) *Yes.*
d. Again. Repeat *b* and *c* until firm.
e. Everybody, put your finger on the ball of the top line.
Check children's responses.
f. Get ready to find the period for the first sentence. Go along
the arrow until you find that period. Check children's responses.

Lesson 77

Groups that are firm on Mastery Tests 13 and 14 should skip this lesson and do lesson 78 today.

SOUNDS

w

l

u

m

TASK 1   Teaching **w** as in **we**

a. Point to **w.** My turn. (Pause.) Touch **w** and say: www.
b. Point to **w.** Your turn. When I touch it, you say it. (Pause.) Get ready. Touch **w.** *www.* Lift your finger.
c. Again. Touch **w.** *wwww.* Lift your finger.
d. Repeat *c* until firm.

TASK 2   Sounds firm-up

a. Get ready to say the sounds when I touch them.
b. Alternate touching **l** and **w.** Point to the sound. (Pause one second.) Say: Get ready. Touch the sound. *The children respond.*
c. When **l** and **w** are firm, alternate touching **l, w, u,** and **m** until all four sounds are firm.

TASK 3   Individual test

Call on different children to identify **l, w, u,** or **m.**

TASK 4   Teacher introduces cross-out game

a. Use acetate and crayon.
b. I'll cross out the sounds on this page when you can tell me every sound.
c. Remember—when I touch it, you say it.
d. Go over the sounds until the children can identify all the sounds in order.

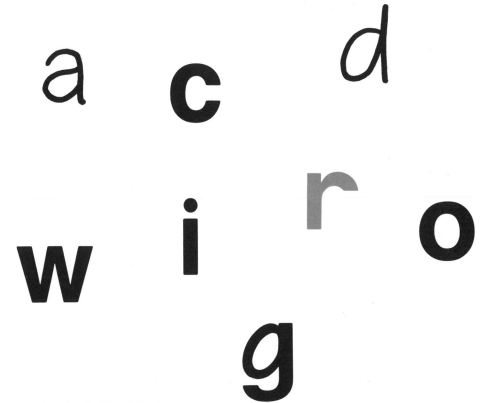

TASK 5   Individual test

Call on different children to identify two or more sounds in task 4.

TASK 6   Teacher crosses out sounds

a. You told me every sound. Get ready to do it again. This time I'll cross out each sound when you tell me what it is.
b. Point to each sound. (Pause.) Say: Get ready. Touch the sound. *The children respond.* As you cross out the sound, say: Goodbye, _____.

131

After you read the words on this page, you'll get to read the words the fast way.

Do not touch any small letters.

TASK 12 Children sound out the word and tell what word

a. Touch the ball for **lāte.** Sound it out.
b. Get ready. Touch **l, ā, t** as the children say *lllāāāt*.
                    If sounding out is not firm, repeat *b*.
c. What word? (Signal.) *Late.* Yes, **late.**

lāte

TASK 13 Children sound out the word and tell what word

a. Touch the ball for **sand.** Sound it out.
b. Get ready. Touch **s, a, n, d** as the children say *sssaaannnd*.
                    If sounding out is not firm, repeat *b*.
c. What word? (Signal.) *Sand.* Yes, **sand.**

sand

TASK 14 Children rhyme with wish

a. Touch the ball for **wish.** Sound it out.
b. Get ready. Touch **w, i, sh** as the children say *wwwiiishshsh*.
    If sounding out is not firm, repeat *b*.
c. What word? (Signal.) *Wish.* Yes, **wish.**
d. Quickly touch the ball for **dish.** This word rhymes with (pause)
    wish.
    Get ready. (Signal.) Move your finger quickly along the arrow. *Dish.*
e. What word? (Signal.) *Dish.* Yes, **dish.**

wish

TASK 15 Children read the words the fast way

a. Now you get to read the words on this page the fast way.
b. Touch the ball for **lāte.** (Pause three seconds.) Get ready.
                    Move your finger quickly along the arrow. *Late.*
c. Repeat *b* for each word on the page.

dish

TASK 16 Individual test

Call on different children to read one word the fast way.

READING VOCABULARY

Do not touch any small letters.

TASK 7   Children sound out the word, then read it the fast way

a. Touch the ball for **rāin.**   Sound it out.
b. Get ready.   Touch **r, ā, n** as the children say *rrrāāānnn.*
                              If sounding out is not firm, repeat *b.*
c. What word?   (Signal.) *Rain.*   Yes, **rain.**
d. Return to the ball.   Get ready to read the word the fast way.
          I'm going to count to five. See if you can remember the word.
e. 1, 2, 3, 4, 5. Get ready.   Move your finger quickly along the arrow.
                              Rain.   Yes, **rain.** Good reading.

f. Again.   Repeat *e* until firm.

TASK 8   Individual test

Call on different children to do *e* in task 7.

TASK 9   Children sound out the word, then read it the fast way

a. Touch the ball for **lāte.**   Sound it out.
b. Get ready.   Touch **l, ā, t** as the children say *lllāāāt.*
                              If sounding out is not firm, repeat *b.*
c. What word?   (Signal.) *Late.*   Yes, **late.**
d. Return to the ball.   Get ready to read the word the fast way.
          I'm going to count to five. See if you can remember the word.
e. 1, 2, 3, 4, 5. Get ready.   Move your finger quickly along the arrow.
                              Late.   Yes, **late.** Good reading.

f. Again.   Repeat *e* until firm.

TASK 10   Individual test

Call on different children to do *e* in task 9.

TASK 11   Children sound out the word, then read it the fast way

Repeat the procedures in task 9 for **fun.**

TASK 12   Individual test

Call on different children to do *e* in task 9 for **fun.**

READING VOCABULARY

After you read the words on this page, you'll get to read the words the fast way.

TASK 6   Children sound out the word and tell what word

a. Touch the ball for **hats.** Sound it out.
b. Get ready. Touch **h, a, t, s** as the children say *haaatsss.*
If sounding out is not firm, repeat *b.*
c. What word? (Signal.) *Hats.* Yes, **hats.**

TASK 7   Children sound out the word and tell what word

a. Touch the ball for **will.** Sound it out.
b. Get ready. Touch **w, i,** between the **l**'s as the children say *wwwiiilll.*
If sounding out is not firm, repeat *b.*
c. What word? (Signal.) *Will.* Yes, **will.**

TASK 8   Children sound out an irregular word (said)

a. Touch the ball for **said.** Sound it out.
b. Get ready. Quickly touch each sound as the children say *sssaaaiiid.*

To correct	If the children sound out the word as **ssseeed** **1.** Say: **You've got to say the sounds I touch.** **2.** Repeat *a* and *b* until firm.

c. Again. Repeat *b* until firm.
d. That's how we <u>sound out</u> the word. Here's how we <u>say</u> the word.
Said. How do we <u>say</u> the word? (Signal.) *Said.*
e. Now you're going to <u>sound out</u> the word. Get ready.
Touch each sound as the children say *sssaaaiiid.*
f. Now you're going to say the word. Get ready. (Signal.) *Said.*
g. Repeat *e* and *f* until firm.
h. Yes, this word is **said.** She **said,** "Hello."

TASK 9   Individual test—Have children do *e* and *f* in task 8.

TASK 10   Children read the words the fast way

a. Now you get to read the words on this page the fast way.
b. Touch the ball for **hats.** (Pause three seconds.) Get ready.
Move your finger quickly along the arrow. *Hats.*
c. Repeat *b* for each word on the page.

TASK 11   Individual test—Have children read one word the fast way.

hats

will

said

TASK 13 Children rhyme with nāme

a. Touch the ball for **nāme.** Sound it out.

b. Get ready. Touch **n, ā, m** as the children say *nnnāāāmmm.*

If sounding out is not firm, repeat *b.*

c. What word? (Signal.) *Name.* Yes, **name.**

d. Quickly touch the ball for **sāme.** This word rhymes with (pause) **name.** Get ready. Touch **s.** *sss.* Move your finger quickly along the arrow. *Sssāme.*

e. What word? (Signal.) *Same.* Yes, **same.**

TASK 14 Children read a word beginning with a stop sound (gāme)

a. Run your finger under **āme.** You're going to sound out this part. Get ready. Touch **ā, m** as the children say *āāāmmm.*

b. Say it fast. (Signal.) *Ame.* Yes, this part says (pause) **āme.**

c. Repeat *a* and *b* until firm.

d. Touch the ball for **gāme.** This word rhymes with (pause) **āme.** Get ready. Move quickly along the arrow. *Game.*

e. What word? (Signal). *Game.* Yes, **game.**

f. Repeat *d* and *e* until firm.

g. Return to the ball. Now you're going to sound out (pause) **gāme.** Get ready. Quickly touch **g, ā, m** as the children say *gāāāmmm.*

h. What word? (Signal.) *Game.* Yes, **game.** Good reading.

i. Repeat *g* and *h* until firm.

TASK 15 Individual test

Call on different children to do *g* and *h* in task 14.

TASK 16 Children read the words the fast way

a. Now you get to read these words the fast way.

b. Touch the ball for **sāme.** (Pause three seconds.) Get ready. Move your finger quickly along the arrow. *Same.*

c. Repeat *b* for the words **gāme** and **nāme.**

d. Have the children sound out the words they had difficulty identifying.

TASK 17 Individual test

Call on different children to read one word the fast way.

Do not touch any small letters.

Lesson 89

Groups that are firm on Mastery Tests 15 and 16 should skip this lesson and do lesson 90 today.

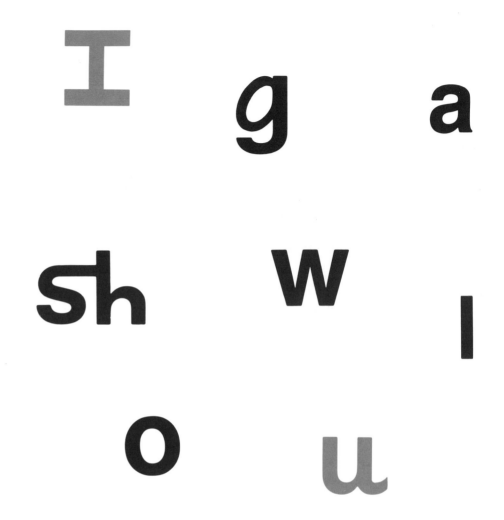

SOUNDS

TASK 1   Teaching I as in **Ice**

a. Point to I. **My turn.** (Pause.)
Touch I and say: III.

b. Point to I. **Your turn. When I touch it, you say it.** (Pause.) **Get ready.** Touch I. *III.*
Lift your finger.

c. **Again.** Touch I. *III.*
Lift your finger.

d. Repeat *c* until firm.

TASK 2   Sounds firm-up

a. **Get ready to say the sounds when I touch them.**

b. Alternate touching I and I. Point to the sound. (Pause one second.) Say: **Get ready.** Touch the sound. *The children respond.*

c. When I and I are firm, alternate touching **I, h, I,** and **i** until all four sounds are firm.

TASK 3   Individual test

Call on different children to identify I, **h, I,** or **i.**

TASK 4   Sounds firm-up

a. Point to I. **When I touch the sound, you say it.**

b. (Pause.) **Get ready.** Touch I. *III.*

c. **Again.** Repeat *b* until firm.

d. **Get ready to say all the sounds when I touch them.**

e. Alternate touching **a, g, I, sh, w, I, o,** and **u** three or four times. Point to the sound. (Pause one second.) Say: **Get ready.** Touch the sound. *The children respond.*

TASK 5   Individual test

Call on different children to identify one or more sounds in task 4.

206

After you read the words on this page, you'll get to read the words in the box the fast way.

Do not touch any small letters.

To correct	For all mistakes, have the children sound out the word and say it fast. Then say: **Remember this word.**

TASK 18   Children sound out the word and tell what word

a. Touch the ball for **in.** Sound it out.
b. Get ready. Touch **i, n** as the children say *iiinnn*.

If sounding out is not firm, repeat *b*.

c. What word? (Signal.) *In.* Yes, **in.**

TASK 19   Children sound out the word and tell what word

a. Touch the ball for **and.** Sound it out.
b. Get ready. Touch **a, n, d** as the children say *aaannnd*.

If sounding out is not firm, repeat *b*.

c. What word? (Signal.) *And.* Yes, **and.**

TASK 20   Children sound out the word and tell what word

a. Touch the ball for **māil.** Sound it out.
b. Get ready. Touch **m, ā, l** as the children say *mmmāāālll*.

If sounding out is not firm, repeat *b*.

c. What word? (Signal.) *Mail.* Yes, **mail.**

TASK 21   Children read the words in the box the fast way

a. Now you're going to read the words in the box the fast way.
b. Touch the ball for **in.** (Pause three seconds.) Get ready.

Move your finger quickly along the arrow. *In.*

c. Repeat *b* for the words **and** and **māil.**
d. Present the series **in, and, māil** at least two times.

TASK 22   Individual test

Call on different children to read one word in the box the fast way.

SUMMARY OF INDEPENDENT ACTIVITY

TASK 27   Introduction to independent activity

a. Hold up Take-Home 88.
b. Everybody, you're going to finish this take-home on your own.
Tell the children when they will work the remaining items.
Let's go over the things you're going to do.

TASK 28   Story copying

Point to the dotted words below the story on side 1. You're going to write the dotted words on this arrow. Then you're going to write those words on the other arrows.

TASK 29   Cross-out game

Point to the boxed word in the Cross-out Game. Everybody, here's the word you're going to cross out today. What word? (Signal.) *Run.* Yes, **run.**

TASK 30   Matching

a. Point to the first column of words in the Matching Game.
b. Everybody, get ready to read each of the words over here.
Reading the fast way.
c. Point to the first word. Get ready. (Signal.) *The children respond.*
d. Repeat *c* for the remaining words.
e. Point to the first column. You're going to make lines for every word over here.

TASK 31   Sound writing

a. Point to the sound-writing exercise on side 2. Here are the sounds you're going to write today. I'll touch the sounds. You say them.
b. Touch each sound. *The children respond.*
c. Repeat the series until firm.

TASK 32   Pair relations

a. Point to the word **shack** in the first row of the pair-relations exercise.
b. Everybody, touch this box on your take-home.
Check children's responses.
c. Get ready to tell me this word. (Pause.) What word? (Signal.)
Shack.
d. You're going to circle the picture that shows a (pause) **shack.**
Do it. Check children's responses.
e. Point to the other boxes. Remember—you're going to circle the picture in each box that shows what the words say.

TASK 33   Story picture

Point to the story picture. After you finish your take-home, you can color the story picture.

END OF LESSON 88

Take-Home 77

STORY

Do not clap for any small letters.

TASK 23   First reading—children sound out each word and tell what word

a. Pass out Take-Home 77. Do not let the children look at the picture until task 25.

b. Get ready to read the story. First word. Check children's responses.

c. Get ready. Clap for each sound. *Hēēē.* What word? (Signal.) *He.*
                                                         Yes, **he.**

d. Next word. Check children's responses.

e. Get ready. Clap for each sound. *Haaasss.* What word? (Signal.)
                                              Has. Yes, **has.**

f. Repeat *d* and *e* for the remaining words in the story.

TASK 24   Second reading—children reread the story and answer questions

a. This time you'll read the story and I'll ask questions.
                          Back to the first word. Check children's responses.

b. Repeat *c* through *f* in task 23. Ask the comprehension questions below as the children read.

After the children read:	You say:
He has fun.	Who has fun? (Signal.) *He has fun.*
He is in the rain	Where does he have fun? (Signal.) *In the rain.*
and the mud.	He has fun in the rain and where? (Signal.) *The mud.*

To correct	If the children do not give acceptable answers, have them reread the sentence that answers the question. Then ask the question again.

TASK 25   Picture comprehension

a. You're going to see somebody in the picture. What do you think he'll be doing? *The children respond.*

b. Turn your take-home over and look at the picture.

c. Ask these questions:
  1. Who is he? *The children respond.* Yes, a pig.
  2. Where is he having fun? *The children respond.*
                                              In the rain and the mud.
  3. Did you ever have fun in the rain and the mud?
                                              The children respond.

TASK 26   Word finding

a. Turn your take-home back to side 1. Everybody, look at the words in the top line. One of the words is **fun**.

b. Get ready to touch **fun** when I clap. (Pause three seconds.)
                    Get ready. Clap. *(The children touch **fun**.)*

c. Repeat *b* for these words: **hē, fun, has, hē, has, hē, fun, has, fun, fun, hē, has.**

TASK 27   Children read the first sentence the fast way

a. Everybody, now you're going to read part of the story the fast way. Finger on the ball of the top line. Check children's responses.

b. Move your finger under the sounds of the first word and figure out the sounds you're going to say. Don't say the sounds out loud. Just figure out what you're going to say. Check children's responses. Prompt children who don't touch under the sounds. (Pause five seconds.) Read the word the fast way. Get ready. Clap. Say **he** with the children. *He.*

c. Next word. Move your finger under the sounds and figure out the sounds. Check children's responses. (Pause five seconds.) Read the word the fast way. Get ready. Clap. Say **has** with the children. *Has.*

d. Repeat *c* for the word **fun.**

e. Let's read the words the fast way again. Everybody, finger on the ball of the top line. Check children's responses. Figure out the first word and get ready to read it the fast way. Say the sounds to yourself. (Pause five seconds.) What word? Clap. *He.* Yes, **he.**

f. Figure out the next word. Say the sounds to yourself. (Pause five seconds.) What word? Clap. *Has.* Yes, **has.**

g. Repeat *f* for the word **fun.**

TASK 24   Children read the second sentence the fast way

a. Everybody, put your finger on the period after **ears**.

Check children's responses.

b. Now move along the arrows until you find the next period.

Check children's responses.

c. Repeat *a* and *b* until firm.

d. Put your finger on the period after **ears**.

Check children's responses.

e. Get ready to read all the words until we come to the next period.

f. Starting with the first word after **ears**.   Check children's responses.

(Pause three seconds.) Get ready.   Clap. *Sam*.

g. Next word.   Check children's responses. (Pause three seconds.)

Get ready.   Clap. *Has*.

h. Repeat *g* for the remaining words in the second sentence.

i. After the children read **tail,** say: Stop. You've read the sentence.

j. Let's read it again. Go back to the period after **ears**.

Check children's responses.
Get ready to read all the words in the sentence.

k. First word.   Check children's responses. Get ready.   Clap. *Sam*.

l. Next word.   Check children's responses. Get ready.   Clap. *Has*.

m. Repeat *l* for the remaining words in the second sentence.

TASK 25   Individual test

a. Everybody, finger on the ball of the top line.

Check children's responses.

b. We're going to have different children read the fast way.

Everybody's going to touch the words.

c. First word.   Check children's responses. Call on a child.

Clap. *The child responds.*

d. Next word.   Check children's responses. Call on a child.

Clap. *The child responds.*

e. Repeat *d* for the remaining word in the first sentence.

TASK 26   Sentence saying

Good reading. Now, everybody, say all the words in that sentence
without looking.   (Signal.) *The children repeat the sentence
at a normal speaking rate.*

77

TASK 28 Individual test

a. Everybody, finger on the ball of the top line.
                                    Check children's responses.
b. We're going to have different children read. Everybody's going
                                    to touch the words.
c. Everybody, touch the first word. Check children's responses.
d. Call on a child. Reading the fast way. Get ready. Clap. *He.*
e. Next word. Check children's responses.
f. Everybody reading. Get ready. Clap. *Has.*
g. Next word. Check children's responses.
h. Call on a child. Get ready. Clap. *Fun.*

SUMMARY OF INDEPENDENT ACTIVITY

TASK 29 Introduction to independent activity

a. Hold up Take-Home 77.
b. Everybody, you're going to finish this take-home on your own.
                Tell the children when they will work the remaining items.
                        Let's go over the things you're going to do.

TASK 30 Story copying

Point to the dotted words below the story on side 1. You're going
            to write the dotted words on this arrow. Then you're going to write
                        those words on the other arrows.

TASK 31 Matching

a. Point to the first column of words in the Matching Game.
b. Everybody, get ready to read each of the words over here.
                Touch the sounds as the children sound out the word.
                Then ask: What word? (Signal.) *The children respond.*
c. Point to the first column. You're going to make lines for every
                                    word over here.

TASK 32 Cross-out game

Point to the boxed sounds in the Cross-out Game. Everybody, what
                sound are you going to circle today? (Signal.) *nnn.*
                What sound are you going to cross out? (Signal.) *uuu.*

TASK 33 Sound writing

a. Point to the sound-writing exercise on side 2. Here are the sounds
            you're going to write today. I'll touch the sounds. You say them.
b. Touch each sound. *The children respond.*
c. Repeat the series until firm.

TASK 34 Pair relations

a. Point to the pair-relations exercise.
b. Everybody, remember the rule. If the picture doesn't show what
                        the word says, you cross out the box.
c. Point to the first box. This word is **fan**. What word? (Signal.) *Fan.*
                Everybody, does the picture show a **fan**? (Signal.) *No.*
                        Are you going to cross it out? (Signal.) *Yes.*
d. If the children's responses are not firm, repeat *c* with one or
                                    more boxes.

TASK 35 Story picture

Point to the story picture. After you finish your take-home,
                        you can color the story picture.

END OF LESSON 77

Take-Home 88

STORY
Do not clap for any small letters.

TASK 19 **First reading—children sound out each word and tell what word**

a. Pass out Take-Home 88. Do not let the children look at the picture until task 21.

b. Get ready to read the story.
c. First word. (Pause.) Get ready. Clap for each sound. *Sssaaammm.* What word? (Signal.) *Sam.* Yes, **Sam.**

d. Next word. (Pause.) Get ready. Clap for each sound. *Haaasss.* What word? (Signal.) *Has.* Yes, **has.**

e. Repeat *d* for the remaining words in the story.

TASK 20 **Second reading—children reread the story and answer questions**

a. This time you'll read the story and I'll ask questions.
b. Repeat *c* through *e* in task 19. Ask the comprehension questions below as the children read.

After the children read:	You say:
Sam has ears.	What does he have? (Signal.) *Ears.* Who has ears? (Signal.) *Sam.*
Sam has a tail.	Sam has ears and what else? (Signal.) *A tail.*
Sam is not a man.	What do you know about Sam? (Signal.) *Sam is not a man.*
Sam is not a cat	Is Sam a man? (Signal.) *No.* What else do you know about him? (Signal.) *Sam is not a cat.*

TASK 21 **Picture comprehension**

a. What do you think Sam is? *The children respond.*
b. Turn your take-home over and look at the picture.
c. Ask these questions:
 1. What is Sam? *The children respond.* Sam is a monkey.
 2. Does he have ears and a tail? *Yes.*
 3. What is he doing? *The children respond.* Eating a banana.
 4. Did you ever eat a banana? *The children respond.*

TASK 22 **Period finding**

a. Turn your take-home back to side 1. Everybody, we're going to read all the words in the first sentence the fast way.
b. Point to the first word. The first <u>sentence</u> begins here and goes all the way to a little dot called a period. So I just go along the arrow until I find a period.
c. Touch **sam.** Have I come to a period yet? (Signal.) *No.* Touch **has.** Have I come to a period yet? (Signal.) *No.* Touch **ēars.** Have I come to a period yet? (Signal.) *Yes.*
d. Again. Repeat *b* and *c* until firm.
e. Everybody, put your finger on the ball of the top line. Check children's responses.
f. Get ready to find the period for the first sentence. Go along the arrow until you find that period. Check children's responses.

TASK 23 **Children read the first sentence the fast way**

a. Everybody, get ready to read all the words in the first sentence the fast way.
b. Touch the first word. Check children's responses. (Pause three seconds.) Get ready. Clap. *Sam.*
c. Next word. Check children's responses. (Pause three seconds.) Get ready. Clap. *Has.*
d. Repeat *c* for the word **ears.**
e. After the children read **ears,** say: Stop. That's the end of the sentence.
f. Let's read the sentence again, the fast way.
g. First word. Check children's responses. Get ready. Clap. *Sam.*
h. Next word. Check children's responses. Get ready. Clap. *Has.*
i. Repeat *h* for the word **ears.**
j. After the children read **ears,** say: Stop. You've read the first sentence.

Lesson 78

w

r

l

m

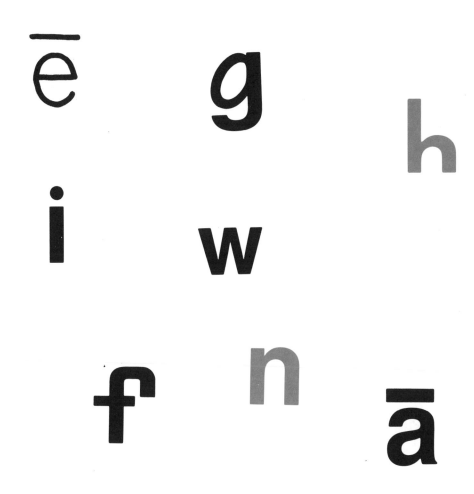

SOUNDS

TASK 1   Teaching **w** as in **we**

a. Point to **w**. **My turn.** (Pause.) Touch **w** and say: www.

b. Point to **w**. **Your turn. When I touch it, you say it.** (Pause.) **Get ready.** Touch **w**. *www.* Lift your finger.

c. **Again.** Touch **w**. *wwww.* Lift your finger.

d. Repeat *c* until firm.

TASK 2   Sounds firm-up

a. **Get ready to say the sounds when I touch them.**

b. Alternate touching **w** and **r**. Point to the sound. (Pause one second.) Say: **Get ready.** Touch the sound. *The children respond.*

c. When **w** and **r** are firm, alternate touching **r, w, l,** and **m** until all four sounds are firm.

TASK 3   Individual test

Call on different children to identify **r, w, l,** or **m.**

TASK 4   Child plays teacher

a. Use acetate and crayon.

b. **[Child's name] is going to be the teacher.**

c. **[He or She] is going to touch the sounds. When** [he or she] touches a sound, you say it.

d. The child points to and touches the sounds. You circle any sound that is not firm.

e. After the child has completed the page, present all the circled sounds to the children.

TASK 5   Individual test

Call on different children. **If you can say the sound when I call your name, you may cross it out.**

137

After you read the words on this page, you'll get to read the words the fast way.

Do not touch any small letters.

TASK 14 Children read a word beginning with a stop sound (tāil)

a. Run your finger under **āil.** **You're going to sound out this part.**
Get ready. Touch **ā, l** as the children say *āāālll.*
b. **Say it fast.** (Signal.) *Al.* **Yes, this part says** (pause) **āl.**
c. Repeat *a* and *b* until firm.
d. Touch the ball for **tāil.** **This word rhymes with** (pause) **āall.**
Get ready. Move to **t,** then quickly along the arrow. *Tail.*
e. **What word?** (Signal.) *Tail.* **Yes, tail.**
f. Repeat *d* and *e* until firm.
g. Return to the ball. **Now you're going to sound out** (pause) **tail.**
Get ready. Quickly touch **t, ā, l** as the children say *tāāālll.*
h. **What word?** (Signal.) *Tail.* **Yes, tail. Good reading.**
The cat has a long tail.
i. Repeat *g* and *h* until firm.

TASK 15 Individual test

Call on different children to do *g* and *h* in task 14.

TASK 16 Children rhyme with not

a. Touch the ball for **not.** **Sound it out.**
b. **Get ready.** Touch **n, o, t** as the children say *nnnooot.*
If sounding out is not firm, repeat *b.*
c. **What word?** (Signal.) *Not.* **Yes, not.**
d. Quickly touch the ball for **hot.** **This word rhymes with** (pause)
not. Get ready. Touch **h.** *h.* Move your finger quickly along
the arrow. *Hot.*
e. **What word?** (Signal.) *Hot.* **Yes, hot.**

TASK 17 Children read the words the fast way

a. **Now you get to read the words on this page the fast way.**
b. Touch the ball for **tāil.** (Pause three seconds.) **Get ready.**
Move your finger quickly along the arrow. *Tail.*
c. Repeat *b* for each word on the page.

TASK 18 Individual test

Call on different children to read one word the fast way.

tāil

not

hot

READING VOCABULARY

Do not touch any small letters.

TASK 6   Children rhyme with **sāil**

a. Touch the ball for **sāil.** Sound it out.
b. Get ready. Touch **s, ā, l** as the children say *sssāāālll.*
  If sounding out is not firm, repeat *b.*
c. What word? (Signal.) *Sail.* Yes, **sail.**
d. Quickly touch the ball for **nāil.** This word rhymes with (pause)
  sail. Get ready. Touch **n.** *nnn.* Move your finger quickly along
  the arrow. *Nnnāil.*
e. What word? (Signal.) *Nail.* Yes, **nail.**

TASK 7   Children sound out the word, then read it the fast way

a. Touch the ball for **gāme.** Sound it out.
b. Get ready. Touch **g, ā, m** as the children say *gāāāmmm.*
  If sounding out is not firm, repeat *b.*
c. What word? (Signal.) *Game.* Yes, **game.**
d. Return to the ball. Get ready to read the word the fast way.
  I'm going to count to five. See if you can remember the word.
e. 1, 2, 3, 4, 5. Get ready. Move your finger quickly along the arrow.
  Game. Yes, **game.** Good reading.
f. Again. Repeat *e* until firm.

TASK 8   Individual test

Call on different children to do *e* in task 7.

TASK 9   Children read the words the fast way

a. Now you get to read these words the fast way.
b. Touch the ball for **sāil.** (Pause three seconds.) Get ready.
  Move your finger quickly along the arrow. *Sail.*
c. Repeat *b* for the words **gāme** and **nāil.**
d. Have the children sound out the words they had difficulty identifying.

TASK 10   Individual test

Call on different children to read one word the fast way.

88

READING VOCABULARY

After you read the words on this page, you'll get to read the words the fast way.

Do not touch any small letters.

TASK 7   Children sound out the word and tell what word

a. Touch the ball for **ēars.** Sound it out.
b. Get ready.   Touch **ē, r, s** as the children say *ēēērrrsss.*
                              If sounding out is not firm, repeat *b.*
c. What word? (Signal.) *Ears.* Yes, **ears.**

ēars

TASK 8   Children sound out the word and tell what word

Repeat the procedures in task 7 for **runs.**

runs

TASK 9   Children sound out the word and tell what word

Repeat the procedures in task 7 for **wins.**

wins

TASK 10   Children read a word beginning with a stop sound (dish)

a. Run your finger under **ish.** You're going to sound out this part.
                  Get ready.   Touch **i, sh** as the children say *iiishshsh.*
b. Say it fast. (Signal.) *Ish.* Yes, this part says (pause) **ish.**
c. Repeat *a* and *b* until firm.
d. Touch the ball for **dish.** This word rhymes with (pause) **iishsh.**
            Get ready.   Move to **d,** then quickly along the arrow. *Dish.*
e. What word? (Signal.) *Dish.* Yes, **dish.**
f. Repeat *d* and *e* until firm.
g. Return to the ball. Now you're going to sound out (pause) **dish.**
            Get ready.   Quickly touch **d, i, sh** as the children say *diiishshsh.*
h. What word? (Signal.) *Dish.* Yes, **dish.** Good reading.
                              I had a **dish** of ice cream.
i. Repeat *g* and *h* until firm.

dish

TASK 11   Individual test—Have children do *g* and *h* in task 10.

TASK 12   Children read the words the fast way

Have the children read the words on this page the fast way.

TASK 13   Individual test—Have children read one word the fast way.

78

TASK 11   Children sound out the word, then read it the fast way

a. Touch the ball for **māil.** Sound it out.

b. Get ready. Touch **m, ā, l** as the children say *mmmāāālll.*

If sounding out is not firm, repeat *b.*

c. What word? (Signal.) *Mail.* Yes, **mail.**

d. Return to the ball. Get ready to read the word the fast way.

I'm going to count to five. See if you can remember the word.

e. 1, 2, 3, 4, 5. Get ready. Move your finger quickly along the arrow.

Mail. Yes, **mail.** Good reading.

f. Again. Repeat *e* until firm.

Do not touch any small letters.

TASK 12   Individual test

Call on different children to do *e* in task 11.

TASK 13   Children sound out the word, then read it the fast way

a. Touch the ball for **sick.** Sound it out.

b. Get ready. Touch **s, i, c** as the children say *sssiiic.*

If sounding out is not firm, repeat *b.*

c. What word? (Signal.) *Sick.* Yes, **sick.**

d. Return to the ball. Get ready to read the word the fast way.

I'm going to count to five. See if you can remember the word.

e. 1, 2, 3, 4, 5. Get ready. Move your finger quickly along the arrow.

Sick. Yes, **sick.** Good reading.

f. Again. Repeat *e* until firm.

TASK 14   Individual test

Call on different children to do *e* in task 13.

TASK 15   Children sound out the word, then read it the fast way

Repeat the procedures in task 13 for **rock.**

TASK 16   Individual test

Call on different children to do *e* in task 13 for **rock.**

Lesson 88

I

i

ā

t

SOUNDS

TASK 1   Teaching I as in Ice

a. Point to **I**. Here's a new sound.

b. My turn. (Pause.) Touch **I** and say: *III.*

c. Again. Touch **I** for a longer time. *IIIII.* Lift your finger.

d. Point to **I**. Your turn. When I touch it, you say it. (Pause.) Get ready. Touch **I**. *III.* Lift your finger.

e. Again. Touch **I**. *IIIIII.* Lift your finger.

f. Repeat *e* until firm.

TASK 2   Individual test

Call on different children to identify **I**.

TASK 3   Sounds firm-up

a. Get ready to say the sounds when I touch them.

b. Alternate touching **I** and **i**. Point to the sound. (Pause one second.) Say: Get ready. Touch the sound. *The children respond.*

c. When **I** and **i** are firm, alternate touching **I**, **i**, **ā**, and **t** until all four sounds are firm.

TASK 4   Individual test

Call on different children to identify **I**, **i**, **ā**, or **t**.

TASK 5   Sounds firm-up

a. Point to **I**. When I touch the sound, you say it.

b. (Pause.) Get ready. Touch **I**. *III.*

c. Again. Repeat *b* until firm.

d. Get ready to say all the sounds when I touch them.

e. Alternate touching **g, o, sh, ē, w, l, u,** and **I** three or four times.
Point to the sound. (Pause one second.) Say: Get ready.
Touch the sound. *The children respond.*

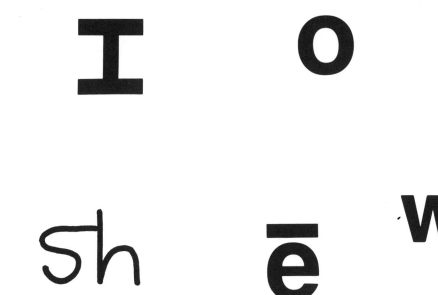

TASK 6   Individual test

Call on different children to identify one or more sounds in task 5.

After you read the words on this page, you'll get to read the words in the box the fast way.

Do not touch any small letters.

To correct	For all mistakes, have the children sound out the word and say it fast. Then say: **Remember this word.**

TASK 17   Children sound out the word and tell what word

a. Touch the ball for **wē.** Sound it out.
b. Get ready.   Touch **w, ē** as the children say *wwwēēē*.
If sounding out is not firm, repeat *b*.
c. What word?   (Signal.) *We.* Yes, **we.**

TASK 18   Children sound out the word and tell what word

a. Touch the ball for **that.** Sound it out.
b. Get ready.   Touch **th, a, t** as the children say *thththaaat*.
If sounding out is not firm, repeat *b*.
c. What word?   (Signal.) *That.* Yes, **that.**

TASK 19   Children sound out the word and tell what word

a. Touch the ball for **sock.** Sound it out.
b. Get ready.   Touch **s, o, c** as the children say *sssoooc*.
If sounding out is not firm, repeat *b*.
c. What word?   (Signal.) *Sock.* Yes, **sock.**

TASK 20   Children read the words in the box the fast way

a. Now you're going to read the words in the box the fast way.
b. Touch the ball for **wē.** (Pause three seconds.) Get ready.
Move your finger quickly along the arrow. *We.*
c. Repeat *b* for the words **that** and **sock.**
d. Present the series **wē, that, sock** at least two times.

TASK 21   Individual test

Call on different children to read one word in the box the fast way.

SUMMARY OF INDEPENDENT ACTIVITY

TASK 26   Introduction to independent activity

a. Hold up Take-Home 87.

b. Everybody, you're going to finish this take-home on your own.
Tell the children when they will work the remaining items.
Let's go over the things you're going to do.

TASK 27   Story copying

Point to the dotted words below the story on side 1. You're going to write the dotted words on this arrow. Then you're going to write those words on the other arrows.

TASK 28   Matching

a. Point to the first column of words in the Matching Game.

b. Everybody, get ready to read each of the words over here.
Reading the fast way.

c. Point to the first word. Get ready.   (Signal.) *The children respond.*

d. Repeat *c* for the remaining words.

e. Point to the first column. You're going to make lines for every word over here.

TASK 29   Sound writing

a. Point to the sound-writing exercise on side 2. Here are the sounds you're going to write today. I'll touch the sounds. You say them.

b. Touch each sound. *The children respond.*

c. Repeat the series until firm.

TASK 30   Pair relations

a. Point to the words **a cat** in the first row of the pair-relations exercise.

b. Everybody, touch this box on your take-home.
Check children's responses.

c. Get ready to tell me the words.   (Pause.) What words?   (Signal.)
A cat.

d. You're going to circle the picture that shows   (pause) **a cat**.
Do it.   Check children's responses.

e. Point to the other boxes. Remember—you're going to circle the picture in each box that shows what the words say.

TASK 31   Story picture

Point to the story picture. After you finish your take-home, you can color the story picture.

END OF LESSON 87

Take-Home 78

STORY
Do not clap for any small letters.

TASK 22 First reading—children sound out each word and tell what word

a. Pass out Take-Home 78. Do not let the children look at the picture until task 24.

b. **Get ready to read the story. First word.** Check children's responses.

c. **Get ready.** Clap for each sound. *Thththaaat.* **What word?** (Signal.) *That.* **Yes, that.**

d. **Next word.** Check children's responses.

e. **Get ready.** Clap for each sound. *Mmmaaannn.* **What word?** (Signal.) *Man.* **Yes, man.**

f. Repeat *d* and *e* for the remaining words in the story.

TASK 23 Second reading—children reread the story and answer questions

a. **This time you'll read the story and I'll ask questions. Back to the first word.** Check children's responses.

b. Repeat *c* through *f* in task 22. Ask the comprehension questions below as the children read.

After the children read:	You say:
That man has the mail.	**Who has it?** (Signal.) *That man.* **What does he have?** (Signal.) *The mail.*
He is late.	**What's wrong?** (Signal.) *He is late.*

To correct	If the children do not give acceptable answers, have them reread the sentence that answers the question. Then ask the question again.

TASK 24 Picture comprehension

a. **What are you going to see in the picture?** *The children respond.*

b. **What will the man have?** (Signal.) *The mail.*

c. **Turn your take-home over and look at the picture.**

d. Ask these questions:
1. **What does the man have?** *The children respond.* **The mail.**
2. **Why is he running?** *The children respond.* **He's late.**
3. **What does that man have on his back?** *The children respond.* **Yes, he's a mail carrier.**

TASK 25 Word finding

a. **Turn your take-home back to side 1. Everybody, look at the words in the top line. One of the words is mail.**

b. **Get ready to touch mail when I clap.** (Pause three seconds.) **Get ready.** Clap. *(The children touch māil.)*

c. Repeat *b* for these words: **man, that, māil, man, māil, man, that, māil, that, māil, that.**

TASK 26 Children read the first sentence the fast way

a. **Everybody, now you're going to read part of the story the fast way. Finger on the ball of the top line.** Check children's responses.

b. **Move your finger under the sounds of the first word and figure out the sounds you're going to say. Don't say the sounds out loud. Just figure out what you're going to say.** Check children's responses. Prompt children who don't touch under the sounds. (Pause three seconds.) **Read the word the fast way. Get ready.** Clap. *That.* **Yes, that.**

c. **Next word. Move your finger under the sounds and figure out the sounds.** Check children's responses. (Pause three seconds.) **Read the word the fast way. Get ready.** Clap. *Man.* **Yes, man.**

d. Repeat *c* for the words **has, thē, mail.**

e. **Let's read the words the fast way again. Everybody, finger on the ball of the top line.** Check children's responses. **Figure out the first word and get ready to read it the fast way. Say the sounds to yourself.** (Pause three seconds.) **What word?** Clap. *That.* **Yes, that.**

f. **Figure out the next word. Say the sounds to yourself.** (Pause three seconds.) **What word?** Clap. *Man.* **Yes, man.**

g. Repeat *f* for the words **has, thē, mail.**

TASK 21 Children read the first sentence the fast way

a. Everybody, get ready to read all the words in the first sentence
the fast way.

b. Touch the first word. Check children's responses.
(Pause three seconds.) Get ready. Clap. *She.*

c. Next word. Check children's responses. (Pause three seconds.)
Get ready. Clap. *Is.*

d. Repeat c for the words **in, thē, rāin.**

e. After the children read **rain** say: Stop. That's the end of
the sentence.

f. Let's read that sentence again, the fast way.

g. First word. Check children's responses. Get ready. Clap. *She.*

h. Next word. Check children's responses. Get ready. Clap. *Is.*

i. Repeat h for the words **in, thē, rāin.**

j. After the children read **rain** say: Stop. You've read the first
sentence.

TASK 22 Children read the second sentence the fast way

a. Everybody, put your finger on the period after **rāin.**
Check children's responses.

b. Now move along the arrows until you find the next period.
Check children's responses.

c. Repeat a and b until firm.

d. Put your finger on the period after **rāin.** Check children's
responses.

e. Get ready to read all the words until we come to the next period.

f. Starting with the first word after **rāin.** Check children's responses.
(Pause three seconds.) Get ready. Clap. *She.*

g. Next word. Check children's responses. (Pause three seconds.)
Get ready. Clap. *Has.*

h. Repeat g for the remaining words in the second sentence.

i. After the children read **sack** say: Stop. You've read the sentence.

j. Let's read it again. Go back to the period after **rāin.**
Check children's responses.
Get ready to read all the words in the sentence.

k. First word. Check children's responses. Get ready. Clap. *She.*

l. Next word. Check children's responses. Get ready. Clap. *Has.*

m. Repeat l for the remaining words in the second sentence.

TASK 23 Individual test

a. Everybody, finger on the ball of the top line.
Check children's responses.

b. We're going to have different children read the fast way.
Everybody's going to touch the words.

c. First word. Check children's responses. Call on a child.
Clap. *The child responds.*

d. Next word. Check children's responses. Call on a child.
Clap. *The child responds.*

e. Repeat d for the remaining words in the first sentence.

TASK 24 Sentence saying

Good reading. Now, everybody, say all the words in that sentence
without looking. (Signal.) *The children repeat the sentence
at a normal speaking rate.*

CROSS-OUT GAME

The children will need pencils.

TASK 25 Children cross out sēē

a. Hold up side 1 of your take-home and point to the Cross-out Game.

b. Everybody, here's the new Cross-out Game.

c. Point to the word in the box. Everybody, read this word the fast
way. (Pause.) Get ready. (Signal.) *See.*

d. This word is **see**. So you're going to cross out every word **see** on
this part of your take-home. Do it. Check children's responses.

TASK 27 Individual test

a. **Everybody, finger on the ball of the top line.**
   Check children's responses.
b. **We're going to have different children read. Everybody's going to touch the words.**
c. **Everybody, touch the first word.** Check children's responses.
d. Call on a child. **Reading the fast way. Get ready.** Clap. *That.*
e. **Next word.** Check children's responses.
f. **Everybody reading. Get ready.** Clap. *Man.*
g. **Next word.** Check children's responses.
h. Call on a child. **Get ready.** Clap. *Has.*
i. Repeat e through h for the remaining words in the first sentence.

SUMMARY OF INDEPENDENT ACTIVITY

TASK 28 Introduction to independent activity

a. Hold up Take-Home 78.
b. **Everybody, you're going to finish this take-home on your own.**
   Tell the children when they will work the remaining items.
   Let's go over the things you're going to do.

TASK 29 Story copying

Point to the dotted words below the story on side 1. **You're going to write the dotted words on this arrow. Then you're going to write those words on the other arrows.**

TASK 30 Matching

a. Point to the first column of words in the Matching Game.
b. **Everybody, get ready to read each of the words over here.**
   Touch the sounds as the children sound out the word.
   Then ask: **What word?** (Signal.) *The children respond.*
c. Point to the first column. **You're going to make lines for every word over here.**

TASK 31 Cross-out game

Point to the boxed sounds in the Cross-out Game. **Everybody, what sound are you going to cross out today?** (Signal.) *iii.*
What sound are you going to circle? (Signal.) *III.*

TASK 32 Sound writing

a. Point to the sound-writing exercise on side 2. **Here are the sounds you're going to write today. I'll touch the sounds. You say them.**
b. Touch each sound. *The children respond.*
c. Repeat the series until firm.

TASK 33 Pair relations

a. Point to the pair-relations exercise.
b. **Everybody, remember the rule. If the picture doesn't show what the word says, you cross out the box.**
c. Point to the first box. **This word is mean. What word?** (Signal.)
   Mean. **Everybody, does the picture show someone who is mean?** (Signal.) *Yes.* **Are you going to cross it out?** (Signal.) *No.*
d. If the children's responses are not firm, repeat c with one or more boxes.

TASK 34 Story picture

Point to the story picture. **After you finish your take-home, you can color the story picture.**

END OF LESSON 78

Take-Home 87

STORY
Do not clap for any small letters.

TASK 17   First reading—children sound out each word and tell what word

a. Pass out Take-Home 87. Do not let the children look at the picture
until task 19.

b. Get ready to read the story.
c. First word. (Pause.) Get ready. Clap for each sound. *Shshshēēē.*
What word? (Signal.) *She.* Yes, **she.**
d. Next word. (Pause.) Get ready. Clap for each sound. *Iiisss.*
What word? (Signal.) *Is.* Yes, **is.**
e. Repeat *d* for the remaining words in the story.

TASK 18   Second reading—children reread the story and answer questions

a. This time you'll read the story and I'll ask questions.
b. Repeat *c* through *e* in task 17. Ask the comprehension questions
below as the children read.

After the children read:	You say:
She is in the rain.	Where is she? (Signal.) *In the rain.*
She has a sack.	What does she have? (Signal.) *A sack.* I wonder what's in the sack. Let's keep reading and find out.
Mail is in that sack.	What is in that sack? (Signal.) *Mail.*
Will she read the mail?	What do you think? *The children respond.* **You** can read, but I don't think **she** can.

TASK 19   Picture comprehension

a. What do you think you'll see in the picture? *The children respond.*
b. Turn your take-home over and look at the picture.
c. Ask these questions:
  1. What is she? *The children respond.* Yes, a dog.
  2. What is she carrying? *The children respond.* Yes, a sack.
  3. Is it raining? (Signal.) *Yes.*

TASK 20   Period finding

a. Turn your take-home back to side 1. Everybody, we're going to
read all the words in the first sentence the fast way.
b. Point to the first word. The first <u>sentence</u> begins here and goes
all the way to a little dot called a period. So I just go along
the arrow until I find a period.
c. Touch **shē.** Have I come to a period yet? (Signal.) *No.*
Touch **is.** Have I come to a period yet? (Signal.) *No.*
Touch **in.** Have I come to a period yet? (Signal.) *No.*
Touch **the.** Have I come to a period yet? (Signal.) *No.*
Touch **rāin.** Have I come to a period yet? (Signal.) *Yes.*
d. Again. Repeat *b* and *c* until firm.
e. Everybody, put your finger on the ball of the top line.
Check children's responses.
f. Get ready to find the period for the first sentence. Go along
the arrow until you find that period. Check children's responses.

Lesson 79

Groups that are firm on Mastery Tests 13 and 14 should skip this lesson and do lesson 80 today.

l i ā

a i o g

u t

ē

s

th

h

d r w c

SOUNDS

TASK 1 Sounds firm-up

a. Point to **l.** When I touch the sound, you say it.
b. (Pause.) Get ready. Touch **l.** */l/.*
c. Again. Repeat *b* until firm.
d. Get ready to say all the sounds when I touch them.
e. Alternate touching **o, i, ā, a, l, g, u,** and **t** three or four times.
        Point to the sound. (Pause one second.) Say: Get ready.
        Touch the sound. *The children respond.*

TASK 2 Individual test

Call on different children to identify one or more sounds in task 1.

TASK 3 Teacher introduces cross-out game

a. Use acetate and crayon.
b. I'll cross out the sounds on this page when you can tell me every sound.
c. Remember—when I touch it, you say it.
d. Go over the sounds until the children can identify all the sounds in order.

TASK 4 Individual test

Call on different children to identify two or more sounds in task 3.

TASK 5 Teacher crosses out sounds

a. You told me every sound. Get ready to do it again. This time I'll cross out each sound when you tell me what it is.
b. Point to each sound. (Pause.) Say: Get ready. Touch the sound. *The children respond.* As you cross out the sound, say: Goodbye, _____.

TASK 11   Children read a word beginning with a stop sound (guns)

a. Run your finger under **uns.**   You're going to sound out this part.
Get ready. Touch **u, n, s** as the children say *uuunnnsss*.
b. Say it fast. (Signal.) *Uns*. Yes, this part says (pause) **uns**.
c. Repeat *a* and *b* until firm.
d. Touch the ball for **guns.** This word rhymes with (pause) **uns**.
Get ready. Move quickly along the arrow. *Guns*.
e. What word? (Signal.) *Guns*. Yes, **guns**.
f. Repeat *d* and *e* until firm.
g. Return to the ball. Now you're going to sound out (pause) **guns**.
Get ready. Quickly touch **g, u, n, s** as the children say *guuunnnsss*.
h. What word? (Signal.) *Guns*. Yes, **guns.** Good reading.

Guns are dangerous.

i. Repeat *g* and *h* until firm.

guns

TASK 12   Individual test—Have children do *g* and *h* in task 11.

TASK 13   Children read a word beginning with a stop sound (got)

a. Run your finger under **ot.** You're going to sound out this part.
Get ready. Touch **o, t** as the children say *ooot*.
b. Say it fast. (Signal.) *Ot*. Yes, this part says (pause) **ot**.
c. Repeat *a* and *b* until firm.
d. Touch the ball for **got.** This word rhymes with (pause) **ot**.
Get ready. Move quickly along the arrow. *Got*.
e. What word? (Signal.) *Got*. Yes, **got**.
f. Repeat *d* and *e* until firm.
g. Return to the ball. Now you're going to sound out (pause) **got**.
Get ready. Quickly touch **g, o, t** as the children say *gooot*.
h. What word? (Signal.) *Got*. Yes, **got**. Good reading. I **got** a bone
for my dog.

got

i. Repeat *g* and *h* until firm.

TASK 14   Individual test—Have children do *g* and *h* in task 13.

TASK 15   Children read the words the fast way

a. Now you get to read the words on this page the fast way.
b. Touch the ball for **guns.** (Pause three seconds.) Get ready.
Move your finger quickly along the arrow. *Guns*.
c. Repeat *b* for **got.**

TASK 16   Individual test—Have children read one word the fast way.

READING VOCABULARY

Do not touch any small letters.

TASK 6 Children sound out the word, then read it the fast way

a. Touch the ball for **lock.** Sound it out.

b. Get ready. Touch **l, o, c** as the children say *lllooоc.*

If sounding out is not firm, repeat *b.*

c. What word? (Signal.) *Lock.* Yes, **lock.**

d. Return to the ball. Get ready to read the word the fast way.

I'm going to count to five. See if you can remember the word.

e. 1, 2, 3, 4, 5. Get ready. Move your finger quickly along the arrow.

Lock. Yes, **lock.** Good reading.

f. Again. Repeat *e* until firm.

TASK 7 Individual test

Call on different children to do *e* in task 6.

TASK 8 Children sound out the word, then read it the fast way

a. Touch the ball for **rut.** Sound it out.

b. Get ready. Touch **r, u, t** as the children say *rrruuut.*

If sounding out is not firm, repeat *b.*

c. What word? (Signal.) *Rut.* Yes, **rut.**

d. Return to the ball. Get ready to read the word the fast way.

I'm going to count to five. See if you can remember the word.

e. 1, 2, 3, 4, 5. Get ready. Move your finger quickly along the arrow.

Rut. Yes, **rut.** Good reading.

f. Again. Repeat *e* until firm.

TASK 9 Children sound out the word, then read it the fast way

a. Touch the ball for **cut.** Sound it out.

b. Get ready. Touch **c, u, t** as the children say *cuuut.*
If sounding out is not firm, repeat *b.*

c. What word? (Signal.) *Cut.* Yes, **cut.**

d. Return to the ball. Get ready to read the word the fast way.

I'm going to count to five. See if you can remember the word.

e. 1, 2, 3, 4, 5. Get ready. Move your finger quickly along the arrow.

Cut. Yes, **cut.** Good reading.

f. Again. Repeat *e* until firm.

READING VOCABULARY

After you read the words on this page, you'll get to read the words the fast way.

Do not touch any small letters.

TASK 4   Children sound out the word and tell what word

a. Touch the ball for **it.** Sound it out.
b. Get ready. Touch **i, t** as the children say *iiit*.
                    If sounding out is not firm, repeat *b*.
c. What word? (Signal.) *It*. Yes, **it**.

TASK 5   Children sound out the word and tell what word

Repeat the procedures in task 4 for **shē.**

TASK 6   Children sound out the word and tell what word

Repeat the procedures in task 4 for **suns.**

TASK 7   Children read a word beginning with a stop sound (tāil)

a. Run your finger under **āil.** You're going to sound out this part.
                    Get ready. Touch **ā, l** as the children say *āāālll*.
b. Say it fast. (Signal.) *Al*. Yes, this part says (pause) **āl**.
c. Repeat *a* and *b* until firm.
d. Touch the ball for **tāil.** This word rhymes with (pause) **āall**.
                    Get ready. Move to **t,** then quickly along the arrow. *Tail*.
e. What word? (Signal.) *Tail*. Yes, **tail**.
f. Repeat *d* and *e* until firm.
g. Return to the ball. Now you're going to sound out (pause) **tail**.
                    Get ready. Quickly touch **t, ā, l** as the children say *tāāālll*.
h. What word? (Signal.) *Tail*. Yes, **tail**. Good reading.
                    The dog wagged his **tail**.
i. Repeat *g* and *h* until firm.

TASK 8   Individual test—Have children do *g* and *h* in task 7.

TASK 9   Children read the words the fast way

Have the children read the words on this page the fast way.

TASK 10   Individual test—Have children read one word the fast way.

TASK 10   Children sound out the word, then read it the fast way

a. Touch the ball for **sag.** Sound it out.
b. Get ready.   Touch **s, a, g** as the children say *sssaaag.*
                              If sounding out is not firm, repeat *b.*
c. What word?   (Signal.) *Sag.* Yes, **sag.**
d. Return to the ball. Get ready to read the word the fast way.
            I'm going to count to five. See if you can remember the word.
e. 1, 2, 3, 4, 5. Get ready.   Move your finger quickly along the arrow.
                              Sag. Yes, **sag.** Good reading.

f. Again.   Repeat *e* until firm.

TASK 11   Individual test

Call on different children to do *e* in task 10.

TASK 12   Children rhyme with ill

a. Touch the ball for **ill.** Sound it out.
b. Get ready.   Touch **i,** between the **l**'s as the children say *iiilll.*
                              If sounding out is not firm, repeat *b.*
c. What word?   (Signal.) *Ill.* Yes, **ill.**
d. Quickly touch the ball for **mill.** This word rhymes with   (pause) **ill.**
            Get ready.   Touch **m.** *mmm.* Move your finger quickly along the
                                       arrow. *Mmmill.*

e. What word?   (Signal.) *Mill.* Yes, **mill.**

TASK 13   Children sound out the word, then read it the fast way

a. Touch the ball for **rock.** Sound it out.
b. Get ready.   Touch **r, o, c** as the children say *rrroooc.*
                              If sounding out is not firm, repeat *b.*
c. What word?   (Signal.) *Rock.* Yes, **rock.**
d. Return to the ball. Get ready to read the word the fast way.
            I'm going to count to five. See if you can remember the word.
e. 1, 2, 3, 4, 5. Get ready.   Move your finger quickly along the arrow.
                              Rock. Yes, **rock.** Good reading.

f. Again.   Repeat *e* until firm.

TASK 14   Individual test

Call on different children to do *e* in task 13.

Do not touch any small letters.

sag

ill

mill

Lesson 87

SOUNDS

TASK 1 Sounds firm-up

a. Point to **i.** When I touch the sound, you say it.
b. (Pause.) Get ready. Touch **i.** *iii.*
c. Again. Repeat *b* until firm.
d. Get ready to say all the sounds when I touch them.
e. Alternate touching **h, n, i, u, t, ē, o,** and **a** three or four times. Point to the sound. (Pause one second.) Say: Get ready. Touch the sound. *The children respond.*

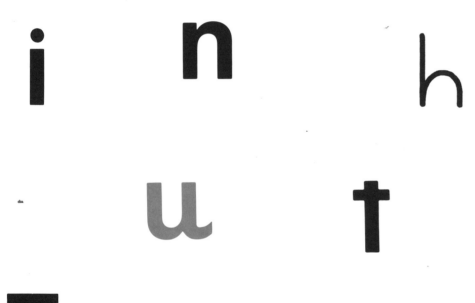

TASK 2 Individual test

Call on different children to identify one or more sounds in task 1.

TASK 3 Teacher and children play the sounds game

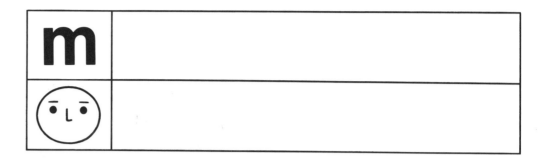

a. Use acetate and crayon. Write the sounds in the symbol box. Keep score in the score box.
b. I'm smart. I bet I can beat you in a game.
c. Here's the rule. When I touch a sound, you say it.
d. Play the game.
Make one symbol at a time in the symbol box. Use the symbols **o, w, sh,** and **ā.**
Make each symbol quickly. (Pause.) Touch the symbol. Play the game for about two minutes. Then ask: Who won? Draw a mouth on the face in the score box.

After you read the words on this page, you'll get to read the words in the box the fast way.

To correct	For all mistakes, have the children sound out the word and say it fast. Then say: **Remember this word.**

TASK 15   Children sound out the word and tell what word

a. Touch the ball for **nut.** Sound it out.
b. Get ready.   Touch **n, u, t** as the children say *nnnuuut.*
                    If sounding out is not firm, repeat *b.*
c. What word?   (Signal.) *Nut.* Yes, **nut.**

TASK 16   Children sound out the word and tell what word

a. Touch the ball for **will.** Sound it out.
b. Get ready.   Touch **w, i,** between the **l**'s as the children say *wwwiiilll.*
                    If sounding out is not firm, repeat *b.*
c. What word?   (Signal.) *Will.* Yes, **will.**

TASK 17   Children sound out the word and tell what word

a. Touch the ball for **lid.** Sound it out.
b. Get ready.   Touch **l, i, d** as the children say *llliiid.*
                    If sounding out is not firm, repeat *b.*
c. What word?   (Signal.) *Lid.* Yes, **lid.**

TASK 18   Children read the words in the box the fast way

a. Now you're going to read the words in the box the fast way.
b. Touch the ball for **nut.** (Pause three seconds.) Get ready.
                    Move your finger quickly along the arrow. *Nut.*
c. Repeat *b* for the words **will** and **lid.**
d. Present the series **nut, will, lid** at least two times.

TASK 19   Individual test

Call on different children to read one word in the box the fast way.

TASK 25   Individual test

a. Everybody, finger on the ball of the top line.
Check children's responses.
b. We're going to have different children read. Everybody's going to touch the words.
c. Everybody, touch the first word. Check children's responses.
d. Call on a child. Reading the fast way. Get ready. Clap. *He.*
e. Next word. Check children's responses.
f. Everybody reading. Get ready. Clap. *Had.*
g. Next word. Check children's responses.
h. Call on a child. Get ready. Clap. *Fun.*

CROSS-OUT GAME
The children will need pencils.

TASK 26   Children cross out rat

a. Hold up side 1 of your take-home and point to the Cross-out Game.
b. Everybody, here's a new Cross-out Game.
c. Point to the word in the box. Everybody, read this word the fast way. (Pause.) Get ready. (Signal.) *Rat.*
d. This word is **rat**. So you're going to cross out every word **rat** on this part of your take-home. Do it. Check children's responses.

SUMMARY OF INDEPENDENT ACTIVITY

TASK 27   Introduction to independent activity

a. Hold up Take-Home 86.
b. Everybody, you're going to finish this take-home on your own.
Tell the children when they will work the remaining items.
Let's go over the things you're going to do.

TASK 28   Story copying

Point to the dotted words below the story on side 1. You're going to write the dotted words on this arrow. Then you're going to write those words on the other arrows.

TASK 29   Matching

a. Point to the first column of words in the Matching Game.
b. Everybody, get ready to read each of the words over here. Reading the fast way.
c. Point to the first word. Get ready. (Signal.) *The children respond.*
d. Repeat c for the remaining words.
e. Point to the first column. You're going to make lines for every word over here.

TASK 30   Sound writing

a. Point to the sound-writing exercise on side 2. Here are the sounds you're going to write today. I'll touch the sounds. You say them.
b. Touch each sound. *The children respond.*
c. Repeat the series until firm.

TASK 31   Pair relations

a. Point to the words **a rat** in the first row of the pair-relations exercise.
b. Everybody, touch this box on your take-home. Check children's responses.
c. Get ready to tell me the words. (Pause.) What words? (Signal.) *A rat.*
d. You're going to circle the picture that shows (pause) **a rat**. Do it. Check children's responses.
e. Point to the other boxes. Remember—you're going to circle the picture in each box that shows what the words say.

TASK 32   Story picture

Point to the story picture. After you finish your take-home, you can color the story picture.

END OF LESSON 86

Take-Home 79

STORY
Do not clap for any small letters.

TASK 20 First reading—children sound out each word and tell what word

a. Pass out Take-Home 79. Do not let the children look at the picture until task 22.

b. **Get ready to read the story. First word.** Check children's responses.
c. **Get ready. Clap for each sound.** *Thththēēē.* **What word?** (Signal.) *Thē.* **Yes, thē.**

d. **Next word.** Check children's responses.
e. **Get ready. Clap for each sound.** *Llloooc.* **What word?** (Signal.) *Lock.* **Yes, lock.**

f. Repeat *d* and *e* for the remaining words in the story.

TASK 21 Second reading—children reread the story and answer questions

a. **This time you'll read the story and I'll ask questions. Back to the first word.** Check children's responses.
b. Repeat *c* through *f* in task 20. Ask the comprehension questions below as the children read.

After the children read:	You say:
The lock is on a rock.	**Where is it?** (Signal.) *On a rock.*
The nut is on the lock.	**The lock is on a rock. Where is the nut?** (Signal.) *On the lock.*

To correct	If the children do not give acceptable answers, have them reread the sentence that answers the question. Then ask the question again.

TASK 22 Picture comprehension

a. **Name some things you think you'll see in the picture.** (Signal.) *Lock, rock, nut.*

b. **Turn your take-home over and look at the picture.**
c. **Show me some things in the picture.**
   1. **Touch the rock.** (The children respond.)
   2. **Touch the lock.** (The children respond.)
   3. **Touch the nut.** (The children respond.)
d. **Ask these questions:**
   1. **Tell me where the lock is.** *On the rock.*
   2. **Tell me where the nut is.** *On the lock.*
   3. **Tell me where the rock is.** *The children respond.* *Yes, in the girl's hand.*

TASK 23 Word finding

a. **Turn your take-home back to side 1. Everybody, look at the words in the top line. One of the words is is.**
b. **Get ready to touch is when I clap.** (Pause three seconds.) **Get ready. Clap.** (The children touch **is**.)
c. Repeat *b* for these words: **lock, is, on, lock, on, lock, is, on, is, lock, is, on.**

TASK 24 Children read the first sentence the fast way

a. **Everybody, now you're going to read part of the story the fast way. Finger on the ball of the top line.** Check children's responses.
b. **Move your finger under the sounds of the first word and figure out the sounds you're going to say. Don't say the sounds out loud. Just figure out what you're going to say.** Check children's responses. Prompt children who don't touch under the sounds. (Pause three seconds.) **Read the word the fast way. Get ready. Clap.** *Thē.* **Yes, thē.**
c. **Next word. Move your finger under the sounds and figure out the sounds.** Check children's responses. (Pause three seconds.) **Read the word the fast way. Get ready. Clap.** *Lock.* **Yes, lock.**
d. Repeat *c* for the words **is, on, a, rock.**

TURN THE PAGE FOR THE REST OF TASK 24.

Take-Home 86

STORY

TASK 20 **First reading—children sound out each word and tell what word**

a. Pass out Take-Home 86. Do not let the children look at the picture until task 22.

b. **Get ready to read the story. First word.** Check children's responses.

c. **Get ready. Clap for each sound.** *Hēēē.* **What word?** (Signal.) *He.* **Yes, he.**

d. **Next word.** Check children's responses.

e. **Get ready. Clap for each sound.** *Haaad.* **What word?** (Signal.) *Had.* **Yes, had.**

f. Repeat *d* and *e* for the remaining words in the story.

TASK 21 **Second reading—children reread the story and answer questions**

a. **This time you'll read the story and I'll ask questions. Back to the first word.** Check children's responses.

b. Repeat *c* through *f* in task 20. Ask the comprehension questions below as the children read.

After the children read:	You say:
He had fun.	**What did he do?** (Signal.) *He had fun.*
She had fun in the sand.	**Where did she have fun?** (Signal.) *In the sand.* **Who else had fun?** (Signal.) *He did.*
And the cat had fun in the sand.	**Name everybody who had fun in the sand.** (Signal.) *He, she, and the cat.*
To correct	If the children do not give acceptable answers, have them reread the sentence that answers the question. Then ask the question again.

TASK 22 **Picture comprehension**

a. **What do you think you'll see in the picture?** *The children respond.*

b. **Turn your take-home over and look at the picture.**

c. Ask these questions:
1. **Where are they?** *The children respond.* **In the sand.**
2. **What are they doing?** *The children respond.* **They're playing.**
3. **Are they having fun?** *Yes.*
4. **Did you ever play in the sand?** *The children respond.*

TASK 23 **Word finding**

a. **Turn your take-home back to side 1. Everybody, look at the words in the top line. One of the words is had.**

b. **Get ready to touch had when I clap.** (Pause three seconds.) **Get ready. Clap.** *(The children touch had.)*

c. Repeat *b* for these words: **had, hē, had, fun, hē, fun, hē, had, fun, fun, hē, had.**

TASK 24 **Children read the first sentence the fast way**

a. **Everybody, now you're going to read part of the story the fast way. Finger on the ball of the top line.** Check children's responses.

b. **Move your finger under the sounds of the first word and figure out the sounds you're going to say. Don't say the sounds out loud. Just figure out what you're going to say.** Check children's responses. Prompt children who don't touch under the sounds. (Pause three seconds.) **Read the word the fast way. Get ready.** Clap. *He.* **Yes, he.**

c. **Next word. Move your finger under the sounds and figure out the sounds.** Check children's responses. (Pause three seconds.) **Read the word the fast way. Get ready.** Clap. *Had.* **Yes, had.**

d. Repeat *c* for the word **fun.**

e. **Let's read the words the fast way again. Everybody, finger on the ball of the top line.** Check children's responses. **Figure out the first word and get ready to read it the fast way. Say the sounds to yourself.** (Pause three seconds.) **What word?** Clap. *He.* **Yes, he.**

f. **Figure out the next word. Say the sounds to yourself.** (Pause three seconds.) **What word?** Clap. *Had.* **Yes, had.**

g. Repeat *f* for the word **fun.**

e. Let's read the words the fast way again. Everybody, finger on the ball of the top line. Check children's responses. Figure out the first word and get ready to read it the fast way. Say the sounds to yourself. (Pause three seconds.) What word? Clap. *Thē.* Yes, **thē.**

f. Figure out the next word. Say the sounds to yourself. (Pause three seconds.) What word? Clap. *Lock.* Yes, **lock.**

g. Repeat f for the words **is, on, a, rock.**

TASK 25 Individual test

a. Everybody, finger on the ball of the top line.
Check children's responses.

b. We're going to have different children read. Everybody's going to touch the words.

c. Everybody, touch the first word. Check children's responses.

d. Call on a child. Reading the fast way. Get ready. Clap. *Thē.*

e. Next word. Check children's responses.

f. Everybody reading. Get ready. Clap. *Lock.*

g. Next word. Check children's responses.

h. Call on a child. Get ready. Clap. *Is.*

i. Repeat e through h for the remaining words in the first sentence.

SUMMARY OF INDEPENDENT ACTIVITY

TASK 26 Introduction to independent activity

a. Hold up Take-Home 79.

b. Everybody, you're going to finish this take-home on your own. Tell the children when they will work the remaining items. Let's go over the things you're going to do.

TASK 27 Story copying

Point to the dotted words below the story on side 1. You're going to write the dotted words on this arrow. Then you're going to write those words on the other arrows.

TASK 28 Matching

a. Point to the first column of words in the Matching Game.

b. Everybody, get ready to read each of the words over here. Touch the sounds as the children sound out the word. Then ask: What word? (Signal.) *The children respond.*

c. Point to the first column. You're going to make lines for every word over here.

TASK 29 Cross-out game

Point to the boxed sounds in the Cross-out Game. Everybody, what sound are you going to circle today? (Signal.) *mmm.* What sound are you going to cross out? (Signal.) *www.*

TASK 30 Sound writing

a. Point to the sound-writing exercise on side 2. Here are the sounds you're going to write today. I'll touch the sounds. You say them.

b. Touch each sound. *The children respond.*

c. Repeat the series until firm.

TASK 31 Pair relations

a. Point to the pair-relations exercise.

b. Everybody, remember the rule. If the picture doesn't show what the word says, you cross out the box.

c. Point to the first box. This word is **sack**. What word? (Signal.) *Sack.* Everybody, does the picture show a **sack**? (Signal.) *No.* Are you going to cross it out? (Signal.) *Yes.*

d. If the children's responses are not firm, repeat c with one or more boxes.

TASK 32 Story picture

Point to the story picture. After you finish your take-home, you can color the story picture.

END OF LESSON 79

TASK 16 Children read a word beginning with a stop sound (got)

a. Run your finger under **ot.** You're going to sound out this part.
     Get ready. Touch **o, t** as the children say *ooot*.
b. Say it fast. (Signal.) *Ot*. Yes, this part says (pause) **ot**.
c. Repeat *a* and *b* until firm.
d. Touch the ball for **got.** This word rhymes with (pause) **ot**.
Get ready. Move quickly along the arrow. *Got*.
e. What word? (Signal.) *Got*. Yes, **got**.
f. Repeat *d* and *e* until firm.
g. Return to the ball. Now you're going to sound out (pause) **got**.
     Get ready. Quickly touch **g, o, t** as the children say *gooot*.
h. What word? (Signal.) *Got*. Yes, **got**. Good reading.
                              Father **got** a new car.

i. Repeat *g* and *h* until firm.

Do not touch any small letters.

got

TASK 17 Individual test

Call on different children to do *g* and *h* in task 16.

TASK 18 Children read a word beginning with a stop sound (hēars)

a. Run your finger under **ēars.** You're going to sound out this part.
                    Get ready. Touch **ē, r, s** as the children say *ēērrsss*.
b. Say it fast. (Signal.) *Ears*. Yes, this part says (pause) **ears**.
c. Repeat *a* and *b* until firm.
d. Touch the ball for **hēars.** This word rhymes with (pause) **ēērss**.
               Get ready. Move to **h,** then quickly along the arrow. *Hears*.
e. What word? (Signal.) *Hears*. Yes, **hears**.
f. Repeat *d* and *e* until firm.
g. Return to the ball. Now you're going to sound out (pause) **hears**.
     Get ready. Quickly touch **h, ē, r, s** as the children say *hēēērrrsss*.
h. What word? (Signal.) *Hears*. Yes, **hears**. Good reading. He **hears**
                                        with his ears.

i. Repeat *g* and *h* until firm.

hēars

TASK 19 Individual test

Call on different children to do *g* and *h* in task 18.

Lesson 80

sh

th

s

h

sh **i** **l**

ē **o**

g **u**

w

SOUNDS

TASK 1   Teaching sh as in she

a. Point to **sh.** Here's a new sound.
b. My turn.   (Pause.) Touch **sh** and say: shshsh.
c. Again.   Touch **sh** for a longer time. shshshshsh.   Lift your finger.
d. Point to **sh.** Your turn. When I touch it, you say it.   (Pause.) Get ready.   Touch **sh.** *shshsh.* Lift your finger.
e. Again.   Touch **sh.** *shshshshshsh.* Lift your finger.
f. Repeat *e* until firm.

TASK 2   Individual test

Call on different children to identify **sh.**

TASK 3   Sounds firm-up

a. Get ready to say the sounds when I touch them.
b. Alternate touching **sh** and **th.** Point to the sound. (Pause one second.) Say: Get ready.   Touch the sound. *The children respond.*
c. When **sh** and **th** are firm, alternate touching **sh, th, s,** and **h** until all four sounds are firm.

TASK 4   Individual test

Call on different children to identify **sh, th, s,** or **h.**

TASK 5   Sounds firm-up

a. Point to **sh.** When I touch the sound, you say it.
b. (Pause.) Get ready.   Touch **sh.** *shshsh.*
c. Again. Repeat *b* until firm.
d. Get ready to say all the sounds when I touch them.
e. Alternate touching **sh, i, l, ē, o, w, g,** and **u** three or four times.
Point to the sound. (Pause one second.) Say: Get ready. Touch the sound. *The children respond.*

TASK 6   Individual test

Call on different children to identify one or more sounds in task 5.

After you read the words on this page, you'll get to read the words the fast way.

TASK 11   Children sound out the word and tell what word

a. Touch the ball for **runs.** Sound it out.
b. Get ready.   Touch **r, u, n, s** as the children say *rrruuunnnsss*.
⠀⠀⠀⠀⠀⠀⠀⠀⠀⠀⠀⠀⠀⠀⠀⠀⠀⠀⠀⠀⠀⠀⠀If sounding out is not firm, repeat *b*.
c. What word?   (Signal.) *Runs*. Yes, **runs.**

TASK 12   Children sound out the word and tell what word

a. Touch the ball for **fan.** Sound it out.
b. Get ready.   Touch **f, a, n** as the children say *fffaaannn*.
⠀⠀⠀⠀⠀⠀⠀⠀⠀⠀⠀⠀⠀⠀⠀⠀⠀⠀⠀⠀⠀⠀⠀If sounding out is not firm, repeat *b*.
c. What word?   (Signal.) *Fan*. Yes, **fan.**

TASK 13   Children sound out the word and tell what word

a. Touch the ball for **did.** Sound it out.
b. Get ready.   Touch **d, i, d** as the children say *diiid*.
⠀⠀⠀⠀⠀⠀⠀⠀⠀⠀⠀⠀⠀⠀⠀⠀⠀⠀⠀⠀⠀⠀⠀If sounding out is not firm, repeat *b*.
c. What word?   (Signal.) *Did*. Yes, **did.**

TASK 14   Children read the words the fast way

a. Now you get to read the words on this page the fast way.
b. Touch the ball for **runs.** (Pause three seconds.) Get ready.
⠀⠀⠀⠀⠀⠀⠀⠀⠀⠀⠀⠀⠀⠀Move your finger quickly along the arrow. *Runs*.
c. Repeat *b* for each word on the page.

TASK 15   Individual test

Call on different children to read one word the fast way.

80

READING VOCABULARY

Do not touch any small letters.

TASK 7   Children sound out the word, then read it the fast way

a. Touch the ball for **lock.** Sound it out.

b. Get ready. Touch **l, o, c** as the children say *lllooc.*

If sounding out is not firm, repeat *b.*

c. What word? (Signal.) *Lock.* Yes, **lock.**

d. Return to the ball. Get ready to read the word the fast way.

I'm going to count to five. See if you can remember the word.

e. 1, 2, 3, 4, 5. Get ready. Move your finger quickly along the arrow.

Lock. Yes, **lock.** Good reading.

f. Again. Repeat *e* until firm.

TASK 8   Individual test

Call on different children to do *e* in task 7.

TASK 9   Children sound out the word, then read it the fast way

a. Touch the ball for **māil.** Sound it out.

b. Get ready. Touch **m, ā, l** as the children say *mmmāāāl.*

If sounding out is not firm, repeat *b.*

c. What word? (Signal.) *Mail.* Yes, **mail.**

d. Return to the ball. Get ready to read the word the fast way.

I'm going to count to five. See if you can remember the word.

e. 1, 2, 3, 4, 5. Get ready. Move your finger quickly along the arrow.

Mail. Yes, **mail.** Good reading.

f. Again. Repeat *e* until firm.

TASK 10   Individual test

Call on different children to do *e* in task 9.

TASK 11   Children sound out the word, then read it the fast way

Repeat the procedures in task 9 for **lid.**

TASK 12   Individual test

Call on different children to do *e* in task 9 for **lid.**

86

READING VOCABULARY
After you read the words on this page, you'll get to read the words the fast way.

Do not touch any small letters.

$\bar{e}_a$rs

TASK 6   Children sound out the word and tell what word

a. Touch the ball for **ēars.** Sound it out.
b. Get ready.   Touch **ē, r, s** as the children say *ēēērrrsss*.
　　　　　　　　　　　　　If sounding out is not firm, repeat *b*.
c. What word?   (Signal.) *Ears.* Yes, **ears.**

TASK 7   Children sound out the word and tell what word

a. Touch the ball for **run.** Sound it out.
b. Get ready.   Touch **r, u, n** as the children say *rrruuunnn*.
　　　　　　　　　　　　　If sounding out is not firm, repeat *b*.
c. What word?   (Signal.) *Run.* Yes, **run.**

run

TASK 8   Children sound out the word and tell what word

a. Touch the ball for **can.** Sound it out.
b. Get ready.   Touch **c, a, n** as the children say *caaannn*.
　　　　　　　　　　　　　If sounding out is not firm, repeat *b*.
c. What word?   (Signal.) *Can.* Yes, **can.**

can

TASK 9   Children read the words the fast way

a. Now you get to read the words on this page the fast way.
b. Touch the ball for **ēars.** (Pause three seconds.) Get ready.
　　　　　　　　Move your finger quickly along the arrow. *Ears.*
c. Repeat *b* for each word on the page.

TASK 10   Individual test

Call on different children to read one word the fast way.

TASK 13   Children sound out the word, then read it the fast way

a. Touch the ball for **rāin.** Sound it out.

b. Get ready.   Touch **r, ā, n** as the children say *rrrāāānnn.*

If sounding out is not firm, repeat *b.*

c. What word? (Signal.) *Rain.* Yes, **rain.**

d. Return to the ball.   Get ready to read the word the fast way.

I'm going to count to five. See if you can remember the word.

e. 1, 2, 3, 4, 5. Get ready.   Move your finger quickly along the arrow.

Rain. Yes, **rain.** Good reading.

f. Again.   Repeat *e* until firm.

Do not touch any small letters.

rāin

TASK 14   Individual test

Call on different children to do *e* in task 13.

TASK 15   Children rhyme with sēē

a. Touch the ball for **sēē.** Sound it out.

b. Get ready.   Touch **s,** between the **ē**'s, as the children say *sssēēē.*

If sounding out is not firm, repeat *b.*

c. What word? (Signal.) *See.* Yes, **see.**

d. Quickly touch the ball for **hē.** This word rhymes with (pause) **see.**

Get ready.   Touch **h.** *h.* Move your finger quickly along the arrow. *He.*

e. What word? (Signal.) *He.* Yes, **he.**

sēē

TASK 16   Children sound out the word and tell what word

a. Touch the ball for **hē.** Sound it out.

b. Get ready.   Touch **h, ē** as the children say *hēēē.*

c. Again.   Repeat *b* until firm.

d. Yes, what word? (Signal.) *He.*

hē

Lesson 86

SOUNDS

TASK 1 Child plays teacher

ā

d

o

th

u

m

a. Use acetate and crayon.
b. [Child's name] is going to be the teacher.
c. [He or She] is going to touch the sounds. When [he or she] touches a sound, you say it.
d. The child points to and touches the sounds. You circle any sound that is not firm.
e. After the child has completed the page, present all the circled sounds to the children.

TASK 2 Individual test

Call on different children.
If you can say the sound when I call your name, you may cross it out.

u

i

n

TASK 3 Teacher introduces cross-out game

a. Use acetate and crayon.
b. I'll cross out the sounds on this page when you can tell me every sound.
c. Remember—when I touch it, you say it.
d. Go over the sounds until the children can identify all the sounds in order.

TASK 4 Individual test

Call on different children to identify two or more sounds in task 3.

TASK 5 Teacher crosses out sounds

a. You told me every sound. Get ready to do it again. This time I'll cross out each sound when you tell me what it is.
b. Point to each sound. (Pause.) Say: Get ready. Touch the sound.
The children respond. As you cross out the sound, say: Goodbye, _____.

After you read the words on this page, you'll get to read the words in the box the fast way.

To correct	For all mistakes, have the children sound out the word and say it fast. Then say: **Remember this word.**

TASK 17   Children sound out the word and tell what word

a. Touch the ball for **wē.** Sound it out.
b. Get ready. Touch **w, ē** as the children say *wwwēēē.*
　　　　　　　　　　　　　If sounding out is not firm, repeat *b.*
c. What word? (Signal.) *We.* Yes, **we.**

TASK 18   Children sound out the word and tell what word

a. Touch the ball for **and.** Sound it out.
b. Get ready. Touch **a, n, d** as the children say *aaannnd.*
　　　　　　　　　　　　　If sounding out is not firm, repeat *b.*
c. What word? (Signal.) *And.* Yes, **and.**

TASK 19   Children sound out the word and tell what word

a. Touch the ball for **will.** Sound it out.
b. Get ready. Touch **w, i,** between the **l**'s as the children say *wwwiiilll.*
　　　　　　　　　　　　　If sounding out is not firm, repeat *b.*
c. What word? (Signal.) *Will.* Yes, **will.**

TASK 20   Children read the words in the box the fast way

a. Now you're going to read the words in the box the fast way.
b. Touch the ball for **wē.** (Pause three seconds.) Get ready.
　　　　　　　　　　　Move your finger quickly along the arrow. *We.*
c. Repeat *b* for the words **and** and **will.**
d. Present the series **wē, and, will** at least two times.

TASK 21   Individual test

Call on different children to read one word in the box the fast way.

Mastery Test 16 after lesson 85, before lesson 86

a. Get ready to read the story.
b. First word. *(The child responds.)* Get ready. Clap for each sound as the child sounds out **wē** one time.
c. **(test item)** What word? (Signal.) *We.*
d. Next word. *(The child responds.)* Get ready. Clap for each sound as the child sounds out **sēē** one time.
e. **(test item)** What word? (Signal.) *See.*
f. **(8 test items)** Repeat d and e for the eight remaining words in the story.

Total number of test items: **10**

A group is weak if more than one-third of the children missed two or more words on the test.

wē ▪ sēē ▪ a ▪ hut. ⟶

wē ▪ will ▪ run ▪ in ⟶

thē ▪ hut. ⟶

WHAT TO DO

If the group is firm on Mastery Test 16 and was firm on Mastery Test 15:

Present lessons 86, 87, and 88, and then skip lesson 89. If more than one child missed two or more words on the test, present the firming procedures specified below to those children.

If the group is firm on Mastery Test 16 but was weak on Mastery Test 15:

Present lesson 86 to the group during the next reading period. If more than one child missed two or more words on the test, present the firming procedures specified below to those children.

If the group is weak on Mastery Test 16:

A. Present these firming procedures to the group during the next reading period. Present each story until the children make no more than one mistake. Then proceed to the next story.
   1. Lesson 83, Story, page 172. Present task 16 two times. Then call on individual children to sound out a word and tell what word.
   2. Lesson 84, Story, page 179. Present task 22 two times. Then call on individual children to sound out a word and tell what word.
   3. Lesson 85, Story, page 185. Present task 19 two times. Then call on individual children to sound out a word and tell what word.
   Duplicate stories for lessons 83, 84, and 85 are provided in the Teacher's Guide. You may reproduce these stories for use in presenting the firming procedures.
B. After presenting the above tasks, again give Mastery Test 16 individually to members of the group who failed the test.
C. If the group is firm (less than one-third of the total group missed two or more words in the story on the retest), present lesson 86 to the group during the next reading period.
D. If the group is still weak (more than one-third of the total group missed two or more words in the story on the retest), repeat A and B during the next reading period.

Take-Home 80

STORY
Do not clap for any small letters.

TASK 22 First reading—children sound out each word and tell what word

a. Pass out Take-Home 80. Do not let the children look at the picture until task 24.

b. Get ready to read the story. First word. Check children's responses.

c. Get ready. Clap for each sound. *Wwwēēē*. What word? (Signal.)
We. Yes, **we**.

d. Next word. Check children's responses.

e. Get ready. Clap for each sound. *Sssēēē*. What word? (Signal.)
See. Yes, **see**.

f. Repeat *d* and *e* for the remaining words in the story.

TASK 23 Second reading—children reread the story and answer questions

a. This time you'll read the story and I'll ask questions.
Back to the first word. Check children's responses.

b. Repeat *c* through *f* in task 22. Ask the comprehension questions below as the children read.

After the children read:	You say:
We see a hut.	What do we see? (Signal.) *A hut.*
We will run in the hut.	Where will we run? (Signal.) *In the hut.*
We will lock the hut.	What will we do to the hut? (Signal.) *Lock it.*

To correct	If the children do not give acceptable answers, have them reread the sentence that answers the question. Then ask the question again.

TASK 24 Picture comprehension

a. What do you think you'll see in the picture? (Signal.)
People and a hut.

b. What do you think the people will be doing in the picture?
(Signal.) *Running in a hut.*

c. Turn your take-home over and look at the picture.

d. Touch the hut in the picture. (*The children respond.*)

e. Ask these questions:
1. What are the people doing? *The children respond.*
Yes, running in the hut.
2. Why are they running? *The children respond.*
Yes, a lion is chasing them.
3. What would you do if a lion was chasing you?
The children respond.

TASK 25 Word finding

a. Turn your take-home back to side 1. Everybody, look at the words in the top line. One word is **will**.

b. Get ready to touch **will** when I clap. (Pause three seconds.)
Get ready. Clap. (*The children touch* **will**.)

c. Repeat *b* for these words: **sēē, hut, sēē, will, hut, will, hut, sēē, will, sēē, hut, will.**

TASK 26 Children read the first sentence the fast way

a. Everybody, now you're going to read part of the story the fast way. Finger on the ball of the top line. Check children's responses.

b. Move your finger under the sounds of the first word and figure out the sounds you're going to say. Don't say the sounds out loud. Just figure out what you're going to say. Check children's responses. Prompt children who don't touch under the sounds. (Pause three seconds.) Read the word the fast way. Get ready. Clap. *We.* Yes, **we.**

c. Next word. Move your finger under the sounds and figure out the sounds. Check children's responses. (Pause three seconds.) Read the word the fast way. Get ready. Clap. *See.* Yes, **see.**

d. Repeat *c* for the words **a, hut.**

TURN THE PAGE FOR THE REST OF TASK 26.

TASK 24 Individual test

a. Everybody, finger on the ball of the top line.
                                        Check children's responses.
b. We're going to have different children read. Everybody's going
                                        to touch the words.
c. Everybody, touch the first word. Check children's responses.
d. Call on a child. Reading the fast way. Get ready. Clap. *He*.
e. Next word. Check children's responses.
f. Everybody reading. Get ready. Clap. *Has*.
g. Next word. Check children's responses.
h. Call on a child. Get ready. Clap. *A*.
i. Repeat *e* and *f* for **shack.**

SUMMARY OF INDEPENDENT ACTIVITY

TASK 25   Introduction to independent activity

a. Hold up Take-Home 85.
b. Everybody, you're going to finish this take-home on your own.
            Tell the children when they will work the remaining items.
                    Let's go over the things you're going to do.

TASK 26   Story copying

Point to the dotted words below the story on side 1. You're going
        to write the dotted words on this arrow. Then you're going to write
                        those words on the other arrows.

TASK 27   Cross-out game

Point to the boxed sounds in the Cross-out Game. Everybody, what
            sound are you going to circle today? (Signal.) *aaa*.
        What sound are you going to cross out? (Signal.) *āāā*.

TASK 28 Matching

a. Point to the first column of words in the Matching Game.
b. Everybody, get ready to read each of the words over here.
                                        Reading the fast way.
c. Point to the first word. Get ready. (Signal.) *The children respond.*
d. Repeat *c* for the remaining words.
e. Point to the first column. You're going to make lines for every
                                        word over here.

TASK 29   Sound writing

a. Point to the sound-writing exercise on side 2. Here are the sounds
            you're going to write today. I'll touch the sounds. You say them.
b. Touch each sound. *The children respond.*
c. Repeat the series until firm.

TASK 30   Pair relations

a. Point to the word **lock** in the first row of the pair-relations exercise.
b. Everybody, touch this box on your take-home.
                                        Check children's responses.
c. Get ready to tell me the word. (Pause.) What word? (Signal.) *Lock*.
d. You're going to circle the picture that shows a (pause) **lock**.
                        Do it. Check children's responses.
e. Point to the other boxes. Remember—you're going to circle the
                        picture in each box that shows what the words say.

TASK 31   Story picture

Point to the story picture. After you finish your take-home,
                                you can color the story picture.

END OF LESSON 85

Before presenting lesson 86, give Mastery Test 16 to each child.
Do not present lesson 86 to any groups that are not firm on this test.

e. Let's read the words the fast way again. Everybody, finger on the ball of the top line. Check children's responses. Figure out the first word and get ready to read it the fast way. Say the sounds to yourself. (Pause three seconds.) What word? Clap. *We.* Yes, **we.**

f. Figure out the next word. Say the sounds to yourself. (Pause three seconds.) What word? Clap. *See.* Yes, **see.**

g. Repeat f for the words **a, hut.**

TASK 27   Individual test

a. Everybody, finger on the ball of the top line.
Check children's responses.

b. We're going to have different children read. Everybody's going to touch the words.

c. Everybody, touch the first word. Check children's responses.

d. Call on a child. Reading the fast way. Get ready. Clap. *We.*

e. Next word. Check children's responses.

f. Everybody reading. Get ready. Clap. *See.*

g. Next word. Check children's responses.

h. Call on a child. Get ready. Clap. *A.*

i. Repeat e and f for **hut.**

SUMMARY OF INDEPENDENT ACTIVITY

TASK 28   Introduction to independent activity

a. Hold up Take-Home 80.

b. Everybody, you're going to finish this take-home on your own. Tell the children when they will work the remaining items. Let's go over the things you're going to do.

TASK 29   Story copying

Point to the dotted words below the story on side 1. You're going to write the dotted words on this arrow. Then you're going to write those words on the other arrows.

TASK 30   Matching

a. Point to the first column of words in the Matching Game.

b. Everybody, get ready to read each of the words over here. Touch the sounds as the children sound out the word. Then ask: What word? (Signal.) *The children respond.*

c. Point to the first column. You're going to make lines for every word over here.

TASK 31   Cross-out game

Point to the boxed sounds in the Cross-out Game. Everybody, what sound are you going to cross out today? (Signal.) *lll.* What sound are you going to circle? (Signal.) *iii.*

TASK 32   Sound writing

a. Point to the sound-writing exercise on side 2. Here are the sounds you're going to write today. I'll touch the sounds. You say them.

b. Touch each sound. *The children respond.*

c. Repeat the series until firm.

TASK 33   Pair relations

a. Point to the pair-relations exercise.

b. Everybody, remember the rule. If the picture doesn't show what the word says, you cross out the box.

c. Point to the first box. This word is **he.** What word? (Signal.) *He.* Everybody, does the picture show **he**? (Signal.) *Yes.* Are you going to cross it out? (Signal.) *No.*

d. If the children's responses are not firm, repeat c with one or more boxes.

TASK 34   Story picture

Point to the story picture. After you finish your take-home, you can color the story picture.

END OF LESSON 80

Before presenting lesson 81, give Mastery Test 15 to each child.
Do not present lesson 81 to any groups that are not firm on this test.

Take-Home 85

STORY
Do not clap for any small letters.

TASK 19 First reading—children sound out each word and tell what word

a. Pass out Take-Home 85. Do not let the children look at the picture until task 21.
b. Get ready to read the story. First word. Check children's responses.
c. Get ready. Clap for each sound. *Hēēē.* What word? (Signal.) *He.* Yes, **he.**
d. Next word. Check children's responses.
e. Get ready. Clap for each sound. *Haaasss.* What word? (Signal.) *Has.* Yes, **has.**
f. Repeat *d* and *e* for the remaining words in the story.

TASK 20 Second reading—children reread the story and answer questions

a. This time you'll read the story and I'll ask questions. Back to the first word. Check children's responses.
b. Repeat *c* through *f* in task 19. Ask the comprehension questions below as the children read.

After the children read:	You say:
He has a shack.	What does he have? (Signal.) *A shack.*
The shack is in the sand.	Where is the shack? (Signal.) *In the sand.*
The man is in the shack.	Where is the man? (Signal.) *In the shack.*
To correct	If the children do not give acceptable answers, have them reread the sentence that answers the question. Then ask the question again.

TASK 21 Picture comprehension

a. What do you think you'll see in the picture? *The children respond.*
b. Where will the shack be? (Signal.) *In the sand.*
c. Where will the man be? (Signal.) *In the shack.*
d. Turn your take-home over and look at the picture.
e. Touch the shack. *(The children respond.)*
f. Show me the sand. *(The children respond.)*
g. Ask these questions:
   1. Where is the man? *In the shack.*
   2. What would you do with a shack like that? *The children respond.*

TASK 22 Word finding

a. Turn your take-home back to side 1. Everybody, look at the words in the top line. One of the words is **he.**
b. Get ready to touch **hē** when I clap. (Pause three seconds.) Get ready. Clap. *(The children touch hē.)*
c. Repeat *b* for these words: **hē, shack, has, hē, has, shack, hē, has, shack, hē, has, shack.**

TASK 23 Children read the first sentence the fast way

a. Everybody, now you're going to read part of the story the fast way. Finger on the ball of the top line. Check children's responses.
b. Move your finger under the sounds of the first word and figure out the sounds you're going to say. Don't say the sounds out loud. Just figure out what you're going to say. Check children's responses. Prompt children who don't touch under the sounds. (Pause three seconds.) Read the word the fast way. Get ready. Clap. *He.* Yes, **he.**
c. Next word. Move your finger under the sounds and figure out the sounds. Check children's responses. (Pause three seconds.) Read the word the fast way. Get ready. Clap. *Has.* Yes, **has.**
d. Repeat *c* for the words **a, shack.**
e. Let's read the words the fast way again. Everybody, finger on the ball of the top line. Check children's responses. Figure out the first word and get ready to read it the fast way. Say the sounds to yourself. (Pause three seconds.) What word? Clap. *He.* Yes, **he.**
f. Figure out the next word. Say the sounds to yourself. (Pause three seconds.) What word? Clap. *Has.* Yes, **has.**
g. Repeat *f* for the words **a, shack.**

Mastery Test 15 after lesson 80, before lesson 81

a. Touch the ball for **rain.** Sound it out. Get ready.
b. **(test item)** Touch **r, ā, n** as the child says *rrrāāānnn.*
c. **(test item)** What word? *Rain.*
d. Touch the ball for **not.** Sound it out. Get ready.
e. **(test item)** Touch **n, o, t** as the child says *nnnooot.*
f. **(test item)** What word? *Not.*
g. Touch the ball for **rug.** Sound it out. Get ready.
h. **(test item)** Touch **r, u, g** as the child says *rrruuug.*
i. **(test item)** What word? *Rug.*
j. Now you're going to read these words the fast way.
k. **(test item)** Touch the ball for **rain.** (Pause three seconds.)
   Get ready. Move your finger quickly along the arrow. *Rain.*
l. **(test item)** Touch the ball for **not.** (Pause three seconds.)
   Get ready. Move your finger quickly along the arrow. *Not.*
m. **(test item)** Touch the ball for **rug.** (Pause three seconds.)
   Get ready. Move your finger quickly along the arrow. *Rug.*

Total number of test items: **9**

A group is weak if more than one-third of the children missed any of the items on the test.

WHAT TO DO

If the group is firm on Mastery Test 15:

Present lesson 81 to the group during the next reading period. If more than one child missed any of the items on the test, present the firming procedures specified below to those children.

If the group is weak on Mastery Test 15:

A. Present these firming procedures to the group during the next reading period.
   1. Lesson 78, Reading Vocabulary, pages 139–140, tasks 11 through 21.
   2. Lesson 79, Reading Vocabulary, page 146, tasks 15 through 19.
   3. Lesson 80, Reading Vocabulary, pages 151–152, tasks 13 through 21.
B. After presenting the above tasks, again give Mastery Test 15 individually to members of the group who failed the test.
C. If the group is firm (less than one-third of the total group missed any items on the retest), present lesson 81 to the group during the next reading period.
D. If the group is still weak (more than one-third of the total group missed any items on the retest), repeat *A* and *B* during the next reading period.

After you read the words on this page, you'll get to read the words the fast way.

TASK 14   Children read a word beginning with a stop sound (did)

a. Run your finger under **id.** You're going to sound out this part.
Get ready. Touch **i, d** as the children say *iiid*.
b. Say it fast. (Signal.) *Id*. Yes, this part says (pause) **id.**
c. Repeat *a* and *b* until firm.
d. Touch the ball for **did.** This word rhymes with (pause) *iid.*
Get ready. Move to **d,** then quickly along the arrow. *Did.*
e. What word? (Signal.) *Did*. Yes, **did.**
f. Repeat *d* and *e* until firm.
g. Return to the ball. Now you're going to sound out (pause) **did.**
Get ready. Quickly touch **d, i, d** as the children say *diiid*.
h. What word? (Signal.) *Did*. Yes, **did.** Good reading.
i. Repeat *g* and *h* until firm.

TASK 15   Individual test

Call on different children to do *g* and *h* in task 14.

TASK 16   Children rhyme with in

a. Touch the ball for **in.** Sound it out.
b. Get ready. Touch **i, n** as the children say *iiinnn*.
If sounding out is not firm, repeat *b*.
c. What word? (Signal.) *In*. Yes, **in.**
d. Quickly touch the ball for **fin.** This word rhymes with (pause)
in. Get ready. Touch **f.** *fff*. Move your finger quickly along
the arrow. *Fffin.*
e. What word? (Signal.) *Fin*. Yes, **fin.**

TASK 17   Children read the words the fast way

a. Now you get to read the words on this page the fast way.
b. Touch the ball for **did.** (Pause three seconds.) Get ready.
Move your finger quickly along the arrow. *Did.*
c. Repeat *b* for each word on the page.

TASK 18 Individual test

Call on different children to read one word the fast way.

did

in

fin

Planning Pages: For Lessons 81–100

Making Progress

	Since Lesson 1	Since Lesson 61
Word Reading	20 sounds 106 regular words	6 sounds 47 regular words Reading words the fast way
Comprehension	**Picture Comprehension** Predicting what the picture will show Answering questions about the picture **Story Comprehension** Answering *who, what, when, where* and *why* questions orally	Answering questions about the picture Answering *who, what, when, where* and *why* questions orally

What to Use

Teacher	Students
Presentation Book B (pages 156–284) **Teacher's Guide** (pages 44–46) **Teacher's Take-Home Book and Answer Key** **Spelling Book**	**Storybook 1** (pages 1–21) **Take-Home Book B** lined paper (Spelling)

Keep in Mind:

When errors occur in story reading, correct the error by having the children sound out the word. Then have them reread the sentence.

What's Ahead in Lessons 81–100

New Skills
- Story length will increase from 15 to 55 words.
- Children identify periods (Lesson 87) and locate the end of a sentence.
- Children identify quotation marks and learn that they indicate that someone is saying the words between the marks (Lesson 94).
- Children identify question marks and discriminate between asking a question and saying the answer (Lesson 98).
- Children begin to work with irregular words (words that are not pronounced the way they are sounded out [Lesson 89]).

New Sounds
- Lesson 88 – **I** (the word *I*)
- Lesson 92 – **k** as in *kiss* (quick sound)
- Lesson 98 – **ō** as in *over*

New Vocabulary
- *Regular words:*

(81) ron, tame	(92) digs, games,
(82) little, she	names, rigs
(83) got	(93) cow, how, mom
(84) shack	(94) shot
(85) did	(95) feel, gate, gates
(86) ears, hears, runs	(97) him, hits, kicks,
(87) guns, suns, tail	nod
(88) dish, wins	(98) hug, kiss, no,
(89) hats, wish	rats, those
(90) sacks, shut,	(99) cakes, for, go,
tacks, with	or, so
(91) licks, now, tears,	(100) nose, old, rocks,
win	socks, teeth

- *Irregular words:*
  - (89) said
  - (94) was

After you read the words on this page, you'll get to read the words the fast way.

Do not touch any small letters.

TASK 9   **Children sound out the word and tell what word**

a. Touch the ball for **shack.** Sound it out.
b. Get ready. Touch **sh, a, c** as the children say *shshshaaac*.
                    If sounding out is not firm, repeat *b*.
c. What word? (Signal.) *Shack.* Yes, **shack.**

TASK 10   **Children sound out the word and tell what word**

a. Touch the ball for **not.** Sound it out.
b. Get ready. Touch **n, o, t** as the children say *nnnooot*.
                    If sounding out is not firm, repeat *b*.
c. What word? (Signal.) *Not.* Yes, **not.**

TASK 11   **Children sound out the word and tell what word**

a. Touch the ball for **got.** Sound it out.
b. Get ready. Touch **g, o, t** as the children say *gooot*.
c. What word? (Signal.) *Got.* Yes, **got.**

TASK 12   **Children read the words the fast way**

a. Now you get to read the words on this page the fast way.
b. Touch the ball for **shack.** (Pause three seconds.) Get ready.
                    Move your finger quickly along the arrow. *Shack.*
c. Repeat *b* for each word on the page.

TASK 13   **Individual test**

Call on different children to read one word the fast way.

Look Ahead

Mastery Tests

Skill Tested	Implications

Test 15 (Lesson 85)
  Reading a story, sounding out
Test 16 (Lesson 90)
  Sounds **w, sh, g, o, l**
Test 17 (Lesson 95)
  Reading a story the fast way
	Bonus Take-Homes, which begin at Lesson 95 and will continue at every fifth lesson, can provide extra practice in reading previously introduced stories.

Test 18 (Lesson 100) Sounds **l, k, sh, u**	Be sure children are firm.

Skills

	Lessons 81–100
Word Reading	3 sounds
	54 regular words
	2 irregular words
	Reading words the fast way
Comprehension	**Story Comprehension** Finding periods, question marks, and quotation marks

Reading Activities

Help children develop comprehension skills by using the following activities.

Scrambled Sentences
(Lesson 83)

Make a word card for every word in each sentence in the lesson story. Mix up all the word cards. Have children take turns picking one card at a time to retell the story. This activity can be done from memory or with the story displayed. Discuss how to tell which word is at the end of a sentence. Have children take turns making up a different story with the words.

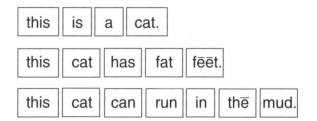

Cartoons and Comic Strips
(Lessons 94–99)

After children have been introduced to quotations in Lessons 94–99, have them draw cartoons using the quotations from a story as dialogue in cartoon bubbles. Children are to write and illustrate the cartoon. This activity can be extended to have children retell a lesson story or create an original cartoon.

READING VOCABULARY

After you read the words on this page, you'll get to read the words the fast way.

TASK 4   Children sound out the word and tell what word

a. Touch the ball for **and.** Sound it out.
b. Get ready. Touch **a, n, d** as the children say *aaannnd.*
If sounding out is not firm, repeat *b.*
c. What word? (Signal.) *And.* Yes, **and.**

TASK 5   Children sound out the word and tell what word

a. Touch the ball for **sand.** Sound it out.
b. Get ready. Touch **s, a, n, d** as the children say *sssaaannnd.*
If sounding out is not firm, repeat *b.*
c. What word? (Signal.) *Sand.* Yes, **sand.**

TASK 6   Children sound out the word and tell what word

a. Touch the ball for **shē.** Sound it out.
b. Get ready. Touch **sh, ē** as the children say *shshshēēē.*
If sounding out is not firm, repeat *b.*
c. What word? (Signal.) *She.* Yes, **she.**

TASK 7   Children read the words the fast way

a. Now you get to read the words on this page the fast way.
b. Touch the ball for **and.** (Pause three seconds.) Get ready.
Move your finger quickly along the arrow. *And.*
c. Repeat *b* for each word on the page.

TASK 8   Individual test

Call on different children to read one word the fast way.

and

sand

shē

Lesson 81

SOUNDS

TASK 1   Teaching sh as in she

a. Point to **sh**. My turn. (Pause.)
Touch **sh** and say: shshsh.

b. Point to **sh**. Your turn. When
I touch it, you say it. (Pause.)
Get ready. Touch **sh**. shshsh.
Lift your finger.

c. Again. Touch **sh**. shshshsh.
Lift your finger.

d. Repeat *c* until firm.

TASK 2   Sounds firm-up

a. Get ready to say the sounds
when I touch them.

b. Alternate touching **s** and **sh**. Point
to the sound. (Pause one second.)
Say: Get ready. Touch the
sound. *The children respond.*

c. When **s** and **sh** are firm, alternate
touching **s, f, sh,** and **th** until all
four sounds are firm.

TASK 3   Individual test

Call on different children to identify **s, f, sh,** or **th**.

TASK 4   Teacher introduces cross-out game

a. Use acetate and crayon.

b. I'll cross out the sounds on this page when you can tell me every
sound.

c. Remember—when I touch it, you say it.

d. Go over the sounds until the children can identify all the sounds
in order.

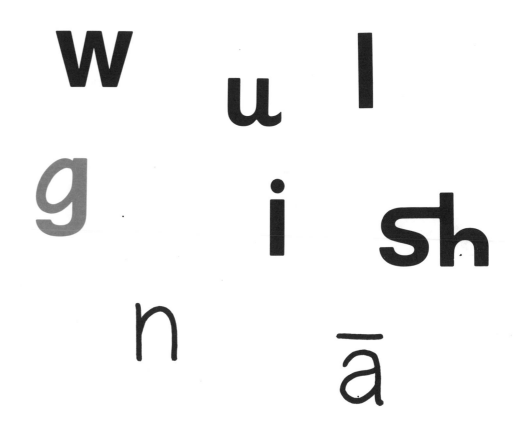

TASK 5   Individual test

Call on different children to identify two or more sounds in task 4.

TASK 6   Teacher crosses out sounds

a. You told me every sound. Get ready to do it again. This time I'll
cross out each sound when you tell me what it is.

b. Point to each sound. (Pause.) Say: Get ready. Touch the sound.
The children respond. As you cross out the sound, say:
Goodbye,_____.

Lesson 85

SOUNDS

TASK 1 Sounds firm-up

a. Point to **sh.** When I touch the sound, you say it.
b. (Pause.) Get ready. Touch **sh.** *shshsh.*
c. Again. Repeat *b* until firm.
d. Get ready to say all the sounds when I touch them.
e. Alternate touching **u, g, ā, sh, d, c, t,** and **o** three or four times.
Point to the sound. (Pause one second.) Say: Get ready.
Touch the sound. *The children respond.*

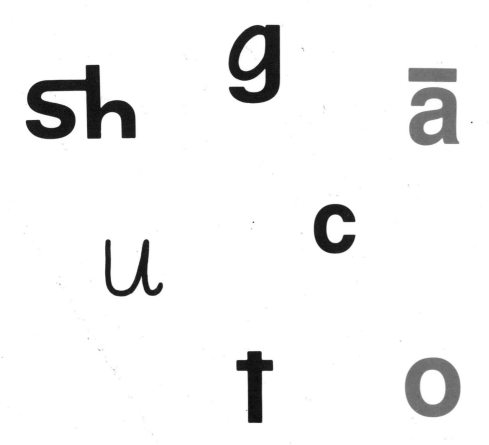

TASK 2 Individual test

Call on different children to identify one or more sounds in task 1.

TASK 3 Teacher and children play the sounds game

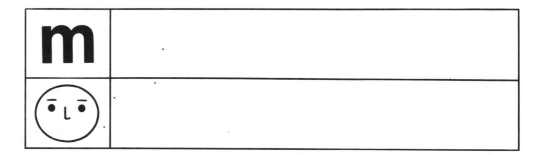

a. Use acetate and crayon. Write the sounds in the symbol box. Keep score in the score box.
b. I'm smart. I bet I can beat you in a game.
c. Here's the rule. When I touch a sound, you say it.
d. Play the game.
Make one symbol at a time in the symbol box. Use the symbols **a, w, m,** and **l.**
Make each symbol quickly. (Pause.) Touch the symbol.
Play the game for about two minutes. Then ask: Who won?
Draw a mouth on the face in the score box.

READING VOCABULARY

After you read the words on this page, you'll get to read the words the fast way.

Do not touch any small letters.

TASK 7   Children sound out the word and tell what word

a. Touch the ball for **at.**   Sound it out.

b. Get ready. Touch **a, t** as the children say *aaat.*

If sounding out is not firm, repeat *b.*

c. What word? (Signal.) *At.*   Yes, **at.**

at

TASK 8. Children sound out the word and tell what word

a. Touch the ball for **nāme.**   Sound it out.

b. Get ready. Touch **n, ā, m** as the children say *nnnāāāmmm.*

If sounding out is not firm, repeat *b.*

c. What word? (Signal.) *Name.*   Yes, **name.**

nāme

TASK 9   Children sound out the word and tell what word

a. Touch the ball for **rāin.**   Sound it out.

b. Get ready. Touch **r, ā, n** as the children say *rrrāāānnn.*

If sounding out is not firm, repeat *b.*

c. What word? (Signal.) *Rain.*   Yes, **rain.**

rāin

TASK 10   Children read the words the fast way

a. Now you get to read the words on this page the fast way.

b. Touch the ball for **at.** (Pause three seconds.)   Get ready.

Move your finger quickly along the arrow. *At.*

To correct	Have the children sound out the word and say it fast.

c. Repeat *b* for each word on the page.

TASK 11   Individual test

Call on different children to read one word the fast way.

TASK 27   Individual test

a. Everybody, finger on the ball of the top line.
Check children's responses.
b. We're going to have different children read. Everybody's going
to touch the words.
c. Everybody, touch the first word. Check children's responses.
d. Call on a child. Reading the fast way. Get ready. Clap. *She.*
e. Next word. Check children's responses.
f. Everybody reading. Get ready. Clap. *Has.*
g. Next word. Check children's responses.
h. Call on a child. Get ready. Clap. *A.*
i. Repeat *e* and *f* for **cat.**

SUMMARY OF INDEPENDENT ACTIVITY

TASK 28   Introduction to independent activity

a. Hold up Take-Home 84.
b. Everybody, you're going to finish this take-home on your own.
Tell the children when they will work the remaining items.
Let's go over the things you're going to do.

TASK 29   Story copying

Point to the dotted words below the story on side 1. You're going
to write the dotted words on this arrow. Then you're going to write
those words on the other arrows.

TASK 30   Cross-out game

Point to the boxed sounds in the Cross-out Game. Everybody, what
sound are you going to cross out today? (Signal.) *mmm.*
What sound are you going to circle? (Signal.) *www.*

TASK 31   Matching

a. Point to the first column of words in the Matching Game.
b. Everybody, get ready to read each of the words over here.
Reading the fast way.
c. Point to the first word. Get ready. (Signal.) *The children respond.*
d. Repeat *c* for the remaining words.
e. Point to the first column. You're going to make lines for every
word over here.

TASK 32   Sound writing

a. Point to the sound-writing exercise on side 2. Here are the sounds
you're going to write today. I'll touch the sounds. You say them.
b. Touch each sound. *The children respond.*
c. Repeat the series until firm.

TASK 33   Pair relations

a. Point to the words **a sack** in the first row of the pair-relations
exercise.
b. Everybody, touch this box on your take-home.
Check children's responses.
c. Get ready to tell me the words. (Pause.) What words? (Signal.)
A sack.
d. You're going to circle the picture that shows (pause) **a sack.**
Do it. Check children's responses.
e. Point to the other boxes. Remember—you're going to circle the
picture in each box that shows what the words say.

TASK 34   Story picture

Point to the story picture. After you finish your take-home,
you can color the story picture.

END OF LESSON 84

After you read the words on this page, you'll get to read the words the fast way.

TASK 12   Children sound out the word and tell what word

a. Touch the ball for **ron.** Sound it out.
b. Get ready. Touch **r, o, n** as the children say *Rrrooonnn*.
　　　　　　　　　　　　　　If sounding out is not firm, repeat *b*.
c. What word? (Signal.) *Ron.* Yes, **Ron.** That's a boy's name.
　(Pause.) **Ron.**

TASK 13   Children sound out the word and tell what word

a. Touch the ball for **run.** Sound it out.
b. Get ready. Touch **r, u, n** as the children say *rrruuunnn*.
　　　　　　　　　　　　　　If sounding out is not firm, repeat *b*.
c. What word? (Signal.) *Run.* Yes, **run.**

TASK 14   Children sound out the word and tell what word

a. Touch the ball for **wē.** Sound it out.
b. Get ready. Touch **w, ē** as the children say *wwwēēē*.
　　　　　　　　　　　　　　If sounding out is not firm, repeat *b*.
c. What word? (Signal.) *We.* Yes, **we.**

TASK 15   Children sound out the word and tell what word

a. Touch the ball for **will.** Sound it out.
b. Get ready. Touch **w, i,** between the l's as the children say *wwwiiilll*.
　　　　　　　　　　　　　　If sounding out is not firm, repeat *b*.
c. What word? (Signal.) *Will.* Yes, **will.**

TASK 16   Children read the words the fast way

a. Now you get to read the words on this page the fast way.
b. Touch the ball for **ron.** (Pause three seconds.) Get ready.
　　　　　　　Move your finger quickly along the arrow. *Ron*.

| To correct | Have the children sound out the word and say it fast. |

c. Repeat *b* for each word on the page.

TASK 17   Individual test

Call on different children to read one word the fast way.

ron

run

wē

will

Take-Home 84

STORY
Do not clap for any small letters.

TASK 22 First reading—children sound out each word and tell what word

a. Pass out Take-Home 84. Do not let the children look at the picture until task 24.
b. Get ready to read the story. First word. Check children's responses.
c. Get ready. Clap for each sound. *Shshsheēē.* **What word?** (Signal.)
She. **Yes, she.**
d. Next word. Check children's responses.
e. Get ready. Clap for each sound. *Haaasss.* **What word?** (Signal.)
Has. **Yes, has.**
f. Repeat *d* and *e* for the remaining words in the story.

TASK 23 Second reading—children reread the story and answer questions

a. This time you'll read the story and I'll ask questions.
Back to the first word. Check children's responses.
b. Repeat *c* through *f* in task 22. Ask the comprehension questions below as the children read.

After the children read:	You say:
She has a cat.	**Who has a cat?** (Signal.) *She does.*
That cat is not little.	**Tell me about the cat.** (Signal.) *He is not little.*
That cat is fat.	**Tell me more about the cat.** (Signal.) *He is fat.*
To correct	If the children do not give acceptable answers, have them reread the sentence that answers the question. Then ask the question again.

TASK 24 Picture comprehension

a. What do you think you'll see in the picture? *The children respond.*
b. Turn your take-home over and look at the picture.
c. Ask these questions:
  1. Is that cat little? *No.*
  2. Who owns that cat? *The children respond.* **The girl does.**
  3. What would you do with a big fat cat like that?
  The children respond.

TASK 25 Word finding

a. Turn your take-home back to side 1. Everybody, look at the words in the top line. One of the words is has.
b. Get ready to touch has when I clap. (Pause three seconds.)
Get ready. Clap. *(The children touch has.)*
c. Repeat *b* for these words: **cat, shē, has, cat, has, cat, shē, has, shē, cat, has, shē.**

TASK 26 Children read the first sentence the fast way

a. Everybody, now you're going to read part of the story the fast way. Finger on the ball of the top line. Check children's responses.
b. Move your finger under the sounds of the first word and figure out the sounds you're going to say. Don't say the sounds out loud. Just figure out what you're going to say. Check children's responses. Prompt children who don't touch under the sounds. (Pause three seconds.) **Read the word the fast way. Get ready.** Clap. *She.* **Yes, she.**
c. Next word. Move your finger under the sounds and figure out the sounds. Check children's responses. (Pause three seconds.) **Read the word the fast way. Get ready.** Clap. *Has.* **Yes, has.**
d. Repeat *c* for the words **a, cat.**
e. Let's read the words the fast way again. Everybody, finger on the ball of the top line. Check children's responses. **Figure out the first word and get ready to read it the fast way. Say the sounds to yourself.** (Pause three seconds.) **What word?** Clap. *She.* **Yes, she.**
f. Figure out the next word. Say the sounds to yourself. (Pause three seconds.) **What word?** Clap. *Has.* **Yes, has.**
g. Repeat *f* for the words **a, cat.**

TASK 18   Children read a word beginning with a stop sound (tāme)

a. Run your finger under **āme.** You're going to sound out this part.
   Get ready. Touch **ā, m** as the children say *āāāmmm.*
b. Say it fast. (Signal.) *Ame.* Yes, this part says (pause) **āme.**
c. Repeat *a* and *b* until firm.
d. Touch the ball for **tāme.** This word rhymes with (pause) **āme.**
   Get ready. Move quickly along the arrow. *Tame.*
e. What word? (Signal.) *Tame.* Yes, **tame.**
f. Repeat *d* and *e* until firm.
g. Return to the ball. Now you're going to sound out (pause) **tāme.**
   Get ready. Quickly touch **t, ā, m** as the children say *tāāāmmm.*
h. What word? (Signal.) *Tame.* Yes, **tame.** Good reading.
i. Repeat *g* and *h* until firm.

TASK 19   Individual test—Have children do *g* and *h* in task 18.

TASK 20   Children read a word beginning with a stop sound (his)

a. Run your finger under **is.** You're going to sound out this part.
                     Get ready.   Touch **i, s** as the children say *iiisss.*
b. Say it fast. (Signal.) *Is.* Yes, this part says (pause) **is.**
c. Repeat *a* and *b* until firm.
d. Touch the ball for **his.** This word rhymes with (pause) **is.**
   Get ready. Move quickly along the arrow. *His.*
e. What word? (Signal.) *His.* Yes, **his.**
f. Repeat *d* and *e* until firm.
g. Return to the ball. Now you're going to sound out (pause) **his.**
               Get ready. Quickly touch **h, i, s** as the children say *hiiisss.*
h. What word? (Signal.) *His.* Yes, **his.** Good reading.
i. Repeat *g* and *h* until firm.

TASK 21   Individual test—Have children do *g* and *h* in task 20.

TASK 22   Children read the words the fast way

a. Now you get to read the words on this page the fast way.
b. Touch the ball for **cat.** (Pause three seconds.) Get ready.
                  Move your finger quickly along the arrow. *Cat.*
c. Repeat *b* for **his.**

TASK 23   Individual test—Have children read one word the fast way.

TASK 16   Children read a word beginning with a stop sound (hit)

a. Run your finger under **it.** You're going to sound out this part.
Get ready. Touch **i, t** as the children say *iiit*.
b. Say it fast. (Signal.) *It*. Yes, this part says (pause) **it**.
c. Repeat *a* and *b* until firm.
d. Touch the ball for **hit.** This word rhymes with (pause) **it**.
Get ready. Move quickly along the arrow. *Hit*.
e. What word? (Signal.) *Hit*. Yes, **hit**.
f. Repeat *d* and *e* until firm.
g. Return to the ball. Now you're going to sound out (pause) **hit**.
Get ready. Quickly touch **h, i, t** as the children say *hiiit*.
h. What word? (Signal.) *Hit*. Yes, **hit**. Good reading.
i. Repeat *g* and *h* until firm.

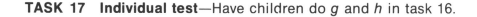

TASK 17   Individual test—Have children do *g* and *h* in task 16.

TASK 18   Children read a word beginning with a stop sound (has)

a. Cover **h**. Run your finger under **as.** This part says (pause) **az**.
b. Uncover **h**. Touch the ball for **h**. Rhymes with (pause) **az**.
Get ready. Move quickly along the arrow. *Has*.
c. What word? (Signal.) *Has*. Yes, **has**.
d. Repeat *b* and *c* until firm.
e. Return to the ball. Now you're going to sound out (pause) **has**.
Get ready. Quickly touch **h, a, s** as the children say *haaasss*.
f. What word? (Signal.) *Has*. Yes, **has**. Good reading.
g. Repeat *e* and *f* until firm.

TASK 19   Individual test—Have children do *e* and *f* in task 18.

TASK 20   Children read the words the fast way

Have the children read the words on this page the fast way.

TASK 21   Individual test—Have children read one word the fast way.

Take-Home 81

STORY

Do not clap for any small letters.

TASK 24 **First reading—children sound out each word and tell what word**

a. Pass out Take-Home 81. Do not let the children look at the picture until task 26.

b. Get ready to read the story. First word. Check children's responses.

c. Get ready. Clap for each sound. *Hiiisss.* What word? (Signal.) *His.* Yes, **his.**

d. Next word. Check children's responses.

e. Get ready. Clap for each sound. *Nnnāāāmmm.* What word? (Signal.) *Name.* Yes, **name.**

f. Repeat *d* and *e* for the remaining words in the story.

TASK 25 **Second reading—children reread the story and answer questions**

a. This time you'll read the story and I'll ask questions. Back to the first word. Check children's responses.

b. Repeat *c* through *f* in task 24. Ask the comprehension questions below as the children read.

After the children read:	You say:
His name is Ron.	What's his name? (Signal.) *Ron.*
He will run. And he will see me.	What two things will he do? (Signal.) *Run and see me.*
To correct	If the children do not give acceptable answers, have them reread the sentence that answers the question. Then ask the question again.

TASK 26 **Picture comprehension**

a. Who do you think you'll see in the picture? (Signal.) *Ron.*

b. What will Ron be doing? *The children respond.*

c. Turn your take-home over and look at the picture.

d. Ask these questions:
1. Who is that? *The children respond.* Yes, Ron.
2. What is he doing? *The children respond.* Running.
3. Who is he looking at? *The children respond.* He's looking right at you.

TASK 27 **Word finding**

a. Turn your take-home back to side 1. Everybody, look at the words in the top line. One of the words is **his.**

b. Get ready to touch **his** when I clap. (Pause three seconds.) Get ready. Clap. *(The children touch* **his.***)*

c. Repeat *b* for these words: **is, his, is, nāme, his, nāme, his, is, nāme, is, nāme, his.**

TASK 28 **Children read the first sentence the fast way**

a. Everybody, now you're going to read part of the story the fast way. Finger on the ball of the top line. Check children's responses.

b. Move your finger under the sounds of the first word and figure out the sounds you're going to say. Don't say the sounds out loud. Just figure out what you're going to say. Check children's responses. Prompt children who don't touch under the sounds. (Pause three seconds.) Read the word the fast way. Get ready. Clap. *His.* Yes, **his.**

c. Next word. Move your finger under the sounds and figure out the sounds. Check children's responses. (Pause three seconds.) Read the word the fast way. Get ready. Clap. *Name.* Yes, **name.**

d. Repeat *c* for the words **is, ron.**

e. Let's read the words the fast way again. Everybody, finger on the ball of the top line. Check children's responses. Figure out the first word and get ready to read it the fast way. Say the sounds to yourself. (Pause three seconds.) What word? Clap. *His.* Yes, **his.**

f. Figure out the next word. Say the sounds to yourself. (Pause three seconds.) What word? Clap. *Name.* Yes, **name.**

g. Repeat *f* for the words **is, ron.**

After you read the words on this page, you'll get to read the words the fast way.

Do not touch any small letters.

TASK 11   Children sound out the word and tell what word

a. Touch the ball for **sand.** Sound it out.
b. Get ready.   Touch **s, a, n, d** as the children say *sssaaannnd*.
　　　　　　　　　If sounding out is not firm, repeat *b*.
c. What word?   (Signal.) *Sand.* Yes, **sand**.

TASK 12   Children sound out the word and tell what word

a. Touch the ball for **not.** Sound it out.
b. Get ready.   Touch **n, o, t** as the children say *nnnooot*.
　　　　　　　　　If sounding out is not firm, repeat *b*.
c. What word?   (Signal.) *Not.* Yes, **not**.

TASK 13   Children sound out the word and tell what word

a. Touch the ball for little. Sound it out.
b. Get ready.   Touch **l, i,** between the **t**'s, **l** as the children say *llliiitlll*.
　　　　　　　　　If sounding out is not firm, repeat *b*.
c. What word?   (Signal.) *Little.* Yes, **little**.

TASK 14   Children read the words the fast way

a. Now you get to read the words on this page the fast way.
b. Touch the ball for **sand.** (Pause three seconds.) Get ready.
　　　　　　　Move your finger quickly along the arrow. *Sand*.
c. Repeat *b* for each word on the page.

TASK 15   Individual test

Call on different children to read one word the fast way.

81

TASK 29 Individual test

a. Everybody, finger on the ball of the top line.
Check children's responses.
b. We're going to have different children read. Everybody's going to touch the words.

c. Everybody, touch the first word. Check children's responses.
d. Call on a child. **Reading the fast way. Get ready.** Clap. *His.*
e. Next word. Check children's responses.
f. Everybody reading. Get ready. Clap. *Name.*
g. Next word. Check children's responses.
h. Call on a child. **Get ready.** Clap. *Is.*
i . Repeat *e* and *f* for **ron.**

SUMMARY OF INDEPENDENT ACTIVITY

TASK 30   Introduction to independent activity

a. Hold up Take-Home 81.
b. Everybody, you're going to finish this take-home on your own.
Tell the children when they will work the remaining items.
Let's go over the things you're going to do.

TASK 31   Story copying

Point to the dotted words below the story on side 1. **You're going to write the dotted words on this arrow. Then you're going to write those words on the other arrows.**

TASK 32   Matching

a. Point to the first column of words in the Matching Game.
b. Everybody, get ready to read each of the words over here.
Reading the fast way.
c. Point to the first word. **Get ready.** (Signal.) *The children respond.*
d. Repeat *c* for the remaining words.
e. Point to the first column. **You're going to make lines for every word over here.**

TASK 33   Cross-out game

Point to the boxed sounds in the Cross-out Game. **Everybody, what sound are you going to circle today?** (Signal.) *shshsh.*
What sound are you going to cross out? (Signal.) *ththth.*

TASK 34   Sound writing

a. Point to the sound-writing exercise on side 2. **Here are the sounds you're going to write today. I'll touch the sounds. You say them.**
b. Touch each sound. *The children respond.*
c. Repeat the series until firm.

TASK 35   Pair relations

a. Point to the pair-relations exercise.
b. Everybody, remember the rule. If the picture doesn't show what the word says, you cross out the box.
c. Point to the first box. **This word is rug. What word?** (Signal.)
Rug. **Everybody, does the picture show a rug?** (Signal.) *No.*
Are you going to cross it out? (Signal.) *Yes.*
d. If the children's responses are not firm, repeat *c* with one or more boxes.

TASK 36   Story picture

Point to the story picture. **After you finish your take-home, you can color the story picture.**

END OF LESSON 81

READING VOCABULARY

After you read the words on this page, you'll get to read the words the fast way.

TASK 5   Children sound out the word and tell what word

a. Touch the ball for **wē.**   Sound it out.
b. Get ready.   Touch **w, ē** as the children say *wwwēēē.*
If sounding out is not firm, repeat *b.*
c. What word?   (Signal.) *We.*   Yes, **we.**

TASK 6   Children sound out the word and tell what word

a. Touch the ball for **shē.**   Sound it out.
b. Get ready.   Touch **sh, ē** as the children say *shshshēēē.*
If sounding out is not firm, repeat *b.*
c. What word?   (Signal.) *She.*   Yes, **she.**

TASK 7   Children sound out the word and tell what word

a. Touch the ball for **and.**   Sound it out.
b. Get ready.   Touch **a, n, d** as the children say *aaannnd.*
If sounding out is not firm, repeat *b.*
c. What word?   (Signal.) *And.*   Yes, **and.**

TASK 8   Children sound out the word and tell what word

a. Touch the ball for **shack.**   Sound it out.
b. Get ready.   Touch **sh, a, c** as the children say *shshshaaac.*
If sounding out is not firm, repeat *b.*
c. What word?   (Signal.) *Shack.*   Yes, **shack.**

TASK 9   Children read the words the fast way

a. Now you get to read the words on this page the fast way.
b. Touch the ball for **wē.** (Pause three seconds.)   Get ready.
Move your finger quickly along the arrow. *We.*
c. Repeat *b* for each word on the page.

TASK 10   Individual test

Call on different children to read one word the fast way.

Do not touch any small letters.

and

Lesson 82

SOUNDS

TASK 1   Teaching **sh** as in **she**

a. Point to **sh.** My turn.   (Pause.)
Touch **sh** and say: shshsh.

b. Point to **sh.** Your turn. When I touch it, you say it.   (Pause.)
Get ready.   Touch **sh.** *shshsh*.
Lift your finger.

c. Again.   Touch **sh.** *shshshsh*.
Lift your finger.

d. Repeat *c* until firm.

TASK 2   Sounds firm-up

a. Get ready to say the sounds when I touch them.

b. Alternate touching **l** and **sh.** Point to the sound. (Pause one second.) Say: Get ready.   Touch the sound. *The children respond.*

c. When **l** and **sh** are firm, alternate touching **th, l, sh,** and **g** until all four sounds are firm.

TASK 3   Individual test

Call on different children to identify **th, l, sh,** or **g.**

TASK 4   Teacher introduces cross-out game

a. Use acetate and crayon.

b. I'll cross out the sounds on this page when you can tell me every sound.

c. Remember—when I touch it, you say it.

d. Go over the sounds until the children can identify all the sounds in order.

TASK 5   Individual test

Call on different children to identify two or more sounds in task 4.

TASK 6   Teacher crosses out sounds

a. You told me every sound. Get ready to do it again. This time I'll cross out each sound when you tell me what it is.

b. Point to each sound. (Pause.) Say: Get ready.   Touch the sound. *The children respond.* As you cross out the sound, say:

Goodbye, _____ .

162

Lesson 84

SOUNDS

TASK 1 Teacher and children play the sounds game

a. Use acetate and crayon. Write the sounds in the symbol box. Keep score in the score box.
b. I'm smart. I bet I can beat you in a game.
c. Here's the rule. When I touch a sound, you say it.
d. Play the game.
   Make one symbol at a time in the symbol box. Use the symbols **sh, w, h,** and **o.**
   Make each symbol quickly. (Pause.) Touch the symbol. Play the game for about two minutes. Then ask: Who won? Draw a mouth on the face in the score box.

TASK 2 Teacher introduces cross-out game

a. Use acetate and crayon.
b. I'll cross out the sounds on this page when you can tell me every sound.
c. Remember—when I touch it, you say it.
d. Go over the sounds until the children can identify all the sounds in order.

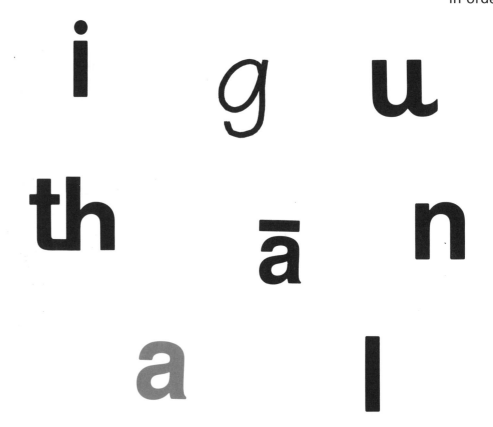

TASK 3 Individual test

Call on different children to identify two or more sounds in task 2.

TASK 4 Teacher crosses out sounds

a. You told me every sound. Get ready to do it again. This time I'll cross out each sound when you tell me what it is.
b. Point to each sound. (Pause.) Say: Get ready. Touch the sound.
   The children respond. As you cross out the sound, say: Goodbye, _____ .

READING VOCABULARY

After you read the words on this page, you'll get to read the words the fast way.

Do not touch any small letters.

TASK 7   Children rhyme with rat

a. Touch the ball for **rat.** Sound it out.
b. Get ready. Touch **r, a, t** as the children say *rrraaat.*
 If sounding out is not firm, repeat *b.*
c. What word? (Signal.) *Rat.* Yes, **rat.**
d. Quickly touch the ball for **hat.** This word rhymes with (pause)
 rat. Get ready. Touch **h.** *h.* Move your finger quickly along
 the arrow. *Hat.*

e. What word? (Signal.) *Hat.* Yes, **hat.**

TASK 8   Children sound out the word and tell what word

a. Touch the ball for **little.** Sound it out.
b. Get ready. Touch **l, i,** between the **t**'s, **l** as the children say *llliiitlll.*
 If sounding out is not firm, repeat *b.*
c. What word? (Signal.) *Little.* Yes, **little.**

TASK 9   Children sound out the word and tell what word

a. Touch the ball for **shē.** Sound it out.
b. Get ready. Touch **sh, ē** as the children say *shshshēēē.*
 If sounding out is not firm, repeat *b.*
c. What word? (Signal.) *She.* Yes, **she.**

TASK 10   Children read the words the fast way

a. Now you get to read the words on this page the fast way.
b. Touch the ball for **rat.** (Pause three seconds.) Get ready.
 Move your finger quickly along the arrow.

To correct	Have the children sound out the word and say it fast.

c. Repeat *b* for each word on the page.

TASK 11   Individual test—Have children read one word the fast way.

rat

hat

littl_e

shē

SUMMARY OF INDEPENDENT ACTIVITY

TASK 23 Introduction to independent activity

a. Hold up Take-Home 83.
b. Everybody, you're going to finish this take-home on your own. Tell the children when they will work the remaining items. Let's go over the things you're going to do.

TASK 24 Story copying

Point to the dotted words below the story on side 1. You're going to write the dotted words on this arrow. Then you're going to write those words on the other arrows.

TASK 25 Cross-out game

Point to the boxed sounds in the Cross-out Game. Everybody, what sound are you going to circle today? (Signal.) *h*. What sound are you going to cross out? (Signal.) *nnn*.

TASK 26 Matching

a. Point to the first column of words in the Matching Game.
b. Everybody, get ready to read each of the words over here. Reading the fast way.
c. Point to the first word. Get ready. (Signal.) *The children respond.*
d. Repeat *c* for the remaining words.
e. Point to the first column. You're going to make lines for every word over here.

TASK 27 Sound writing

a. Point to the sound-writing exercise on side 2. Here are the sounds you're going to write today. I'll touch the sounds. You say them.
b. Touch each sound. *The children respond.*
c. Repeat the series until firm.

TASK 28 Pair relations

Point to the pair-relations exercise. Remember—you're going to circle the picture in each box that shows what the words say.

TASK 29 Story picture

Point to the story picture. After you finish your take-home, you can color the story picture.

END OF LESSON 83

After you read the words on this page, you'll get to read the words the fast way.

Do not touch any small letters.

TASK 12   Children sound out the word and tell what word

a. Touch the ball for **run.** Sound it out.
b. Get ready.   Touch **r, u, n** as the children say *rrruuunnn*.
    If sounding out is not firm, repeat *b*.
c. What word?   (Signal.) *Run.* Yes, **run.**

TASK 13   Children sound out the word and tell what word

a. Touch the ball for **māde.** Sound it out.
b. Get ready.   Touch **m, ā, d** as the children say *mmmāāād*.
    If sounding out is not firm, repeat *b*.
c. What word?   (Signal.) *Made.* Yes, **made.**

TASK 14   Children sound out the word and tell what word

a. Touch the ball for **ram.** Sound it out.
b. Get ready.   Touch **r, a, m** as the children say *rrraaammm*.
    If sounding out is not firm, repeat *b*.
c. What word?   (Signal.) *Ram.* Yes, **ram.**

TASK 15   Children sound out the word and tell what word

a. Touch the ball for **cat.** Sound it out.
b. Get ready.   Touch **c, a, t** as the children say *caaat*.
    If sounding out is not firm, repeat *b*.
c. What word?   (Signal.) *Cat.* Yes, **cat.**

TASK 16   Children read the words the fast way

a. Now you get to read the words on this page the fast way.
b. Touch the ball for **run.** (Pause three seconds.) Get ready.
    Move your finger quickly along the arrow. *Run*.

To correct	Have the children sound out the word and say it fast.

c. Repeat *b* for each word on the page.

TASK 17   Individual test

Call on different children to read one word the fast way.

run

māde

ram

cat

TASK 20 Children read the first sentence the fast way

a. Everybody, now you're going to read part of the story the fast way. Finger on the ball of the top line.   Check children's responses.

b. Move your finger under the sounds of the first word and figure out the sounds you're going to say. Don't say the sounds out loud. Just figure out what you're going to say.   Check children's responses. Prompt children who don't touch under the sounds. (Pause three seconds.) Read the word the fast way. Get ready. Clap. *This.* Yes, **this.**

c. Next word. Move your finger under the sounds and figure out the sounds.   Check children's responses. (Pause three seconds.) Read the word the fast way. Get ready.   Clap. *Is.* Yes, **is.**

d. Repeat *c* for the words **a, cat.**

e. Let's read the words the fast way again. Everybody, finger on the ball of the top line.   Check children's responses. Figure out the first word and get ready to read it the fast way. Say the sounds to yourself. (Pause three seconds.) What word?   Clap. *This.* Yes, **this.**

f. Figure out the next word. Say the sounds to yourself.   (Pause three seconds.) What word?   Clap. *Is.* Yes, **is.**

g. Repeat *f* for the words **a, cat.**

TASK 21   Individual test

a. Everybody, finger on the ball of the top line.
                    Check children's responses.

b. We're going to have different children read. Everybody's going
                    to touch the words.

c. Everybody, touch the first word.   Check children's responses.

d. Call on a child. Reading the fast way. Get ready.   Clap. *This.*

e. Next word.   Check children's responses.

f. Everybody reading. Get ready.   Clap. *Is.*

g. Next word.   Check children's responses.

h. Call on a child. Get ready.   Clap. *A.*

i. Repeat *e* and *f* for **cat.**

PAIR RELATIONS
The children will need pencils.

TASK 22   Children circle the correct picture in each box

a. Point to the first box in the pair-relations exercise on side 2.

b. I'll read this word. **Hut.** What word?   (Signal.) *Hut.* Yes, **hut.**

c. One of the pictures in the box shows a   (pause) **hut.**

d. Point to the picture of the truck. Does this picture show a **hut**? (Signal.) *No.* What does it show?   (Signal.) *A truck.* Is that the right picture?   (Signal.) *No.*

e. Point to the picture of the hut. Does this picture show a **hut**? (Signal.) *Yes.* That's the right picture. So I'll circle it.

f. Point to the second box **(a lock).**

g. Everybody, touch this box on your take-home.
                    Check children's responses.

h. Everybody, get ready to tell me the words.   (Pause four seconds.) What words?   (Signal.) *A lock.* Yes, **a lock.**

i. You're going to touch the picture that shows   (pause) **a lock.** (Pause.) Get ready.   (Signal.) Check children's responses.

j. Point to the third box **(a fan).** Repeat *g* through *i* for the third box.

k. Everybody, read the words in the top row to yourselves; then circle the picture in each box that shows what the words say.
                    Check children's responses.

l. You'll do the rest of the boxes later.

TASK 18 Children read a word beginning with a stop sound (can)

a. Run your finger under **an.** You're going to sound out this part.
Get ready. Touch **a, n** as the children say *aaannn.*

b. Say it fast. (Signal.) *An.* Yes, this part says (pause) **an**.

c. Repeat *a* and *b* until firm.

d. Touch the ball for **can.** This word rhymes with (pause) **an.**
Get ready. Move quickly along the arrow. *Can.*

e. What word? (Signal.) *Can.* Yes, **can.**

f. Repeat *d* and *e* until firm.

g. Return to the ball. Now you're going to sound out (pause) **can.**
Get ready. Quickly touch **c, a, n** as the children say *caaannn.*

h. What word? (Signal.) *Can.* Yes, **can.** Good reading.

Can a boy sing?

i. Repeat *g* and *h* until firm.

can

TASK 19 Individual test

Call on different children to do *g* and *h* in task 18.

Take-Home 83

STORY

TASK 16 First reading—children sound out each word and tell what word

a. Pass out Take-Home 83. Do not let the children look at the picture until task 18.

b. Get ready to read the story. First word. Check children's responses.

c. Get ready. Clap for each sound. *Thththiiisss.* What word? (Signal.) *This.* Yes, **this**.

d. Next word. Check children's responses.

e. Get ready. Clap for each sound. *Iiisss.* What word? (Signal.) *Is.* Yes, **is**.

f. Repeat d and e for the remaining words in the story.

TASK 17 Second reading—children reread the story and answer questions

a. This time you'll read the story and I'll ask questions. Back to the first word. Check children's responses.

b. Repeat c through f in task 16. Ask the comprehension questions below as the children read.

After the children read:	You say:
This is a cat.	What is this? (Signal.) *A cat.*
This cat has fat feet.	What does the cat have? (Signal.) *Fat feet.*
This cat can run in the mud.	What can this cat do? (Signal.) *Run in the mud.*

To correct	If the children do not give acceptable answers, have them reread the sentence that answers the question. Then ask the question again.

TASK 18 Picture comprehension

a. What do you think you'll see in the picture? *The children respond.*

b. What will the cat be doing? (Signal.) *Running in the mud.*

c. Turn your take-home over and look at the picture.

d. Ask these questions:

1. What's that cat doing? *The children respond.* *Running in the mud.*

2. What's that stuff on the cat's feet? *The children respond.* Mud.

3. What kind of feet does this cat have? *The children respond.* Fat feet.

4. Did you ever get your feet covered with mud? *The children respond.*

TASK 19 Word finding

a. Turn your take-home back to side 1. Everybody, look at the words in the top line. One of the words is **this**.

b. Get ready to touch **this** when I clap. (Pause three seconds.) Get ready. Clap. *(The children touch **this**.)*

c. Repeat b for these words: **is, cat, this, is, this, a, cat, this, cat, a, this, cat.**

Take-Home 82

STORY

TASK 20 First reading—children sound out each word and tell what word

a. Pass out Take-Home 82. Do not let the children look at the picture
until task 22.
b. Get ready to read the story. First word. Check children's responses.
c. Get ready. Clap for each sound. *Wwwēēē*. What word? (Signal.)
We. Yes, **we**.
d. Next word. Check children's responses.
e. Get ready. Clap for each sound. *Haaad*. What word? (Signal.)
Had. Yes, **had**.
f. Repeat *d* and *e* for the remaining words in the story.

TASK 21 Second reading—children reread the story and answer questions

a. This time you'll read the story and I'll ask questions.
Back to the first word. Check children's responses.
b. Repeat *c* through *f* in task 20. Ask the comprehension questions
below as the children read.

After the children read:	You say:
We had a ram.	Who had a ram? (Signal.) *We did.*
That ram ran.	What did he do? (Signal.) *He ran.*
We ran and he ran.	Who ran? (Signal.) *We ran and he ran.*

To correct	If the children do not give acceptable answers, have them reread the sentence that answers the question. Then ask the question again.

TASK 22 Picture comprehension

a. What do you think you'll see in the picture? *The children respond.*
b. What will the ram be doing? (Signal.) *Running*.
c. Turn your take-home over and look at the picture.
d. Ask these questions:
   1. Who is running? *The children respond.*
   Yes, the children and the ram are running.
   2. Why are those children running? *The children respond.*
   The ram is chasing them.
   3. What do you think that ram will do if he catches up to them?
   The children respond.

TASK 23 Word finding

a. Turn your take-home back to side 1. Everybody, look at the words
in the top line. One of the words is **had**.
b. Get ready to touch **had** when I clap. (Pause three seconds.)
Get ready. Clap. *(The children touch* **had***.)*
c. Repeat *b* for these words: **had, ram, had, we, ram, we, ram, had,
we, ram, had.**

After you read the words on this page, you'll get to read the words the fast way.

TASK 10   Children sound out the word and tell what word

a. Touch the ball for **that.** Sound it out.
b. Get ready. Touch **th, a, t** as the children say *thththaaat.*
                              If sounding out is not firm, repeat *b.*
c. What word? (Signal.) *That.* Yes, **that.**

that

TASK 11   Children sound out the word and tell what word

a. Touch the ball for **shē.** Sound it out.
b. Get ready. Touch **sh, ē** as the children say *shshshēēē.*
                              If sounding out is not firm, repeat *b.*
c. What word? (Signal.) *She.* Yes, **she.**

shē

TASK 12   Children sound out the word and tell what word

a. Touch the ball for **cat.** Sound it out.
b. Get ready. Touch **c, a, t** as the children say *caaat.*
                              If sounding out is not firm, repeat *b.*
c. What word? (Signal.) *Cat.* Yes, **cat.**

cat

TASK 13   Children sound out the word and tell what word

a. Touch the ball for **can.** Sound it out.
b. Get ready. Touch **c, a, n** as the children say *caaannn.*
                              If sounding out is not firm, repeat *b.*
c. What word? (Signal.) *Can.* Yes, **can.**

can

TASK 14   Children read the words the fast way

a. Now you get to read the words on this page the fast way.
b. Touch the ball for **that.** (Pause three seconds.) Get ready.
                        Move your finger quickly along the arrow. *That.*

| To correct | Have the children sound out the word and say it fast. |

c. Repeat *b* for each word on the page.

TASK 15   Individual test—Have children read one word the fast way.

TASK 24   Children read the first sentence the fast way

a. Everybody, now you're going to read part of the story the fast way. Finger on the ball of the top line.   Check children's responses.

b. Move your finger under the sounds of the first word and figure out the sounds you're going to say. Don't say the sounds out loud. Just figure out what you're going to say.   Check children's responses. Prompt children who don't touch under the sounds. (Pause three seconds.)   Read the word the fast way. Get ready. Clap. *We.*   Yes, **we.**

c. Next word. Move your finger under the sounds and figure out the sounds.   Check children's responses. (Pause three seconds.)   Read the word the fast way. Get ready.   Clap. *Had.*   Yes, **had.**

d. Repeat c for the words **a, ram.**

e. Let's read the words the fast way again. Everybody, finger on the ball of the top line.   Check children's responses.   Figure out the first word and get ready to read it the fast way. Say the sounds to yourself.   (Pause three seconds.)   What word? Clap. *We.*   Yes, **we.**

f. Figure out the next word. Say the sounds to yourself.   (Pause three seconds.)   What word? Clap. *Had.*   Yes, **had.**

g. Repeat f for the words **a, ram.**

TASK 25   Individual test

a. Everybody, finger on the ball of the top line.
                                            Check children's responses.

b. We're going to have different children read. Everybody's going
                                            to touch the words.

c. Everybody, touch the first word.   Check children's responses.

d. Call on a child.   Reading the fast way. Get ready. Clap. *We.*

e. Next word.   Check children's responses.

f. Everybody reading. Get ready. Clap. *Had.*

g. Next word.   Check children's responses.

h. Call on a child.   Get ready. Clap. *A.*

i. Repeat e and f for **ram.**

PAIR RELATIONS
The children will need pencils.

TASK 26   Children circle the correct picture in each box

a. Point to the first box in the pair-relations exercise on side 2.

b. I'll read these words. **A nut.** What words? (Signal.)
                                            A nut.   Yes, **a nut.**

c. One of the pictures in the box shows (pause)   **a nut.**

d. Point to the picture of the ball.   Does this picture show **a nut**?
                    (Signal.) *No.*   What does it show? (Signal.) *A ball.*
                        Is that the right picture? (Signal.) *No.*

e. Point to the picture of the nut.   Does this picture show **a nut**?
                    (Signal.) *Yes.*   That's the right picture. So I'll circle it.

f. Point to the second box **(a man).**

g. Everybody, touch this box on your take-home.
                                            Check children's responses.

h. Everybody, get ready to tell me the words. (Pause four seconds.)
                            What words? (Signal.) *A man.*   Yes, **a man.**

i. You're going to touch the picture that shows (pause)   **a man.**
                    (Pause.)   Get ready. (Signal.) Check children's responses.

j. Point to the third box **(rock).** Repeat g through i for the third box.

k. Everybody, read the words in the top row to yourselves; then circle
                        the picture in each box that shows what the words say.
                                            Check children's responses.

l. You'll do the rest of the boxes later.

READING VOCABULARY

After you read the words on this page, you'll get to read the words the fast way.

TASK 4   Children sound out the word and tell what word

a. Touch the ball for **not**. Sound it out.
b. Get ready.   Touch **n, o, t** as the children say *nnnooot*.
                              If sounding out is not firm, repeat *b*.
c. What word?   (Signal.) *Not*. Yes, **not**.

TASK 5   Children sound out the word and tell what word

Repeat the procedures in task 4 for **little**.

TASK 6   Children sound out the word and tell what word

Repeat the procedures in task 4 for **got**.

TASK 7   Children rhyme with this

a. Touch the ball for **this**. Sound it out.
b. Get ready.   Touch **th, i, s** as the children say *thththiiisss*.
                              If sounding out is not firm, repeat *b*.
c. What word?   (Signal.) *This*. Yes, **this**.
d. Quickly touch the ball for **miss**. This word rhymes with   (pause)
     this. Get ready.   Touch **m**. *mmm*. Move your finger quickly along
                              the arrow. *Mmmis*.
e. What word?   (Signal.) *Miss*. Yes, **miss**.

TASK 8   Children read the words the fast way

a. Now you get to read the words on this page the fast way.
b. Touch the ball for **not**. (Pause three seconds.) Get ready.
                    Move your finger quickly along the arrow. *Not*.

| To correct | Have the children sound out the word and say it fast. |

c. Repeat *b* for each word on the page.

TASK 9   Individual test—Have children read one word the fast way.

Do not touch any small letters.

not

littl e

got

this

miss

SUMMARY OF INDEPENDENT ACTIVITY

TASK 27   Introduction to independent activity

a. Hold up Take-Home 82.
b. Everybody, you're going to finish this take-home on your own.
Tell the children when they will work the remaining items.
Let's go over the things you're going to do.

TASK 28   Story copying

Point to the dotted words below the story on side 1. You're going
to write the dotted words on this arrow. Then you're going to write
those words on the other arrows.

TASK 29   Cross-out game

Point to the boxed sounds in the Cross-out Game. Everybody, what
sound are you going to cross out today? (Signal.) *shshsh.*
What sound are you going to circle? (Signal.) *ththth.*

TASK 30   Matching

a. Point to the first column of words in the Matching Game.
b. Everybody, get ready to read each of the words over here.
Reading the fast way.
c. Point to the first word. Get ready. (Signal.) *The children respond.*
d. Repeat *c* for the remaining words.
e. Point to the first column. You're going to make lines for every
word over here.

TASK 31   Sound writing

a. Point to the sound-writing exercise on side 2. Here are the sounds
you're going to write today. I'll touch the sounds. You say them.
b. Touch each sound. *The children respond.*
c. Repeat the series until firm.

TASK 32   Pair relations

Point to the pair-relations exercise. Remember—you're going to
circle the picture in each box that shows what the words say.

TASK 33   Story picture

Point to the story picture. After you finish your take-home,
you can color the story picture.

END OF LESSON 82

Lesson 83

SOUNDS

TASK 1 Teacher and children play the sounds game

a. Use acetate and crayon. Write the sounds in the symbol box. Keep score in the score box.
b. *I'm smart. I bet I can beat you in a game.*
c. *Here's the rule. When I touch a sound, you say it.*
d. Play the game.
Make one symbol at a time in the symbol box. Use the symbols **l, f, ē,** and **ā.**
Make each symbol quickly. (Pause.) Touch the symbol.
Play the game for about two minutes. Then ask: *Who won?*
Draw a mouth on the face in the score box.

TASK 2 Sounds firm-up

a. Point to **w.** *When I touch the sound, you say it.*
b. (Pause.) *Get ready.* Touch **w.** *www.*
c. *Again.* Repeat *b* until firm.
d. *Get ready to say all the sounds when I touch them.*
e. Alternate touching **u, w, sh, i, o, t, g,** and **a** three or four times.
Point to the sound. (Pause one second.) Say: *Get ready.* Touch the sound. *The children respond.*

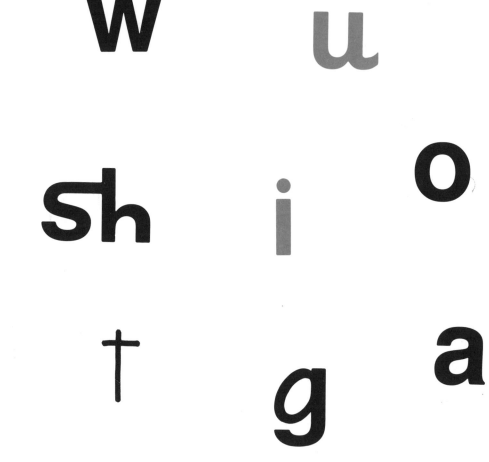

TASK 3 Individual test

Call on different children to identify one or more sounds in task 2.